Deaf Mental Health Care

This volume presents a state of the art account of the clinical specialty of mental health care of deaf people. Drawing upon some of the leading clinicians, teachers, administrators, and researchers in this field from the United States and Great Britain, it addresses critical issues from this specialty such as:

- deaf/hearing cross-cultural dynamics as they impact treatment organizations;
- clinical and interpreting work with deaf persons with widely varying language abilities;
- adaptations of best practices in inpatient, residential, trauma, and substance abuse treatment for deaf persons;
- overcoming administrative barriers to establishing state-wide continua of care;
- university training of clinical specialists;
- the interplay of clinical and forensic responses to deaf people who commit crimes;
- an agenda of priorities for Deaf mental health research.

Each chapter contains numerous clinical case studies and places a heavy emphasis on providing practical intervention strategies in an interesting, easy to read style. All mental health professionals who work with deaf individuals will find this to be an invaluable resource for creating and maintaining culturally affirmative treatment with this population.

Neil S. Glickman, PhD, is the former Unit Director of the Mental Health Unit for Deaf Persons at Westborough State Hospital in Massachusetts. He currently works as a psychologist with Deaf Services for Advocates, Inc., in Framingham, MA, and consults with Deaf Schools, rehabilitation programs, and mental health programs nationwide.

COUNSELING AND PSYCHOTHERAPY:
INVESTIGATING PRACTICE FROM SCIENTIFIC, HISTORICAL,
AND CULTURAL PERSPECTIVES

A Routledge book series
Editor: Bruce Wampold, University of Wisconsin

This innovative new series is devoted to grasping the vast complexities of the practice of counseling and psychotherapy. As a set of healing practices delivered in a context shaped by health delivery systems and the attitudes and values of consumers, practitioners, and researchers, counseling and psychotherapy must be examined critically. By understanding the historical and cultural context of counseling and psychotherapy and by examining the extant research, these critical inquiries seek a deeper, richer understanding of what is a remarkably effective endeavor.

Published

Counseling and Therapy with Clients Who Abuse Alcohol or Other Drugs
Cynthia E. Glidden-Tracy

The Great Psychothearpy Debate
Bruce Wampold

The Psychology of Working: Implications for Career Development, Counseling, and Public Policy
David Blustein

Neuropsychotherapy: How the Neurosciences Inform Effective Psychotherapy
Klaus Grawe

Principles of Multicultural Counseling
Uwe P. Gielen, Juris G. Draguns, Jefferson M. Fish

Beyond Evidence-Based Psychotherapy: Fostering the Eight Sources of Change in Child and Adolescent Treatment
George Rosenfeld

Cognitive Behavioral Therapy for Deaf and Hearing Persons with Language and Learning Challenges
Neil S. Glickman

Pharmacology and Treatment of Substance Abuse: Evidence and Outcome Based Perspectives
Lee Cohen, Frank Collins, Alice Young, Dennis McChargue, Thad R. Leffingwell, Katrina Cook

IDM Supervision: An Integrated Developmental Model for Supervising Counselors and Therapists, Third Edition
Cal Stoltenberg and Brian McNeill

Culture and the Therapeutic Process: A guide for Mental Health Professionals
Mark M. Leach and Jamie Aten

The Resilient Practitioner: Burnout Prevention and Self-Care Strategies for Counselors, Therapists, Teachers, and Health Professionals
Thomas M. Skovholt and Michelle Trotter-Mathison

Deaf Mental Health Care
Neil S. Glickman

Forthcoming

The Handbook of Therapeutic Assessment
Stephen E. Finn

The Great Psychotherapy Debate, Revised Edition
Bruce Wampold

Deaf Mental Health Care

Edited by Neil S. Glickman

Routledge
Taylor & Francis Group

NEW YORK AND LONDON

First published 2013
by Routledge
711 Third Avenue, New York, NY 10017

Simultaneously published in the UK
by Routledge
27 Church Road, Hove, East Sussex BN3 2FA

Routledge is an imprint of the Taylor & Francis Group, an informa business

Library of Congress Cataloging in Publication Data
Glickman, Neil S.
Deaf mental health care / Neil S. Glickman.
p. cm.
ISBN 978-0-415-89474-6 (hardback : alk. paper) — ISBN 978-0-415-89475-3 (pbk. : alk. paper) 1. Deaf—Mental health services—Massachusetts. 2. Deaf—Mental health—Massachusetts. I. Title.
RC451.4.D4G56 2013
362.4'2009744—dc23
2012029653

ISBN: 978-0-415-89474-6 (hbk)
ISBN: 978-0-415-89475-3 (pbk)
ISBN: 978-0-203-81054-5 (ebk)

Typeset in Garamond
by EvS Communication Networx, Inc.

Printed and bound in the United States of America
by Edwards Brothers, Inc.

Contents

Series Editor's Foreword

This series is devoted to understanding the complexities of the practice of counseling and psychotherapy. As a set of healing practices, delivered in a context molded by health delivery systems and the attitudes and values of consumers, practitioners, and researchers, counseling and psychotherapy must be examined critically. Volumes in this series discuss counseling and psychotherapy from empirical, historical, anthropological, and theoretical perspectives. These critical inquiries avoid making assumptions about the nature of counseling and psychotherapy and seek a deeper understanding of the bases of what is a remarkably effective endeavor.

The predominant model of psychotherapy involves finding evidence-based treatment for particular disorders. However, increasingly, there is a recognition that treatments, regardless of their evidence base, need to be adapted to patient populations if they are to be acceptable and effective. Increasingly, we see such treatments described and tested. An important population, not often discussed, is the deaf population. Neil S. Glickman, the editor of *Deaf Mental Health Care*, has put together a volume that comprehensively covers the topic of mental health care for deaf persons, from individual patient care to systems of care, including training of therapists and conducting research. As the reader will learn, Deaf people are a linguistic and cultural group, and Deaf mental health care is a clinical specialization requiring additonal training, personal and cultural self-awareness, a distinct knowledge base, and unique skill set.

Bruce Wampold, PhD, ABPP
Series Editor
University of Wisconsin–Madison

About the Contributors

Alison L. Aubrecht, MA, DCC, LPCC is a White Deaf female who recently transitioned from the mental health field to work full time as a social justice activist with a non-profit organization. She has previously worked in school settings and as a mental health specialist with the Deaf and Hard of Hearing Services Division in Minnesota. Much of her work involves deaf-hearing cross-cultural mediation.

Sally Austen is the lead editor of two of the most important books on Deaf mental health care published in Great Britain. These are *Deafness and Challenging Behavior* (co-edited with Dave Jeffery) and *Deafness in Mind* (coedited with Susan Crocker). She is a Consultant Clinical Psychologist who has worked with deaf people for over 18 years. She is employed by Birmingham and Solihull Mental Health Trust and works at Denmark House, National Deaf Mental Health Service, Birmingham, England.

Karen Bishop's career since 1990 has been dedicated to working with deaf children and youth faced with emotional and behavioral challenges at The Walden School, the residential treatment program at The Learning Center for the Deaf in Framingham, Massachusetts. She has worked as a teacher, an education director, and, for the past five years, as the director. Karen holds a Master of Education degree from Boston University in Deaf Education and is a licensed teacher of the deaf. She recently completed the Certificate of Leadership Program at Suffolk University in the Master of Public Administration Program.

Patrick J. Brice received his PhD in Clinical and Developmental Psychology in 1983, and has been at Gallaudet University since then. He first completed a post-doctoral fellowship in Psychology at Gallaudet in 1983, taught in the Department of Counseling from 1984 until 1995, and since 1995 has been a Professor in the Department of Psychology. He has been the Clinical Psychology PhD Program Director since 2001. In addition to his teaching at Gallaudet, Dr. Brice has studied various aspects of development in deaf children, including social cognition; self-regulation and executive functions; social-emotional development; and parent-child attachment. He is an Associate Editor for the *Journal of Deaf Studies and Deaf Education* and a reviewer for the *Journal of the American Orthopsychiatric Association*, and also serves as a grant reviewer for various funding agencies. Dr. Brice has also been a consulting psychologist to the Lab School of Washington, St. Elizabeth's Hospital, the National Health Care Foundation for the Deaf, and the Family Service Foundation in Maryland.

Charlene Crump is the state Mental Health Interpreter Coordinator in Alabama. She is responsible for the Mental Health Interpreter Training initiative and developing state standards for mental health interpreting. Charlene is an Adjunct Instructor at Auburn University in Montgomery, Alabama and currently serves as President of the Alabama Chapter of the American Sign Language Teachers Association. She has served as Chair of the Alabama Licensure Board and contributed to the Registry of Interpreters for the Deaf Standard Practice Paper focusing on Mental Health Interpreting. She has served on several national expert focus groups on mental health interpreting.

Steve Hamerdinger is the Director of the Office of Deaf Services in the Alabama Department of Mental Health. Previous to moving to Alabama, he was the Director of the Office of Deaf and Linguistic Services at the Missouri Department of Mental Health and also held several clinical positions. Steve is past president of the American Deafness and Rehabilitation Association and the New Mexico Association of the Deaf. He has been adjunct faculty and visiting lecturer at several colleges and universities. Gallaudet Alumni Association awarded him its Alice Cogswell award for his more than 25 years of service to deaf people. Steve has played a leadership role in many national initiatives pertaining to the development of culturally affirmative mental health services for deaf people.

Wendy Heines, MSW, LCSW, is Chief Executive Officer for Salisbury Behavioral Health, which she joined in 2003 as the Director of the newly formed Deaf Services Center, now known as PAHrtners Deaf Services. Under her leadership, the staff has grown from 12 to more than 120 employees, and several programs have been added, including: interpreting, outpatient, case management, community living arrangements for individuals who are deaf with co-occurring developmental disabilities, and a residential treatment facility for adolescents who are deaf. The number of individuals served in these programs continues to grow. Ms. Heines is a 1991 graduate of Rutgers University with a Master's in Social Work. She has over 20 years of experience establishing and operating behavioral healthcare programs for deaf persons in New Jersey and Pennsylvania.

Neil S. Glickman, PhD, is a licensed psychologist and certified vocational and psychiatric rehabilitation counselor in Massachusetts. He was co-founder (along with Sherry Zitter) of the Mental Health Unit for Deaf Persons, a Deaf psychiatric inpatient unit at Westborough State Hospital in Massachusetts, where he worked for 17 years, 14 as unit psychologist and director. He is the author of *Cognitive Behavioral Therapy of Deaf and Hearing Persons with Language and Learning Challenges* (Routledge, 2009), and co-editor (with Michael Harvey) of *Culturally Affirmative Psychotherapy with Deaf Persons* (Lawrence Erlbaum, 1996) and (with Sanjay Gulati) of *Mental Health Care of Deaf Persons: A Culturally Affirmative Approach* (Lawrence Erlbaum, 2003). He currently works as a psychologist with Deaf services at Advocates, Inc. in Framingham and also teaches psychiatric rehabilitation at the Institute for Social and Rehabilitative Services at Assumption College, in Worcester, Massachuestts. He serves on the editorial board for the *Journal of Deaf Studies and Deaf Education*. He teaches and consults on the subject of Deaf mental health care and cognitive behavioral psychotherapy.

Michael John Gournaris is a Deaf licensed psychologist in the state of Minnesota and currently works as the Mental Health Program Director with the Minnesota Department of Human Services, Deaf & Hard-of-Hearing Services Division. Since April 2007, he has been responsible for overseeing the statewide mental health delivery system for deaf and hard-of-hearing adults. Prior to his appointment as director, Dr. Gournaris worked in residential treatment centers in Florida for two years, as a clinical psychologist with the Tampa Bay Academy and National Deaf Academy (NDA). Before that, he worked as a clinician with the University of Miami/Jackson Memorial Hospital in Miami, Florida and Family Services Foundation, Inc. in Maryland. He is currently serving as an advisory board member of the NDA and the committee chair in the Mental Health Committee within the National Association of the Deaf (NAD). Dr. Gournaris has coordinated and co-composed several NAD Position Statements on various mental health topics.

Debra Guthmann, EdD, is the Director of Pupil Personnel Services at the California School for the Deaf, Fremont where she oversees all clinical services. She is the founding Director of the Minnesota Chemical Dependency Program for Deaf and Hard of Hearing Individuals, one of the first inpatient treatment programs of uts kind in the country. Dr. Guthmann has made over 200 national and international presentations, written numerous articles and several book chapters focusing on ethical issues, substance abuse, and treatment models to use with the deaf and hard of hearing. Dr. Guthmann has also been involved in developing a number of curriculum and materials including an anti-tobacco curriculum, HIV prevention curriculum and a training DVD for clinicians working with deaf clients. She is on the adjunct faculty at Gallaudet University, is a past President for the National Association on Alcohol, Drugs and Disability (NAADD), and past President of the American Deafness and Rehabilitation Association (ADARA), which is one of the largest organizations for professionals serving deaf and hard of hearing individuals.

Irene W. Leigh, PhD, a deaf psychologist, has done high school teaching, psychological assessment, psychotherapy, and mental health administration. Currently she is Professor Emerita and former Chair of the Department of Psychology at Gallaudet University. Her numerous presentations, research, and publications have focused on deaf people and issues related to identity, multiculturalism, parenting, attachment, depression, and cochlear implants. She is a Fellow of the American Psychological Association and was an Associate Editor for the *Journal of Deaf Studies and Deaf Education*. Her most recent book is *A Lens on Deaf Identities* (2009).

Sue O'Rourke has worked in Deaf mental health care for 20 years. She is a Consultant Clinical Psychologist currently in private practice working mainly with deaf people in the criminal justice system. Prior to this she was Clinical and Operational Director for St. George Healthcare Group, Great Britain, providing secure and open rehabilitation for deaf people with forensic histories. She has published important book chapters in the three leading books on Deaf mental health care in Great Britain.

Robert Q Pollard, Jr., PhD, is a Professor of Psychiatry at the University of Rochester School of Medicine where he founded and directs the Deaf Wellness Center (DWC). The DWC is home to numerous initiatives pertaining to mental health, sign language interpreting, public health, and professional education opportunities for deaf people. Dr. Pollard's work has been recognized with many national and international awards and honors. He has been principal investigator on 48 federal, state, foundation, and local grants totaling over $5M, has published 86 articles and book chapters, and produced 15 films in American Sign Language for Deaf audiences. Dr. Pollard's scholarship interests include psychopathology, psychological testing, sign language interpreting, forensic evaluation, intimate partner violence, and public health issues affecting the deaf population. He is active in several national organizations, especially the American Psychological Association, where he founded a Special Interest Section on Deafness.

Martha Sheridan is a Professor in the Department of Social Work at Gallaudet University. Bringing extensive experience in mental health, school social work, and private practice, Dr. Sheridan joined the graduate faculty at Gallaudet in 1997. Her administrative experience includes clinical supervision, as well as program development, management, evaluation, and consultation. Dr. Sheridan is engaged in ongoing research on the developmental experiences of deaf and hard-of-hearing people across the lifecycle. She is the author of *Inner Lives of Deaf Children: Interviews and Analysis* (2001) and *Deaf Adolescents: Inner Lives and Lifeworld Development* (2008). Other publications cover social work assessment and practice with deaf and hard-of-hearing people, deaf women, deaf parenting with hearing children, adolescents with Ushers Syndrome, suicide prevention, and existential transcendence among deaf and hard-of-hearing people. She has lectured extensively on these topics as well as on family issues, spirituality in social work practice, aging, domestic violence, deaf women, health and mental health services. She has served in various capacities with the Council on Social Work Education. She also serves as Co-Director of the U.S. Department of Education grant supporting the school social work specialization within the MSW Program.

Kendra Smith, PhD, LPC, is an Associate Professor in the Department of Counseling at Gallaudet University and serves as Director of the Mental Health Counseling degree program. Prior to teaching, she was a mental health counselor at Gallaudet University's Mental Health Center. Dr. Smith has authored articles and book chapters and presented at international and national conferences on such topics as cross-cultural issues in supervision, ethical responsibility of clinical supervisors, and counseling college students. Dr. Smith is a past member of the Board of Directors of Deaf Abused Women's Network in Washington, DC, and served on the Subcommittee on Mental Health, Office of the Deaf and Hard of Hearing for the State of Maryland. She was also the chairperson of the Mental Health Special Interest Section of ADARA from 2001–2007.

Cynthia Sternfeld is a Licensed Professional Counselor in Lambertville, New Jersey. Her practice serves deaf, hearing, and hard-of-hearing clients with diverse mental health needs. Ms. Sternfeld worked at the New Jersey's Katzenbach School for the Deaf from 1985 until 2010. Her professional roles at the school included, classroom teacher, independent living coordinator, state-wide school based mental health counselor, and finally Director of Campus Life. In her time at the school she developed multiple programs and curricula for deaf and hard-of-hearing individuals including HIV prevention, substance abuse prevention and independent living. She is an Adjunct Professor at The College of New Jersey and has taught Analysis of Drug Dependencies, Foundations of Sex Education, and American Sign Language. She has authored and co-authored multiple projects including anti-tobacco curriculum, HIV prevention curriculum, independent living programs and a training DVD for clinicians working with deaf clients.

Roger C. Williams is currently employed by the South Carolina Department of Mental Health as the Director of Services for the Deaf and Hard of Hearing. He was previously employed as the Program Manager for Deaf Services at the Piedmont Center for Mental Health Services. He is a South Carolina Licensed Master Social Worker and holds an RID Certificate of Transliteration and an SCAD/NAD IAP Level 5 Interpreting Certificate. He is the 1989 winner of the N.C. Governor's Advocacy Council for Persons with Disabilities Distinguished Service Award, the 1979 winner of the Robert D. Frisina Award for deaf/hearing integration and the 1996 winner of the "Outstanding Transition to the Community" Award from the South Carolina Mental Health Association. In 2009, he was appointed as the United States Representative to the International Institute for Mental Health Leadership's Task Force for the Deaf and Hard of Hearing.

Acknowledgments

Deaf mental health care was not the invention of any one person. Many people (clinicians, researchers, teachers, scholars, and the people we serve), deaf and hearing, have contributed to this developing clinical specialization. As a hearing person who is a second language learner of ASL, I am always aware that for me this work is cross-cultural, and that I can only work effectively with deaf people to the extent they allow me the privilege of partnering with them. I have tried very hard in this book to make it clear that this developing specialization grows out of the contributions, over many years, of many individuals. I believe an edited work, where many experts can make new contributions, is the best venue for advancing this effort. I've seen my role, through this work and my previous two edited works, as mainly that of organizing these contributions so that the outlines, themes, and controversies of this specialization become more clear. For instance, I've seen many excellent Deaf mental health clinicians (that is, clinicians, deaf and hearing, who specialize in work with deaf people) work to adapt mental health approaches for deaf clients. I know this adaptation work goes on wherever deaf people are served. In this book, I've worked with the chapter contributors to describe how many such adaptations have been done. I hope this makes it easier for all of us, our specialization, to refine these adaptations. As noted in the last chapter, there is so much more work we need to do.

This is my first edited work where I didn't have a colleague as co-editor, yet I had many people offer me essential help throughout the process. To begin with, I had the work of all these wonderful contributors, all experts in this field. I asked several of these contributors, especially Robert Pollard, Michael Gournaris, Alison Aubrecht, Steve Hamerdinger, Roger Williams, and Charlene Crump to comment on sections I wrote. Four of the chapters which bear my name were collaborations (with Charlene Crump, Wendy Heines, Sue O'Rourke, Sally Austen, and Robert Pollard). I sought out these collaborations because I knew I couldn't write these chapters alone, and I knew that these particular people were the top in their field. Chapter 1 is my summary of the collective work of probably 100 colleagues over a 23-year period. Other people who offered invaluable feedback on chapters I contributed to were Michael Harvey, Sherry Zitter, Robyn Dean, Susan Jones, McCay Vernon, and Ellen Vershbow.

I've had the good fortune to work in a few "centers of excellence" for Deaf mental health care. Most recently, I've been at Advocates, Inc., an agency which provides community-based psychiatric rehabilitation services, and which has a commitment to strong, culturally affirmative Deaf programming. Key leadership people at Advocates promoting that commitment include Bill Taylor, Chris Gordon, Keith Scott, Diane Gould, Beth Lacey, Brenda Mele-Soares, and Amy Morgan. Deaf Services colleagues I've had the pleasure to work there with include Eveleen Cunningham, Dara Baril, Jonathan LeJeune, Gloria Farr, Ronda Mothersell, Paul O'Rourke, Sanjay Gulati, Anthony Patrowicz, Denise Paro, James Jones, Sandy Martins, Shane Fuller, Jordan Ray, Kevin Ahern, Jayne Galiazzo, Bryan Baitazar, Andrew Veith, Joseph Karnolisz, William Stratemeier, Jennifer Marichal, Joseph Smith, Marco Gonzalez, Christina O'Neill, Steven Ropp, Jayne Galiazzo, Lisha Weeks, Sharon MacLean, Ellen Vershbow, Karen Melo, and Amory Wallace. At the Massachusetts Department of Mental Health, Coordinator of Deaf Services Lucille Traina has been a prime mover and valued colleague for many projects in Deaf mental health care in Massachusetts.

Chapter 10, written with Robert Pollard, addresses Deaf mental health research. That chapter draws heavily upon a conference organized by Dr. Pollard and includes appendices describing the conference results. The National Association of State Mental Health Program Directors (NASMHPD) was the prime sponsor of this conference, and Executive Director Robert Glover and Associate to Executive Director Meighan Haupt have been enthusiastic supporters of Deaf mental health care and Deaf mental health research at NASMHPD for many years. As discussed in Chapter 4, most Deaf mental health care work is done in the public sector and depends heavily on having informed and skillful allies in state and federal government. The NASMHPD leadership has been particularly responsive to the call for culturally and clinically competent mental health services for deaf persons.

This is my second book with Routledge, and in both cases I've felt well taken care of by my colleagues there, especially, for this book, Dana Bliss, Christopher Tominich, Anna Moore, Katharine Earwaker, Eleanor Reading and, at EVS, Lynn Goeller. Routledge is a first class operation from start to finish.

My husband and life partner Steven Riel has been my chief supporter in all things I do. He has seen me through the ups and downs of this and my other writing projects, and, in the most fundamental way, makes all things possible for me.

The deaf people I've had the pleasure to work with and serve are the true heroes of Deaf mental health care. I'm old enough now, and have been working in one place long enough, to have worked with some of these persons for over two decades. I've seen many people move from hospital to community to independent functioning so I know that people get better, recover, grow, and sometimes amaze others with what they are capable of accomplishing. Quality Deaf mental health care works. Yes, we need to provide culturally and clinically competent care, but the true source of progress always rests in the individual finding the strength, courage and capacity to make life better. That capacity is always there, and the real skill in mental health specialists is partnering with persons served to draw out these capacities for growth. I am thankful to all these deaf persons, and I hope the stories of resiliency and recovery found here convey the respect and admiration that I, and all the book contributors, have for them.

Introduction

What Is Deaf Mental Health Care?

Neil S. Glickman

In 1996, psychologist Robert Pollard, director of the Deaf Wellness Center at the University of Rochester School of Medicine, published an article entitled "Professional Psychology and Deaf People: The Emergence of a Discipline." Speaking primarily to psychologists, he described the cases of Daryl, a deaf patient at a psychiatric center, and Karen, a deaf doctoral student in psychology. He argued that Daryl needed mental health treatment from clinical specialists trained to work with deaf people. He also argued that Karen could become one of these specialists if the field of psychology opened its doors to deaf students. Pollard went on to describe some aspects of the emerging discipline of professional psychology and deaf people. This included the ability to assess and treat deaf persons who are fluent in American Sign Language (ASL) and, just as importantly, dysfluent in any language. It included "an intimate knowledge of the potentials and pitfalls of translation between ASL and English" (p. 391). Pollard argued on both practical and ethical grounds that this emerging discipline must include full institutional supports for the development of deaf psychologists. Whether psychologists were treating clients or training new professionals, there was enough distinct and new about work with deaf people to make this work a discipline or clinical specialty. Pollards' seminal article is one of the seeds of this book.[1]

Also in 1996, Michael Harvey and I edited a book called, *Culturally Affirmative Psychotherapy with Deaf Persons*. This book was centered on one key theme. By 1996, the cultural model of the Deaf Community was well established as the contrast to the older, "medical-pathological" model of deaf people. The Deaf Community was increasingly being understood as people with a language and cultural difference, not a disability. Harvey and I took this paradigm shift in the understanding of deaf people as the premise for this book on psychotherapy. If we viewed deaf people as linguistic and cultural minorities, *not* people with a disability, we asked, what would this imply for the practice of psychotherapy? We and our contributors went on to draw out some of these implications.

My own interest in the cultural model of deaf people began when I was a graduate student in counseling at then Gallaudet College in the early

1980s (Glickman, 1983, 1986). I am hearing, and, like many others, I was drawn to work with deaf people primarily by the beauty of ASL. I later realized that, also like many other hearing people, I was working through some of my own identity issues vicariously through this interest in deaf people. I subsequently studied the development of cultural identity in deaf people relating it quite consciously to my own identity development as a gay man. I knew that cultural identity development was an important part of any "culturally affirmative" work with minority people, and it seemed to me logical to think that ways cultural identity developed in deaf persons would follow the same overall psychological principals as are seen in other minority persons (Glickman, 1996). The idea that deaf people would not define themselves by their hearing loss but rather by their language, culture, and relationship to a community made sense to me as it resonated with everything I knew, from experience and study, about living as a minority in contemporary America.

The 3 Dimensions of Deaf Mental Health Care

In our book (Glickman & Harvey, 1996), there is one chapter, which I wrote which I've continued to work on since in my mind. That chapter is titled "What Is Culturally Affirmative Psychotherapy?" What I tried to do there was survey the field of culturally affirmative psychotherapy with other cultural, linguistic, and minority groups and then draw parallels to the treatment of culturally Deaf persons in psychotherapy. In doing this, I depended heavily upon an important paper put out by the leading researchers/clinicians of culturally affirmative psychotherapy of that day in which they described the culturally skilled counselor as showing three kinds of special abilities. Because their conceptualization guides this present work also, I requote the key passage here:

> First, a culturally skilled counselor is one who is actively in the process of becoming aware of his or her own assumptions about human behavior, values, biases, preconceived notions, personal limitations, and so forth. They understand their own world views, how they are the product of their cultural conditioning, and how (they) may be reflected in their counseling and work with racial and ethnic minorities. The old adage "counselor, know thyself" is important in not allowing biases, values, or "hang-ups" to interfere with the counselor's ability to work with clients. Prevention of ethnocentrism is a key ingredient to effective cross-cultural counseling.

> Second, a culturally skilled counselor is one who actively attempts to understand the world view of his or her culturally different client without negative judgments. It is crucial that counselors understand and share the world views of their culturally different clients with

respect and appreciation. This statement does not imply that counselors have to hold the world views as their own, but can accept them as another legitimate perspective.

Third, a culturally skilled counselor is one who is in the process of actively developing and practicing appropriate, relevant, and sensitive intervention strategies and skills in working with his or her culturally different clients. Studies consistently reveal that counseling effectiveness is improved when counselors use modalities and define goals consistent with the life experiences and cultural values of clients. It is recognized that extrapsychic as well as intrapsychic approaches may be more appropriate and that differential helping strategies may be needed. (Sue, Arredondo, & McDavis, 1992, p. 481)

My 1996 book with Michael Harvey was my first attempt to lay out a framework for mental health care with deaf people. In my mind, then and now, the structure of any Deaf mental health care (DMHC) specialty would consist of elaboration on these three themes. This would make it consistent with other mental health treatment efforts with minority group members. That effort is continued in this book where all three dimensions are addressed.

Personal and Cultural Self-awareness

The self-awareness dimension is the most overlooked. The self-awareness dimension is what is missing when a psychologist wants to know, "what psychological tests should I use with deaf people?" as if that were all there was to psychological evaluations of deaf people. It is missing whenever hearing clinicians think that they just need to take some workshops about deaf people and never realize that just as important is to learn about themselves as culturally hearing people. It is missing whenever clinicians uncritically apply the medical model to assessment and treatment of deaf people, and never consider the viewpoint that members of the Deaf Community hold about themselves, which is that they are culturally different, not disabled. The paradigm difference is comparable to older notions of homosexuality, once well enshrined within psychiatry, as deviation or perversion, compared with the views that self-accepting gay and lesbian people held of themselves. It is comparable to older notions, once widespread among White Americans, of slavery or racial segregation as the natural, God-given state of relations between White and Black Americans. In each case, fundamental identity questions were at stake for both minority and majority persons, and health affirming psychological approaches could only emerge out of a new sociological context which affirmed the minority persons.

While it may seem like common sense to hearing people, especially those trained in the medical professions, to view deaf people as disabled, it is crucial for them to understand that such viewpoints immediately distance them from many of the people they want to serve. The context of deaf-hearing relationships, the way we relate to each other and manage power, all bear directly on any mental health enterprise directed at deaf people. Just as it has been for White Americans with regard to people of color, heterosexuals with regard to sexual and gender minorities, men with regard to women, etc., hearing people who work with deaf people are challenged to reconsider very fundamental assumptions about who we are. In this case, the assumptions have to do with notions of ability and disability, of what constitutes cultural and language difference, of best ways of communication, and even more fundamentally, of what it means to help.

The self-awareness dimension addresses the issue of cross cultural interactions between deaf and hearing people. It addresses the power dynamics, the struggles that deaf people, like all minority persons, have faced to have a "voice" in organizations designed to help them, the communication challenges, the biased perceptions that both hearing and deaf people can bring to this work. Pollard, in the same article as cited above, speaks about the importance for hearing persons of developing "cross cultural legitimacy" in working with deaf person:

> Hearing persons pursuing careers working with and for this population increasingly recognize that they are beholden to the Deaf community for two critical characteristics needed to be effective—sign language fluency and what might be termed *cross-cultural legitimacy*. While professional education is important to be sure, it is not enough to serve this population well. These two additional qualities are equally necessary. Hearing professionals in the deafness field must recognize that sign fluency and cross-cultural legitimacy are things that are not gained through school. These essential qualities only come from consistent and culturally appropriate interaction with persons who are deaf. Sign fluency and cross-cultural legitimacy are given to hearing people by the Deaf community, or really earned from them, and they constitute an investment that the community has made in the hearing person, an investment that is due a particular standard of return. (Pollard, 1996, p. 393)

In my experience, this topic of how hearing and deaf people relate to each other is unquestionably the most difficult domain in DMHC to discuss because it elicits defensiveness. Hearing people don't like to think about how they may hold prejudicial ideas and behave in oppressive manners. Neither do deaf people. It's much safer to talk about the other group, to diagnose or blame them, and to consider oneself innocent and good.

As a hearing psychologist, it is not difficult at all for me to discuss issues like "mental health care of deaf people" as long as I keep the focus on deaf people. If I give a lecture in a hospital on this subject, most of the hearing people will be very comfortable with the talk. They will see me as an objective expert on the subject. If there are deaf people present, especially educated, articulate deaf people, they will often have a different view. They will object to what they see as me making any link between deaf people and psychopathology. They will also object to a hearing person presenting himself as expert on the lives of deaf people. If, on the other hand, I start by saying that one should never discuss psychopathology in deaf people until one fully understands normality and health in deaf people, and if I state further, that one cannot understand psychopathology in deaf people without first understanding what hearing people *have done* to deaf people, I will get a very different response. The deaf people present are more likely to feel affirmed and see me as an ally. The hearing people, especially those from the medical professions, may see me as ideologically biased, as non-objective, as pushing a political agenda, and some will tune me out. Because deaf people, like other minorities, are struggling in their personal and collective liberation, Deaf mental health care is political. There is no safe, objective, medically-neutral ground on which to stand.

The discussion is difficult but necessary. More than any other issue, and just as with other majority-minority relationships, the development of truly empathic, respectful cross cultural partnerships trumps any other issue in terms of making or breaking a treatment program. If you are hearing, there is a lot for you to learn about deaf people in order to do this work. But even more important than what you know is how you relate to the deaf people you meet.

Addressing well the issue of deaf/hearing cross cultural conflict has been the most difficult part of this book to write about because it involved taking personal risks and perhaps exposing organizational dynamics that some would prefer to remain hidden. We had more case stories we wanted to include but had to remove because people objected to their dirty laundry being aired. I have never known a Deaf mental health program or organization that didn't face these conflicts, yet talking about them openly can be dangerous. For one thing, it is difficult to be objective about conflicts one is part of. For another, there is almost always organizational pressure to pretend that "we all get along fine because, in our organization, we are all very enlightened people." The *real* enlightened position is not to pretend there are no conflicts in our organization, but to address them honestly and skillfully. Because this aspect of the work is very sensitive, it is addressed several places in this book through imaginary dialogues. Such dialogues enable us to more safely represent different points of view. Dialogues are also, I believe, a more culturally affirmative way to teach ideas to deaf people.[2] Imaginary cross cultural dialogues illustrating common conflicting points of view are found in Chapters 1, 2, 5, and 9.

As specialists in this field know well, the oppression of deaf people is "storied" within the medical model in which hearing people, presumably whole, strive to fix or correct deaf people, presumably disabled. The playing field has historically been one in which hearing people hold all the power, designing and administering programs to "help" deaf people. The central theme in this history has been language oppression; the deliberate, systematic, effort to prevent deaf children from acquiring sign language and from affiliation with other deaf people (Lane, 1992). Another theme is that of "fixing" hearing loss, a goal which might be less problematic did it not go along with denial and suppression of everything considered Deaf (i.e., the Deaf Community, culture and language).

Deaf people hold feelings and beliefs about themselves and the majority culture that are very comparable to those of other oppressed groups. They struggle against the majority for their own individual and collective empowerment, and in that battle they encounter some majority persons who strive to be allies, others that actively resist them, and others that hold ambivalent views. Deaf people themselves, like other minority persons, hold the full range of opinions regarding what it means to be a minority. Some identify strongly with the Deaf Community. Others identify with hearing people or with other minority communities. Others are bicultural or multicultural. These identities often develop and change over time (Glickman, 1996; Leigh, 2009).

The identities of hearing people, as hearing people, develop also, just as those of White people develop, and in that process, as we come to understand, to "get it," we become more effective as potential helpers and healers. The naïve hearing person comes to this encounter with no awareness that he or she, as a hearing person, is a cultural being (Lane, 1996). H-Dirksen L. Bauman describes eloquently his process of identity change as he moved from being a person who could hear to a person who was hearing:

> I was born as a *person who could hear;* which is different from being born *hearing.* Like any identity, hearing identity is a social construction. I became *hearing* at the age of twenty-one, when I was hired as a dormitory supervisor for the Colorado School for the Deaf and Blind (CSDB). Suddenly, my world changed: It was no longer *my* world. I was an outsider, a foreigner in my own land. My identity was constructed for me; long before I ever began working at CSDB, a whole discourse on the meanings of being hearing had evolved in the Deaf world. Growing up, the thought that I was a hearing person never crossed my mind; hearing was so normal it went unnoticed. It was just the way things were. Only after a ten-year-old Deaf boy told me that I was hearing did the realization strike me. This is more than a residential school I have wandered into; this is a profoundly different way of being in the world. (Bauman, 2002, p. viii)

The process *of becoming hearing* is often painful, especially for those who begin with unrealistic expectations about being welcomed by deaf people as helpers. Many a well-intentioned hearing person, initially enthusiastic about "helping the deaf," has stepped away once they realized that genuine helping would take a different course. They would have to struggle with *being hearing* in a world where that marks you, not as a helper, but as an outsider and often as an oppressor.

In 2012, as Deaf mental health care emerges as its own field, the days when there were no qualified deaf professionals to employ are past. There are an ever growing number of deaf persons with graduate degrees and licenses, people who have struggled mightily to gain access to their professions, so this field can no longer be about hearing people establishing, defining and administering programs. It has to be about a creation of genuine partnerships between deaf and hearing colleagues, a real sharing of power, and this must involve for hearing people the same kind of fearless self-examination as it has for White people working with non-Whites, men accepting women in leadership roles, heterosexuals accepting people with different sexual and gender identities, etc.

Hearing and deaf persons working together, then, inevitably have cross-cultural conflicts, and developing self-awareness is the first step in addressing such conflicts. A further complication is that for hearing people who want to do this work, there is no alternative but to struggle to learn the language well. Most of the hearing people I've known, including myself, who have learned American Sign Language as adults have not found this easy. At Westborough State Hospital, which had a Deaf inpatient unit for 23 years,[3] many people expressed interest in learning sign language, but very few persisted through a rigorous course of study and practice. Pretty soon after beginning, their fantasies about the ease of learning sign language were dispelled. They realize this would be just as hard as learning any other language; harder perhaps, because they would also have to learn to use their bodies in whole new ways.

When deaf people are conceptualized solely as having a medical problem, when hearing people are conceptualized solely as helpers and healers of this medical problem, it is a small step indeed to conceptualizing other problems deaf people have as medical problems, ignoring their social context, over-pathologizing and over-medicating, and to repeating patterns of domination and oppression of deaf people within the treatment context. This dynamic was one of many "lessons learned" on the Westborough State Hospital Deaf Unit, discussed in Chapter 1. This is why the identification of some new "Deaf program" or the arrival of some new "expert on deaf people" is frequently met with suspicion and guardedness by deaf people and their allies. Put another way, the problem is not that deaf people are more paranoid, as hearing clinicians sometimes assume, but rather that hearing people collectively have been far more destructive to deaf people than we want to believe. Our medical preoccupation with fixing deafness has blinded us to the socio-cultural aspects of this work (Lane, 1992).

That said, the contributors to this volume do not argue that deaf people have all the answers, that Deaf mental health care is simply about putting deaf people in power. This point is emphasized in Chapter 5 where Wendy Heines and I argue that cultural and clinical competence are not the same thing and that having a culturally competent program is no guarantee of having a clinically competent program. We try to illustrate there what both cultural and clinical competence look like in Deaf residential treatment programs. A parallel discussion occurs in Chapter 7 where Karen Bishop, the director of the Walden School, a program for deaf children with emotional and behavioral problems, describes the interplay of clinical and communication/cultural competence which are both essential to treatment of severely traumatized deaf children.

The self-awareness dimension is addressed in several other places in this book. It is addressed most directly in Chapter 2 by Gournaris and Aubrecht, deaf clinicians working in Minnesota. Gournaris and Aubrecht suggest that deaf and hearing people respond to each other in very familiar and predictable ways. They each develop a set of characteristic "relational postures" towards the other, and when people assuming different relational postures come into contact with each other, very predictable conflict patterns emerge. Developing self-awareness about these relational postures, understanding one's own motivation for doing this work, and working very consciously to be effective across cultural boundaries, become essential ingredients for DMHC. As Gournaris and Aubrecht stress, this is just as important a process for deaf people as it is for hearing people.

The self-awareness dimension is also addressed in Chapter 5 in the form of an imaginary dialogue between a deaf and hearing program leader in which common complaints that hearing and deaf employees have of each other are voiced. Work in any Deaf treatment program today and you are bound to find variations on the themes addressed in this dialogue. The dimension is illustrated in Chapter 1 where several cross cultural Deaf/hearing conflicts are presented. It is addressed further in the Chapter 8 by Brice, Leigh, Sheridan, and Smith on preparation of mental health professionals to work with deaf people. All four of these program leaders prepare students at Gallaudet University, and all argue that the personal experiences that students have in this Deaf centered place are crucial parts of their professional preparation to work with deaf clients. Finally, the self-awareness dimension is addressed in Chapter 9 by O'Rourke, Austen, and myself when we discuss all the biases that hearing people hold that interfere with their ability to respond well to deaf people with challenging and sometimes criminal behaviors.

The Knowledge Dimension: Deaf Studies and Knowledge of Deaf People

The knowledge dimension refers most immediately to knowledge of the world view(s) of persons with whom one works. I understand the knowledge dimension more broadly to refer to the body of specialized knowledge about a group of people that one needs to acquire in order to work well with them. This brings us to the commonly voiced concern that one cannot generalize about deaf people. There is certainly no "psychology of deafness" in the sense of their being any set of personality traits or other attributes that one can subscribe to all deaf people. Deaf people, like other minority groups, have widely varying experiences. Variation among deaf people is as great as variation between deaf and hearing people. The deaf child raised by deaf parents in a signing home, the deaf immigrant to the United States who was raised without any schooling or language exposure, the hearing young adult who suddenly loses his hearing following a head trauma in a motorcycle accident, the elderly woman whose hearing begins to decline in her later years, may have little in common; and this says nothing for the endless other kinds of differences deaf people have from one another. Given these differences, how can one speak about Deaf mental health care as if there were just one systematic approach to working with deaf people?

The diversity among deaf people speaks to how large the body of specialized knowledge is that one must acquire to do this work competently. If one is hired to work as a mental health specialist with deaf persons in an outpatient mental health center, the expectation will likely be that one works well with all the deaf people who come along. Some of these persons will see themselves as culturally Deaf. Others will want nothing to do with the Deaf Community. One's clients will vary widely in communication skills, as already noted. Some will have cochlear implants and hearing aids. Some will be severely mentally ill or personality disordered. Some will have addiction problems. Some will have less serious problems with stress or relationships. Some will want to talk with you. Others will be dragged there by someone else who thinks they need to see a counselor. They will be children, teenagers, young and older adults. They will have varying ethnic, religious, and sexual orientations. Some will be adjusting to their loss of hearing. Others will have problems that are completely unrelated to their hearing status. Some will want to be served as a couple or family. Others will want you to advocate for them in social situations and to help them with challenges of daily life. I always remember the deaf young man who called the clinic I worked in asking for an appointment. He wasn't looking for counseling. His very first words to me on the TTY, the telecommunication device then in use, even before he gave his name, were, "I need a girlfriend."

On the Westborough State Hospital Deaf Unit, we served enormously diverse deaf clientele who nonetheless had much in common. They were all deaf or hard of hearing, 14 years of age or older, and had problems severe enough to get them into a psychiatric hospital. Most, if they had to receive treatment in a psychiatric hospital, preferred a program which had deaf and signing staff. The population we saw was skewed heavily in the direction of signing deaf people, a good percentage of whom I describe using the phrase "language and learning challenged" (Glickman, 2009). Deaf mental health care, while it must serve all people with hearing impairments, is unquestionably skewed in focus towards people who became deaf at birth or early in life, who live their lives as deaf or hearing impaired persons, and who sign. Most of what specialists learn has to do with working with signing people who have some relationship with the Deaf Community. This group of signing deaf people is itself hugely diverse. Anyone who enters this field needs to be able to work with this diverse group even though they may also be called upon to also work with non-signing, late deafened, and hard-of-hearing people.

The diversity among deaf people must not lead us to miss the forest for the trees. Yes, there is this diversity, but there are also commonalities. There is a body of knowledge to acquire about the psychological themes and issues in the lives of deaf people. Some of this knowledge is to be found in the emerging discipline of Deaf Studies (Bauman, 2002; Marschark & Spencer, 2011). This includes studies of the history and culture of deaf peoples as well as personal narratives about the deaf experience, both written and signed. Some of it comes from books that have titles like "psychology of deafness" (Levine, 1960; Paul & Jackson, 1993; Vernon & Andrews, 1990) and from related studies about psychological and social development of deaf people (Levine, 1960; Marschark, 1993; Scheetz, 2004; Schlesinger & Meadow, 1972). Even if one rejects the idea of a "psychology of deafness," specialists in this field need to familiarize themselves with this literature.

We should examine in this context the words we use to reference this group of people. The words we choose to describe deaf people are just as loaded as words like Negro, Black, African American, Hispanic American, Latino, Gay, Lesbian, Queer, homosexual, etc. The words matter. As Gournaris and Aubrecht note in Chapter 2, the words "the deaf," "hearing impaired," and "deafness" are all problematic because they are part of the medical storying about what it means to be deaf. To ask about a psychology of deafness is already to highlight the medical fact of hearing loss as the central, organizing issue in the lives of deaf people. It would be the same as asking about a "psychology of homosexuality" or the "psychology of race" as if it were the sexual behavior or race, and not the life experiences and socio-cultural context that organize, an identity.

It is interesting to contrast the term "deafness" with the newer term "deafhood," coined by Deaf activist Paddy Ladd (Ladd, 2003). As Ladd, writes, the contrast is specifically related to the difference between a medical and a cultural/experiential understanding of what it means to be Deaf.

> As I absorbed these stories and emotions (of deaf people), I found myself coining a new label of "Deafhood." Deafhood is not, however, a "static" medical condition like "deafness." Instead, it represents a process—the struggle by each Deaf child, Deaf family and Deaf adult to explain to themselves and each other their own existence in the world. (p. 3)

"Deafhood" is a Deaf-centered term even if not all deaf people embrace it. "Deafness" is a hearing/medical centered term. There is no "psychology of deafness," no one way that hearing loss effects psychological development. But deaf people have many experiences in common, and out of these experiences develop some perceptions, beliefs, attitudes, and psychological themes that are common, but not universal. This is important, because in DMHC, clinicians need to understand these common experiences, beliefs attitudes and psychological themes and to work with them. Inevitably, then, there will be a tension in this work between the pursuit of knowledge of commonalities, which might, carefully, be called a "psychology of deaf peoples" and a recognition of diversity and individual differences.

One of these themes in this psychology is the variations in Deaf cultural identity development (Glickman, 1996; Leigh, 2009; Maxwell-McCaw, 2001). In Chapter 2, Gournaris and Aubrecht move away from what they see as a narrow cultural identity perspective to describe several "relational postures," longer term patterns of attitudes, beliefs and behaviors, which they believe are found commonly among deaf and hearing people. It would seem that even with all this diversity, deaf and hearing people, who work together in educational, rehabilitation and mental health programs, still find themselves in fairly predictable kinds of conflicts with each other. My experience as a hearing man working with deaf people for over 30 years has been that this is very true, so much that I've come to believe that how deaf and hearing people handle these predictable areas of conflicts ultimately make or break a treatment program. If there were no common psychology and sociology to this work, no common themes and issues that deaf and hearing people face whenever we interact, then it would be hard to explain why these same kinds of cross cultural conflicts happen again and again, or to devise a way forward towards more effective cross cultural partnerships. The knowledge dimension concerns what deaf and hearing people need to know about each other so that we can achieve this bridge, creating the successful and culturally affirmative treatment programs we all want.

Prior to 1970, alleged differences between deaf and hearing people were cast as deficiencies in deaf people. Based on the early work of Pintner and Myklebust (Myklebust, 1964; Pintner, Eisenson, & Stanton, 1941;

Pollard, 1992), these descriptions of the alleged deficiencies in deaf people (e.g., deaf people are language impaired, immature, impulsive, impulsive, concrete, aggressive, less intelligent) were part of what (hearing) authorities thought of as a "psychology of deafness." The work of the next two to three decades was corrective to this, establishing that deaf people have the same range of intelligence as hearing people, that ASL is a real language, and members of the Deaf Community are culturally different, that deaf children from deaf families did as well as hearing children in hearing families on a range of variables. The need to correct the prior pathological view of deaf people prevented people from asking questions about what real differences may exist between the thinking and learning patterns of deaf and hearing people (Pollard, 1992; Schlesinger & Meadow, 1972). Hauser and Marschark (2008) note,

> In an effort to demonstrate that sign language was fully comparable to spoken language and that deaf children from deaf families were as developmentally advantaged as hearing children from hearing families, consideration of differences between deaf and hearing children and even explanations of the considerable diversity among deaf children relative to hearing age-matched peers were largely banished from the research agenda. Where did this self-imposed research censorship get us? (p. 441)

The distaste developed among professionals who work with deaf people for any attempt to describe a psychology of deafness works against our pursuit of knowledge of what is similar in the deaf experience. A generation of scholars has argued emphatically against any notion that deaf people are different, especially when the differences point to deficiencies relative to hearing people. Lane's 1992 critique of an "audist psychology of the deaf" is the most emphatic on this point. One result of this desire to present deaf people in a culturally affirmative way is that it becomes challenging to find the right way to describe psychopathology when it does exist. In mental health settings, one works with deaf people who have various kinds of psychopathology, and one needs a language for this that doesn't build upon negative stereotypes and mistaken beliefs about deaf people.

I believe it is possible to respect and work from the cultural model of deaf people while still appreciating that the experiences of some deaf people in a hearing society, especially the experiences of language deprivation and communication isolation, do create disadvantages, deficits, even additional disabilities. I also believe it is crucial to recognize that most of the causes of hearing loss in birth or early life can also cause other medical, neurological, and cognitive problems. For the first few years of my work with deaf people, I thought it was inappropriate and offensive to ask, as part of an intake, about the cause of the person's hearing loss. I've changed my view of that even though I know it is a culturally insensitive question. In a clinical context, the question is relevant.

Like hearing people, deaf people have problems rooted in both biology and environment. One can recognize, in some deaf people, the presence of disabilities while still appreciating Deaf ways of being in the world as different, not deficient, and sometimes as advantageous. The beauty of sign language, the benefits of communication in this visual means, and the strong sense of community and culture entice many hearing people into contact with deaf people and the Deaf world. Many hearing people decide to work with deaf people not because we want to fix or help people we see as less than us, but because we are drawn to a language, culture, and world we see as very appealing. We seek contact with deaf people because of what this adds to our lives. It is striking just how many hearing people see involvement with deaf people as enriching our lives, and how many of us become crusaders for deaf people, whether or not this is welcomed by deaf people themselves. Indeed, many hearing people in this field, far from wanting deaf people to become more hearing, seem to want themselves to become more Deaf. As Hoffmeister and Harvey (1996) described, and as reviewed in Chapter 2 in this book, this "confusion of boundaries" posture may be part of a psychology of hearing people who are drawn to deaf people because they are searching for an identity themselves.

The disadvantages that some deaf people face include the high prevalence of neurologically based learning disabilities, the systemic obstacles to learning sign language, the resulting fact that many deaf children begin school without native language skills in any language, the fund of information gaps that make it hard to associate new learning with old learning and relatively low levels of literacy overall. It also appears to be the case that deaf people experience higher levels of traumatic and abusive experiences.[4] The advantages that many signing deaf people have over hearing people include superior performance in visual spatial organization and memory, the ability to read facial expressions for emotion, visual attention, and certain kinds of mental manipulation (Marschark & Hauser, 2008). Belonging to a close cultural community can give one a strong sense of identity and a network of friends, family and associates such that one never feels alone. Again, this draws many hearing people who don't feel a similar connection to their own communities. Other differences between deaf and hearing persons are neither advantages nor disadvantages. They are just differences. An example is a visual as opposed to an auditory orientation towards the world. Whether one attributes these differences to the contrasts between spoken and sign languages, auditory or visual learning, or common life experience differences between deaf and hearing people; they all attest to an apparent reality that there are distinctions between how deaf and hearing people think and function that apply some of the time.

The Marschark and Hauser (2008) text on "Deaf cognitions" explores cognitive differences between deaf and hearing people and their implications for deaf education. The authors there argue, for instance, that deaf students are at a huge disadvantage when mainstreamed in hearing classrooms where no accommodations are made for their learning style and, crucially, that the presence of interpreters does not overcome this disadvantage. The differences between a visual and an auditory orientation to the world, and between spoken and signed language, may call for a different teaching style.

> Even if we cannot yet be sure what kinds of educational interventions would be optimal for deaf students, the difference in outcomes when teachers know how deaf students think and learn is now clear. Several studies have demonstrated that deaf students tend to learn significantly less in mainstream college classrooms than their hearing peers, despite having highly skilled interpreters and instructors who utilize appropriate classroom techniques for teaching deaf students (e.g., collaboration with interpreters, providing notes; Marschark & Wauters, 2008, p. 313)

Why should deaf students in hearing classrooms learn less than hearing students when skilled interpreters are present? Perhaps it has to do with the interpretation process itself as opposed to learning directly from teachers who use one's language. Perhaps it has to do with differences in how teachers who know deaf people teach. Whatever the reasons, the same dynamics occur in mental health settings where many deaf persons appear to do better when working with clinicians who sign themselves and who use counseling techniques that resonate with deaf people. In this book, considerable attention is directed to describing and illustrating counseling approaches that are more closely aligned with a visual orientation to the world, the grammatical features of ASL, and these Deaf cognitive processes.

Deaf cognitions are also referred to by Leigh, Pollard and others (Leigh & Pollard, 2011; Namy, 1977) as different "thought worlds":

> The unique visual-gestural modality of sign languages, their substantial structural and production differences from spoken languages, the behavioral norms of Deaf culture, and the very experience of growing up and living life with versus without the sense of hearing combine to yield quite different "thought worlds" between Deaf and hearing people. (Leigh & Pollard, 2011, p. 271)

If differences in Deaf cognition are pertinent for Deaf education, then certainly they are also pertinent for mental health and rehabilitation efforts. If the last generation of Deaf mental health specialists had to argue that deaf persons are capable of benefiting from any style of psychother-apy, then perhaps this generation can argue that, yes, while this is true, certain kinds of adaptations to best practices in mental health care appear to resonate well with many deaf consumers. This appears to be due to many factors, some of which are disadvantages, some of which are advan-tages, and most of which are just different ways of being-in-the-world.

The fact that women are individually different from each other does not prevent modern feminist scholars from exploring differences between female and male experiences and sensibilities. The fact that individual African Americans can have little in common does not mean that the experience of growing up a racial minority in a White dominant society is not relevant to a "psychology of African Americans" and other racial minorities. Any discussion of mental health care with minority groups will describe generalizations, including shared sensibilities, that apply to many members of that group (Sue & Sue, 2008), even while they point out individual differences. It would be nice to believe that we are now historically far enough away from the early theorists who saw deaf people as inferior to hearing people, that we no long have to insist that "we are all the same," and instead can explore, respectfully, deaf experiences and deaf sensibilities without apology. This may be naïve, and one must be ever on guard that discussions about how deaf and hearing people may be differ-ent do not slide into the old paradigm about deaf people being inferior. Nonetheless, this exploration of, for example, how to make mental health care work better for deaf people requires this search for commonalities in the deaf experience.

A Brief Digression into the History of the Development of Deaf Mental Health Care[5]

Knowledge in a field includes knowledge of its history. Therefore it is worthwhile reviewing briefly the pioneering works and literature that brought us to this point.

Prior to the 1970s, the small literature that existed on mental health care of deaf people worked exclusively from the medical-pathological model of deafness. Deaf people were understood only as people with a medical disability. They were presumed to be disabled and psychological evaluations began with the assumption of deafness as pathology.

In the first half of the 20th century, the main research into psychol-ogy and deaf people was published by Rudolf Pintner and associates (Pol-lard, 1992). Reflecting the interest in newly developing intelligence tests, they published over 80 papers comparing deaf and hearing samples on intelligence and personality. Using highly biased measures such as written English tests, they found, not surprisingly, lower intelligence and more psychopathology in the deaf samples (Vernon, 1995). Pintner's conclu-sions on the relative intellectual inferiority of deaf people were reinforced later by Helmer Myklebust, whose own studies of deaf people using English based personality tests such as the MMPI concluded that deaf people showed greater psychopathology (Pollard, 1992). More recently, we've come to understand how these results come from biased tests and testing procedures (Pollard, 2002). A study by Rosen (1967) found, for instance, that deaf Gallaudet College freshmen often produced psychotic MMPI profiles.

In the 1950s and early 1960s, five specialty mental health programs for deaf persons were established. The first was the mental health project for the deaf established at the New York State Psychiatric Institute by Franz Kallman, John Rainer, and Ken Altshuler. This was followed by the St. Elizabeth Hospital unit in Washington, DC founded by Luther Robinson; a program at the Michael Reese Hospital in Chicago founded by Roy Grinker, McCay Vernon, and Eugene Mindel; the University of California San Francisco's Center on Deafness founded by Hilde Schlesinger and Kay Meadow, and a psychiatric inpatient program for the deaf in Manchester, England, established by John Denmark. These programs all focused on the most severely disturbed deaf people. They provided the first contexts in which psychotherapy with deaf adults was discussed.

In the 1970s and 1980s, coincident with the recognition of American Sign Language (ASL) as a genuine language and the Deaf Community as a subculture, a number of mental health clinicians, some of whom were deaf, pioneered new "culturally affirmative" approaches to psychotherapy with deaf persons. They challenged the stereotypes about deaf people being incapable of insight oriented psychotherapies as well as the presumed connection between deafness and psychopathology.

In the 1970s, psychologist Edna Levine conducted a survey of psychological service providers working with hearing impaired people and found that most were practicing without special training or knowledge, including knowledge of sign language. Her survey resulted in the important 1975 Spartanburg Conference on the Functions, Competencies and Training of Psychological Services to the Deaf,[6] which she later reported on in a groundbreaking monograph (Levine, 1977). At this conference, standards were proposed for professionals who work with deaf people. Dr. Levine was involved in founding the New York State Psychiatric Institute's mental health program for the deaf and New York University's research and training center for deafness rehabilitation. One of her books, *The Ecology of Early Deafness* (1981), is noteworthy for the emphasis she places on the "ecology" or environment that deaf children need to thrive. She was very clear that such an ecology had to include sign language. She also describes the nature of psychological examination of deaf people and qualifications for examiners. Levine could easily be considered the mother of what we are now calling Deaf mental health care. She died in 1992, but she would be thrilled to see the development of her field, especially the growing number of deaf psychologists.

The first text on counseling deaf people was a small monograph with that name edited by two pioneering deaf psychologists, Allen Sussman and Larry Stewart (1971). This text contained chapters describing the social and psychological problems of deaf people, the then current status and principles of counseling with deaf people, the role and function of the counselor, and counselor preparation. Patterson and Stewart, in their chapter on principles of counseling with deaf people, argued that … "the nature and principles of counseling with deaf people are no different than those that characterize counseling with other people. Rather, it is their implementation that differs" (p. 55). They argued that for counseling to be successful with deaf people, "the counselor must 1. understand certain facts about deaf people; 2. be aware of the special problems experienced by the deaf; 3. know the impact of these problems so that their impact on the counseling relationship may be minimized; 4. be able to communicate with deaf people in their language; and 5. be aware of ways that deaf clients can be helped to better express themselves" (p. 56).

Counseling with Deaf People (1971) addressed such basic questions as whether deaf people face unique problems, what qualifies counselors to work with deaf people, whether standard methods of psychotherapy could be applied with deaf clients, and how one trains counselors to work with deaf people. At the end of their preface, the editors hoped that "this book will be the first of many on the subject of counseling the deaf" (p. 9).

The 1960s and 1970s were a time of fast growth in the world of psychotherapies beyond the psychodynamic and behavioral models which dominated the field in the first half of the 20th century. Sussman and Brauer (1999) noted how deaf people were excluded from this burgeoning of psychotherapies. Part of the reason was the lack of qualified clinicians, but this

> slow progress … was further exacerbated by negative attitudes of mental health professionals and avowed experts in deafness regarding the ability of deaf individuals to benefit from psychotherapy. The prevailing attitude at the time was that deaf people, due to their traditionally imputed deficiencies such as language difficulties, communication problems, lack of English skills, inability to reason on the abstract level, and personality issues, were not appropriate or feasible candidates for in-depth insight-developing, affectively oriented, psychoanalytically oriented, and cognitively oriented psychotherapies. It was believed that only the highly educated, the highly verbal, post-lingually deafened individuals could benefit from such forms of therapy. (p. 3)

Also in 1971, Eugene Mindel and McCay Vernon published, *They Grow in Silence.* This was followed the next year by Hildle Schlesinger and Kathryn Meadow's, *Sound and Sign.* Both of these books had profound influence over the fields of education, rehabilitation and mental health care with deaf people. These three books, along with Levine's (1981) *Ecology of Early Deafness* and her monograph on the Spartanburg conference (Levine, 1977), can be considered the first "Deaf affirmative" psychology books published in the United States.

They Grow in Silence, The Ecology of Early Deafness, and *Sound and Sign* all reinforced the importance of sign language in deaf education. Schlesinger and Meadow in *Sound and Sign* (1972) presented research showing that almost five times as many deaf as hearing students displayed severe behavioral problems. They described numerous deaf individuals who received psychotherapy services in their specialized Deaf mental health care outpatient mental health program. Like Levine, they made the then radical claim that staff members working in such a Deaf mental health care program needed special training in order to understand the language and the special needs of the Deaf Community. Professionals working with deaf individuals needed to acquaint themselves with the manual sign language of the deaf, with the cultural factors, the conflicts, and the developmental stresses to which deaf individuals are subjected. They needed also to understand, and be ready to try to reduce, the stigma attached to deafness by persons with normal hearing (Schlesinger & Meadow, 1972, p. 230).

It was another decade before the next book on this subject, an edited volume called *Deafness and Mental Health* (Stein, Mindel, & Jabaley, 1981) appeared. This book contains a chapter on "Insight Oriented Psychotherapy with the Deaf" (F. Levine, 1981). Levine made the then groundbreaking claim that "psychoanalytically oriented psychotherapy may be the treatment of choice for the intelligent deaf adult with emotional problems" (p. 113). While this certainly represented an advance over the early stereotypes about the alleged inability of deaf people to do insight oriented treatment, the author still made assumptions suggesting they had not yet moved beyond a hearing, ethnocentric viewpoint. For instance, a new deaf patient, in a waiting room with a receptionist who did not sign, about to meet a therapist who is also a novice signer, is described like this: "An incipient paranoia exploded in the waiting room, where she frightened the receptionist by signing with the fury of a boxer throwing punches" (p. 117). The notion of deaf people being paranoid is evoked here along with the suggestion that use of sign language reflects hostility. The metaphor of a "boxer throwing punches" isn't a particularly culturally attuned way of describing someone using sign language. Was this client truly paranoid or did she have legitimate reasons to be concerned about whether she would be understood and well treated?

In a second case, the psychiatrist interprets a deaf patient with excellent speech dropping his voicing as an attempt to make the psychiatrist feel, "awkward and helpless. This led me to an appreciation of how helpless and awkward (he) felt in relation to the hearing world" (p. 118).

When the psychiatrist finally commented on the patient's tendency to drop his voice,

> his anger at being deaf emerged. Thereafter, he resorted much less often to lowering his voice, but the helpless rage at being deaf that had been touched upon scared him greatly and could not be contained by the therapeutic alliance. We met for yet another 6 months, dealing at times with his frustration at being deaf. He terminated treatment with only a vague plan to start again with me later. And without ever fully working through the fear of his rage or the helplessness behind it. (pp. 118–119)

We see here a problem with psychotherapies that place much emphasis upon the importance of making psychodynamic interpretations of client motivations. Interpretations are subject to the bias of the interpreter. The bias implicit in these and other cases is that the deaf client must accommodate to the communication needs of the clinician and that failure to do so represents some pathology on the clients' part. This is a hearing bias in people who imagine themselves to be objective. Another bias is that clinical interpretations revolve around presumed feelings of loss and rage at being deaf and about the need for clients to mourn the loss of hearing (as opposed to, for instance, anger against the therapist for being unable to communicate well in the client's own language). The abrupt termination by the client of his therapy is presumed to be due to his inability or unwillingness to work through these negative feelings about his hearing loss and not, for instance, at his frustration with his therapists inability to understand him. While the deaf clients described here probably had the capacity for insight oriented psychotherapy, it seems the therapists were still limited both by inadequate self-awareness, knowledge of deaf people, and communication skills.

A more successful chapter was written by Larry Stewart, co-editor of the 1971 volume referenced above (Stewart, 1981). Stewart was the first person to demonstrate that non-directive counseling could be done with "traditionally underserved" deaf clients. Stewart, like fellow pioneer Allen Sussman, argued that "many deaf clients experience no difficulty in participating in the counseling process exactly as a hearing client of comparable abilities would, provided the counselor possesses the communication skills and empathy level necessary for effective interaction with the client" (p. 136). Stewart provides transcripts of sessions demonstrating counseling (primarily client centered and reality therapy) with deaf clients with very different language and functional abilities. His most striking examples are of his work with clients who have limited language abilities.

The next significant publication was an edited monograph published by the Arkansas Rehabilitation and Training Center on Deafness and Hearing Impairment (Anderson & Watson, 1985). This monograph included one of the first discussions of cross cultural variables in counseling with deaf people (Anderson & Rosten, 1985). The chapters on how to apply psychodynamic psychotherapy (Rayson, 1985), Adlerian counseling (Farrugia, 1985), Reality therapy (McCrone, 1985), Structural family therapy (Scott & Dooley, 1985), and structured group therapy (Danek, 1985) review basic principles of these treatment approaches and describe their applicability with deaf consumers. This monograph, along with *Deafness and Mental Health* (Stein et al., 1981), brought consideration of deaf people into the world of rapidly expanding psychotherapies. The main theme was that deaf people could be worked with successfully in many styles of psychotherapy.

In the 1980s, coincident with the explosion of interest in Deaf Culture, the first articles on cross cultural psychotherapy with deaf persons appeared (Anderson & Rosten, 1985; Glickman, 1983, 1986; Sussman, 1988). These were followed in the 1990s and early 2000s by other articles on this topic (Freedman, 1994) as well as books taking an explicitly "culturally affirmative" view of counseling and mental health care of deaf persons (Glickman, 2009; Glickman & Gulati, 2003; Glickman & Harvey, 1996; Leigh, 1999). The psychotherapy with deaf persons literature of this time consisted overwhelmingly of theoretical arguments and case studies, not empirical research (Leigh & Pollard, 2003). A representative article by Peterson and Gough (1995) discusses the principals of Gestalt Therapy such as the goal of creating greater self-awareness, and relates this to work with deaf clients. Some Gestalt techniques are reviewed and then an account of a Gestalt therapy session with a deaf client is presented. No research is cited; just a theoretical argument and case example.

The late 1980s saw the publication of the first book addressing systemic and family therapy interventions with deaf persons (Harvey, 1989). This text provided a conceptualization of functional and dysfunctional behaviors that individual deaf people showed as located, not within the deaf individual, but rather within patterns of interaction between them and people in their family, personal and professional networks. Accordingly, several systemic interventions were described. As with the new emphasis on culturally affirmative treatment, Harvey's text moved the perspective clinician's view when treating deaf persons away from any presumed connection between deafness and psychopathology. Harvey argued that deafness has no inherent meaning, *but the meaning that people assign to deafness has great psychological impact.* Deaf people could not be understood apart from how they were understood and treated in their families, schools, jobs, network of professional helpers, and the larger society's cultural influence. Therefore, Harvey demonstrated, it was often most useful to intervene with family, school, and professional helpers; to change their interaction with the deaf "identified patient," than to sit with the lone deaf person in the relative isolation of the therapy office.

Harvey went on to produce two more books on psychotherapy with deaf persons, particularly non-culturally deaf persons and those with acquired hearing loss (Harvey, 1998, 2001). Unlike his book on systemic and family therapy, both of these books were written for lay persons. They consisted of case studies (stories) about deaf persons from diverse walks of life going through the psychotherapy process. Counter transference factors were also illustrated.

Deaf Mental Health Literature from Great Britain

The literature review thus far has focused on the United States but there has also been a growth of specialty programs and literature in Europe, especially in Great Britain. The chief pioneer of Deaf mental health programs in Britain was John Denmark. As the son of a headmaster of a school for deaf children, he grew up knowing British Sign Language. He later established the first psychiatric unit for deaf persons (Denmark & Warren, 1972) and wrote an important book called *Deafness and Mental Health* (Denmark, 1994) in which he provided a broad overview of the psychological, sociological and cultural aspects of being deaf. He also reviewed the specialized knowledge base and skills clinicians must have. At first the only signing clinician in his specialty Deaf unit, he had a deep understanding of the importance for clinicians of being able to assess and treat using sign language themselves.

While Denmark advocated for the development of more specialized programs for deaf consumers, he said relatively little about psychotherapy per se. His primary concerns were that clinicians be properly trained, that they could sign competently themselves or at least work well with interpreters, that they understood the problems and abilities of deaf people and made appropriate assessments.

Three recent British edited texts have included chapters addressing aspects of psychotherapy with deaf persons. Two of these texts, *Mental Health and Deafness* (Hindley & Kitson, 2000) and *Deafness in Mind* (Austen & Crocker, 2004) contain chapters on psychodynamic, cognitive behavioral and family systemic psychotherapies. Another recent British volume, *Deafness and Challenging Behavior* (Austen & Jeffery, 2007) is the first book to focus on the challenge of helping deaf persons with severe behavior problems. The problems are understood from varying viewpoints (neurological, psychodynamic, developmental, and linguistic) and varying techniques and approaches to managing them are discussed. The connection between language deprivation and behavioral problems is well explored in this book.

Also from Great Britain, Mairian Corker's (1994) book, *Counselling: The Deaf Challenge*, has the benefit of being written from the point of view of an astute deaf professional. This book is especially useful for persons doing insight oriented psychotherapy with deaf persons. Corker's premature death silenced an emerging Deaf voice with much to offer the Deaf mental health field.

More on the Knowledge Dimension

In Chapter 8 of this volume, the knowledge dimension is addressed further by Patrick Brice, Irene Leigh, Martha Sheridan, and Kendra Smith, all department chairs of various mental health training programs at Gallaudet University. When I approached them about writing this chapter, my question to them was how they prepared students to become Deaf mental health specialists. I knew that they had to impart the body of knowledge specific to each discipline, but beyond this they had to also teach students specifically what they needed to know to work with deaf people. If we are ever going to have a credential for Deaf mental health specialists, there will some day be a qualifying exam, an idea proposed by the National Association of the Deaf in an important position statement concerning culturally affirmative and linguistically accessible mental health services (National Association of the Deaf, 2003). This exam would have to be based on an accepted body of specialized knowledge. These educators are in the forefront of preparing such specialists.[7] What do they think professional preparation for such specialists should look like? What body of knowledge and set of specialized skills must students acquire during their graduate educations? What is different about the preparation of Deaf mental health specialists, and what are the particular challenges and benefits to training deaf persons for such roles? These questions provide the content for Chapter 8.

Specialists in Deaf mental health care have to familiarize themselves with the growing research and scholarship in this field. One center of such scholarship has been the various mental health programs at Gallaudet, with many important texts coming from scholar/educator/clinicians in this faculty. Psychology Department Chairperson Irene Leigh has been particularly prolific. Two of her texts, *Psychotherapy with Deaf Persons from Diverse Groups* (Leigh, 1999, 2010) and *A Lens on Deaf Identities* (Leigh, 2009), should be required reading for all counselors of deaf people. Other noteworthy Deaf mental health texts from Gallaudet faculty include *Ethics in Mental Health and Deafness* (Gutman, 2002) and Martha Sheridan's two books *Inner lives of Deaf Children* (2001) and *Deaf adolescents* (2008).

The knowledge dimension should also include awareness of how Deaf mental health programs are created. Deaf mental health specialists advocate for the creation of specialized Deaf mental health programs. In the United States, most such programs have required support from the federal or state governments. Deaf mental health programs typically serve a large geographic area. They bring together clinicians from different disciplines, striving to create signing environments attuned to the communication and clinical needs of deaf persons. Several such specialized programs are represented in this book: the Westborough State Hospital Deaf Unit and Advocates Deaf residential programs that I have been affiliated with; the Walden School program for deaf children with emotional and behavioral problems in Framingham, Massachusetts; the Deaf Services Center (now called PAHrtners Deaf Services) from outside Philadelphia, Pennsylvania; and the Minnesota Chemical Dependency Program for Deaf and Hard of Hearing Persons from Minneapolis, Minnesota.

In Chapter 4, three of the most prominent state coordinators for public mental health services for deaf persons; John Gournaris from Minnesota, Steve Hamerdinger from Alabama, and Roger Williams from South Carolina, describe how Deaf mental health services were created in their respective states, what they look like and how they compare and contrast. They draw out the difficult lessons learned from several state efforts to develop such services. This includes the synergistic role of organized advocacy, threats or realities of litigation, strategic use of compelling individual stories, data, and knowledge of what works and what definitely does not. They describe the core principal of the need to create Deaf-specific, culturally affirmative treatment programs and to hire clinicians with the specialized communication and clinical skills.

Because the numbers of deaf persons needing specialized services is usually small, DMHC clinicians and programs must serve a wide diversity of deaf clientele in a broad geographic area. This principal is always challenged by fiscal and administrative realities which dictate that only certain people can be served by a service and which make it difficult to recruit, hire, and supervise persons with unique skills and life experiences. In one way or another, Deaf mental health specialists are always fighting to create specialized Deaf programs and services against the torrent of forces that push for mainstreamed or integrated programs, without specialized expertise. Gournaris, Hamerdinger, and Williams have all had to struggle against limited funds, arbitrary practices and widespread ignorance that interfere with the creation of quality mental health care for deaf people. In the face of these forces, what have they, and other advocates in these states, been able to fashion? Their knowledge and collective wisdom can inform the efforts of other advocates so that they don't have to all re-invent the wheel. At this stage in our collective experience, we do have a pretty good idea of what needs to be done. Indeed, standards of care for Deaf mental health care were organized by Randall Myers, and published by the National Association of the Deaf, as long ago as 1995 (Myers, 1995).

Knowledge about the special clinical and communication needs of deaf people emerges when they are served together in Deaf treatment programs. We could make observations about language dysfluency and about the possibility of a specialized clinical disorder in some deaf people[8] because there have been various deaf inpatient treatment units where similar observations were made again and again. We know very little about the experiences of deaf people in the Criminal Justice System (CJS) because they are so rarely brought together, but in Chapter 9, O'Rourke, Austen, and I discuss a key study emerging out of one state where Deaf prison units exist revealing some vitally important information about the language skills of deaf prisoners, information directly bearing on the possibility of providing them with due process in our legal system (Miller, 2004). If deaf people are poorly served by most mental health systems, their plight is certainly far worse within the CJS which may not even attempt to offer rehabilitation. Much of we are learning about Deaf mental health care applies to work with deaf defendants in court and deaf incarcerated people, and we have an even longer way to go before such institutions respond to deaf people constructively.

In Chapter 9, again through use of an imagined dialogue, O'Rourke, Austen, and I explore what a culturally affirmative response to deaf people within the CJS would look like. Because we are talking here about deaf persons who commit crimes, we also address directly the question that many people will ask; whether such specialized prison programs should even be attempted. Criminals, whatever their background and status, don't elicit the same sympathy and support as people seen as struggling with disabilities and disorders.

Whenever one does search through the research literature that exists, one encounters the name McCay Vernon again and again. Through his books and seminal articles, no one person has done more to assemble and publish what is known about deaf people than McCay Vernon. If Edna Levine is the mother of Deaf mental health care, then McCay Vernon would be the father. Both of these pioneers were key figures in restoring sign language to Deaf schools, a monumental contribution in itself. Ask yourself what is known on almost any topic relevant to deaf education, rehabilitation and mental health care, and you will quickly discover that McCay Vernon has described the state of the art. In the last decade or so, he has also championed the cause of deaf people in the criminal justice system, and has been a key figure in publishing most of what we know about that group and advocating for change (Vernon, 2010; Vernon & Greenberg, 1999; Vernon & Miller, 2001, 2005; Vernon & Raifman, 1997; Vernon, Steinberg, & Montoya, 1999; Vernon & Vernon, 2010). If we are ever to produce a more culturally affirmative response to deaf persons in the criminal justice system, such as that discussed in Chapter 9, McCay Vernon will also be the father and hero of that effort.

Finally, I would be remiss not to acknowledge a sad reality of the Deaf mental health field which is that quality scientific research that explores dimensions of the challenges, and creates and validates best practices, is sorely needed. We don't really know, for instance, such basic questions, always asked, about the prevalence of various kinds of psychiatric, substance abuse and developmental disorders among deaf people. We can speculate and estimate. We can extrapolate from a few small samples, but we don't really know.

In the past 25 years, Robert Pollard has emerged as the leading figure in Deaf mental health research. Dr. Pollard and his team at the Deaf Wellness Center (DWC) in Rochester, New York have produced a steady stream of ground-breaking research and practice papers regarding topics such as epidemiology, mental health interpreting, training and preparation for deaf psychologists, psychological evaluation and treatment of deaf persons, and adapting psychological treatments and health educational practices for deaf persons. The work of the Westborough Deaf Unit adapting cognitive behavioral therapy for deaf persons with language and learning challenges drew upon best practices pioneered by the DWC team (Glickman, 2009 and Chapter 1, this volume). Their research citations alone are far too numerous to include here but are available on their informative website (www.urmc.rochester.edu/dwc). It is no exaggeration to say that Deaf mental health would be a shadow of its current self without all the ground-breaking scholarship and materials coming out of the DWC.

The Skills Dimension

Deaf Mental Health Care also involves clinicians who bring to their work highly specialized skills. In this book, three kinds of skills are emphasized. These are:

1. Skills in handling very complex and unique communication challenges;
2. Skills in managing deaf/hearing cross cultural relationships;
3. Skills in adapting best practices in evaluation and treatment for a diversity of deaf people.

Two kinds of communication skills are widely recognized: the ability to sign competently and to work well with interpreters. But even these two foundational skills are far more complex than they first appear to be. Our deaf clients know how different their communication skills are from each other. A deaf resident of a group home I work with at present, all of whose roommates are signing deaf people, complains to me that he can't talk to any of them because they don't make any sense. "You sign and they sign," I respond to him playfully. "Yes," he says, "but I don't understand them."

It takes a great deal of sign language skill to judge whether a communication problem between a signing consumer and a signing clinician is due to skill deficiencies in the consumer, the clinician, or both. For example, I'm in a hospital with a deaf patient and deaf staff person explaining to the doctor that a Certified Deaf Interpreter is needed for communication with the deaf patient. I'm signing while I'm speaking because there is no interpreter present. The doctor sees me signing and says, "You are doing fine." I reply, "You can't judge that. You can't judge the level of signing skill of me or (this deaf patient)," but the doctor is unconvinced. To him, signing is signing. If I were speaking Japanese, he would probably be more willing to appreciate that he can't evaluate how well I speak Japanese, but his standards for signing is that it is all "good enough." The simultaneous communication (speaking and signing at the same time) that I'm using looks very clear to him, but I know that most of it is incomprehensible to the deaf patient in the room. The nursing administrators at Westborough State Hospital counted anyone who signed at any level as a "signer" for the purposes of staffing, and nuances about communication skill differences were lost on many of them. Usually, there is a financial incentive (lower overtime costs, not hiring interpreters) for the lower standards.

To complicate this further, people who know a little sign language often think they sign much better than they do. They often become psychologically invested in being considered someone who knows sign language, who is qualified to help "the deaf." The problem of beginning signers and their employers overestimating their ability to serve deaf persons is common and is one reason that Deaf mental health programs need to have a position like that of Communication Specialist, someone who establishes appropriate standards for communication skills and assists when those standards are not met. This is not to say, of course, that beginning and intermediate signers (deaf and hearing) should never be employed, but rather that there is quality control to assure that the appropriate communication resources are drawn upon to assist them. I've personally known many superb clinicians who did first rate work with deaf persons even though they didn't sign well or at all, but in all cases these persons worked alongside of a qualified communication team consisting of interpreters, certified Deaf interpreters, and deaf staff who monitored and assisted with the communication process. These non-signing clinicians also tend to be exceptionally sensitive to deaf/hearing cross cultural dynamics.

The most sophisticated Deaf mental health programs today recognize the extraordinary skills it takes to communicate effectively with every deaf person referred, including the problem of deaf persons who are very dysfluent sign communicators, and have staff who are genuine communication experts. These persons are *in addition to* interpreters and signing staff.

Working well with interpreters involves knowing a great deal about the language skills of deaf and hearing people, the interpreting process, the interplay of language and thought, the training and skills of interpreters, and the clinical impact of introducing one (or more!) interpreters into the treatment setting. Examples of this are presented in Chapter 3. The topic there is how interpreters and clinicians work together when the deaf consumer is very language dysfluent. Interpreting for persons whose language and thinking is not clear is a challenge on order of magnitude more difficult than interpreting for fluent, clear language users. Clinicians, especially when doing mental status assessments, need to understand *how* the consumer is thinking, *how* he or she uses language. When working with interpreters, they only receive what the interpreter conveys. If the interpreting process cleans up dysfluent language, making the consumer appear more clear, organized and sensible than they really are, this can affect the evaluations clinicians make. Indeed, many hearing non-signing clinicians never "see" the language dysfluency of these clients because the language errors were corrected in the interpreting process. How, then, should interpreters handle unclear language?

Sometimes a second interpreter, a certified deaf interpreter (CDI) is brought in, which makes the communication dynamics even more complex, and increases the likelihood that unclear language will be corrected in the interpreting process. What, if any, information about the consumers' language skills do the interpreters share with clinicians? What do clinicians need to know about the diversity of communication abilities of deaf people and the possible meanings of dysfluent sign language? How can clinicians distinguish dysfluent language that suggests a thought disorder from dysfluent language that suggests language deprivation or other problems? What does best practice in interpreter(s)/clinician collaboration look like? These questions are in addition to the more familiar questions raised about the presence of interpreters in mental health situations. These familiar questions have to do with how interpreters can impact the treatment process (Harvey, 1982, 1989). The risks and benefits of work with a CDI is discussed further in Chapter 3.

As with so many other areas of Deaf mental health care and research, the Deaf Wellness Center has advanced the specialty of mental health interpreting by developing standards and training materials, through conceptualizing interpreting in new ways, and by training interpreters in challenges like interpreting for language dysfluent persons (Dean & Pollard, 2001, 2005, 2012; Pollard, 1998). Some of this training is conducted in a yearly mental health interpreting program conducted by the Alabama Office of Deaf Services. In Chapter 3 of this book, the skills involved for both interpreters and clinicians when working with language dysfluent persons are considered from both perspectives.

Thus, "signing well" is a more complicated skill than it first appears because of the diversity of ways that deaf people communicate and the large numbers of language dysfluent deaf consumers. When one is hired as a mental health specialist to work with deaf people, with the presumption that one "signs well," one may have a hard time acknowledging that one needs help to communicate well with certain deaf clients. Unless they are native signers themselves, very few clinicians who specialize in work with deaf people ever reach the standard of communication skill needed to work well with every deaf person that they meet. As the complexity of the communication challenges faced in this field becomes clearer, there is increasing recognition that effective communication often requires this team effort. More and more, specialists in mental health care of deaf people recognize the importance of having a genuine Communication Specialist on the treatment team. This person, again, is in addition to interpreters and signing staff. Whenever one thinks about adapting a treatment approach for deaf persons, especially those who are sign language dysfluent, a Communication Specialist should be involved in the planning and implementation of this effort.

Hearing people who know nothing about deaf people usually believe they've handled the cross cultural and language challenges sufficiently by hiring a sign language interpreter or a "signer." They see no need for accommodations beyond this one act. This is a very naïve stance and much attention is spent in this book debunking it. Deaf mental health care involves the skill of expert collaboration between genuine communication and clinical experts. It involves, as Pollard stated above, "an intimate knowledge of the potentials and pitfalls of translation between ASL and English." This is not the same thing as bringing an interpreter or signer into the room.

Skills in handling communication are also at the heart of forensic evaluations and court procedures, as discussed in Chapter 9. The matter of whether or not a deaf person receives due process in court hangs on this issue being handled well, and there is good reason to believe that 20 to 50% of deaf persons do not receive due process because of poor handling of communication (Miller, 2004). As in clinical settings, court personnel often do not know anything more than "bring in an interpreter" and they assume that, with the interpreter there, all communication matters are well handled, and that this will satisfy the Americans with Disability Act and other laws. Advocates struggle to get interpreters provided and may not themselves always realize that genuine communication access, especially for the language dysfluent defendant, will require more than this. A deaf defendant can appear competent or incompetent based on how expertly communication is handled and whether the court is willing to accommodate the changes to process that allow adequate communication to occur (Vernon & Miller, 2001, 2005).

The second specialized skill area is the ability to handle deaf/hearing cross cultural dynamics well. Again, this is rarely attended to sufficiently. It's very easy for naïve hearing people to assume that they will not have to undergo any personal self-examination when working with culturally Deaf people, that their good intentions should not be challenged. For instance, a hearing supervisor who is not familiar with deaf people provides supervision to a culturally Deaf counselor. The hearing supervisor is frustrated because the deaf counselor does not seem receptive to taking his suggestions or following what he knows to be best practice in their field. What he doesn't grasp is that the culturally Deaf counselor may be resistant to taking direction from a culturally naïve, non-signing hearing person who he perceives as "not getting" the language and cultural challenges he faces. The supervisor is also not attuned to just how easily misunderstandings happen and how much effort it takes to communicate well across this language and cultural barrier. The deaf and hearing persons also sometimes have such contrasting life experiences and world views that they can talk past each other without understanding why. The deaf/hearing cross cultural *stuff* is always there just as it is in other majority/minority dynamics. It is often the "elephant in the room." The culturally competent clinician or administrator working with deaf and hearing people will have the skills to manage this process. Again, this is addressed most directly in Chapters 1, 2, 5, and 8.

Finally, a good deal of attention is given in this book to the issue of adapting best practices in mental health and substance abuse treatment for deaf people. In the past, it has been difficult to talk about making adaptations for many deaf consumers because the implication was that one had to "dumb down" treatment to fit deaf people, all stereotyped as "low functioning." Deaf people naturally objected to such depictions, especially the well-educated deaf people who read and write in the professional literature. It must always be remembered that no such generalizations about deaf people are valid, that there is more diversity among deaf people than between deaf and hearing people, and that cultural differences do not reflect differences in intelligence or ability. As noted above, adaptations may or may not need to be made for language and cultural differences, learning style, fund of information gaps, and language and learning challenges. We make progress when we can recognize and work with this complex clinical reality without making unfair generalizations that stereotype deaf people.

That said, deaf and hearing signing clinicians everywhere adapt treatment methods for many deaf consumers. This is a clinical reality, and some of our most talented and creative deaf clinicians give workshops on how to do this.[9] They do so because they know intuitively and from experience what works. Everywhere you go in the Deaf mental health field, you find skilled clinicians adapting practices for deaf consumers. The problem is that most of the time they don't publish what they do so that others will learn from them and not have to reinvent the wheel. I hope this book will partially correct that problem.

In this book, we study adaptations that have been made to best practices in psychiatric rehabilitation (Chapter 5), substance abuse treatment (Chapter 6), and residential treatment of traumatized children (Chapter 7) in order to discover commonalities in how talented clinicians adapt treatment for a diversity of deaf clients.

Once again, much of the ground work for this was done by the staff of the Deaf Wellness Center in their work adapting dialectical behavior therapy and psychoeducation regarding health care matters (O'Hearn & Pollard, 2008; Pollard, Dean, O'Hearn, & Hayes, 2009). The DWC has been meticulous in providing documentation for their efforts and also producing materials such as the DVD's on DBT groups.

The DWC staff also developed even more ground-breaking educational materials for the Center for Disease Control (CDC) and in that process illustrated principals relevant to any efforts to adapt educational and treatment materials for signing deaf people. These materials, on educational topics like asthma, chemical agents, dirty bombs, chlorine, lead poisoning, and emergency communication for deaf people, go well beyond translation. The way the information is presented is designed for deaf learners. One key adaptation is to convey information through dialogue between two or more deaf people. On the DVD presentation on asthma management, for example, DWC staff took the key learning points and created new materials, using deaf actors, where one actor explains the information to other actors. These other actors ask questions, and the information is conveyed through this conversational give and take. The actual dialogue between them adds information that is not always present in the English source materials but takes into account common fund of information gaps in less educated deaf people. For instance, the actors stop to elaborate on key concepts like "triggers" and "asthma management plan," which may be new for these consumers. Information is presented through dialogue in the form of a story. It is signed by deaf native or near native signers. All actors are deaf so to convey the idea of deaf people learning from each other, not from hearing people (Pollard et al., 2009).

In the examples of adaptations given in this book, a few themes keep reappearing. These include:

1. The multiple kinds of adaptations for language. These include careful attention and matching to the communication abilities of consumers, the simplification or avoidance of English language based materials, the utilization of visual and pictorial aids.
2. Pre-treatment efforts to inform and engage clients, especially the need to provide clients with a schema or map of the treatment process.
3. The attention to fund of information differences.
4. The reliance upon storytelling and visual metaphors.
5. Teaching concepts through examples.
6. The use of active treatment strategies, like role playing and therapeutic activities, as a basis for generating discussions and insights.
7. Creative uses of technology.

Storytelling and Clinical Examples

Efforts are made throughout this book to present information in a manner that is consumer friendly. I encouraged all the chapter authors to search for clinical examples and stories, and to be willing to share personal experiences when appropriate. Wherever they felt it was appropriate, I encouraged them to talk in the first person. In Chapters 2, 5, and 9, information is presented through invented dialogues. We couldn't completely avoid an academic presentation, especially with regard to situating this work within the context of the mental health literature, but I hope this effort, which parallels some of the adaptations that are made to the treatment process, will make the book more accessible and interesting for most readers. I've come to be fully convinced of the power of teaching through examples, metaphors,[10] and stories. It's "deaf friendly," but it's "hearing friendly" too.

The heavy reliance upon case examples throughout this book brings up the important issue of confidentiality. How could we present clinical examples, so necessary to describing this work, while still protecting confidentiality within the close knit Deaf world? Every contributor to this book struggled with this and kept concerns about protecting client confidentiality in the forefront. The answer is that every case example is very significantly disguised. Not only names, but all identifying information is changed, and in many instances the characteristics of multiple consumers are blended into one for the purpose of the story. While this may sacrifice some of the validity of the case studies, I think the essential points remain valid. The consumers we describe are representative of the kinds of persons served in Deaf mental health programs, and if particular people seem to remind the reader of someone they know, this is probably because we've captured well commonalities in the clinical population. Again, deaf people differ in every conceivable way, and all efforts at generalizations must be balanced by this appreciation of client diversity. We've done our best to capture this balance, present case scenarios that are clinically useful, protect confidentiality, and still respect the diversity in the population.

A Concluding Metaphor

Fred Astaire and Ginger Rogers were famous, mid-20th century Hollywood performers best known for their spectacular dancing. Fred Astaire was the more celebrated of the pair, but it is often said that his partner Ginger Rogers performed all same dance steps equally well, only she did them backwards and in heels.

Doing Deaf mental health care is something like taking the role of Ginger Rogers in a dance routine. One has to master all the same techniques as every other performer but then one has to do so much more. One needs, as we have seen, additional kinds of cultural self-awareness and personal humility. One must learn a substantial body of new knowledge. One needs to be at least bilingual, in the spoken and signed languages of one's community, and just as importantly be able to work with people who have enormously varying language skills. The sophisticated communication skills one needs extend to the ability to work well with different kinds of interpreters and communication specialists, understanding the linguistic and clinical implications of such work. Whatever the clinical domain in which one works, be it trauma, mood disorders, substance abuse, couples and family therapy, or any other, one needs to learn "best practice" as it is currently understood, and then one has to know how to make creative adaptations to match the skills and needs of the particular consumers with whom one works. This is a daunting challenge, but many people are up for it, and, like Ginger Rogers, though underappreciated, with their multiple talents, match and sometimes outshine their contemporaries.

It seems fitting then to conclude with an appreciation of all my Deaf mental health care colleagues, past, present, and future, who perform all the same dance steps as "regular" mental health professionals, but who do these steps backwards and in heels.

Notes

1. In this book, extending a convention, Deaf with a capital D is used to describe the Deaf Community, Deaf Culture, Deaf programs, Deaf mental health care or explicit references to culturally Deaf people. The lower case deaf is used in all other circumstances.
2. See Chapter 5 and the ground-breaking work from the Deaf Wellness Center referenced in that chapter.
3. See Chapter 1.
4. See Chapters 9 and 10.
5. Much of this section is reprinted with permission from JADARA (see Glickman & Harvey, 2008).
6. This conference is discussed further in Chapter 8.
7. This is also addressed in the NAD 2008 supplemental paper on this issue (http://www.nad.org/issues/health-care/mental-health-services/access).
8. See Chapter 1.
9. I'm thinking here of Joseph (TJ) Batiano and Melissa Watson, both formally of the National Deaf Academy.
10. See Chapter 6 for discussion of the use of visual metaphors with clients.

References

Anderson, G. B., & Rosten, E. (1985). Towards evaluating process variables in counseling deaf people: A cross cultural perspective. In G. B. Anderson & D. Watson (Eds.), *Counseling deaf people: Research and practice* (pp. 1–22). Fayetteville: Arkansas Rehabilitation Research and Training center on Deafness and Hearing Impairment

Anderson, G. B., & Watson, D. (Eds.). (1985). *Counseling deaf people: Research and practice*. Fayetteville: Arkansas Rehabilitation Research and Training Center on Deafness and Hearing Impairment.

Austen, S., & Crocker, S. (Eds.). (2004). *Deafness in mind*. London: Whurr Publishers, Ltd.

Austen, S., & Jeffery, D. (Eds.). (2007). *Deafness and challenging behavior*. West Sussex, England: Wiley.

Bauman, H-Dirksen L. (Ed.). (2002). *Open your eyes: Deaf studies talking*. Minneapolis: University of Minnesota Press.

Corker, M. (1994). *Counselling: The deaf challenge*. London: Jessica Kingsley.

Danek, M. (1985). Structured group counseling with deaf adolescents. In G. B. Anderson & D. Watson (Eds.), *Counseling deaf people: Research and practice* (pp. 235–249).

Fayetteville: Arkansas Rehabilitation Research and Training Center on Deafness and Hearing Impairment.

Dean, R., & Pollard, R. (2001). The application of demand-control theory to sign language interpreting: Implications for stress and interpreter training. *Journal of Deaf Studies and Deaf Education, 6*(1), 1–14.

Dean, R., & Pollard, R. (2005). Consumers and service effectiveness in interpreting work: A practice profession perspective. In M. Marschark, R. Peterson & E. Winston (Eds.), *Interpreting and interpreter education: Directions for research and practice* (pp. 259–282). New York, NY: Oxford University Press.

Dean, R. K., & Pollard, R. Q. (2012). Beyond "interesting": Using demand control schema to structure experiential learning. In K. Malcolm & L. Swabey (Eds.), *In our hands: Educating healthcare interpreters* (pp. 77–104). Washington, DC: Gallaudet University Press.

Denmark, J. (1994). *Deafness and mental health.* London: Jessica Kingsley Publishers.

Denmark, J., & Warren, F. (1972). A psychiatric unit for the Deaf. *British Journal of Psychiatry, 120,* 423–428.

Farrugia, D. (1985). Adlerian counseling and the deaf client. In G. B. Anderson & D. Watson (Eds.), *Counseling deaf people: Research and practice* (pp. 145–166). Fayetteville: Arkansas Rehabilitation Research and Training Center on Deafness and Hearing Impairment.

Freedman, P. (1994). Counseling with deaf clients: The need for culturally and linguistically sensitive interventions. *JADARA, 27*(4), 16–28.

Glickman, N. (1983). A cross-cultural view of counseling with deaf clients. *Journal of Rehabilitation of the Deaf, 16*(3), 4–15.

Glickman, N. (1986). Cultural identity, deafness and mental health. *Journal of rehabilitation of the Deaf, 20*(2), 1–10.

Glickman, N. (1996). The development of culturally Deaf identities. In N. Glickman & M. Harvey (Eds.), *Culturally affirmative psychotherapy with deaf persons* (pp. 115–153). Mahwah, NJ: Erlbaum.

Glickman, N. (2009). *Cognitive behavioral therapy for deaf and hearing persons with language and learning challenges.* New York, NY: Routledge.

Glickman, N., & Gulati, S. (2003). *Mental health care of Deaf people: A culturally affirmative approach.* Mahwah, NJ: Erlbaum.

Glickman, N., & Harvey, M. (1996). *Culturally affirmative psychotherapy with deaf persons.* Mahwah, NJ: Erlbaum.

Glickman, N., & Harvey, M. (2008). Psychotherapy with Deaf adults: The development of a clinical specialization. *JADARA, 41*(3), 129–186.

Gutman, V. (2002). *Ethics in mental health and deafness* (2nd ed.). Washington, DC: Gallaudet University Press.

Harvey, M. (1982). The influence and utilization of an interpreter for deaf persons in family therapy. *American Annals of the Deaf, 127*(7), 821–827.

Harvey, M. (1989). *Psychotherapy with deaf and hard of hearing persons: A systemic model.* Hillsdale, NJ: Erlbaum.

Harvey, M. (1998). *Odyssey of hearing loss: Tales of triumph.* San Diego, CA: Dawn Sign Press.

Harvey, M. (2001). *Listen with the heart: Relationships and hearing loss.* San Diego, CA: Dawn Sign Press.

Hauser, P. C., & Marschark, M. (2008). What we know and what we don't know about cognition and deaf learners. In M. Marschark & P. C. Hauser (Eds.), *Deaf Cognition: Foundations and Outcomes* (pp. 439–457). New York, NY: Oxford University Press.

Hindley, P., & Kitson, N. (Eds.). (2000). *Mental health and deafness*. London: Whurr.

Hoffmeister, R., & Harvey, M. (1996). Is there a psychology of the hearing? In N. Glickman & M. Harvey (Eds.), *Culturally affirmative psychotherapy with Deaf persons*. Mahwah, NJ: Erlbaum.

Ladd, P. (2003). *Understanding Deaf culture: In search of deafhood*. Clevedon, England: Multilingual Matters, Ltd.

Lane, H. (1992). *The mask of benevolence*. New York, NY: Knoff.

Lane, H. (1996). Cultural self-awareness in hearing people. In N. Glickman & M. Harvey (Eds.), *Culturally affirmative psychotherapy with Deaf persons* (pp. 57–72). Mahwah, NJ: Erlbaum.

Leigh, I. (1999). *Psychotherapy with deaf clients from diverse groups*. Washington, DC: Gallaudet University Press.

Leigh, I. (2009). *A Lens on Deaf Identities*. New York, NY: Oxford University Press.

Leigh, I. (Ed.). (2010). *Psychotherapy with deaf persons from diverse groups* (2nd ed.). Washington, DC: Gallaudet University Press.

Leigh, I. W., & Pollard, R. Q (2003). Mental health and deaf adults. In M. Marschark & P. E. Spencer (Eds.). *Oxford handbook of deaf studies, language, and education* (pp. 203–215). New York, NY: Oxford University Press.

Leigh, I. W., & Pollard, R. Q. (2011). Mental health and deaf adults. In M. Marschark & P. E. Spencer (Eds.), *Oxford handbook of deaf studies, language and education* (2nd ed., pp. 214–226). New York, NY: Oxford University Press.

Levine, E. (1960). *The psychology of deafness*. New York: Columbia University Press.

Levine, E. (1977). *The preparation of psychological service providers to the deaf: A report of the Spartanburg conference on the functions, competencies and training of psychological service providers to the deaf*: PRWAD Monograph No. 4.

Levine, E. (Ed.). (1981). *The ecology of early deafness*. New York, NY: Columbia University Press.

Levine, F. (1981). Insight oriented psychotherapy with the Deaf. In L. Stein, E. Mindel, & T. Jabaley (Eds.), *Deafness and mental health* (pp. 113–132). New York, NY: Grune & Stratton.

Marschark, M. (1993). *Psychological development of deaf children*. New York, NY: Oxford University Press.

Marschark, M., & Hauser, P. C. (Eds.). (2008). *Deaf cognition: Foundations and outcomes*. New York, NY: Oxford University Press.

Marschark, M., & Spencer, P. (Eds.). (2011). *The Oxford handbook of deaf studies, Language and education* (2nd ed. Vol. 1). New York, NY: Oxford University Press.

Marschark, M., & Wauters, L. (2008). Language comprehension and learning by deaf students. In M. Marschark & P. C. Hauser (Eds.), *Deaf cognition: Foundations and outcomes* (pp. 313). New York, NY: Oxford University Press.

Maxwell-McCaw, D. (2001). *Acculturation and psychological well-being in deaf and hard of hearing people* (Unpublished doctoral dissertation). George Washington University, Washington, DC.

McCrone, W. (1985). Reality therapy applications with hearing-impaired clients. In G. B. Anderson & D. Watson (Eds.), *Counseling deaf people: Research and practice* (pp. 167–186). Fayetteville: Arkansas Rehabilitation Research and Training Center on Deafness and Hearing Impairment.

Miller, K. R. (2004). Linguistic diversity in a Deaf prison population: Implications for due process. *Journal of Deaf Studies and Deaf Education, 9*(1), 112–119.

Mindel, E. D., & Vernon, M. (1971). *They grow in silence.* Silver Spring, MD: National Association for the Deaf Press.

Myers, R. R. (1995). *Standards of care for the delivery of mental health services to deaf and hard of hearing persons.* Silver Spring, MD: National Association of the Deaf.

Myklebust, H. (1964). *The psychology of deafness.* New York, NY: Grune and Stratton.

Namy, C. (1977). Reflections on the training of simultaneous interpreters: A metalinguistic approach. In D. Gerver & H. W. Sinaiko (Eds.), *Language interpretying and communication* (pp. 22–33). New York. NY: Plenum.

National Association of the Deaf. (2003). Position statement on mental health services. Retrieved from http://www.nad.org/issues/health-care/mental-health-services/position-statement

O'Hearn, A., & Pollard, R. (2008). Modifying dialectical behavior therapy for deaf individuals. *Cognitive and behavioral practice, 15,* 400–414.

Patterson, C. H., & Stewart, L. G. (1971). Principles of counseling with deaf people. In A. E. Sussman & L. G. Stewart (Eds.), *Counseling with deaf people* (pp. 43–86). New York, NY: Deafness Research and Training Center.

Paul, P. V., & Jackson, D. W. (1993). *Toward a psychology of deafness: theoretical and empirical perspectives.* Boston. MA: Allyn and Bacon.

Peterson, D. B., & Gough, D. L. (1995). Applications of Gestalt therapy in deafness rehabilitation counseling. *JADARA, 29*(1), 17–31.

Pintner, R., Eisenson, J., & Stanton, M. (1941). *The psychology of the physically handicapped.* New York, NY: Croffs and Company.

Pollard, R. Q. (1992). 100 years in psychology and deafness: A centennial retrospective. *Journal of the American Deafness & Rehabilitation Association, 26*(3), 32–46.

Pollard, R. Q. (1996). Professional psychology and deaf people: The emergence of a discipline. *American Psychologist, 51*(4), 389–396.

Pollard, R. (1998). *Mental health interpreting: A mentored curriculum* [Videotape and users' guide]. Rochester, NY: University of Rochester School of Medicine.

Pollard, R. Q. (2002). Ethical conduct in research involving deaf people. In V. Gutman (Ed.), *Ethics in mental health and deafness* (pp. 162–178). Washington, DC: Gallaudet University Press.

Pollard, R. Q., Dean, R. K., O'Hearn, A., & Hayes, S. (2009). Adapting health education material for Deaf audiences. *Rehabilitation Psychology, 54*(2), 232–238.

Rayson, B. (1985). Psychodynamic psychotherapy with deaf clients. In G. B. Anderson & D. Watson (Eds.), *Counseling deaf people: Research and practice* (pp. 123–144). Fayetteville: Arkansas Rehabilitation Research and Training center on Deafness and Hearing Impairment.

Rosen, A. (1967). Limitations of personality inventories for assessment of deaf children and adults as illustrated by research with the Minnesota Multiphasic Personality Inventory. *Journal of Rehabilitation of the Deaf, 1,* 47–52.

Scheetz, N. A. (2004). *Psychosocial aspects of deafness.* Boston, MA: Pearson/A & B.

Schlesinger, H. S., & Meadow, K. P. (1972). *Sound and sign: Childhood deafness and mental health.* Berkeley: California University Press.

Scott, S., & Dooley, D. (1985). A structural family therapy approach for treatment of deaf children. In G. B. Anderson & D. Watson (Eds.), *Counseling deaf people: Research and practice* (pp. 211–234). Fayetteville: Arkansas Rehabilitation Research and Training Center on Deafness and Hearing Impairment.

Sheridan, M. (2001). *Inner lives of deaf children: Interviews and analysis.* Washington, DC: Gallaudet University Press.

Sheridan, M. (2008). *Deaf adolescents: Inner lives and life world development.* Washington, DC: Gallaudet University Press.

Stein, L., Mindel, E., & Jabaley, T. (Eds.). (1981). *Deafness and mental health.* New York, NY: Grune & Stratton.

Stewart, L. (1981). Counseling the Deaf client. In L. Stein, E. Mindel, & T. Jabaley (Eds.), *Deafness and mental health* (pp. 133–159), New York, NY: Grune & Stratton.

Sue, D. W., Arredondo, P., & McDavis, R. (1992). Multicultural counseling competencies and standards: A call to the profession. *Journal of Counseling and Development, 70*(4), 477–486.

Sue, D. W., & Sue, D. (2008). *Counseling the culturally diverse: Theory and practice* (5th ed.). Hoboken, NJ: Wiley.

Sussman, A. (1988). Approaches to counseling and psychotherapy revisited. In D. Watson, G. Long, M. Taff-Watson & M. Harvey (Eds.), *Two decades of excellence: A foundation for the future* (pp. 2–15). Little Rock, AR: American Deafness and Rehabilitation Association.

Sussman, A. E., & Brauer, B. A. (1999). On being a psychotherapy with deaf clients. In I. Leigh (Ed.), *Psychotherapy with deaf clients from diverse groups* (pp. 3–22). Washington, DC: Gallaudet University Press.

Sussman, A. E., & Stewart, L. G. (Eds.). (1971). *Counseling with deaf people.* New York, NY: Deafness Research and Training Center.

Vernon, M. (1995). An historical perspective on psychology and deafness. *JADARA, 29*(2), 8–13.

Vernon, M. (2010). The horror of being deaf and in prison. *American Annals of the Deaf, 155*(3), 311–321.

Vernon, M., & Andrews, J. F. (1990). *The psychology of deafness.* New York, NY: Longman.

Vernon, M., & Greenberg, S. F. (1999). Violence in Deaf and hard of hearing people: A review of the literature. *Aggression and Violent Behavior, 4*(3), 259–272.

Vernon, M., & Miller, K. (2001). Linguistic incompetence to stand trial: A unique condition in some deaf defendants. *Journal of Interpretation*, 99–120.

Vernon, M., & Miller, K. (2005). Obstacles faced by deaf people in the criminal justice system. *American Annals of the Deaf, 150*(3), 283–291.

Vernon, M., & Raifman, L. J. (1997). Recognizing and handling problems of incompetent deaf defendants charged with serious offenses. *International Journal of Law and Psychiatry, 20*(3), 373–387.

Vernon, M., Steinberg, A., & Montoya, L. (1999). Deaf murderers: Clinical and forensic issues. *Behavioral Science and the Law, 17*, 495–516.

Vernon, M., & Vernon, M. (2010). *Deadly charm: The story of a Deaf serial killer.* Washington, DC: Gallaudet University Press.

1 Lessons Learned from 23 Years of a Deaf Psychiatric Inpatient Unit[1]

Neil S. Glickman

The Deaf Unit at Westborough State Hospital was a specialty psychiatric inpatient unit for deaf persons established in a state mental hospital in Massachusetts. It opened in January, 1987, and I was hired as co-director, along with Sherry Zitter. I worked there for 3 years until I left to pursue my doctorate in Psychology. I returned in 1996 as the unit director and psychologist and worked there for another 14 years until Westborough State Hospital closed in the Spring of 2010.

The vision that guided the creation of this unit was that of a "culturally affirmative" treatment program for deaf persons (Glickman & Zitter, 1989). This meant creating, as much as we could, a Deaf space, with American Sign Language (ALS) used as the language of treatment, large numbers of deaf staff at all levels of the organization, and a Deaf sensitivity brought to everything we did. These efforts at creating culturally affirmative treatment were documented in the first book that emerged from the unit's work (Glickman & Gulati, 2003). The unit never relinquished this vision of cultural affirmation though in practice achieving it was easier said than done. I think most of the staff would agree that, at our best, we were a well-functioning bicultural, bilingual program, where cross-cultural conflicts were often handled skillfully.

In the 23 years of its' existence, the Westborough Deaf Unit provided psychiatric care for, I would estimate, around 200 deaf people, many of whom were hospitalized numerous times. In the Spring of 2010, as Westborough State Hospital closed, the Deaf Unit was moved with most of its' staff to Worcester State Hospital, about a half hour further west. I chose at that time to retire from the unit. At that time, I also decided to reflect back on our 23-year history. We learned a number of important lessons about the problems of deaf psychiatric clients, about how to adapt assessment and treatment for them, and about the creation of culturally affirmative and clinically competent treatment environments. This chapter presents my summary of these lessons.

What Did We Learn about Deaf Psychiatric Clients?

I'd like to begin by describing three of our clients.[2]

Roberto was a 32-year-old deaf male who had been living with his mother and stepfather. He was born and raised in Puerto Rico where he attended school, but Roberto learned very little formal sign language and virtually no English or Spanish. His large, protective hearing family kept him at home most of the time and communicated with him in simple "home signs" and gestures. Roberto assisted with simple tasks around the house. Because his family could not communicate any important issue with him, they tended to give him things he wanted so as to avoid a tantrum or aggressive behavior. His demands, and their inability to satisfy them, became more of a serious problem as he grew into a large, strong adolescent and adult. Every now and then, he'd have some kind of behavioral meltdown, breaking things, threatening people, and sometimes pushing and hitting people. He was referred to the Deaf Unit after a particularly bad explosion. His mother reluctantly called the police. They arrived but could not communicate with him. They subdued him physically, and then brought him to an emergency room. Nobody in the emergency room could do any kind of clinical assessment. Reluctant to release him, they referred him instead to the Deaf Unit for an evaluation.

Omar was a 35-year-old deaf male living in a hearing group residence at the time of his referral. He was friendly and pleasant most of the time and was not usually physically aggressive. He had Bipolar Disorder, and as long as he took his medicine and avoided alcohol and marijuana, he was usually safe. However, he didn't think he needed the medicine and he liked to drink and get high. When he stopped taking his medicine, he became manic. He would be awake all night, his language became more confused, and he went out and did things that got him into trouble. He borrowed money and got into debts he couldn't pay off. He became very defiant with staff. He went cruising for young women and, even more concerning, young teenage girls. Omar didn't have the social skills to get romantic partners, and he tended to push himself on women. He had grabbed the breasts and buttocks of several female counselors and staff. He expressed an interest in young girls but, as far as staff knew, he had not actually sexually assaulted one. Staff in the programs that served him worried about what this apparent interest in young girls meant and how they should respond. They asked us whether his inappropriate sexual behavior was due to poor language and social skills, to being off his medication and on drugs, or whether it reflected problem of pedophilia and criminal sex offending. He was brought to the hospital after a period of being off his medication when he sexually assaulted a staff person. Omar's account of the event was that (a) it didn't happen, (b) she grabbed him, and (c) he wouldn't do it again.

Joe was a 16-year-old student in a Deaf residential program nearby at the time of his hospitalization on the Deaf Unit. The police arrested him and brought him to the emergency room after he threatened a teacher with a knife and threw rocks at her car. The reason he gave was that he was mad because the teacher postponed the trip to the mall.

Joe started in this school at age 12 after being kicked out of three other less restrictive placements. "Less restrictive" meant hearing mainstreamed programs where most people couldn't communicate with him. He was kicked out because of severe behavior problems: fights with peers, threatening, and sometimes punching staff. Due to his late exposure to sign, Joe had very basic sign skills. He only read simple words. His intelligence tested around 75, in the borderline mentally retarded range. Joe was removed from his biological family at age 4 following confirmation of physical abuse and neglect. His stepfather may have also sexually abused him. He lived in two foster placements before an adoptive family was found for him at age 8. The adoptive parents were kind, caring hearing people who knew some sign but Joe was so difficult to manage that they had to place him in a residential school. They were supportive and involved and took Joe home whenever they could. Joe could be quite friendly and funny at times, and he was especially good at taking care of animals. He wanted to be a vet, but at this time he had difficulty attending any academic class and was frequently disruptive. He carried diagnoses of Attention Deficit Hyperactivity Disorder, Oppositional Defiant Disorder, and Post-traumatic Stress Disorder. The school did not want to take him back until we evaluated his medication and stabilized his behavior.

Roberto was an unusual client for us in that, when he was first admitted, he had almost no functional language skills. Omar and Joe were more representative in that they had more signing skills though they were not fluent signers. However, over time we came to realize something vitally important about our clients. More than half of them were not effective language users in any language. They were language dysfluent, some quite severely, in their best language, which was almost always ASL. This made us very dependent upon other people to gather basic history, and sometimes these people were also poorly informed. They also had poor ability to communicate with our clients. Records were sometimes available, but their quality was uneven.

Reports of sexual and physical abuse were common, but they were often not detailed or substantiated and may have reflected little more than the suspicions of the person writing the report. In a 7-year review of all 94 deaf clients served on the Deaf Unit at that time, we were reasonably confident that some kind of physical abuse occurred in 15% of clients, some kind of sexual abuse occurred in 21%, and a combination of physical and sexual abuse occurred in another 16%. That means that we were reasonably certain that just over half of our clients (52%) had experienced some kind of abuse. We suspected abuse in another 11% of clients. For 19% of clients, we didn't know and couldn't find out (Glickman, 2009, p. 30). This meant that it was extremely likely that a large majority of our clients had experienced physical, sexual abuse, or both, but it was also very common that we could not obtain a clear, reliable account of what actually happened. Our clients' poor language skills prevented them from developing a coherent narrative about their lives. It also interfered with the treatment and recovery process.

From its beginning, the Deaf Unit staff included a deaf communication specialist. Initially, that person's job was primarily concerned with providing sign language training when needed and helping to assure a treatment environment that was culturally affirmative for deaf people. Over time, as we paid more attention to the problem of language dysfluency in our clients, the communication specialist came to function more as a deaf relay interpreter, assisting with interviews and treatment sessions with our many language disordered clients.

The communication specialist helped us establish communication standards and protocols. Many of our hearing staff, especially new signers, had difficulty appreciating the vast differences between the communication abilities of our clients. They thought that signing was signing, and they couldn't appreciate who signed well and who signed badly. Nor could they appreciate that their own signing abilities were usually nowhere near as skilled as they thought they were. The tendency of staff to overestimate the communication abilities of anyone who signs was reinforced by administration officials anxious to minimize overtime costs associated with ensuring that staff with a particular level of signing competency were always present. It was also reinforced by union officials who resisted our efforts to establish sign language standards for staff. Given this confusion about the actual communication abilities of both clients and staff, we needed badly to have a genuine communication expert. We were able to hire a succession of these experts into the communication specialist position.

A common scenario went something like this: We had a deaf client who was particularly difficult to understand, and one day the interpreters, deaf staff and others were discussing this problem. We were trying to figure out how to communicate to him some important issues. At that moment, a counselor who had just completed his first sign language class came over and announced confidently that *he* had no difficulty communicating with the client. Similarly, it was reasonably common for staff who were grossly unqualified to interpret nonetheless to offer to do so creating *cross-cultural* tensions with the deaf staff and members of the Communication Department. In the domain of communication with deaf people, it is certainly true that *a little knowledge is a dangerous thing*.

Communication problems are the bread and butter of Deaf treatment programs. They provide daily challenges and opportunities. For instance, it sometimes happened that one deaf client would accuse another one of

sexual assault. These situations almost always called for formal investi-
gations including, sometimes, medically oriented assessments. One time,
such an incident occurred when our interpreters, communication specialist, and deaf social worker were not present. A nurse with beginner level
signing skills, working alongside a hearing mental health worker with
slightly better signing skills, and a doctor who knew little about deaf
people, misunderstood the client, jumped to conclusions, and sent the
client for the sexual assault evaluation. The next day we had to call in the
appropriate communication and clinical resources, and painstakingly go
through the whole interview process again. We concluded that no such
assault had occurred, and the client had gone through this invasive, and
potentially traumatizing, medical procedure unnecessarily.

The problems of working with language dysfluent deaf clients brings
new meaning to a phrase attributed to the English playwright George
Bernard Shaw: "The single biggest problem in communication is the illusion that it has taken place."

In the Westborough Deaf Unit's last few years, spurred on at first by the
dissertation research of psychologist Patricia Black, we spent a lot of time
analyzing the particular language errors our deaf clients made (Black,
2005, p. 196; Black & Glickman, 2005, 2006). Our deaf communication specialist Michael Krajnak would interview them and videotape the
interview, and then he and the interpreters would evaluate the language
samples. This led us to notice that certain kinds of language problems
were common. These included:

1. Very limited (impoverished) vocabulary, with many signs used
   incorrectly.
2. Poor ability to communicate time and sequencing. This includes
   an absence of grammatical indicators for tense (e.g., LAST-YEAR,
   THRRE-MONTHS-FUTURE), inaccurate use of the FINISH sign
   to indicate tense, an absence of references to time, a lack of sequential
   reasoning (first this happened, then this, then this) and a tendency to
   mix up past, present and future events. Sometimes a person was not
   clear as to whether something actually happened or whether this was
   something they wanted to happen. Asking questions like WHEN?
   would not work, and when we introduced specifics (YESTERDAY,
   MONDAY, ONE-WEEK-AGO), we couldn't be confident we were
   not suggesting the response.
3. Absence or inaccurate use of key grammatical features such as subject,
   verb, and object. Clients would say something happened but leave out
   the subject. They were not clear as to who did what to whom. One client would sign TEACH repeatedly when she meant LEARN. We've
   often found ourselves asking repeatedly, WHO?, and not getting a
   clear answer. Related to this would be the inability to inflect verbs
   correctly (to move verbs to show actor and receiver and qualities of

action) or to use the spatial properties of ASL to indicate subjects and objects. ASL syntax would be absent or confused.

4. Mixture of established signs, home signs, sometimes signs from foreign sign languages, gestures, English words and sometimes words from Spanish. In some cases, where clients had grown up outside the United States, we weren't sure if they were using a local sign variant or a home sign.

In the Deaf mental health literature, sign language dysfluency has been discussed primarily in four contexts.[3] First, sign language disorders, like spoken language disorders, are assumed to have neurological causes related to the etiology of deafness (Vernon & Andrews, 1990). Second, Howard Poizner, Edward Klima, and Ursula Bellugi studied the sign language abilities of deaf fluent ASL users who lost some communication abilities due to strokes. They were able to show that acquired aphasias in deaf fluent signers resemble those in hearing users of spoken English. (Poizner, Klima, & Belllugi, 1987). Third, in Great Britain, Alice Thacker studied the sign language production of deaf persons with schizophrenia and found that thought disorders can influence sign production just as they can influence spoken language production (Thacker, 1994, 1998). Fourth, sign language dysfluency is related to inadequate exposure to ASL rich environments in childhood. Our own work built on Thacker's but placed greater emphasis on this sign language dysfluency related to language deprivation (Black, 2005; Black & Glickman, 2005, 2006; Glickman, 2007, 2009).

Very few of our clients were fluent ASL users who suffered language loss due to a severe mental illness. Much more commonly, they were persons who had dysfluent language all their lives. Through careful review of numerous videotaped language samples from clients, we tried to parse out the kinds of language problems most likely to be related to language deprivation as distinct from those most likely related to thought disorder. This differential diagnosis is very difficult and as a field we have barely begun to articulate how this task can be accomplished (Glickman, 2007).

The key lesson learned here is about the prevalence and clinical significance of the problem of language dysfluency in deaf mental health and rehabilitation clients. Serving deaf persons who are fluent signers presents one kind of challenge. Many deaf clients are dysfluent or poor signers, and serving them presents a much greater challenge. Programs that serve deaf people need to staff with this understanding that they will serve people with greatly varying degrees of language competency in both sign and spoken language. The appropriate standard has been set by the Office of Deaf Services in the Alabama Department of Mental Health. The expectation set there is that all clinicians sign fluently *and* that they work alongside a qualified communication specialist when evaluating and treating deaf persons with severe language disorders. Even deaf clinicians are expected to work with the communication specialist.

The high numbers of language dysfluent deaf clients was one way in which our clientele differed from the hearing clientele in the hospital. Returning to the three clients cited above, Omar had a bona fide severe mental illness: Bipolar Disorder. Joe carried working diagnoses of Attention Deficit Hyperactivity Disorder, Oppositional Defiant Disorder, and Post-traumatic Stress Disorder but no psychotic disorder. Joe had severe attention and behavioral problems, compounded by a history of multiple forms of trauma and poor language skills. Omar had a similar history of trauma, poor language development and other developmental deficits, but he also had a serious mental illness. Roberto didn't have a major psychiatric disorder (unless we fudge a diagnosis by adding the tag "not otherwise specified"). He had a history of severe language deprivation, and lifelong behavioral problems. It's possible he had undiagnosed brain injury at birth. Using performance IQ measures, he tested in the borderline range for mental retardation. Like the majority of our clients, he was hospitalized because of a severe behavioral incident and the lack of community resources to contain or help him.

We had higher functioning deaf people on the unit; persons who were fluent in ASL and/or English, some of whom had Bachelor's and even Master's degrees. But they were not typical clients. For a variety of reasons, higher functioning deaf people often chose not to be hospitalized in our program. They had concerns about confidentiality. They knew many of the staff socially. Some had worked as counselors to some of the lower functioning persons on the unit and they didn't want to now be treated as those persons' peers. Many higher functioning deaf persons actually would select a non-deaf setting, with all its communication problems, because they were more likely to have intellectual peers and because they had to worry much less about confidentiality. When in crisis, they faced an unfair dilemma: a Deaf Unit would provide good communication access and sensitivity to Deaf Culture but sometimes a lack of intellectual peers and real concerns regarding confidentiality. For some, accessing hearing programs through an interpreter was the better option. This contributed to a skew in the population of deaf persons we served towards those who could be considered more "low functioning."

The hearing clients at Westborough State Hospital, a state psychiatric hospital, were primarily adults who developed a severe mental illness like schizophrenia. Many had trauma histories, problems with alcohol and drugs, and personality disorders. However, by and large, they were not people who had the kinds of language and developmental disorders that many deaf clients had. Many of our deaf clients had shown emotional, behavioral and learning difficulties their entire lives. About a quarter had mild levels of mental retardation, and we could have increased the size of this cohort if we changed our admission policies. Hearing clients admitted to the hospital had to be persons in the public mental health system, primarily persons with severe mental illnesses who could not be served adequately in private, acute care hospitals. By contrast, any deaf person needing inpatient care could be referred to us, so we had clients with a much greater range of clinical problems. On the milder end were relatively well-functioning deaf people who suffered an acute psychiatric crisis and needed a brief hospitalization, the kind of client that is usually served in private mental health hospitals. Some of our clientele were deaf persons with severe addiction problems who became suicidal or dangerous to others in the context of substance abuse. Some were deaf people with major mental illnesses like schizophrenia, but these constituted only about a third of our clients whereas they were nearly 90% of the hearing clients in the hospital.

The whether they had a severe mental illness or not, the largest cohort of our clients were deaf people with emotional and behavioral disorders associated with language deprivation and sometimes with neurological problems related to the cause of their deafness. This group had a low baseline level of functioning and was not easily made safe to return to community living. For some of these clients, medication would play a relatively small role in their recovery. Many of these persons took psychiatric medication, sometimes quite a bit of it. Our role as a Deaf program was to try to get the medication right, and commonly this meant reducing or simplifying medication plans. More important than medication would be the establishment of the proper rehabilitative (skill building) focus for treatment.

The challenges of serving deaf persons on our specialty Deaf Unit were, first, that we served clientele with a huge range of functional and language abilities while, second, the population was skewed towards "lower functioning" persons, with severe learning and language challenges, like Roberto, Omar, and Joe. This diversity meant that on any particular day, we would have to provide programming for intelligent, linguistically competent deaf persons who, could, for instance, explore in cognitive therapy how their thoughts contribute to their emotions; while having other deaf, mentally retarded, language disordered clients with whom the goal was that they use a rocking chair to calm themselves down. This meant that the content of any particular treatment group, such as coping skills, was constantly being shifted "up or down." It meant struggling to meet the needs of more competent deaf persons who complained, rightly, that they had no peer group. It meant great difficulty getting a meaningful quorum for any particular treatment group as the functional abilities, language skills, intellectual sophistication as well as treatment problems of the group members differed so dramatically.

In the deaf mental health literature, "low functioning" deaf persons are also referred to as "high risk" or "traditionally underserved deaf." I have used the terms "psychologically unsophisticated" and "language and learning challenged" to describe the same group (Glickman, 2003, 2009). Poor language abilities in their best language are the first and most significant characteristic of persons from this group. Other commonly cited characteristics are difficulties in school and work life; behavioral, social and emotional adjustment problems; health, mental and physical limitations, and inabilities to live independently (Dew, 1999; Long, Long, & Ouellette, 1993).

This cohort of deaf persons is also discussed in the literature on psychiatric inpatient treatment of deaf people. In fact, it's in this literature that one finds speculation as to whether these deaf people have a unique clinical syndrome. Possibly the earliest speculation on this matter was from a Norwegian psychiatrist, Terje Basilier (1964). He postulated that some deaf clients might have a "certain personality structure" he called *surdophrenia*. A similar argument was made by American pioneering psychiatrists John Rainer and Kenneth Altshuler. They noted that a subgroup of the deaf clients they treated did not appear to fit any of the established diagnostic categories. They talked about deaf people having "primitive personalities" and "impulsive disorders" (Rainer & Altshuler, 1967), and they were not always careful in distinguishing this subgroup of the clinical population from deaf people as a whole. These two notions, of surdophrenia and primitive personality disorder, have been roundly criticized, especially when they are misapplied to deaf people as a whole (Lane, 1992). However, Vernon, whose work has done much to legitimize the importance of sign language use with deaf children, has embraced the diagnosis of primitive personality disorder, while being very clear about the subgroup of deaf persons to whom it applies (Vernon & Andrews, 1990). He has written extensively and eloquently on the problems involved when such persons commit crimes and interact with police and courts (Vernon & Miller, 2001, 2005; Vernon & Raifman, 1997). Vernon has championed this diagnosis because a large percentage of the deaf persons he assesses in forensic settings meet the criteria, and this diagnosis helps courts understand their special needs and limitations.

These clinicians are not alone. Another pioneering psychiatrist with deaf persons, Roy Grinker, with whom Vernon worked early in his career, discussed how common it was for deaf clients to have no adequate means of communication, including sign language (Grinker et al., 1969). They noted that two thirds of the deaf clients they studied displayed patterns of "inadequate and marginal functioning" (p. 42). They described these persons as suffering essentially from developmental delays and noted the treatment was better characterized as developing basic psychosocial skills than as treatment of psychiatric disorders per se. Grinker and colleagues used the term "borderline syndrome" to describe this group. They were not thinking of "borderline personality disorder" as it is understood today but rather of persons with very marginal communication and psychosocial development.

In Great Britain, the pioneering work on mental health care with deaf persons was done by psychiatrist John Denmark. He also pointed out that most of the deaf clients seen were referred due to communication and behavioral difficulties. He called such problems "developmental disorders of communication" and also "problems related to deafness (Denmark, 1985, 1994).

More recently, Haskins presented a study of 43 deaf clients treated on another specialty Deaf psychiatric unit. Among her findings was the higher percentage of clients diagnosed with *Pervasive Developmental Disorder Not Otherwise Specified*. Clients with this disorder have difficulty befriending fellow clients who are deaf, have a history of job failure because of an inability to grasp the implicit social demands that are present on most job sites, and often end up in altercations because of their rigid cognitive styles and inability to appreciate another's point of view (Haskins, 2004). This is one diagnosis that can be used to describe this group although this gives the impression that neurologically we are seeing a variant of autism, and this is probably not true most of the time.

Another recent study of deaf psychiatric inpatients found compatible results. Landsberger and Diaz (2010) reviewed archival data comparing 30 deaf and hard-of-hearing inpatient adults with 60 hearing inpatient adults. "Significant differences were found between deaf and hearing inpatient groups in the frequency of impulse control disorders (23% versus 2%), pervasive developmental disorders (10% versus 2%), substance use disorders (20% versus 45%), mild mental retardation (33% versus 3%) and personality disorders (17% versus 43%). The deaf group had a larger proportion of diagnoses of psychotic disorders not otherwise specified (17% versus 2%)" (p. 196).

In this author's experience, the difficulty clinicians have in diagnosing deaf clients is evident in the heavy reliance upon the tag "not otherwise specified" or "NOS" One sees this in *developmental disorder NOS, psychotic disorder NOS, impulse control disorder NOS, pervasive developmental disorder NOS and personality disorder NOS*. Another recent study of schizophrenia in deaf inpatients found that the largest number of deaf persons diagnosed with schizophrenia were categorized as having *undifferentiated schizophrenia* (Mompremier, 2009). The qualifier *undifferentiated* is similar to the qualifier *not otherwise specified*. It means that the person doesn't fit into established categories. It's an acceptable way of admitting, "this diagnosis isn't quite right" or even "I don't really know."

The consistency in findings of every major study of deaf psychiatric inpatients, with regard to a large subgroup of "low functioning," language impaired, developmentally delayed and behaviorally disordered clients, cannot simply be attributed to the prejudice and ignorance referred to as audism (Humphries, 1977; Lane, 1992). The audist conclusion is that this group represents deaf people as a whole or that there is something like a deaf personality with these attributes. This is obviously not true. However, the persons discussed here *are* a significant cohort of the deaf persons served in clinical settings. They *do not* represent deaf people as a whole, but they are a significant percentage of deaf people referred for mental health and rehabilitation treatment. *Indeed, I believe the strongest argument we have for the need for specialized Deaf friendly treatment programs is that it is only such programs that have a chance of serving these persons well.* Arguably, higher functioning deaf persons such as all those who chose not to be served in our program have some chance of benefiting from a non-specialized treatment setting. The cohort we are describing now, I believe, virtually never benefit from treatment in non-specialized settings.

Is there a unique psychiatric disorder at play here? Having treated so many of these clients on the Deaf Unit, and seeing how often other Deaf mental health care (DMHC) clinicians have described and struggled to diagnose persons with these characteristics, I believe all of us are describing a clinical reality, a set of co-occurring problems. However, I don't like any of the diagnostic labels, such as primitive personality disorder, that have been proposed so far because they are unnecessarily stigmatizing. I read into all the discussions of diagnostic challenges found in the DMHC literature as well as the literature on traditionally underserved deaf persons the attempt to define this disorder. Essentially, these are deaf people who experienced severe language deprivation and never developed mastery of any language. Some of them have neurological compromises. Some have attachment problems related to poor communication between child and parents. They have experienced education deprivation. Primarily because of severe language deprivation, they develop an array of psychosocial deficits and display problem behaviors in every setting. *These problems are developmental.* They do not suddenly appear in adulthood (as major mental illnesses usually do) but have been present all their lives. By the time they reach adulthood, they have "failed" in school, work, home, and independent living settings, and pose major treatment challenges. In the worst cases, some of these clients are so aggressive and dangerous that even the best treatment programs cannot manage or treat them safely. More often, their behavioral and emotional problems are treatable with the right combination of cultural, communication and clinical expertise. In essence, treatment and rehabilitation programs are asked to make up for the disastrously poor environments these persons were raised in, including the foolishness, short sightedness and arrogance involved in not exposing them sufficiently to ASL.

My own attempt at a name for this disorder is *language deprivation with deficiencies in behavioral, social and emotional adjustment* (Glickman, 2009).

The criteria I proposed were:

1. The person is born with a hearing loss severe enough so as to preclude the ability to comprehend oral language or the child loses that ability before the acquisition of oral language.
2. The hearing loss cannot be remediated, or is not remediated, sufficiently for the person to be able to acquire and comprehend oral language effectively.
3. The child is not exposed to American Sign Language (or other sign languages) sufficiently so as to acquire it as a native user.
4. The person is severely dysfluent in their best language or communication modality, either receptively, expressively or both, as measured by objective tests or determined by expert evaluators of that language. The person is functionally illiterate in the spoken/written language of the larger community.
5. From early childhood, the child displays a pattern of behavioral, social and emotional disturbances such as aggression, self-harm, a gross lack of social skills, and poor school performance. These problems usually occur in every setting.
6. The person demonstrates an enormous deficit in fund of information about the world (e.g., social norms, knowledge of history, government, current events, rights and responsibilities of being a citizen.)
7. As an adult, the person experiences great difficulties developing work skills, particularly in the interpersonal and attitudinal aspects of work, and learning to live independently.
8. The person is at least 14 years of age.
9. The person does not have mental retardation, schizophrenia or another psychotic disorder. If adolescent, they do not have a conduct disorder; and if adult, they do not have anti-social personality disorder (Glickman, 2009).

When formulating these proposed diagnostic criteria, the most difficult part was being clear about criteria 9, the rule-outs. The heart of the disorder, and the key issue which distinguishes this group of deaf clients from hearing psychiatric clients, are the language problems and associated developmental deficits and behavioral problems. However, these problems often accompany more recognized clinical disorders, and pure cases, where there is no co-morbid problem, are less common. This criterion, therefore, may be more useful for research purposes than in clinical settings where co-morbidity is the rule.

Deaf people with these language and developmental deficits are easy to misdiagnose. The language and behavioral problems make them appear more mentally ill than they really are. Clinicians working exclusively from a medical model can easily decide that these persons are primarily in need of psychiatric medication as opposed to language and skill development. In addition, diagnosing them with major mental illnesses may be the only way to get them services like residential or day treatment. All these forces pull for psychiatrists to treat these person as if their primary problem is a brain disorder, and their primary need is for psychiatric medication. This is not to say that such medications don't sometimes help, especially when there is co-morbidity, but the real need is usually for rehabilitative treatment resources that are scarce. More often than psychiatrists like to admit, medications given to these clients have no benefit apart from sedation, and sometimes that is their real purpose (Whitaker, 2010). The psychiatrists presume the clients have some major mental illness, but the bottom line is that they, and their teams, are searching desperately for ways to contain and treat dangerous behaviors. Over 50 years ago, Grinker, one of the pioneers of Deaf mental health treatment in the United States, got it right when he noted that the most important treatment paradigm is the development of psychosocial skills (Grinker et al., 1969). If no such linguistically and clinically appropriate treatment program is available, psychiatrists will use the only other tool available to them: medication.

The result is something else we see often in the inpatient treatment of deaf persons: grossly overmedicated people. Over time, medication gets added to medication, so that it is not uncommon to find deaf persons who have taken multiple kinds of very powerful medications for many years. Indeed, some deaf patients accumulate diagnosis alongside medications, and the presence of long list of diagnoses alongside of a long list of medications is a good indication that the person probably has this particular combination of language and behavioral problems that isn't in the *Diagnostic and Statistical Manual*. Heavy dosages of psychotropic medications, along with causing sedation, can contribute to cognitive and serious health problems. (Moncrieff, 2009; Whitaker, 2010). In time, they may become part of the reason the person is functioning badly. Once people are on such medications, however, it can be quite hard to take them off of them, especially when their coping skills and social supports are poor.

This developmental disorder confounds all discussions in the literature on questions such as the prevalence of schizophrenia in deaf persons. So many deaf people who end up in psychiatric hospitals have these developmentally based language and behavioral problems that look, to the eye untrained in work with deaf people, like major mental illnesses, that research studies that attempt to quantify the number of deaf persons given such diagnoses should be considered unreliable and invalid right from the start. The fact is that psychiatry as a profession does such a poor job of diagnosing major mental illnesses in deaf people that we really have no idea about these prevalence rates. The experience of the Deaf Unit, and other such programs, supports the notion that many of the deaf people served who do have major mental illness also have this developmental disorder. They get classified, as we have seen, with undifferentiated schizophrenia or with some condition NOS.

The key lessons learned about our clients were the pervasiveness and significance of language deprivation and the likelihood that we were working with many persons who had a unique clinical disorder. The disorder combined language and other developmental deficits, as described above, and sometimes occurred alongside more recognized clinical disorders. In essence, we saw more clients with language and developmentally based behavioral problems and fewer clients with major mental illnesses than would normally be expected in a psychiatric inpatient setting. To serve these persons adequately, we had to have staff with exceptional communication abilities, not just "signers," and we had to be extremely mindful and expert about communication procedures. We also had to adapt considerably our approach to psychiatric rehabilitation.

What Did We Learn about Adapting Mental Health Treatment for this Population?

The language, learning, and behavioral problems of so many of our clients forced us to adapt our treatment approaches. The majority of our clients were not people who made good use of verbal, insight oriented psychotherapies even if they were carried out in fluent ASL. Their sign language impairments, very limited fund of information about the world, developmental deficits, lack of experience with the idea of using language to solve problems, along with their cultural differences, meant we had a huge chasm of understanding to overcome before we could treat them effectively. Facing this chasm honestly eventually lead to embrace of a concept we called "pretreatment."

"Treatment" refers to a process that occurs when clients and counselor(s) share an understanding of a problem, a set of relevant goals, and the procedure for achieving those goals, *and the client says, "yes, I want that."* Mental health treatment is collaborative. It is done *with* clients, and it assumes some informed understanding and commitment from clients. Many of the problems counselors working with such clients face when treatment doesn't work are due to the fact that the client does not understand, value or know how to use mental health treatment. Other problems occur when the client does understand, but doesn't want, or is ambivalent, about change. When clinicians try to influence persons who do not understand and have not agreed to mental health treatment, they are not doing mental health treatment. They are doing social control. In mental health, where clients may engage in very dangerous behaviors, practitioners do have some social control responsibilities. If we know that a person is planning to harm someone, we have a legal responsibility to intervene against the persons will to prevent it. However, there is very little that can be accomplished in treatment without a persons' informed consent. Mental health practitioners must spend a great deal of time with some consumers in pretreatment activities, trying to elicit informed engagement. We found that on the Deaf Unit, because of the language and fund of information deficits that so many clients had, we had to devote considerable attention to pretreatment. Once we truly grasped how unprepared many of our clients were for the process of collaborating effectively in mental health treatment, our work actually became easier. We just had to adopt a pretreatment, as opposed to a treatment, orientation.

Pretreatment work refers to the process of trying to educate and motivate clients for mental health and rehabilitation interventions. It is the process of trying to bridge this gap and fashion a form of treatment that is meaningful and useful. Because our clients may lack a schema or map for the treatment process, a central pretreatment task is to give them one. That is, we need to find a way to conceptualize treatment that makes sense to them and elicits their engagement. For most clients, the most useful map we could give them was found in a focus upon *skills*. We explained that treatment, in a nutshell, boiled down to the process of developing skills. In ASL, there is no one sign corresponding to the English word "treatment." Sometimes the sign for HELP is initialized with a "t" handshape, but this English sign is also used for "therapy," and doesn't capture the multiple components of mental health treatment.

In fact, neither the concept of therapy nor of treatment is needed much of the time. There is an ASL sign for COUNSELING, but we found it simpler and more compelling to just invite clients to PRACTICE SKILLS. We talked to clients about skills; those they already had and those they needed to acquire; and this became the treatment language of the milieu. We found it is much easier to build a treatment program around the notion of skills than it was, for instance, around the idea of insight or around the idea, central to psychiatric rehabilitation, of recovery.[4] It was also preferable to any notion of treatment as helping with mental illnesses, a concept that was both stigmatizing and, for some clients, overly abstract. Skills is a more user friendly concept. There is no stigma associated with it. It is easier to explain. Our most common discussions focused on skills for managing internal experiences like emotions. We called these coping skills. We also discussed with clients skills for dealing with other people. This included social, conflict resolution, problem solving, communication, assertiveness and other skills. With some clients, we focused on basic activities of daily living (ADL) skills such as taking a bath, making your bed and doing your laundry.

This emphasis upon skills brought us right into the world of psychiatric rehabilitation and cognitive behavioral therapy (especially that form of it developed by Donald Meichenbaum (Meichenbaum, 1977a, 1977b, 1985, 1994, 1996, 2001, 2007; Meichenbaum & Biemiller, 1998; Meichenbaum & Goodman, 1971; Meichenbaum & Turk, 1987). We also drew heavily upon Marsha Linehan's dialectical behavior therapy (Linehan, 1993a, 1993b) and Ross Greene's collaborative problem solving (Greene, 1998; Greene & Ablon, 2006). All these approaches recognize skill deficits as the principal reason for client problems and all present different ways of helping clients develop psychosocial skills. Working within this skill building model, we could be confident we were doing best practice as currently understood. All these models, however, would need to be adapted considerably to fit the language and conceptual world of our clients (Glickman, 2009).

The principal way we adapted these skill building treatments was by approaching them developmentally. Dialectical behavior therapy, for instance, with its highly didactic treatment approach, formal curriculum, heavy reliance upon abstract concepts and written materials, was developmentally inappropriate for most of our clients, yet we could borrow many ideas from it. For instance, the DBT notion of "distress tolerance" could be simplified to the idea of "coping." The DBT emphasis on "mindfulness" could be incorporated into a skill we called "red, yellow, green" (from the traffic light), with the red light signifying "stop and notice." Rather than expecting clients to sit through lectures on skills, we'd use treatment approaches more developmentally appropriate such as role playing and therapy games.

We also conceptualized each skill using a picture. Our communication specialist Michael Krajnak drew hundreds of these pictures and produced two CD-ROMS on which they are available (Glickman, 2009; Glickman & Gulati, 2003). These pictures were posted everywhere in the milieu. They were in the day hall and referred to each morning during community meeting when each client was asked to look at the pictures and select a skill for the day. They were reproduced into sets of laminated "skill cards" which were incorporated into therapy games (e.g., "Pick a card and act it out. Then others guess the skill, and the winner gets a prize."). Clients drew their own skill cards in art therapy. They built cardboard traffic lights ("red, yellow, green" skills) to bring home. Many clients asked for sets of the skill cards to take home with them on discharge and brought these to their group and family homes. These pictures became so popular that the hearing adolescent and adult units in the hospital started using them. Other staff told us that many hearing clients had severe language and learning challenges (Gaines, Meltzer, & Glickman, 2009), and these simple, clear pictures provided for them also a practical and appealing map for the treatment process. Since the publications of the CD-ROMs, Michael's skill cards have been reproduced in treatment programs around the world.

One other developmental adaptation was noteworthy. This was the heavy reliance upon sensory movement interventions to develop coping skills. Sensory movement interventions were pioneered by occupational therapists originally for use with children with developmental disorders like autism but more recently have been brought into the mental health field (Ayres, 1979; Champagne, 2006; Champagne & Stromberg, 2004; Moore, 2005). Sensory interventions that we used on the Deaf Unit included heavy blankets, vests, and wrist bracelets, and toy animals stuffed with rice so they became very heavy. We also used a variety of mechanical massagers (which clients would self-administer) and rocking chairs.

Figure 1.1 Skills cards for simple coping skills.

Clients at all ability levels would draw upon these tools as their coping skills but for clients with severe language impairments, sensory based interventions were sometimes the only coping skills accessible. We had many clients identify "rocking in a chair" or "using the heavy blanket" as their favorite coping skill. Not only did these interventions often work, but they became the occasion for success stories being built about how clients were able to calm themselves down. Nursing staff came to embrace these tools because they were practical, minimally dependent upon language, and effective (Trikakis, Curci, & Strom, 2003). Sensory strategies are included in sophisticated treatment approaches like DBT but they are not emphasized there. With our concern with developmental adaptations and language impairments, sensory strategies took center stage.

When clients were able to calm themselves down by, for instance, recognizing they were agitated (the red light skill), going to their room or our "comfort room" to wrap themselves in a heavy blanket and lie on a soft mattress (the yellow light skill), or tell themselves to calm down (the green light skill), then staff would converse with them about their successful use of such skills. (i.e., *"Look what you just did! You were angry and upset. You used the red light skill. You stopped and noticed and then you went to the comfort room. Then, you used the heavy blanket skill and the lying on the mattress skill. Wow. What success!"*) After our staff were trained to see such developmentally simple activities as skills, they became able, in fact, to see skills everywhere. They could see skills when clients went for a walk, played with a dog, used a videogame, or tossed around a basketball. When they could see these skills everywhere, they could talk about what they saw. This created a strength based program with clients many of whom were very "low functioning" and had severe behavior problems. This framework opened up for us treatment possibilities with clients that were otherwise very difficult to reach.

Over time, the main discourse with clients in our milieu became "look what skill you used." This kind of shared discourse served many functions. It served the pretreatment function of bring clients into dialogue regarding a practical treatment strategy. With so much of a focus upon what clients did well, it became easier to introduce discussions of what they could do better; what new skills they could learn. These discussions of skills set the foundation for many skill building techniques that are available in the cognitive behavioral therapy world (Glickman, 2009). They also serve a function consistent with cognitive therapy of changing a client's self-talk and beliefs about their own abilities. In other words, they change clients "story" about themselves. For instance, we had one client, a deaf male with schizophrenia, who would say to his treatment providers: *"when I'm upset, I go to my room and rock on my bed. Don't worry. That's my coping skill."* This client had a skill and a story about his successful use of skills. Both the skill and the story were important parts of his recovery.

While clients are still pretreatment, particular strategies for developing skills are most effective. The easiest way to begin is to simply notice and label skills clients already use. We paid attention to any time a client did *not* show a particular problem and attributed their success in that instance to particular skills. We engaged clients in a discussion of how they did so well. What enabled them to use this particular skill in this stressful situation? When clients are referred for behavioral problems, and they haven't acknowledged their behaviors as problems, or haven't accepted responsibility for changing their behaviors, we focused on times *they did something* to stay in control. How did they do that? What does this say about their skills?

David was an adolescent client referred from a residential school after a particularly bad episode in which he pushed a teacher down a flight of stairs. On admission, he blamed everyone but himself. It was the teacher's fault because she was mean to him. It was the other students' fault because they provoked him. It was the doctor in the emergency rooms fault for sending him to the hospital. If people were nicer to him, he'd behave fine. *They* should be in the hospital, not him.

David was pretreatment. He wouldn't go into anything called "therapy" to work on changing his behaviors. However, in the hospital, David had to deal with a number of new stressors. He was on a locked unit. His freedom was much more curtailed than it was at school. He had to eat food he didn't like according to a schedule he didn't like. He couldn't use the videophone whenever he wanted. He was expected to attend certain activities and keep his behavior under control.

As expected, David had difficulty with these new stressors, but not all the time. Even clients with the most severe behavioral problems do not show these problems all the time. Sometimes they accept a rule, limit or structure. They also do things which help them cope with these stressors.

In David's case, as with many other adolescents we have served, he coped with these new stressors by using videogames.

Earlier in our history, we would have called his preoccupation with videogames a problem and limited his access. This usually provoked escalation in the behavior problems. We came to learn that there was much more therapeutic payoff to seeing his use of videogames as a skill, and talking to him about how he used this skill to manage the stressors of this environment. Did he notice, for instance, how he was feeling (angry, frustrated, sad, etc.) and then how he felt when he was using the videogames? Did he notice that this helped him keep from blowing up? Could he show us what he could do on the videogame? Could he teach us?

Our goal, of course, was not to reinforce videogame playing but rather to get him engaged in a conversation about coping skills. We learned that this was done best by recognizing the realities of the skills he already had. Often, this got our foot in the therapeutic door. Our next steps would be to engage him in a problem solving conversation related to use of skills? We'd ask questions like:

"What other skills do you have? What else do you do that helps you cope when you are stressed? Do you use these skills all the time? What happens when you don't use these skills? Is that what you want? Did you use your videogame skills when the teacher at school told you that you couldn't join the trip? If you had used that skill, instead of pushing the teacher down the stairway, what would have happened? Would you be stuck in this hospital then? If you used your videogame skills and stayed in control, didn't hurt anybody, would your life be better now? What if you learned other skills? What if you had a lot of skills for staying in control when you are stressed? Would your life be better then? Would you be able to do more of what you want, like go on trips to the mall?"

Naturally, the questions we could ask depended on the language skills of the client. It was much easier to do this work with clients who had better language skills. When their language skills were poor, we would need to draw upon communication experts. Often, we couldn't ask hypothetical questions (i.e., what would happen if …"). Sometimes clients could not understand or use conditional phrasing (i.e., if this, then that). This made the work harder, and makes collaboration with communication experts essential. Staff that non-signers imagine sign "good enough," could not communicate with these clients, or teach them skills, without help from genuine expert signers.

Implicit in this style of work is a second means of developing skills in pretreatment individuals. That is doing what psychologist Ross Greene calls "collaborative problem solving" (Greene & Ablon, 2006). If we can present a client with a problem and help them think it through, we will be developing their problem solving skills and affirming their abilities. In David's case, as with so many others, we were aiming to help him to think through the consequences of his behavior. If he continued to behave aggressively, what would happen? If he used these and other skills, what would happen? Which outcome was better?

In our strength-based treatment mode, we interpreted many outcomes as success. When David was merely able to have the conversation without blowing up, *that* showed use of skills (e.g., listening, turn taking, respectful communication, managing feelings), and was evidence of what he was capable of. Of course, this conversation *is the treatment. It is the therapy.* The fact that it occurred outside a designated therapy hour, sitting in the day hall alongside the videogame, was irrelevant. We were working in that conversation on the development of an array of psychosocial skills. This would be reflected on our treatment plan and documentation to insurance providers. As we engaged David, we could move these sessions into formal, designated, treatment venues like a counselor's office.

Through this process of engaging David and other clients, we learned something else. We learned to work from a "one down" stance. In essence, we recognized his abilities, asked him questions which put him in the position of being the authority, and invited him to work with us to learn more skills. This was different than our previous "one up" stance in which staff told clients what was right and wrong, set and enforced rules, imposed limits and consequences. The one down stance, though not appropriate for every occasion, was far more effective at soliciting engagement, at moving clients from pretreatment to treatment.

Learning to work "one down" was also a key element of culture change on the unit, resulting in a far less triggering environment for clients and a dramatic, sustained reduction in our decisions to restrain clients. Early in the unit's history, we restrained clients an average of about 40 times a year. Some deaf persons have complained of being traumatized by the use of restraint in our program. We had a signing environment, but they still had a bad experience because they were restrained. In our last year and a half, we had one restraint. We had stepped out of the older psychiatric culture in which restraints were a default response to dangerous behaviors (National Association of State Mental Health Program Directors Medical Directors Council, 2002). Staff learning to work "one down" was a key element of this culture change.

The key lesson here is that we could help many persons who would normally be considered "poor candidates for therapy" but who we saw as "pretreatment." We found a number of best practices from cognitive behavioral therapy, especially those concerned with developing psychosocial skills, that were applicable. We created a strength-based model by founding conversations with clients on our recognition of skills they already showed, even such basic skills as rocking in a chair, playing videogames or drawing pictures. The Deaf Unit moved from a program that was reasonably culturally affirmative, which it strove to be from the beginning, to one that was also clinically effective, when it learned these lessons.

What Did We Learn about Staff and Program Development?

We started our program with a commitment to cultural affirmation of deaf people, but it took about 15 years before our clinical approach solidified. Eventually, I came to appreciate that cultural competence is the necessary, but not sufficient condition for Deaf treatment programs. In the first book that emerged from the Unit's work, we were able to operationalize what we meant by "culturally affirmative" treatment for Deaf people (Glickman, 2003).

1. Culturally affirmative programs serve only Deaf people, usually from a large geographic area.
2. Culturally affirmative programs strive to hire large numbers of competent deaf staff at all levels of the organization.
3. Culturally affirmative programs need genuine communication excellence. They strive to create signing environments and have some staff who are communication experts.
4. Culturally affirmative programs create an affirmative physical environment including for deaf persons with vision and mobility limitations.
5. In culturally affirmative programs, deaf people manage the communication dynamics. The judges of whether effective communication is occurring must be deaf people.
6. A culturally affirmative program works mindfully with deaf/hearing cross-cultural transference, counter transference as well as cultural biases.
7. A culturally affirmative program adapts treatment methods to fit the skills and needs of clients.

When the Deaf Unit was created in 1987, we began with a political commitment to culturally affirmative services, but the lesson we learned subsequently was that *we could not be clinically effective unless we provided a treatment environment grounded in the Deaf experience.* Without a culturally affirmative approach, we wouldn't have the communication resources we needed. We wouldn't have the talented deaf staff and their unique abilities to join and communicate with very impaired deaf people and model more healthy psychosocial skills. We'd also have been far more vulnerable to the over-pathologizing of deaf people that occurs when clinicians work exclusively within the medical pathological framework.

Fortunately, the administration of Westborough State Hospital promoted a culture of psychiatric rehabilitation. A psychiatric rehabilitation model, focused on skill development, sets the stage for creation of a program in which there can be skill based strategies for most problems. By contrast, the medical model, which locates all client problems in some presumed illness or disorder that clients have, and assumes that staff are experts with the ability to fix these disorders, easily replicates patterns of domination and oppression between deaf and hearing people. Because for most people trained in the medical disciplines, being deaf is "storied" within a medical framework, it can be dangerous when Deaf treatment programs are administered by people working only from a medical model. It is dangerous because the disempowerment of deaf people emerges out of the medical model of deafness. *It is dangerous because most of the work of Deaf treatment programs is rehabilitative or habilitative, involves teaching psychosocial skills, not fixing a medical problem, even when clients do have major mental illnesses.* And it is dangerous because the medical model reinforces a hierarchical culture, with everyone reporting through their discipline heads and a physician in charge, and it will be rare for deaf people to have leadership roles in this hierarchy. This hierarchical structure is much less likely to be attuned to the skills and strengths of deaf people compared to the egalitarian cultures promoted within psychiatric rehabilitation programs.

While we were fortunate on the Deaf Unit to work with many physicians and nurses who could see beyond their medical training to embrace Deaf Culture, we also struggled with others who could not do so. Programs that serve deaf people have historically been far more likely to have deaf staff in lower paid, paraprofessional roles. This is changing as deaf people gain access to the professions. When culturally insensitive, domineering doctors and nurses run such programs, deaf people will not want to work there. Communication will be poor, and management of the communication dynamics is probably the core skill Deaf programs need to master. This power imbalance is still, I believe, the rule, not the exception, in mental health programs that serve deaf people. It is especially the rule in programs that work strictly from a medical model because this model allows hearing clinicians to continue to see themselves as benevolent helpers who fix deaf people. This means that many Deaf treatment programs are still places of profound disrespect for deaf people. The hearing people who work there don't usually perceive the injustices. They may well imagine themselves to be providing culturally affirmative treatment services simply because an interpreter or deaf staff person is present. The deaf staff in their midst, if there are any, likely consider these claims to be nonsense. They commonly feel very disempowered and disrespected. I've heard this many times from deaf staff in various programs, including the program I ran. Many times, the deaf staff in our program would say that we were not as culturally affirmative as we liked to believe we were.

There is another lesson that isn't evident until you do have a reasonably culturally affirmative treatment program. That lesson is that cultural affirmation is not a sufficient condition for good clinical care. Until you have it, you may always imagine that *if we just got the communication right, everything would be fine.* Once you have a reasonably culturally affirmative milieu, it becomes possible to see that getting the culture, communication and deaf/hearing relationships right still does not solve all clients problems. Cultural affirmation creates one essential context, but one still has to provide competent and effective treatment.

It should also be noted that Deaf treatment programs serve some extraordinarily challenging clients, some of whom are very violent, and that very commonly the police and courts refuse to set limits on these clients.[5] No hearing program, serving difficult hearing clients, is successful 100% of the time, yet Deaf programs, because there are so few of them, are expected to serve well every deaf person referred. They are expected to do this even in the face of severe language and behavioral challenges, of non-collaboration from clients, of refusal, often, of legal authorities to get involved, and in the absence of community resources readily available to hearing persons.

Deaf people, like hearing people, need to be trained in mental health care. Individual deaf clinicians may or may not be competent, and sometimes the deaf candidate is not the best choice for a job. As the Deaf Unit matured, we found that we struggled to get both the cultural and the clinical dynamics right, and that sometimes (such as with many personnel decisions), we might meet one goal at the expense of the other. This was one reason we never escaped cross-cultural conflicts.

Depending so heavily upon paraprofessional staff to manage a treatment milieu also presented challenges. When people are raised in family and school environments where authoritarian rule setting, not language-based negotiation, is the norm (an unfortunate reality for many deaf people), they will tend to copy what they know, and they will need supervision and training to work with clients in the collaborative decision making style so essential to psychiatric rehabilitation. Both deaf and hearing people can be authoritarian. Both can show poor work attitudes and skills, a lack of work ethic and commitment to patient care. However, when offered proper supervision and training, many staff learned to behave differently. I remember talking to one deaf male staff person who had a very bossy manner with clients. I asked him how he was raised, and he told me about his abusive, bullying father. I asked him if he liked how he was raised and if he wanted to raise his own children in the same way. He answered without hesitation, "No! No! I don't want to be like my father!" It wasn't hard to help him see the parallels to how we relate with our clients. However, not all staff, deaf or hearing, can make good use of supervision to overcome an authoritarian style of relating that they learned as children.

Over time, we found that the concept of *skills* gave us a framework equally effective for both client treatment and staff development. This was one shared concept that every discipline could use and that was equally applicable to staff as well as clients. With clients, even when we are treating bona fide mental illnesses such a schizophrenia, the treatment could be conceptualized as developing a variety of skills (understanding and managing symptoms, coping with unpleasant emotions and dealing with other people, for instance). Staff conflicts with clients, with each other, with administration, also require coping and conflict resolution skills. This skill language is relatively easy to understand, can be conceptualized in pictures, and is compatible with the world views of most of our deaf clients and staff. Skills can also be taught through stories, and when clients are helped to use skills, their use of skills itself becomes a story. It becomes the story of their developing abilities. Therefore, I'd argue that the adoption of a skill based treatment approach is itself an example of culturally affirmative treatment for deaf people. It is through helping clients develop skills that we create with them a culturally affirmative story. The theme of this story is "I can do this. We can do this."

The most advanced social skill that I asked Deaf Unit staff to practice was cross-cultural conflict resolution. In multicultural settings, such as programs employing deaf and hearing people (and many other culturally different people), cross-cultural misunderstandings and conflicts are common. The conflicts take many forms. When hearing people think about personnel matters, for instance, they usually value clinical competence most. They value clinical training and credentials. When deaf people think about personnel matters, they usually prioritize good communication in sign. This is because they understand in a far more profound way the crippling experience of having poor communication throughout one's life. They also know much more clearly than hearing people usually do what effective communication in sign language actually looks like.

These respective biases were behind many of the cross-cultural conflicts between deaf and hearing people that occurred in our setting. They commonly played out in staffing decisions. Who should be hired and promoted? How do we weigh the relative importance of communication and clinical skills? How important is it that large numbers of deaf people are employed by this organization? Who is qualified to work here? Who decides this? The social context for these biases is usually one in which hearing people hold more institutional power. This was the case at Westborough, where all the hospital and Department of Mental Health administrators were hearing. In its 23 years at Westborough State Hospital, the Deaf Unit had only one deaf director whose tenure was only a year or two.

Another context for personnel decisions was the collective bargaining agreements that the hospitals four unions negotiated with state officials. Most of the time, the unions were not particularly attuned to, or supportive of, the particular staffing needs of our small Deaf program. For instance, when the economic crisis hit and department-wide layoffs occurred, the question arose over whether deaf or signing staff, working on the Deaf Unit, would have protection from layoffs. Three of the four unions took the position that the only important consideration in layoffs was seniority, how long someone had worked for the state. They argued that hearing persons with seniority but no prior interest or skill in working with deaf people had priority in layoff decisions over deaf staff with less seniority, *even for work on a Deaf Unit*. Incredible as this may sound, three of our four unions took this position explicitly. Some of the union stewards who had already worked with deaf members backed us, but they were overruled. When challenged about how this would devastate care for our deaf clients, most of the union officials argued using the old, tired cliché that anyone could learn sign language on the job. We had over two decades of experience demonstrating how this wasn't the case, how many hearing people assigned to a Deaf unit *never* became competent signers, but these union officials really had no interest in challenging the time honored principal of seniority or of departing from the collective bargaining agreements that were developed state wide and didn't address the needs of small specialized programs like ours. The exception was the Social Workers union where union officials had a more developed clinical understanding of deaf client needs. They maintained support for the idea that the social worker and case managers had to be competent signers and that they would let us be the judge of signing competence. The difference, I think, was that the union leadership in the Social Workers union were also clinicians.

Consider how these respective cultural biases played out in some deaf/hearing cross-cultural conflicts I know of, occurring in different Deaf treatment settings:

1. A hearing nurse, new to work with deaf people, approaches a deaf developmentally delayed client and speaks to him as she would a hearing person. She doesn't sign. She also approaches a deaf-blind client and, to the astonishment of deaf staff, speaks to him as if he could see and hear. One of the deaf mental health workers interrupts her and tells her, in sign, gesture, and with unclear speech that she can't do that. He is visibly annoyed and impatient with her. He gets an interpreter and tells her very bluntly that she is not communicating respectfully with deaf people. She takes this as a scolding from someone who, in this setting, is her "inferior," and she complains about his rudeness. She writes him up for disciplinary action. This triggers a rage response from the deaf person who sees multiple forms of hearing oppression occurring. He also complains that this nurse is culturally insensitive and unsuitable for work with deaf people. He doesn't appreciate that while he was right about the nurse's ignorance about communicating with deaf and deaf-blind persons, his manner of expressing this was rude, insulting and, yes, insubordinate. When the nurse hears about the complaint against her, this triggers her own rage response. She's also in the middle of a difficult divorce and custody battle with a "bossy" husband, and the behavior of the deaf male staff person triggers her feelings of anger with her husband. She feels victimized as a woman. The male deaf mental health worker feels victimized as a deaf person.

2. In a Deaf treatment program, a board meeting was held that was run by a hearing administrator and psychiatrist. Several deaf staff were present including the staff person who recently created a Deaf awareness program for the agency. The subject of the Deaf awareness program came up, and board members asked the program staff to describe it. The hearing psychiatrist immediately jumped in to do so. Because of the 5-second time lag for those watching the interpreter, the psychiatrist had the opportunity to comment before the deaf staff person who actually created and ran this program. The deaf staff member raised his hand to speak after the psychiatrist had started talking, and a board member asked that the deaf staff person be able to address this issue. The psychiatrist then stopped talking and the deaf staff person described the program. Later, it became clear that the hearing psychiatrist felt that the deaf staff person had rudely interrupted him. The deaf staff person was counseled for his "unprofessional" behavior. However, the issue of who interrupted whom is open to interpretation. Because the hearing psychiatrist did not attend to the interpreter time lag, it could just as easily be argued that he interrupted the deaf staff person. Second, it was the deaf staff person who was more qualified to talk on that topic, so, arguably, it was the psychiatrist whose behavior was, if not unprofessional, at least non-collegial. The hearing psychiatrist was speaking for the deaf staff about a program they created and ran. However, because the deaf staff person had less power, it was he who was disciplined.

3. In a residential treatment setting, one of the deaf staff who is loudest in his criticism of the "oppression" coming from the administration is widely known to have a poor work attitude, abusing sick time, spending much work time on the Internet or his mobile pager, and being negligent and disrespectful of clients. A promotional opportunity comes up, and he isn't considered for it. To add fuel to the fire, a hearing staff person, who has much poorer signing skills but is seen by administration to be more dedicated to high quality client care, receives the promotion. For the deaf employee, this is further proof of hearing biases of this "audist" organization. For the hearing administrators, the attitude of the deaf employee is infuriating. They believe they are also dedicated to cultural affirmation for deaf people, but not if it means promoting deaf staff who aren't doing good work. The bottom line for them is who is providing the best care and treatment of clients. They don't see this as a deaf or hearing matter but rather a matter of individual competence and dedication which either a deaf or hearing person may show. Many of the deaf staff, and their hearing allies, grumble amongst themselves that this hearing person, with marginal signing skills, was promoted over a deaf person with native signing abilities. Some could see that the deaf applicant had poor work attitudes and behaviors but they still perceive that, when push comes

to shove, the communication abilities that deaf staff usually have are not valued by hearing administrators on par with other qualities that applicants for hire and promotion possess. They object that someone who doesn't have good sign communication skills is promoted over other people who do. They suspect that the hearing administrators think all signing is "good enough" and don't appreciate what a truly excellent sign communicator contributes to client care.

The important lesson we learned about administering Deaf mental health programs is that these cross-cultural conflicts are built in. They are bound to happen, but it is rare for the personnel involved, at any level of the organization, to have the cross-cultural conflict resolution skills needed to manage these conflicts well. This is not an inconsequential matter. I believe that all Deaf treatment programs and schools struggle with variations on these cross-cultural tensions, and some programs have fallen apart because they were not handled well. Thus, an important, rarely discussed dimension of culturally affirmative programming is preparing the staff with such essential skills as listening, cross culturally, with empathy; recognizing common hearing and deaf biases; and managing the power imbalances to ensure that deaf viewpoints are well represented in decision making forums.[6] The lesson is that one cannot create an effective Deaf treatment program without attending to the cross-cultural dynamics between deaf and hearing people.

Conclusion

In Chapter 4 of this book, Gournaris, Hamerdinger, and Williams, three statewide directors of Deaf mental health services, argue that specialized Deaf inpatient units are not absolutely necessary, and that when funding is tight, the resources are better directed to community based treatment programs. They note that Deaf inpatient programs were established and then closed in several states when the decision was made that more deaf people could be served better by funding community programs like group homes, day and work programs, outreach, and mental health specialists. To their well-reasoned arguments one could add one more point. When Deaf inpatient programs are created in the absence of community based residential programs, deaf persons who are homeless become stuck on the units for months or even years at a time. We saw this happen many times at Westborough. For the deaf clients involved, being stuck in a state psychiatric hospital, even one with deaf and signing staff, was no victory. They wanted to live normally, as other people do, in the community.

It is difficult to argue with this position, but I want to try. A quality specialized Deaf inpatient program offers many things to Deaf mental health care. In Massachusetts, the creation of this service gave deaf people visibility within the Department of Mental Health. Having a deaf inpatient program brought deaf people with severe mental health needs into the service system. They were referred to the program, evaluated appropriately, and then staff could advocate for the community based services they needed. While many deaf people did become stuck on the Deaf Unit for much too long, the end result is that Massachusetts developed a network of residential treatment programs unrivaled anywhere else in the world. At the time of this writing, there are well over a dozen such programs in this small state.

The Deaf Unit was also able to model a standard of care for community based treatment programs. The idea of culturally affirmative programs, hiring many deaf staff and having specialized communication and clinical competence, spread from the Deaf Unit into these community resources. Over time, many Department of Mental Health commissioners, state legislators, and other officials toured the program, talked with deaf patients and staff, and became educated about the service needs of deaf people. It is unlikely that the Massachusetts DMH would have the ongoing commitment to serving deaf people that it has had for more than a quarter century without the existence of this key Deaf program.

Deaf psychiatric inpatient programs also have the potential to assemble a team of qualified staff. There is no guarantee this will happen because there are many obstacles to these programs recruiting and hiring qualified staff. If these programs do not have a director who is knowledgeable and empowered to advocate for the specialized needs of such a program, a Deaf program can be Deaf in name only. A Deaf program which does not really have expertise in serving deaf people can do more damage than good. Somewhere, the standard for best practice in Deaf mental health care has to be set, and a quality Deaf inpatient program can be such a place with the right combination of qualified staff and support from the hospital, agency and Deaf Community.

Another benefit of such programs is that they can provide a place for staff development, including practica and internships. Although the Deaf Unit was never able to obtain the resources to provide a psychology internship for a deaf psychology student, we had deaf and hearing interns from counseling, social work, interpreting, nursing and expressive therapies work on the unit. We also had many medical and psychiatry residents work with our clients and sometimes they went on to present grand rounds and write papers on the subject. Many deaf and hearing staff persons began as direct care staff persons on the unit and went on to undergraduate and graduate studies in the mental health field. They took the treatment strategies they learned on the unit, the ways we adapted cognitive behavioral therapy (Glickman, 2009), into other treatment programs. Some of our deaf mental health workers learned about deaf interpreting and went on to become certified deaf interpreters.

Deaf inpatient programs are also places where crucially needed research can be done. For instance, the work done by Thacker (1994, 1998) and ourselves on language dysfluency was done in inpatient settings, and our hypothesis about the syndrome *of language deprivation with deficiencies in behavioral, social and emotional adjustment* comes from this inpatient setting. If we are going to advance our knowledge about the treatment needs of deaf persons with mental illness, we do need such specialized treatment settings where a critical mass of deaf persons and the right kind of staff expertise can be brought together.

Finally, there is the ongoing need for inpatient treatment resources for deaf persons who do have either very severe behavioral problems or genuine psychiatric crises where safety is at stake. In Massachusetts, the referrals to the Deaf Unit, now at Worcester State Hospital, have decreased as a result of the array of residential treatment programs available, but even with such programs, clients still go into crisis and need inpatient treatment. One reason the unit is rarely full with deaf people now is because these community-based programs make it far less likely that deaf people will become stuck on the unit, occupying a bed unnecessarily. Now the unit can be used as it should be used, as a short-term treatment resource for all but the most seriously disturbed deaf people.

The future for the Deaf Unit in Massachusetts at this time looks mixed. On the one hand, the DMH has maintained its commitment to deaf inpatient services. On the other hand, there have not been the number of referrals to justify continuing a full inpatient program. System wide, funds are shifting from an inpatient to a community focus, and there is no reason this shouldn't apply to services for deaf persons as well. For years now, the unit has had to mix deaf and hearing clients. This may be better than no inpatient treatment resource at all, but mixed units have their own set of challenges. It's especially difficult to create a signing environment in a mixed unit, and inevitably the deaf and hearing clients and staff clash. On the other hand, we had hearing clients who loved being placed on the Deaf Unit, who took great interest in signing, and one even went on to major in Deaf studies in his college program. We also had deaf clients, especially some of the higher functioning people, who did quite well in small treatment groups with hearing peers. There is no one size that fits all. A Deaf inpatient unit, even if it must shift its shape to fit the changing demand, reflects a commitment to serve deaf people with severe mental health needs well and to promote the development of Deaf mental health care. If a state is developing deaf services for the first time, there is good reason to start with such a specialized center of excellence, create a beachhead of deaf services, establish standards of care, and then move from there towards establishing less intensive outpatient programs.

Notes

1. An earlier version of this chapter was published by JADARA and is reprinted with permission. Glickman, N. (2010), Lessons learned from 23 years of a Deaf

psychiatric inpatient unit: Part 1. *JADARA, 44*(1), 255–239; and Glickman, N. (2001), Lessons learned from 23 years of a Deaf psychiatric inpatient unit: Part 2. *JADARA, 44*(2), 82–100.

2. As noted in the book Introduction, all case histories have been altered to protect confidentiality.
3. See Chapter 3.
4. The paradigm of "recovery" might be a more useful map if discussed in terms of personal life goals. See the discussion of this in Chapter 5.
5. See Chapter 9 for a fuller discussion of this issue.
6. See Chapters 2 and 5 for more on this.

References

Ayres, J. A. (1979). *Sensory integration and the child*. Los Angeles, CA: Western Psychological Services

Basilier, T. (1964). Surdophrenia: the psychic consequences of congenital or early acquired deafness. *Acta Psychiatrica Scandinavica, 40*, 362–372.

Black, P. (2005). Language dysfluency in the Deaf inclient population (Unpublished doctoral dissertation). Fielding University, Santa Barbara, California.

Black, P., & Glickman, N. (2005). Language deprivation in the Deaf inclient population. *JADARA, 39*(1), 1–28.

Black, P., & Glickman, N. (2006). Demographics, psychiatric diagnoses, and other characteristics of North Amnerican Deaf and hard-of-hearing inclients. *Journal of Deaf Studies and Deaf Education, 11*(3), 303–321.

Champagne, T. (2006). *Sensory modulation and environment: Essential elements of occupation* (2nd ed.). Southampton, MA: Champagne conferences and consultation

Champagne, T., & Stromberg, N. (2004). Sensory approaches in inpatient psychiatric settings: Innovative alternatives to seclusion and restraint. *Journal of Psychosocial Nursing, 42*(9), 35–44.

Denmark, J. (1985). A study of 250 clients referred to a department of psychiatry for the deaf. *British Journal of Psychiatry, 146*, 282–286.

Denmark, J. (1994). *Deafness and mental health*. London: Jessica Kingsley.

Dew, D. W. (Ed.). (1999). *Serving individuals who are low-functioning deaf.* Washington, DC: The George Washington University Regional Rehabilitation Continuing Education Program.

Gaines, J., Meltzer, B., & Glickman, N. (2009). Language and learning challenges in adolescent hearing psychiatric inpatients. In N. Glickman (Ed.), *Cognitive behavioral therapy for deaf and hearing persons with language and learning challenges* (pp. 213–224). New York, NY: Routledge.

Glickman, N. (2003). Culturally affirmative inpatient treatment with psychologically unsophisticated Deaf people. In N. Glickman & S. Gulati (Eds.), *Mental health care of deaf people: a culturally affirmative approach* (pp. 145–201). Mahwah, NJ: Erlbaum.

Glickman, N. (2007). Do you hear voices?: Problems in assessment of mental status in deaf person with severe language deprivation. *Journal of Deaf Studies and Deaf Education, 12*(2), 127–147.

Glickman, N. (2009). *Cognitive behavioral therapy for deaf and hearing persons with language and learning challenges*. New York, NY: Routledge.

Glickman, N., & Gulati, S. (2003). *Mental health care of Deaf people: A culturally affirmative approach*. Mahwah, NJ: Erlbaum.

Glickman, N., & Zitter, S. (1989). On establishing a culturally affirmative psychiatric unit for deaf people. *JADARA, 23*(2), 46–59.

Greene, R. (1998). *The explosive child.* New York, NY: Harper Collins.

Greene, R. W., & Ablon, J. S. (2006). *Treating explosive kids: the collaborative problem-solving approach.* London: Guilford Press.

Grinker, R., Vernon., M., Mindel, E., Rothstein, D., Easton, H., Koh, S., et al. (1969). *Psychiatric Diagnosis, Therapy and Research on the Psychotic Deaf* (No. Research Grant number RD-2407-S). Washington, DC: U.S. Department of Health, Education and Welfare.

Haskins, B. G. (2004). Serving deaf adult psychiatric inclients. *Psychiatric Services, 55,* 439–441.

Humphries, T. (1977) Communicating across cultures (Deaf/Hearing) and language learning (Unpublished doctoral dissertation). Union Graduate School, Cincinnati, OH.

Landsberger, S., & Diaz, D. (2010). Inclient psychiatric treatment of deaf adults: Demographic and diagnostic comparisons with hearing inclients. *Psychiatric Services, 61*(2), 196–199.

Lane, H. (1992). *The mask of benevolence.* New York, NY: Knoff.

Linehan, M. (1993a). *Cognitive behavioral treatment of borderline personality disorder.* New York, NY: Guilford Press.

Linehan, M. (1993b). *Skills training manual for treating borderline personality disorder.* New York, NY: Guilford Press.

Long, G., Long, N., & Ouellette, S. E. (1993). Service provision issues with traditionally underserved persons who are deaf. In O. M. Welch (Ed.), *Research and practice in deafness: Issues and questions in education, psychology and vocational service provision* (pp. 107–126). Springfield, IL: Charles C. Thomas.

Meichenbaum, D. (1977a). *Cognitive-behavioral modification: an integrative approach.* New York, NY: Plenum Press.

Meichenbaum, D. (1977b). *Stress-inoculation training. In Cognitive-behavior modification.* New York, NY: Plenum Press.

Meichenbaum, D. (1985). *Stress Inoculation Training.* Elmsford, NY: Pergamon Press.

Meichenbaum, D. (1994). *A clinical handbook/practical therapist manual for assessing and treating adults with post-traumatic stress disorder.* Waterloo, Canada: Institute Press.

Meichenbaum, D. (1996). *Mixed anxiety and depression: a cognitive-behavioral approach. On The Newbridge assessment and treatment of psychological disorders series.* New York, NY: Newbridge Communications, Inc.

Meichenbaum, D. (2001). *Treatment of individuals with anger-control problems and aggressive behaviors: a clinical handbook.* Clearwater, FL: Institute Press.

Meichenbaum, D. (2007). Stress inoculation training: A preventative and treatment approach. In P. M. Lehrer, R. L. Woolfolk & W. S. Sime (Eds.), *Principles and practice of stress management* (3rd ed., pp. 131–142). New York, NY: Guilford Press.

Meichenbaum, D., & Biemiller, A. (1998). *Nurturing independent learners: Helping students take charge of their learning.* Newton, MA: Brookline Books.

Meichenbaum, D., & Goodman, J. (1971). Training impulsive children to talk to themselves: A means of developing self-control. *Journal of Abnormal Psychology, 77,* 115–126.

Meichenbaum, D., & Turk, D. (1987). *Facilitating treatment adherence: a practitioner's guide.* New York, NY: Plenum Press.

Moncrieff, J. (2009). *The myth of the chemical cure: A critique of psychiatric drug treatment.* New York, NY: Palgrave Macmillan/St. Martin's Press.

Moore, K. M. (2005). *The sensory connection program*. Framingham, MA: Therapro, Inc.

Mompremier, L. (2009). A descriptive phenomenological study of symptoms of schizophrenia in deaf clients (Unpublished doctoral dissertation). Gallaudet University, Washington, DC.

National Association of State Mental Health Program Directors Medical Directors Council. (2002). *Reducing the use of seclusion and restraint. Part III, Lessons from the deaf and hard of hearing communities.* Alexandria, VA: National Technical Assistance Center or State Mental Health Planning (NTAC).

Poizner, H., Klima, E. S., & Belllugi, U. (1987). What the hands reveal about the brain. Cambridge, MA: The MIT Press.

Rainer, J. D., & Altshuler, K. Z. (1967). *Psychiatry and the deaf.* New York, NY: Columbia University Press.

Thacker, A. (1994). Formal communication disorder: Sign language in deaf people with schizophrenia. *British Journal of Psychiatry, 165,* 818–823.

Thacker, A. (1998). The manifestation of schizophrenic formal communication disorder in sign language (Unpublished doctoral dissertation). St. George Hospital Medical School, London, England.

Trikakis, D., Curci, N., & Strom, H. (2003). Sensory strategies for self-regulation: Non-linguistic body-based treatment for deaf psychiatric patients. In N. Glickman & S. Gulati (Eds.), *Mental health care of deaf people: A culturally affirmative approach* (pp. 68–81). Mahwah, NJ: Erlbaum.

Vernon, M., & Andrews, J. F. (1990). *The psychology of deafness.* New York, NY: Longman.

Vernon, M., & Miller, K. (2001). Linguistic incompetence to stand trial: A unique condition in some deaf defendants. *Journal of Interpretation,* 99–120.

Vernon, M., & Miller, K. (2005). Obstacles faced by deaf people in the criminal justice system. *American Annals of the Deaf, 150*(3), 283–291.

Vernon, M., & Raifman, L. J. (1997). Recognizing and handling problems of incompetent deaf defendants charged with serious offenses. *International Journal of Law and Psychiatry, 20*(3), 373–387.

White paper on addressing the trauma treatment needs of children who are deaf or hard of hearing and the hearing children of deaf parents. (2006). Los Angeles, CA: National Child Traumatic Stress Network.

Whitaker, R. (2010). *Anatomy of an epidemic.* New York, NY: Crown.

2 Deaf/Hearing Cross-cultural Conflicts and the Creation of Culturally Competent Treatment Programs[1]

Michael John Gournaris and Alison L. Aubrecht

Introduction

The psychological motivation and traits of hearing people who work with deaf people have been explored by several authors (Baker-Shenk & Kyle, 1990). Hoffmeister and Harvey (1996) refer to these as the "psychology of the hearing," contrasting their work with the much more extensive literature about a presumed "psychology of deafness" (Levine, 1960; Myklebust, 1964; Paul & Jackson, 1993; Vernon & Andrews, 1990). Lane (1992) has challenged the whole notion of a "psychology of deafness" as "audist," and while we agree that there are no psychological traits common to all deaf people, there are several unidentified or unlabeled "relational postures" which deaf people may commonly assume towards hearing people. Relational postures involve both attitudes and behaviors. The relational postures that deaf people assume towards hearing people are often triggered by the relational postures that hearing people commonly assume towards them. These contrasting perspectives, stemming from widely different experiences and worldviews, foster what Glickman (2009) refers to as cross-cultural conflicts between deaf and hearing people.

Our intent in this chapter is to expose and explore these relational postures and potential conflicts revealing their forms and patterns. These deaf/hearing cross-cultural conflicts are very common and destructive to both individuals and organizations. Many Deaf mental health and rehabilitation programs' working environments have deteriorated because both deaf and hearing staff did not recognize and manage these cross-cultural conflicts competently (Glickman, 2009). We hope that such exposure will promote treatment environments where deaf and hearing people have more successful relationships.[2]

We begin by reviewing the literature about common shared employment experiences of deaf people. Such work experiences may elicit deep emotional reactions ranging from frustration to powerlessness, distrust to rage, particularly when working within programs whose missions center around providing treatment to deaf people. It is important for people to understand what deaf people often experience at work, even in designated

Deaf treatment programs. It is also important for people to understand how hearing people in these programs think and feel. We recognize that at times, this process of self-examination may be uncomfortable for the reader.

Similar to other minority and majority groups, deaf and hearing individuals frequently misread each other. The implications of hearing privileges and oppressive behaviors often create power imbalances between deaf and hearing individuals, which in turn may foster conflicts, mutual distrust, and the development of widely contrasting narratives about shared experiences. Deaf and hearing people frequently do not see eye to eye. Their communication problems go well beyond that of using different languages. Influenced by their own cultural upbringing and worldview, persons from each group may unintentionally act in ways that reinforce the prejudices and stereotypes of the other. If such behaviors go unexplored, resulting consequences may range from staff burn out to ineffective treatment strategies, or worse, treatment that may be harmful for clients.

Our discussion regarding deaf/hearing conflicts is followed by examples of successful deaf/hearing partnerships. The creation of such partnerships is far more complex than people assume. Successful partnerships require personal and cultural self-awareness, a great deal of knowledge and specialized skills (Corker, 1994; Glickman, 1996). Openness to critical investigation of one's own biases, a genuine interest in self-improvement, an authentic commitment to creating opportunities for equality, and the capacity for compassion and empathic listening across a cultural and power barrier are key ingredients in fostering that equity. The payoff is a culturally competent treatment setting. Such environments are essential for an effective system of mental health care in which deaf individuals have the opportunity to thrive.

Common Employment Challenges Experienced by Deaf Workers in Cross-cultural Environments

Research on the employment experiences of deaf people presents three common themes: discrimination, communication problems, and prejudicial attitudes. Resistance from employers to initially hiring deaf people, providing reasonable accommodations, training and promoting them appears to be largely based on misunderstanding, prejudice, and communication barriers.

A national study of workplace discrimination revealed that between July 26, 1992 and September 30, 2003, as many as 8,936 complaints were filed with the Equal Employment Opportunity Commission (EEOC) by people with hearing loss (Bowe, McMahon, Chang, & Louvi, 2005). These authors found that the discrimination cases by individuals with hearing loss were mostly related to hiring, promotion, training, and conditions of discharge. Other complaints were related to work assignment, demotion, discipline, and suspension.

Luft (2000) found that the lack of appropriate and clear communication, as well as limited opportunities for professional growth within an organization were likely to contribute to poor employment and retention rates among deaf employees. Scherich (1996) described how communication difficulties caused problems for deaf employees in six specific workplace situations: in-service/training, socializing with hearing co-workers, department/staff meeting, work related social functions, receiving instructions and supervision, and performance evaluation. Scherich concluded that proper communication accommodations are essential for deaf employees' career maintenance and advancement.

Employers' lack of willingness to work with deaf employees also appears to be relevant (Scheetz, 1993). Scheetz concluded that after examining several employment-related studies, resistive attitudes (i.e., having deaf employees is not desired) and permissive attitudes (i.e., considering deaf applicants only if she fit in the organization without the need for any job accommodations) cause many of the employment problems deaf people face. Moores (1996) found that, despite good work performance evaluations, many hearing supervisors believed that deaf employees should not advance within the organization and therefore did not offer further training. This finding supports Welsh's (1993) conclusion that deaf employees were less likely to advance even when they were perceived to be qualified. While deaf people are increasingly obtaining leadership positions within various organizations, recruiting deaf professionals with both adequate training and experience is often difficult because of the lack of developmental opportunities (Benedict & Sass-Lehrer, 2007). This may mean the résumés of deaf candidates often are not as strong as hearing candidates. The hearing candidate may be hired based on a resume that lists more experience, in part because the deaf candidate did not have the same opportunities. The fact that the deaf candidate does not have as strong of a resume will give the employer a rational basis for turning down the "less qualified applicant."

The attitudes toward deaf applicants appears to be a widespread problem as indicated in a television show that broadcasted on February 4, 2011 (Yee, 2011) on ABC News's "What Would You Do?" with John Quinones. The show uses hidden cameras to depict actors doing controversial things and to capture people's reactions to dilemmas. ABC News hired two deaf female students from Rochester Institute of Technology's National Technical Institute for the Deaf (NTID) to be actors for the production, in which situation they would pretend to apply for a job opening at a small coffee shop in New Jersey. The manager, also an actor, immediately told the students that they would not be hired because they were deaf using these statements:

- "We don't hire deaf people here."
- "I'm sure you can do lots of things. But this is not the job for you."
- "The next time you come in here, bring an interpreter."
- "I think you people would rather work with people of your own kind."
- "I'm not going to hire a deaf person; I'll let you know right now, I'm not going to waste your time."

Actual customers witnessing the discrimination gave blank stares and some rolled their eyes, but only three reportedly spoke up to defend the students (only one supportive customer's reaction was aired on the show). As the day progressed, the manager/actor became bolder with his discrimination using these statements:

- "Go ahead and fill out the application. I'm going to write 'DEAF' across the top of it."
- "Isn't there another place you'd feel more comfortable working? I think you'd be more comfortable someplace else."
- "I'm trying to run a business, and that type of impairment would be a nuisance."
- "It would make things uncomfortable for our customers."
- "Is there a deaf school around? Maybe you should find a job there."

The comments above did not appear to invoke many responses from the customers, as they did not defend the deaf students. Even more troubling was the two professionals with human resources background who approached the manager at separate times and actually tried to educate him how to "legally" discriminate, by accepting the applications but not to call them back. One stated, "You don't have to hire her, but you need to be careful how you communicate that," she said. "This is a very litigious society."

Two other segments were shown on the same ABC News show that night. In one, a situation involving racial profiling was staged in Arizona. A hired actor dressed in a security guard uniform approached two Hispanic actors (one was John Quinones himself) at a restaurant asking for identification to see if the Hispanics are legal residents. Many Caucasian customers erupted in anger and aggressively confronted the security guard accusing him for racial profiling and some actually threatened the actor. Some used profanity. One female customer even offered the Hispanic actors to escape with her in the car to avoid deportation. In the other segment, ABC News filmed people's reactions when waitresses' tips were stolen by an actor/patron. More people protested about the actor's improper behavior. In these segments, job discrimination against deaf people did not generate the same strong reactions in people, as did discrimination against

Hispanic persons and waitress tips being stolen. Gerry Buckley (NTID President) said it best, "When President (George H.W.) Bush signed the Americans with Disabilities Act, many of us hoped that that would be the last barrier." He further noted, "What we found out, though, is that attitudinal barriers were still there, and that we have much work to do to educate people" (NTID News, 2011).

The Value of Deaf Staff and Strong Deaf-Hearing Partnerships

With so much of the literature focused on difficulties that deaf people face, it was a pleasant surprise to find a book chapter that centers on strengths that deaf staff bring to the deaf-hearing collaboration in mental health settings. Klein and Kitson (2000) wrote extensively about strengths that deaf staff bring to the partnership. They recounted stories of situations where patients were not understood until a native signer was brought in. They noted that deaf staff communicate with more ease in situations involving deaf people with "limited or odd" communication.

Additionally, Klein and Kitson (2000) discussed credibility that deaf staff have with the community and ways that this relationship is vital in terms of establishing an authentic, effective practice where deaf individuals feel confident utilizing services. They state that when deaf staff return to the community, their sharing stories "demystifies and destigmatizes mental health" (p. 289).

Klein and Kitson ask:

> If they had deaf colleagues, would psychiatrists for deaf people (as recently as the mid-1980's) have over-generalized from their deaf patients to say that deaf people exhibit concrete thinking, rigidity, decreased empathy, projection of responsibility on to others, lack of insight or self-reproach, unrealistic views of their own abilities, increased demands and impulsivity with poor control of rage? (2000, p. 289)

Backenroth (1998) offered an excellent analysis of hearing and deaf people in bi-cultural work groups. She evaluated the social interactions between the two groups, noting their individual and collective responses. On the individual level, both deaf and hearing people demonstrated motivation for contact and positive attitudes toward one another. For example, individuals from both groups reported that, despite their differences in language and culture, they want to be open to each other, empathic, able to make jokes and laugh, have good eye contact, be curious about each other, and be included in conversations. On a group level, both deaf and hearing people stated how important it was for hearing people to sign well if the two groups were to communicate effectively and avoid misunderstandings.

Challenges of Creating Deaf and Hearing Partnerships

Deaf and hearing partnerships and collaborations are unsuccessful when people feel they are not being respected, trusted, valued, and supported. Deaf and hearing interactions that are not based on open and frank communication in which difficult issues are open for dialogue, will eventually lead to missed opportunities for both parties to learn more about each other's experiences and perspectives. Snyder (1987) demonstrates how emotional responses to cross-cultural conflicts, when unexamined, result in necessary discussions being avoided and important decisions being delayed. She provided an example of cross-cultural conflict at an agency serving deaf people in Hawaii. She described how a deaf staff member repeatedly blamed the hearing director of the agency for not sharing crucial information with her. This deaf employee also questioned the director's motives for what she interpreted to be exclusion of deaf staff. The deaf employee rightly noted that the usual language outside of staff meetings and the office was spoken English. Therefore, deaf staff often missed informal discussions within the agency where crucial information could be passed along. Direct conversation with the director required the use of an interpreter. What the deaf employee wanted and needed was some affirmative outreach, some visible attempt to include her in the information flow. This could be done in many ways, and would require some effort on the part of the hearing administration and staff beyond scheduling an interpreter for occasional meetings. In this situation, the deaf employee saw the lack of such affirmative inclusion efforts as discrimination. The hearing employer probably felt that the deaf employee was making unreasonable demands or perhaps that she was acting in an "entitled" manner. The employer may have felt that provision of occasional interpreters, which can be major expenses, was already going "above and beyond" what was necessary.

This situation could be understood using different narratives such as "a difficult employee," "a difficult employer," "job discrimination," or "cross-cultural conflict." However one sees it, there was no venue for discussion of what is, after all, a very common experience, at least for deaf employees. The real solution may not even have been a particular communication policy, though that could help, but a more empathic and respectful dialogue and attempt at collaborative problem solving.

Socio-emotional and Political Dynamics

The following categories are all common consequences of oppressive behaviors and environments in which hearing people are perceived as having more privileges. Understanding these dynamics may allow for more profound awareness of potential barriers to efficient collaboration in cross-cultural environments.

Audism

Deaf people are frequently confronted by the need to assert their right to equality. There has been much discussion about dynamics of oppression within the Deaf Community. Oppression of deaf individuals has been termed "audism" (Humphries, 1977). Humphries, in a 1977 dissertation, defined audism as "the notion that one is superior based on one's ability to hear or behave in the manner of one who hears." Discussions regarding audism have included: ways that hearing environments create barriers for deaf people, hearing people making decisions about and for deaf people, and English having privileged status over ASL.

The following is an example of a person demonstrating audist behavior: A therapist (hearing) working in a program serving deaf individuals was approached by a deaf colleague (also a program therapist). The deaf therapist had some ideas for improving some of the agency forms. Wanting to engage co-workers in brainstorming ways to improve program efficiency, the deaf therapist invited the hearing therapist to add his input. Rather than simply doing so, the hearing therapist took over the project, took the suggested revisions from the deaf therapist, revised them, worked further with hearing colleagues on the project, and then submitted the final proposal to their supervisor, all without involving the deaf therapist who initially raised the idea.

Hearing Privilege

Hearing people generally control the direction of mental health services and the treatment decisions of deaf clients. Benedict and Sass-Lehrer (2007) explained that hearing people, because they are members of the social majority, have powerful influence over decisions that affect legislation, policies, professional organizations, and research agendas. Hearing people are also perceived by many deaf people as having more power or advantages over them even when the organization serving deaf individuals has many more deaf employees.

Hearing privilege is an important concept in illustrating one aspect of deaf/hearing cultural dynamics. Tiffany Tuccoli discussed this concept in an unpublished master's thesis in 2008. She defined hearing privilege as "advantages or entitlements that are enjoyed by people who can hear which are denied to those who are deaf" (p. 23) and explained that hearing people have many "unearned advantages and privileges" that create a situation of unequal opportunities for those who are deaf. Bryant (2010) has popularized this concept through the workshops he has given throughout the United States. He defined hearing privilege as a set of advantages enjoyed by hearing people beyond those commonly experienced by non-hearing people in the same social, political, and economic spaces (e.g., country, community, or workplace). In addition, Bryant emphasized that hearing privilege differs from audism or prejudice in that people benefiting from hearing privilege do not necessarily hold audist beliefs or prejudices and can be oblivious to the privileges that they experience. To give an example of hearing privilege: a hearing coordinator unintentionally "forgets" to schedule for an ASL interpreter for an important two-hour meeting, and then decides not to change the meeting time, stating that the issues are important and it is not feasible to wait the minimum amount of time required to arrange an interpreter. Another example of hearing privilege may be found in hearing people who, with less than native sign language abilities, accept jobs to teach sign language classes when there are more qualified deaf candidates. Audism can be found in an organization that very deliberately decides not to hire deaf applicants, preferring a hearing applicant with ASL skills, and rationalizing that this will allow them to use staff more "flexibly." The hearing applicant, who takes the job, even if unaware of the audist intentions of the agency, is benefiting from hearing privilege.

The majority of programs that serve deaf individuals (i.e., schools of the deaf, organizations, agencies) have hearing administrators. Much of the time, decisions are made without input from deaf people. In a real life example, a program supervisor (hearing woman) of a Deaf Services agency sets up a work group whose mission is to develop a Deaf mentor program. She then selects five hearing employees who will collaborate in developing mentoring services for hearing families with deaf children. No deaf employees are included in the work group despite the fact that there are several qualified deaf employees working within the program.

These situations reflect the privileges that hearing people have and sometimes take advantage of for self-enrichment, not realizing that such decisions will seriously impact their relationships with people. Although the two terms, "audism" and "hearing privilege" share some common characteristics, there is one significant difference. While hearing privilege is often an unconscious acceptance of ways that the environment is unfairly biased for the hearing individual, audism reflects attitudes and behavior that actively oppress deaf people.

The Dominance of English over Signed Languages

Deaf people often observe that hearing people (and some deaf people) appear to make little effort to acquire skills in ASL when they work with deaf people. They also quite frequently assume their signing abilities are much better than they actually are. At the same time, it is expected that deaf people be fluent in English and they are criticized when they are not. This double standard is often a prominent factor in promotional decisions. While literacy in English is required for most supervisory and management positions in English speaking countries, there is no such expectation about ASL fluency, or there are sloppy standards for what constitutes ASL fluency, even in programs serving deaf people.

Deaf people can understand why reading and writing are important, but it is just as obvious to them that signing well is a crucial skill in any Deaf agency or service. Why then do people who don't sign well get promoted? And why is it reasonable to accommodate hearing individuals by providing interpreters but not to accommodate deaf individuals by providing proofreaders and/or editors? How is this fair or in the interest of quality client care?

Many deaf professionals and clients have concerns about working with hearing mental health professionals who work with deaf clients but are not skilled signers. Several deaf research participants in Smith's 2007 dissertation, like Autumn, who are mental health counselors addressed this issue, "I am surprised that many hearing counselors who go to conferences about treating deaf clients cannot even sign" (p. 132). Amber shared similar thoughts as Autumn: "I have noticed lately wherever I go I see hearing counselors working with deaf clients and these counselors do not seem to sign well. They may have important experience and training, but the language is not there and I assume the understanding of the client's experience is not there" (p. 132).

Competency Concerns

Deaf individuals, even when they are well trained and have the proper credentials, often worry about their competence levels being viewed positively by hearing people even in settings designed to serve deaf people. An example is found in Smith (2007) where Autumn works with hearing professionals who do not know ASL: "In general, they do treat me as an equal professional," Autumn shared, "But the process of meetings feels different. I feel equal and professional in a group using ASL, but here in staff meetings I do not feel professional and often doubt myself." She later expanded her comment, "Previously, when I was working with deaf staff members, I felt more confident in what I was doing, but trying to fit with hearing colleagues is difficult. But this is a hearing world. And it goes both ways. I think the environment influences how you feel about yourself and how you present yourself influences the environment, too.... I work with clients alone, but I co-lead a group with a hearing therapist and all crisis interventions require another therapist to provide a second opinion. I am confident in my work with deaf clients ... but in staff meetings that confidence seems to vanish. I question myself" (p. 128). Smith further explained that the comments made by Autumn illuminated the fact that despite having proper credentials and high fluency in ASL, she, like many other deaf professionals, believes that her hearing colleagues do not view her as competent.

One reason many deaf people struggle with feeling less competent is because they are aware that many hearing people assume deaf people are less competent. These hearing people see the deaf condition as a disability, feel sorry for deaf people, and sometimes equate hearing loss with lesser intelligence or other presumed deficits. Though education and training opportunities for deaf people have increased dramatically over the years, barriers continue to exist due to biases about deaf people. This puts deaf people at a competitive disadvantage in the employment market place. Also, because they miss out on a lot of the incidental information flow between hearing people, they may not be aware of what they don't know. The flip side of this is that deaf people often bring an expert, insider knowledge of the needs and abilities of deaf people, yet even here their experiences can be devalued by hearing people who like to think of themselves as experts on deaf-related issues. Thus, the issue of competence is a highly sensitive one for deaf workers. When deaf workers find themselves working in designated Deaf programs and feel devalued and disrespected as workers, it can be particularly painful, and as such may trigger intense reactions.

Being Expendable

Deaf people are aware that they are often perceived as a financial burden at their job sites. Some may fear losing a position, believing that they will be replaced by a hearing person. Such experiences give deaf people a reason to tread cautiously with hearing co-workers and supervisors whom they need to recruit as allies. The narratives provided by Smith (2007) are prime examples. Autumn commented, "Hearing agencies still seem to look at deaf people from a pathological perspective and it is very likely that agencies providing services to deaf clients would rather hire hearing counselors with 'deaf experience' than deaf counselors. There seems to be little value given to the experiences that deaf counselors bring to their work" (p. 125).

Many deaf mental health professionals also experience difficulty gaining employment or internship opportunities, even at sites that specialize in treating deaf individuals (Hauser, Maxwell-McCaw, Leigh, & Gutman, 2000; Pollard, 1996). Along with the stress of feeling expendable, deaf people also often experience the additional distress of not being able to change jobs with the same ease as hearing people. For instance, a deaf clinician who lost his job due to agency-wide layoffs would most likely have to move out of the area (often out-of-state) to obtain a similar position working specifically with deaf consumers, while a hearing clinician most likely would search for the same position within his home area due to a higher volume of available positions.

Ignorance

Deaf individuals often become irritated with hearing people when they appear to lack sensitivity to the norms and experiences of deaf people. Janet (Smith, 2007) shared her experience of observing continual tension between the hearing staff working outside of the Deaf program and those staff members within the Deaf program: "The other hearing staff members were respectful and they tried to see me as a peer, but they complained about me and other deaf staff having equipment, like TTYs (text telephones) and pagers. I wanted them to understand how long it took to communicate with the insurance company via TTY, but they did not understand that ... During staff meetings, I would raise my hand repeatedly to try to interrupt, but would be ignored. But when I was signing, they would interrupt, using their voice, constantly ... their supervisor, my hearing equivalent, would send email to my staff and not carbon copy me. That is an example of how I was ignored, but eventually that improved" (p. 127). Sophia also shared information about the tension with hearing staff who did not sign, "Often the hearing staff did not want to write with me. They wanted other staff to interpret. I did not think that was fair. I wanted to hear directly from them" (Smith, 2007, p. 128).

Additional examples of hearing persons insensitivity to and ignorance about deaf people are: (a) Failing to ask deaf people about matters pertaining to deaf people and ignoring them at all other times, or only ever asking about matters pertaining to deaf people and not about any other topics; (b) insisting their signing is good when any native user of ASL can see their signing is poor; and (c) making statements, such as, "I like to help the deaf, " or "You write well for a deaf person!" Hearing people also make paternalistic assumptions about what they think deaf people can and can't do. They may assume a job assignment is too difficult for a deaf person. They may also excuse inappropriate behavior from a deaf client on the assumption that the client didn't really understand the situation. Indeed, many deaf people are smart enough to take advantage of the fact that they know hearing people don't expect much of them.

Hostility and Resentment toward Hearing People

Some deaf people resent hearing people because of years of mistreatment. More than a few harbor a secret hatred of hearing people. Many deaf individuals especially resent hearing individuals and organizations speaking for the Deaf Community. They find it offensive that some doctors, audiologists, and teachers make a living by defining and adopting a pathological approach in treating what they term "deafness". They feel that they have become subjects of study or treatment for the benefit of hearing people, not themselves. These feelings and experiences may predispose deaf people to acting in an unfriendly, even hostile manner with hearing people. Deaf people often asked, "Are you deaf or hearing?" when they encountered signers, but this question really asked, "Are you with us or with the other?" (Andrews, Leigh, & Weiner, 2004). Andrews et al. explained that these questions raised "the issue of belongingness and the issue of cultural values" (p. 226).

Resentment also stems from the perception that hearing people are taking over jobs that deaf people tend to apply for. Others may feel that hearing people are simply taking advantage of deaf people for their own personal gain. Klein and Kitson (2000) noted in their observations of deaf-hearing partnerships that deaf individuals have several common attitudes towards hearing staff, including the idea that "Hearing staff are pursuing their careers at the expense of deaf patients and staff" (p. 293).

A deaf staff member at a Deaf mental health treatment facility commented, "I have seen instances of deaf staff responding pejoratively or rudely to hearing staff when they felt the hearing staff was not being sensitive to their needs/culture." In other words, the hostility that a deaf person may express towards particular hearing people may not always be fair. Unconstructive criticism of hearing people who could otherwise become natural allies is counterproductive.

Tokenism

Many deaf people feel they are treated like a token. In the workplace, while most decisions are made by a team of hearing people, deaf people (usually one person) are occasionally invited to be involved in committees to gain a deaf person's point of view, though their input is often ignored or dismissed. Pete, a mental health clinician, discusses this dynamic in Smith (2007): "They seemed to delay incorporating my ideas, but now are agreeing with me … I always look at how they treat me. I am considered the highest level deaf person in this agency … but I do not think I am recognized as an equal by the other administrators" (p. 124). These deaf individuals who serve as tokens may achieve a position of power, but still feel they have no influence. Pete adds: "They say we are peers, and yes, we technically are, but they do not respect my role. I sometimes feel like a token" (p. 124).

Despite feelings of powerlessness, deaf tokens often value the power that they derive from their position and try to sometimes placate deaf peers who are less privileged. At times, they may feel pressured by hearing people to "keep other deaf people in line" in order to maintain the additional power they have. This contributes to their lack of trust and resentment towards hearing people. These dynamics parallel those of other minorities in the workforce.

Postures Influencing Cross-cultural Interaction

Many challenges are inherent in cross-cultural interactions between hearing and deaf individuals. Both deaf and hearing people have characteristic attitudes and behaviors or "relational postures" in how they interact with each other. We will first review some of the literature on hearing relational postures with deaf people. We will follow up with new material on common relational postures we believe deaf people assume towards hearing people. Then, we will describe what often happens when hearing and deaf people with different relational postures interact with each other.

Common Hearing Relational Postures towards Deaf People

In a book chapter entitled "Is There a Psychology of the Hearing?" Hoffmeister and Harvey (1996) discusses what they termed "relational postures" that hearing people assume with deaf people. They defined relational postures as "patterns of perception and behavior that hearing professionals have toward deaf persons." Five of the postures they described are summarized as follows:

The Freedom Fighter Posture

Hoffmeister and Harvey (1996) describe the Freedom Fighter Posture as an individual who is "focused on righting the wrongs of society that have been perpetrated on deaf people." They describe individuals who are likely to assume this posture, such as children of deaf adults (CODAs). The Freedom Fighter may have as a child observed helplessly situations where a deaf person, perhaps a parent or sibling, was treated unfairly. As an adult, this person feels a need to correct the wrongs that were observed in the past. The Freedom Fighter also may be outspoken and driven while at other times be the mediator or peacemaker. Freedom Fighters often experience a wide range of emotions, such as empathy, compassion, helplessness, and guilt.

Jay, a CODA, recently graduated from an Interpreter Training Program and joined a county mental health service as a staff interpreter. He quickly noticed that his two co-workers who are deaf social workers were largely ignored by hearing co-workers and county administrators. In addition, the deaf social workers did not have any working space in their cramped department. To his great surprise, Jay was assigned to an office with his own computer when hired. He immediately confronted the county administrators about his deaf co-workers not having working space and told them that he was willing to give up his office for them. Jay also decided to host an office potluck once a month for the purpose of including the deaf social workers in the conversations with hearing co-workers.

The Pathological Posture

Hoffmeister and Harvey (1996) describe the Pathological Posture as an individual who "believes that the deaf need the help of a hearing person in order to function well in the hearing world and avoid the horrors that may otherwise befall them" (p. 81). It is from this perspective that a hearing person may feel compelled to "help" deaf people lead better lives, perhaps by developing policies and theories about them, or constructing specific approaches that are deemed a good fit for the supposedly helpless deaf individual. The hearing person with this relational posture is often totally unaware of the cultural, linguistic, and personal practices of deaf people. For instance, many medical organizations and boards include information about "hearing-impaired people," yet they do not have deaf professionals as faculty or even have them on advisory or policy boards.

A culturally Deaf adult makes an appointment with Linda, an audiologist, for an updated audiogram, which is required for some paperwork she is filling out. Linda does not know any ASL and does not intend to learn the language. They communicated through paper and pen. With the audiogram result in her hands, Linda wholeheartedly recommends this deaf adult for a cochlear implant despite the fact that she has never expressed interest in the procedure.

Blame the Victim Posture

Hoffmeister and Harvey (1996) describe the Blame the Victim Posture as a person who, like the Freedom Fighter, is struggling to come to terms with oppression that they have witnessed towards deaf people. Unlike the Freedom Fighter, however, the Blame the Victim Posture is an individual who "rather than attempting to make the world more just … instead blame(s) the victim. The deaf must deserve their lowly status" (p. 82). People with this posture are inclined to make generalizations about deaf people being unintelligent, concrete, socially unskilled, having poor language abilities, etc. They ignore the social context of deaf people's lives and present the limitations that some deaf people develop as an inevitable result of their hearing loss, rather than an avoidable consequence of poor parenting and misguided educational policies. Many hearing people who present themselves as authorities on deaf people display this posture.

Deanna works as an addiction counselor and her agency was awarded with a grant to provide chemical dependency services to deaf consumers living in the city. She has survival ASL skills. Deanna was asked by her supervisor to set up an Alcohol Anonymous (AA) group for deaf individuals on Tuesday nights. After two AA meetings, deaf members became frustrated with the lack of progress due to Deanna's limited ASL skills and her ability to understand their signs which significantly slowed down the group process. A deaf member e-mailed to Deanna's supervisor asking for an interpreter for the AA meetings. When Deanna was informed about this new arrangement, she was upset. She stated that her ASL skills are just fine and she can understand the deaf members without much difficulty. After thinking about this situation for a few hours, Deanna met her supervisor again and blamed the deaf person who requested an interpreter for the communication difficulties. She also stated that this deaf person really doesn't have good insight into his alcoholism.

Klein and Kitson (2000) discussed similar dynamics in terms of attitudes or postures towards deaf staff in mental health settings. They noted that there is a common sentiment that "Deaf staff are lazy … always off sick … do not want to serve patients" (p. 293). In addition they noted that "Deaf staff just dump their 'emotional baggage' on to hearing people, especially staff" (p. 291).

Idealization and Betrayal Posture

Hoffmeister and Harvey (1996) describe the Idealization and Betrayal Posture as individuals who "at the beginning stages of their involvement with the Deaf Community, idealize deaf people … (which) sets the stage for hearing professionals to experience betrayal" (p. 85). The authors discuss ways that the media has given a false impression of deaf people. For instance, actor Marlee Matlin is portrayed as a deaf person who lip reads with astounding fluency and can understand people even when they are signing behind her. Hearing individuals with this posture, then, have preconceived ideas about deaf people. Their ideas are easily proven wrong leaving the individuals to feel betrayed by deaf people for not meeting their expectations.

Henry decided to become a Rehabilitation Counselor working with deaf people and applied for a specific graduate program in the West Coast as he wanted to study under a well-known deaf professor who was a Rehabilitation Counselor for 30 years. This professor also authored a popular college textbook on this particular field. Henry bought this book months early and immediately started reading before he had his first class with this professor. Henry thoroughly enjoyed the case studies and discussions listed in the book. He sees this deaf professor as a giant in the field. Henry thought that this deaf professor would be a lively lecturer with excellent speech skills. He saw several television shows where deaf people were portrayed as excellent lip-readers. With that mindset and upon meeting the deaf professor for the first time in a classroom, he was stunned that the deaf professor wasn't particularly interested in interacting with hearing students and didn't speak at all. The deaf professor's lectures were often dull and difficult to follow. Throughout the semester, the deaf professor also was critical of Henry's progress in mastering ASL. Henry's preconceived idealization posture sets the stage for him to experience betrayal. Henry started to realize this deaf professor did not live up to his expectations. He started to have feelings of being let down and betrayed. Because of these feelings, he became more frustrated and alienated. His passion to master ASL dispersed.

Confusion of Boundaries Posture

Hoffmeister and Harvey (1996) describe the Confusion of Boundaries Posture as professionals who sometimes "overidentify and seek to become totally integrated in the Deaf Community" (p. 89). The authors go on to discuss ways that overidentifying may eventually lead to burnout and vicarious trauma. An example given is that of an interpreter who feels that she is too important to her students to take a day off in order to attend a wedding. At the other end of the boundary spectrum, the authors note, professionals may become too rigid in their boundaries. An example given involved a teacher of the deaf who rigidly stuck to signing English as opposed to being open to learning other ways of communicating, such as ASL.

Paula has a deaf sister whom she is close to. Paula has excellent ASL skills and immersed herself in the Deaf Community at young age. She met a deaf man and decided to marry him. From that point, Paula started frequenting Deaf clubs as well as being part of her local Deaf club bylaws committee and hosting deaf-related social gatherings. Enamored with Deaf Culture, she became more active with the National Association of the Deaf. She participated in their meetings on policy changes and became one of the most voracious voices for states to issue special license to teach deaf and hard-of-hearing children. Paula was also very engaged in and outspoken about Gallaudet's presidential selection process. Many deaf individuals became annoyed by Paula's behavior and questioned why she, as a hearing individual, was overly involved in the business of Deaf Community.

Common Deaf Relational Postures

Most of the literature on how deaf people perceive hearing people has been presented in the context of cultural identity development in deaf people (Glickman, 1996; Leigh, 2009). Glickman's model of deaf identity development presents four basic identity stages, which he terms "culturally hearing," "culturally marginal," "immersion," and "bicultural." Identity development theory assumes cultural identity changes in fairly predictable ways. Nash and Nash (1981) were possibly the first to discuss attitudes that deaf individuals assume in relating to hearing people. Their 1981 book includes a chapter entitled "How the Deaf See the Hearing," in which they discuss three types: Type I, The Almost Deaf; Type II, The Mostly Hearing; and Type III, The Completely Hearing. Their conception of "types" assumes more attitudinal and behavioral stability than identity development models do.

Deaf peoples' experiences with hearing individuals vary widely. Some are born into hearing families while others do not encounter hearing ways of being until they enter school. These experiences influence the development of specific responses or behavioral patterns towards hearing individuals. Cultural identity certainly plays a part. At the same time, we believe that the identity development framework does not account for all of the ways in which deaf people approach hearing people. We think that some of the relational postures that deaf people assume with hearing people are more entrenched in social context and psycho-social dynamic than is indicated by current identity development theory.

Hoffmeister and Harvey's (1996) discussion of hearing relational postures describes a majority group's observations and experiences with deaf individuals. In most cases, those observations are not based on deeply rooted childhood experiences with deaf individuals. In the case of deaf individuals, by contrast, there is an incorporation of lifelong experience with hearing individuals. This dynamic creates a reasonably stable pattern of thoughts, attitudes and behaviors, at least with regard to interactions with hearing people. Presented below are some of what we believe to be the more common "relational postures" of deaf individuals. We acknowledge that not everyone will identify with the postures below. In addition, some people may identify with more than one. The postures below are intended to be an introduction to exploring ways that deaf people approach and interact with hearing people.

The Submissive Posture

Some deaf individuals have internalized audist attitudes. They have adopted the belief that hearing people are superior. Gertz (2008) has termed this concept "dyconscious audism." She used this term to describe people who feel inferior, experience a state of helplessness and powerlessness, and either feel or behave like victims. Klein and Kitson (2000) documented similar behaviors, stating that "Often they have an unconscious assumption that Deaf people, including themselves, cannot achieve" (p. 289). Discussing deaf inpatients, they noted, "Initially patients did not approach the Deaf staff and questioned their ability, as they felt safe with the hearing staff, whom they saw as 'clever, skilled and confident'" (p. 289).

Submissive postures include deaf individuals who do not trust other deaf individuals, instead depending on hearing people to do things for them and resenting them when they are not helpful. The submissive generally looks to hearing people to validate and affirm their work and behavior. They tend to be very protective of hearing people. They are quick to rush to their defense.

Janet has worked at a unit for deaf clients with chemical dependency issues for the past 12 years. For several years, Janet was the only deaf staff member working in the unit. In the recent years, a few deaf people have joined the staff. These deaf people have noticed how the communication problems with hearing poor signers have contributed to the behavioral problems in the patients, and they have pointed this out. Before these new deaf staff were hired, communication difficulties were buried under the rug either by ignoring the situation or by making comments like, "She has a good heart!" or "He's trying his best!" One of the newly hired deaf staff person requested a meeting with the other deaf staff to raise these concerns. During the meeting, Janet became enraged by the discussion, stating that it was "totally inappropriate to blame hearing people," and that the deaf staff were "trying to push out hearing people." Janet rushed over to her hearing supervisor and reported this "unauthorized" meeting.

The Militant Posture

Some deaf individuals strongly dislike and distrust all things that are conceptualized as "hearing." The Militant is quick to stereotype hearing and deaf people, to think in black and white, "us versus them" terms, and to be highly confrontational. Their attacks on hearing people are often irrational and unfair. They are more concerned with expressing their feelings than with being effective change agents and their handling of cross-cultural conflicts is often unskillful. Both deaf and hearing people tend to consider them to be trouble makers and disregard their input, which infuriates them further. However, Militants can sometimes intimidate other people. This person may be stuck in what Glickman (1996) describes as the immersion identity stage.

Ellen, a behavioral aide at a treatment center, is perceived by her peers as "an angry deaf militant person." She is argumentative during meetings, challenging any policies that she feels are unfair to her and other deaf individuals. Many hearing colleagues steer clear of her. Whenever new people are hired, Ellen is the first to approach them. With a confrontational manner, she questions their background and affiliation with the Deaf Community. She judges whether they are sufficiently skilled, have the right attitudes, even whether they are "Deaf enough." When people don't meet her rigid expectations, she writes them off, complains about them, and undermines their work.

The Activist Posture

Some deaf individuals strive to understand and skillfully combat the oppression that deaf people face. They make this a focus, if not a purpose, in their lives. These people are constantly alert for signs of oppression and may be quick to challenge statements and policies made by hearing people. Activists expend a tremendous amount of energy fighting perceived injustice, and sometimes this leads other deaf and hearing people to feel uncomfortable working with them. Even when Activists work very skillfully and professionally (such as following the chain of command to file a complaint), they are often seen as "rocking the boat" or even as "trouble makers." Activists are often misread as unreasonable or even militant. Activists try to work the system, in collaboration with hearing allies. They struggle to combat oppression while remaining attentive to relational dynamics. Above all, they want to be effective in creating change.

Cody is a deaf student in a community counseling program. Fluent in ASL, Cody is passionate about language development and visual strategies for working with deaf clients. To his disappointment, his class on advanced therapy techniques is taught by a hearing professor who has rudimentary sign skills (despite having worked in the program with deaf students for more than 15 years). After two classes with the professor, Cody decides to request an interpreter for the remainder of the semester and files a complaint with the Department Chair regarding this professor's signing skills.

The Native Posture

Some deaf individuals prefer to live as much of their lives as they can among other deaf individuals. The Natives do not have strong positive or negative feelings about hearing people. They simply are not interested in interacting with them most of the time. They consider them "outsiders" and prefer to interact with "their own people." Comfortable and content with being a deaf person, the Native has no interest in becoming hearing or behaving as hearing people do. They deal with hearing people in a business-like manner as they must, but the pleasures they find in life are among other deaf people. In Smith (2007), Amber comments on the support she receives from deaf co-workers, "It is a benefit because we work with hearing colleagues in our workplace and we have each other to support when we feel oppressed or neglected in a way. We are able to understand how each other feel because of our experiences in the outside society where the majority of people are hearing" (p. 126). Additionally, Autumn states, "Often the hearing therapist misses so much in the deaf client's communication because he or she looks away or does not get the whole picture due to lack of cultural and linguistic awareness ..." (p. 128). When they observe deaf individuals receiving inadequate care from hearing therapists, Natives tend to feel very protective. The Native also believes that deaf people are experts on deaf experiences and is skeptical of any research or publications written by hearing people on the topic of "deafness" or "the deaf." An example of a deaf person with Native relational posture is illustrated below.

Jill is a school counselor working at a school for the deaf. She has worked there for over 10 years and is involved on many committees. One of her parents is deaf. Her partner and their children are also deaf. Jill is actively involved in Deaf organizations and frequently attends National Deaf Association conferences. Jill is also on the board of Deaf Women United. All of Jill's friends are deaf. Jill sometimes interacts briefly with hearing individuals, such as teachers and other counselors and works well with hearing colleagues. However, she prefers to spend her time with deaf peers. Jill will interact with hearing people who have excellent ASL skills, but has no interest in them if they do not sign.

The Objectifier Posture

With the rise of deaf executives, we are beginning to notice phenomena where deaf leaders use their Deaf identity for both personal and organizational benefit and behave in ways that show a subtle affiliation with hearing people such as using speech even when there are deaf people around, and being very focused on what hearing people can do for them. We call this posture the "Objectifier."

The Objectifiers are exquisitely attuned to the power dynamics at play at the institutions in which they work, in particular the ways that being both deaf and hearing can be strategic assets. As managers, for instance, they often hire a hearing subordinate as their "right hand" because they perceive that this hearing subordinate can bolster their own standing or do things for them that they think other deaf people cannot do. Objectifiers, while they claim to have an insider's knowledge about deaf people, often hold some of the same biases as the hearing majority (that English language skills are more important than ASL skills, that hearing people are more capable than deaf people). These biases can mean that they discriminate against deaf employees even while they boast about their Deaf organization's cultural competence.

Objectifiers tend to see both deaf and hearing people more as objects than subjects, treating people as representative of a group and not as individuals. This posture often pays off as the person becomes very successful and both hearing and deaf people may look up to them. Some deaf and hearing colleagues and subordinates may perceive these Objectifiers as hypocritical. They often observe that Objectifiers do not really give deaf people the same opportunities they provide hearing people.

Mary is a deaf CEO of an organization that provides advocacy services to deaf individuals who are victims of domestic violence. Mary is a charismatic and innovative leader. She appointed a hearing woman as a vice-president because this person has a large network of contacts within the Women's Advocacy community. While Mary has also hired a large number of deaf employees to work in her organization, she prefers to use hearing employees in specific situations such as grant writing or lobbying the state legislators despite having several talented deaf employees who have the skills these jobs require. Mary has assisted other states in setting up domestic violence programs for deaf individuals and people on the committee have noted that Mary tends to pick hearing people for high profile, high stakes assignments even when there are qualified deaf persons available.

Application of Relational Postures: Case Studies

Deaf and hearing people who have certain relational postures, when interacting with each other, exhibit patterns of interaction that are reasonably predictable. The stance each takes often elicits a counter-stance from the other party, again in predictable ways. The patterns here parallel those with other majority/minority group dynamics; for instance, White people with unexamined racism interacting with activist African Americans. If one knows the patterns, the interactions that follow are easy to anticipate. Developing self-awareness about these common dynamics will improve cross-cultural collaboration.

In this section, we examine some of these predictable cross-cultural conflicts and offer ideas for solutions. We will illustrate this with several case studies. We begin by exploring two individuals: a hearing administrator with an Idealization and Betrayal Posture and a deaf employee with a Native Posture.

Marquise is a hearing woman from an upper-middle-class, well-educated family. After graduating from Smith College, where she had a deaf classmate and learned sign language. Marquise went on to become a professor of Psychology and later the chairperson of her department at a university.

Natalie is a third generation deaf individual. After graduating from a school for the deaf, she went on to graduate from Gallaudet University with a doctorate in Clinical Psychology. She then moved to a different state, where she took a position as a professor/researcher in the department of Psychology. Marquise became her supervisor.

Initially, Marquise was excited about hiring Natalie. She remembered the deaf classmate from Smith College. This deaf classmate used her voice when signing and sometimes didn't sign at all, and Marquise formed the impression that this was the best way for deaf people to communicate. Her education at Smith, located next door to staunchly oral Clarke school for the deaf, reinforced this impression. After several meetings with Natalie, Marquise began to feel disillusioned about her. Natalie never used her voice even in one-on-one meetings with Marquise and would request an interpreter. Natalie frequently inserted feedback regarding cultural norms during discussions about deaf clients, and some of the more seasoned psychologists reported that they felt she was questioning their expertise (which, in fact, she sometimes did). Marquise began to feel she made a mistake in hiring Natalie and began to focus more on evaluative actions that would result in transferring or terminating her.

Although Natalie eventually wanted to return to work at her alma mater, she was excited about the opportunity to work with Marquise and her department. She had been told that the department was doing innovative research and felt welcome when she met Marquise. At first, Marquise invited her to several meetings and introduced her around. Gradually, however, Natalie began to feel that Marquise was growing distant and critical of her work. Natalie started to feel that Marquise was picking on her and approached the Human Resources Office to ask them to intervene. Subsequent meetings revealed that Natalie's supervisor and co-workers perceived her as an abrasive and insubordinate. Natalie was eventually asked to leave the department.

Marquise (hearing department chair) and Natalie (deaf professor), are two individuals who perceive one another based on conflicting cultural values and experiences resulting in tension and misunderstanding. Marquise had a very specific idea that deaf people communicate using spoken English and rarely utilize interpreting services. In the past, Marquise experienced a relationship with a deaf person who had a similar background to her own, whereas Natalie's background involved growing up in a native Deaf household, where the cultural norms are significantly different. Natalie was very accustomed to being in an environment where her straightforward approach was welcome. She became frustrated when encountering some of the more indirect communication patterns that hearing people use, especially in politically charged situations. Natalie was unprepared for the politics of a university department and needed Marquise to mentor her, not turn against her. Natalie knew she had insight into the needs of deaf clients and was shocked and astounded that her expertise was not recognized. She could not understand why Marquise, whom she thought was an advocate for deaf people, would object so strongly to her use of her native language and insistence that communication between them be clear. Marquise, whose knowledge of deaf people was very limited and skewed, misread Natalie completely and mistreated her as a result.

Marquis and Natalie would benefit from the opportunity to explore how their experiences and values have put them into conflict with one another. If Marquise were to meet with a supervisor or consultant who is familiar with deaf/hearing cross-cultural dynamics, she may be able to identify some of the idealization and possibly some stereotypes that interfere with her ability to see Natalie's skills and strengths. This type of introspection promotes the self-awareness that she may have unintentionally been sabotaging Natalie's efforts to establish herself in the department, For her part, Natalie needs to feel safe to raise concerns she may have about cross-cultural biases. She needs to know about the university policies that protect her, including any options for drawing upon outside mediators such as the University Ombudsman, but more helpfully, she needs to know from Marquise that she can raise with her such sensitive issues.

Another example of cross-cultural conflict explores challenges experienced by two individuals: a hearing woman with Blame the Victim Posture and a deaf man with Activist Posture.

Shirley is a hearing child of deaf parents. Her parents do not sign fluently and neither graduated from high school. Shirley is an only child. Her mother stayed at home with her and her father worked for a printing company. Shirley became interested in the medical profession after attending several doctor appointments with her parents and acting as a go-between during those appointments even though her ASL skills were rudimentary. Shirley now works as a psychiatric nurse at an in-patient treatment facility where 90% of the patients are deaf. Her ASL skills remain rudimentary. Bob, a deaf child of deaf parents, had a similar upbringing. Although his father graduated from high school, his mother dropped out during her middle school years to help out on the family farm. Bob's family quickly figured out that he had an aptitude for language and would ask him to help out with important paperwork at a young age. Bob became passionate about accessibility for deaf individuals as a result of what he saw with his own parents and their friends. Bob and Shirley work together on the same psychiatric inpatient unit serving deaf individuals.

Bob and Shirley, both strong personalities, "hit it off" when they first met on the job. Gradually, however, Bob began to observe how Shirley became impatient with some of the deaf patients, and this impatience triggered outbursts from them which sometimes lead staff to physically restrain the patients. Bob and the other deaf staff became increasingly vocal about how Shirley's poor signing was fostering bad care.

After one of the staff meetings, Bob approached Shirley and asked if they could discuss a few things, Bob then described some of the patterns that he was noticing. Because they initially had a strong rapport, he was expecting that his feedback would be well received. Shirley, however, became defensive and hostile, stating that his feedback was inappropriate and "medically unnecessary." She insisted that the patient behaviors were not her fault. In a moment of anger, Shirley added, "Deaf people can't just get away with everything. We have to help them, show them that their behavior is not acceptable." Bob, noticing that he was becoming angered by her comments, put an end to the meeting. He then requested the assistance of the program administrator (a hearing man) for the purpose of mediating the conflict. During the meeting, Bob attempted to explain how her comments were offensive to him as a deaf person. Shirley, however, broke down crying and stated, "I can't believe you're doing this to me. I work so hard to help out, and I do good work. All you ever do is criticize me." The program administrator ended the meeting, noting that Bob needed to be more sensitive and to leave the task of giving feedback to the administrators.

Several issues are contributing to this cross-cultural conflict. Shirley and Bob have had similar experiences of taking care of their deaf parents. This shared experience has the potential to create a strong connection between them but on closer look, these experienced affected them very differently. Shirley appears to have been left with some deep-seated anger towards deaf people while Bob feels much more protective of them and is likely to champion their cause. Shirley's unconscious hostility towards deaf people and Bob's protective attitude were bound to clash, all the more because each saw themselves as well-informed experts about deaf people.

Both Bob and Shirley need a supervisor or consultant who can help them identify the life experiences responsible for their current attitudes and interpersonal conflict. One would hope a program administrator could assume this role. The administrator would also have to be concerned and prepared to intervene immediately if staff behaviors were triggering patient behavior problems leading to restraints.

When a supervisor demonstrates a willingness to ensure that the environment is one that promotes equality and security, employees are less likely to feel the need to take it upon themselves to "fix" things. Individual supervision is not usually enough to solve these conflicts. Effective program leadership needs to model cross-cultural conflict resolution. This includes respectful and empathic listening, exploring one's own role in creation of a conflict, and a search for the Win, Win, Win solution (Glickman, 2009; Weeks, 1992). Equally important is an awareness of how some of the power imbalances may result in giving the hearing person more power during conflict resolution meetings, especially if the facilitator is also hearing. Becoming aware of such a dynamic will allow the facilitator to better structure the discussion, possibly even going as far as to invite a deaf person to co-facilitate.

Bob and Shirley's employer could consider forming a Cultural Awareness and Sensitivity committee whose goal would be to identify specific problem areas and give balanced perspectives of effective solutions. Committees like this, with representation from all groups, and when well lead, can be effective promoters of cross-cultural collaboration. On the other hand, committees that are not taken seriously, that are perceived by the minority workers as "window dressing" covering up oppressive practices, may well make minority employees feel even more powerless. An alternative to committees would be an open dialogue group where the intention is also to explore cross-cultural dynamics in a way that allows participants to examine internal biases and perceptions with the goal of becoming more self-aware as well as building a stronger alliance.

The communication issue has to be addressed in a forthright manner. Hearing people like Shirley who work regularly with deaf people are at a great disadvantage if they do not learn ASL with relative fluency. Their inability to sign poses barriers that go beyond language differences. In addition to difficulty with language, the person who does not sign will also miss important non-verbal and cultural cues that supplement communication. Deaf people who work alongside hearing people who make no effort to sign or improve their ASL skills cannot help but feel resentful. Cooperation between hearing and deaf employees requires adequate communication in sign language. Without language skills, there is only so far that a hearing counselor, supervisor, or colleague of deaf people can go in understanding and helping deaf people. Even when hearing people never master the language, they learn volumes about deaf people, and themselves, through the struggle to learn it.

In a final example, some employment challenges are explored in a cross-cultural interaction between a hearing employee who is operating from a Pathological Posture and the deaf supervisor who is operating from a Militant Posture. This is probably the most toxic mix of orientations possible.

George, a hearing man, comes from a large Catholic family. As the eldest child, he has always felt a sense of responsibility and assumed a caretaking role with his younger siblings. While attending college, George dated a woman who had a culturally Deaf mother. As a result, George became fascinated by deaf people and decided that he would like to work with them. George eventually finished college with a degree in psychology and applied for his first job as a mental health technician at a mental health facility that provided residential services to deaf adolescents and young adults.

Matthew, a deaf man, comes from a hearing family. His three siblings are also deaf. Matthew's parents worked full time and did not spend much time with their children. Matthew and his brothers attended the state school for the deaf. Matthew has a long history of not getting along with hearing peers.

Excited to begin working with deaf people, George immediately started developing activities for the adolescents he was working with. Thinking that deaf people do better with less complex activities, George put together several activities that are traditionally used with younger children. George was determined to connect with the teens in his unit and felt that he would be able to help them. George began to see himself as something of a father-figure and was confident that the boys would be happy to have his help.

Although Matthew did not get along with hearing people as a rule, he was especially hostile towards George. Matthew immediately picked up on George's paternalistic attitude and concluded that George did not respect deaf people. He frequently called George in for meetings where he would criticize his work and scold him for "spoon feeding" the adolescents on his unit. George felt that Matthew was ungrateful and unfair. At one point, George described Matthew to another staff member, saying that "Matthew seems almost militant in his determination to shoot down any of my ideas … it's like he just hates hearing people."

As George became more and more uncomfortable with Matthew, he grew cool towards him. He distanced himself by increasing his use of English terminology which he suspected Matthew would not know. This only served to antagonize Matthew further. George also took advantage of his hearing privilege by meeting frequently with Matthew's supervisor and engaging him in a discussion about how angry and hostile Matthew was. He elicited from the supervisor a shared narrative about Matthew as "the angry deaf person."

George would talk to Matthew's supervisor with minimal signs when Matthew was around, which prevented Matthew from being included in the conversation. This communication choice pushed Matthew's emotional buttons, resulting in the loss of his temper, which served to reinforce the narrative of Matthew as an angry, out of control person.

In the case of Matthew (deaf supervisor) and George (hearing mental health technician), there are several cross-cultural issues present that may be preventing both individuals from forming an effective working relationship.

Matthew has deep-seated conflicts that are preventing him from being an effective supervisor. His behaviors are creating a hostile work environment, and this needs to be addressed. Matthew might benefit from therapy, and would probably be more open to seeing a deaf therapist. He would likely believe that only a deaf therapist could understand him, and possibly be too angry to work well with a hearing therapist. At the same time, it is critical that Matthew's supervisor immediately address the hostile ways he is approaching hearing staff. Whatever the psychological reasons, Matthew is discriminating, and this is unacceptable in any workplace.

Matthew might also benefit from some mentoring about how to be an effective supervisor and elicit the best work performance from his supervisees. Matthew has some legitimate reasons to be concerned that George's paternalistic attitudes towards deaf people would prevent the students under his care from reaching their potential. However, Matthew isn't addressing these work performance issues well.

George, on the other hand, would benefit from a few supervision sessions focused on identifying how his tendency to "help" is two sided. In George's case, as with many paternalistic helpers, their fantasies about protecting, taking care of or rescuing people perceived as more limited may actually be ways to bolster his own self-esteem. Sometimes such paternalistic attitudes occur in a religious context, where helping becomes a way for one to feel morally superior or right with God. This may be the case for George. Whatever the motivation, George's behavior may actually be disempowering the people he serves. He may unintentionally be sending a message to his deaf colleagues that he perceives deaf people as less intelligent and capable. This is certainly the message that Matthew received. A competent, culturally informed supervisor in a Deaf program needs to be on the lookout for, and interrupt, this fairly common dynamic.

George also went over Matthew's head to his supervisor, and elicited from him a narrative about Matthew's hatred of hearing people. By joining in the construction of this narrative, Matthew's supervisor allowed George to undermine Matthew's authority. He should have resisted such efforts at collusion and spoken with Matthew privately.

Examples of Effective Cross-cultural Relationships

Andrews, Leigh, and Weiner (2004) reported that positive deaf and hearing partnerships exist in research groups and schools for the deaf. Jones and Pullen (1992) and Benedict and Sass-Lehrer (2007) offered their personal successes with conflict resolution in working together as deaf and hearing colleagues. Seeing themselves as each embedded in a culture, they were able to make cultural exchange part of their ongoing dialogue, and this greatly facilitated conflict resolution. Jones and Pullen (1992) emphasized that both deaf and hearing partners must accept each other as individuals, discuss things, and laugh at things together. Benedict and Sass-Lehrer (2007) explained that as collaborators in research, writing, and teaching, they have striven to accomplish a partnership of shared decision making and responsibility. Learning to work together has helped them trade off leadership roles. Examples of their partnership include an instance when the deaf person (Benedict) was involved on the local, state, national and international level in the field of early intervention and the hearing person (Sass-Lehrer) had contacts that facilitated the deaf person in receiving speaking engagements, writing projects, and opportunities to participate in many outside groups such as boards and committees. Andrews et al. (2004) also provided several good examples of deaf and hearing partnerships and emphasized that it is up to deaf and hearing professionals "to set examples and train future generations to recognize this as status quo" (p. 232).

The first author (Gournaris) has observed in many employment settings the practice of using interpreters in mixed deaf/hearing meetings even when all of the members could sign competently. Some hearing members prefer this practice as they are not confident in their signing abilities and struggle to understand all that is signed to them. Gournaris found that as long as hearing people had the option of not signing, they continued to follow disrespectful practices such as speaking to each other without signing or signing and speaking, a practice that still can exclude ASL using adults. When hearing people had the option of not signing, an unfair dynamic occurred. Hearing people who sign could always oversee conversations between deaf people, but deaf people could not overhear the conversations between hearing people. Thus, the practice of allowing hearing people who can sign to opt out and use interpreters still fostered an unequal power imbalance between deaf and hearing people.

Both authors of this chapter feel that in agencies and organizations where there is a mix of deaf and hearing staff, it is reasonable to expect that staff communicate using American Sign Language at all times (even when no deaf staff are present). Doing so promotes fluency and reduces tokenism behavior. More importantly, it lessens the differentiation between the two groups, leading to more cohesiveness. Ultimately, language does not become "deaf language" and "hearing language" and is instead about common language. The authors are aware that many people feel that this is not a "realistic" expectation. However, when a group that has power and privilege deems something "realistic," they may just be doing what is easy for them. "Realistic" expectations should be open to alternative perspectives. Deaf and hearing partnerships can accomplish a great deal when all people bring the right set of skills and attitudes and where dialogue about cultural differences is "grist for the mill."

Another instance of cross-cultural interaction occurred at a school for the deaf, where the second author (Aubrecht) had a hearing clinical supervisor who was also a hearing parent of a deaf child. During one discussion, Aubrecht and the supervisor got in a tense discussion about the term "disability" being applied to deaf people. Aubrecht insisted that she did not consider herself disabled and the supervisor persisted in insisting "but you *are* disabled." The discussion went back and forth a bit until Aubrecht asked, "Why is it so important to you that I be labeled disabled?" At this point, her supervisor realized that labeling deaf people as "disabled" had psychological value to her. Challenging the "common sense" idea that deaf people are disabled disoriented the supervisor, and put her sense of herself, her known reasons for working with deaf people, in question. Fortunately, this supervisor was able to explore this non-defensively. The whole discussion was very productive for both individuals and created a closer working relationship between them.

Predictable Cross-cultural Conflicts: A Dialogue

In the following imaginary dialogue, we present what we believe is a very representative cross-cultural conflict, present in many settings that serve deaf persons. We've placed into this dialogue five persons representing five of the stances we've described above. The Objectifier (O), Submissive (S), and Militant (M) are deaf persons. The Confusion of Boundaries (CB) and Pathological (P) postures are taken by hearing persons. The subject is "how shall we communicate in meetings or in the presence of deaf employees?" The topics discussed here may seem to hearing people unfamiliar with deaf people like trivial matters but communication and language policy and practice are the most emotionally loaded and meaningful matters for deaf people, as well as hearing people who are immersed in the Deaf Community. Conflicts like this actually get to the heart of the matter of how deaf and hearing people relate with each other.

The topics being discussed are whether hearing and deaf people must always sign in the presence of deaf people, or even when deaf people are not around; and how they should sign. Is the use of simultaneous communication (i.e., speaking and signing at the same time) an acceptable compromise? Even more important is the issue of how such policies and practices are determined. This gets to the issue of power. How we communicate will have immediate and powerful ramifications for how power is shared between deaf and hearing people in the organization.

M: I think we should write in the communication policy that all individuals must use ASL AT ALL TIMES while at this agency.

O: My observation has been that hearing employees, who are given the choice of communicating without the additional stress of worrying too much about their second language, work more efficiently.

M: Excuse me! What about deaf people's comfort? So what if hearing people have to experience a little bit of discomfort—we have to live with that all day, every day!

P: I think we need to acknowledge that the main language of the United States is English. The reality is this is a hearing world and we have a lot of people who speak working here as well as coming through here and we need to respect that. We also have hard-of-hearing employees, who do not use ASL or do not have strong ASL skills.

CB: I think we're forgetting that this is an agency serving deaf people who communicate in ASL. I think it is completely realistic to expect that within this agency, we use ASL in order to be inclusive of everyone. I'm perfectly comfortable with this. I even use ASL when no deaf people are around. If everyone signs, everyone has access. It's that simple. We can't come in and throw around our "hearing world" weight. Because this agency serves a large group of deaf persons, and has a Deaf focus, we must use the language of the Deaf Community.

S: I am concerned about how hearing employees will feel about forcing the communication issue on them. I do agree we should sign, but I do not want this to cause more problems within the agency. Hearing people have a right to their own language also and we shouldn't be forcing our language on them.

O: Okay it looks like we have two points of agreement: that we should sign in the presence of deaf people and that we need to be inclusive. So I guess the question is what do we mean when we say inclusive?

CB: Hold, on, I don't think we agree. I never said we should sign only in the presence of deaf people. I think we should use ASL at all times while in this agency and I would add that we should use ONLY ASL, and not speak and sign at the same time.

M: I second that!

S: But don't you think we should let hearing people use the language they are most comfortable with?

P: Yes, exactly. We can't force people to use one communication mode over another. Again you have to remember …

M: (interrupts) Well, hearing people have been forcing their language and communication mode on deaf people for hundreds of years. Welcome to our world!

P: The bottom line is that we need to respect individual rights to choose. There are people of all kinds of disability here and each person has a different thing that works best for them. We shouldn't be forcing ASL on anyone.

CB: You don't really get it. Hearing people can choose to sign or speak, to use English or to learn ASL. Many deaf people don't have these options. They can't choose English as easily as a hearing person can choose ASL. They can't choose to speak clearly if they don't have that ability. When you set up this false equation between the language choices of deaf and hearing people, you oppress deaf people. A deaf affirmative agency is one that respects and uses the language of the Deaf Community. This office should respect deaf people, just as if we were all deaf.

P: I don't think it's realistic to ask me not to be hearing. English is my native language, and I have a right to it also. The simple fact is, it's easier to speak than sign.

O: My sense is that some deaf people feel excluded at times if hearing employees do not sign in presence of deaf employees. If we have a Deaf service agency where hearing people who can sign don't do so in front of deaf people, the agency will look bad to the Deaf Community and the stakeholders. We won't have credibility. We'll lose consumers and then eventually the contracts and grants.

S: Well, I admit I do feel left out when I see signing hearing people not signing, but then I understand how they feel. It's hard for them to have to accommodate to me all the time.

CB: This is why a communication policy should be established agency-wide. It is about respecting deaf employees and the consumers we serve.

O: I see your point. (turns to P) I understand that English is your native language. Please understand that many in this agency use ASL to communicate …

M: (interrupts and speaks to P directly) You do not respect deaf people!

O: (turns to M) Wait! I am not done talking. (turns back to P) Can we agree that ASL is one of the languages used here and this is an agency that serves deaf people?

CB: (interrupts O): I don't think you're being fair to M. You just cut him off.

O: We'll come back to M, let me finish up. I'm trying to keep us on track here. Let me talk with some employees to get their input. This has to work for the hearing employees too. We don't want to alienate them. They don't all sign. This has to work for the whole company.

P: Yes, we should set up a survey to check the agency climate and I think it is a fantastic idea to give agency members the opportunity to give input.

M: That's not going to work. You know there are more hearing staff here at the agency than deaf staff. That will skew the results. (CB nodding in agreement)

O: You are turning this into deaf vs. hearing. That's not the objective of our committee. I'd like to hear feedback from some of the hearing employees before setting up a policy, because this agency employs two-third hearing individuals. I am sure the vice-president, who is hearing, will appreciate that we ask hearing employees first for feedback. Hearing employees holding important positions may decide to leave the agency because of the communication policy.

P: I think I can speak on behalf of many hearing people here in the agency that this communication policy is a bad idea. (Turns to CB) You are being meddlesome in the agency affairs, telling us how to communicate with each other. I do not like it at all. I'm not willing to be oppressed by deaf people.

O: We need to focus on what's best for the agency. We have a reputation to defend....

CB (to the Objectifier and yelling) I think you are just a little bit too concerned with how certain hearing people feel, how the agency looks, and how you appear to the Deaf Community. See, in my experience ...

O: (interrupts) Ok, clearly we are not getting anywhere. We're just going in circles around the same issues. Why don't we take a break, talk to some of the other people here and get a sense of what they are thinking, and then we can reconvene?

In between the meetings, all of the individuals check in with co-workers. The Objectifier also talks with administration to share that the committee meeting did not go well and asks if it is absolutely necessary to set up a communication policy for the good of the agency. Administration indicates that there has been a complaint through Human Resources that deaf employees feel they are excluded from key agency meetings and that it is necessary to set up a communication policy. Administration also shares that the committee is simply to make recommendations and that management (along with a HR representative) will make final decisions regarding the policy.

During the in-between time, P confronts CB privately in her office. P states that she feels that CB is trying to be deaf. CB does not respond. P also makes a comment about how she has seen "people like CB" in the agency over the years and the person never lasts long. "You will burn out," she says, "because you are not being true to who you are. You are over involved with deaf people and in the end you will not find a place in the Deaf Community and will tire of all of this nonsense." In the meantime,

M also approaches O privately and "vents." He shares that he feels that hearing people are taking over and that he feels that P is very oppressive. O listens and then comments that "Many people feel the way you do." M also mentions to O that several agency employees question O's loyalty to deaf employees. They state quietly that O only looks after himself as being in power. O responds that he looks out for what is the best for the agency regardless the employee's hearing status.

Noting that there appeared to be more tension present, administration decided to bring in a consultation team that specializes in facilitating cross-cultural dialogues. The team (one deaf and one hearing facilitator) engaged the committee members in a lengthy open dialogue process, during which time individual employees had the opportunity to talk about their own values and biases, as well as listen to each other. This process, although somewhat raw for many people, allowed employees to process some of the frustrations and fears that they were experiencing. Committee members who participated in this process noted that it was very helpful and made the observation that it would be beneficial for all agency employees to have the opportunity to participate in such a cross-cultural, problem solving dialogue.

For the second meeting, all five members were present. In addition, someone from administration joined the meeting to facilitate the process and provide structure. This person set up ground rules for the meeting. Those rules were: no personal comments targeting each other, stay on topic, understand ideas fully before judging them, and focus on agency-wide efficiency as opposed to personal preferences. He used a white board to outline three communication areas: (a) communication on day-to-day basis in informal areas, (b) communication during meetings, and (c) Information dissemination. He explained that he wants all committee members to share information about one area at a time and brainstorm freely.

After brainstorming, the group discussed pros and cons of each suggestion made. The group then outlined a communication policy based on the areas with the most pros and least cons and sent it in to the administration.

This dialogue is a fairly common example of cross-cross cultural conflict at agencies where there are deaf and hearing staff. The tension that was present during the first meeting carried over into agency-wide functions. Instead of attempting to brush things under the rug or to just tell staff to move on, the administration in this case decided to tackle the issue head on by giving employees a safe space to process their cultural and personal experiences. This process, although not speedy, laid the foundation for a more genuine deaf-hearing partnership. Employees felt "heard" and supported. They were more willing to cross invisible cultural boundaries in order to work together more efficiently. Employees participated more fully in the second committee meeting, actively brainstorming, and left the meeting feeling a sense of accomplishment.

The authors understand that cross-cultural conflicts are inevitable when people from different cultures interact. Success is having venues and mechanisms for addressing such conflicts well. Success is also greatly facilitated when staff persons have personal and cultural self-awareness and cross-cultural communication skills. We have observed that deaf/hearing cross-cultural relations generally improve when there is a critical mass of deaf people to create the power base needed to get the issues placed on the table. One or two deaf employees in a large office or agency, even one supposedly dedicated to serving deaf people, are easily overwhelmed and overpowered. Cross-cultural conflicts are easier to address when power is more equally distributed.

Conclusions

In the spirit of transparency, the authors of this chapter would like to disclose our own identities, which always have the potential to influence the lens from which we present theories. The first author is a deaf White man from a Deaf family. He attended a mainstream school until fifth grade and moved to a state school for the deaf from grades 6–12. He also graduated from Gallaudet University. The second author is a deaf White female from a hearing family. She attended mainstream schools and graduated from Gallaudet University.

Our intent in this chapter is to expose the socio-emotional and political dynamics and explore the relational postures, behaviors, and cross-cultural conflicts between deaf and hearing people. We identified five postures that we feel are commonly seen in deaf people when they interact with hearing people. Some of these deaf and hearing relational postures, particularly those that clash with each other, are destructive to both individuals and organizations. Many mental health and rehabilitation programs that serve deaf consumers have been weakened or destroyed because these cross-cultural conflicts were handled poorly. This is in fact a huge problem in our field that is rarely attended to well. We have tried here to offer examples of these conflicts being handled both badly and well. The key points we have emphasized are:

1. Deaf/hearing cross-cultural conflicts are normal and expected in every employment settings where deaf and hearing people work. They occur in mental health settings where many clinical situations may be stressful and highly charged. Awareness of cross-cultural conflicts and efforts not to take any such cross-cultural conflicts personally must be continually reinforced and practiced.
2. Deaf people, as cultural minorities, have common work and life experiences that influence their perceptions of hearing people, whether or not they are aware of them. Confronting those biases objectively and skillfully is an important step in resolving any cross-cultural conflict.

3. Deaf and hearing people often have predictable attitudes and behaviors toward each other. Because these patterns in deaf individuals are based on life-long experiences, these orientations may solidify into relational postures five of which (Submissive, Activist, Militant, Native, and Objectifier) are presented here. Deaf identity development is a factor, but many deaf people have patterns of interaction with hearing people that are more stable than Deaf identity development theory predicts. Hearing people have experiences that impact how their identities as hearing people develop, and in some cases these identities may also reflect stable relational postures. This could be an area for new research.

4. Because these interactions are common and predictable, so are the cross-cultural conflicts that occur when deaf and hearing individuals with different orientations relate to each other. This chapter has offered a few examples of predictable conflicts that were handled both badly and well.

5. Deaf/hearing cross-cultural conflicts can make or break a program. Conflict resolution skill building in staff and teams can lessen the conflicts. However, deaf and hearing individual must demonstrate a key ingredient for such conflict resolution efforts to succeed: *genuineness*. Ignoring the conflicts, dealing with conflicts grudgingly, or applying "window dressing" to hide conflicts (like establishing a Deaf cultural awareness committee but ignoring the recommendations) are recipes for program failure. Furthermore, power imbalances must be taken into consideration in using a conflict-resolution approach. Creating venues for open dialogue may minimize the impact of those power imbalances.

Many people talk about the importance of having a "positive attitude" at work but what exactly does a positive attitude consist of? We do not believe that a positive attitude means that hearing people defer to deaf people on every issue or vice versa. Rather, a positive attitude involves the recognition that cross-cultural conflicts are normal and common. It involves the search for an empathic connection across personal and cultural barriers. It involves a willingness to examine non-defensively both personal and cultural biases (and recognition that deaf and hearing people hold biases, as deaf and hearing people, just as other cultural groups do). It involves the willingness to strive for ever greater cross-cultural knowledge and skill. Finally, it involves a commitment to the use of respectful, empathic dialogue to address differences. Many of the conflicts between deaf and hearing employees within organizations revolve around communication and recur often. When communication procedures for these bilingual settings are established and followed, and when there is a sense that it is safe to offer feedback, relationships between hearing and deaf people improve significantly.

The authors of this chapter, inspired by Bryant (2010), present the following recommendations that hearing individuals, deaf individuals, and agencies may adopt as a framework for taking steps to create effective deaf and hearing treatment teams and culturally competent treatment programs.

Recommendations for Hearing Individuals

1. Demonstrate an ongoing and sincere commitment to improve your signing skills and Deaf cultural awareness.
2. Remain open and non-defensive with regard to exploring ways in which being hearing gives you "privileges" in settings that serve deaf people. A humble and respectful attitude will help you develop better relationships with others in the agency. Strive to work with deaf colleagues even when this means you taking more of a supportive or back seat role. Resist the pull to become identified as an "expert" on deaf people.
3. When conflicts with deaf individuals arise related to cross-cultural dynamics, be willing to listen compassionately and avoid personalizing the conflict. Give deaf individuals the benefit of the doubt and listen openly to their feelings and reasoning.
4. Continue to engage in cross-cultural training and frequently check-in with deaf and hearing colleagues as a means of ensuring that you are not crossing cultural boundaries. Explore your reasons for wanting to work with deaf individuals.

Recommendations for Deaf Individuals

1. Explore and understand how your experiences with hearing individuals colors your perceptions of them. Have you come to think that all hearing people behave in similar ways or have similar motives? Consider that your reactions to particular hearing people will be influenced by your previous experiences with them, and that you might not be fair or objective. Give hearing people the benefit of the doubt.
2. Be aware that the power structure tends to favor hearing individuals. Be prepared to present your case in a calm and objective manner. When you see unfair practices, seek support from advocates and/or trusted allies who may be able to assist you in strategizing the best way to present your concerns. Learn how to advocate skillfully, which includes adjusting your advocacy style for different audiences.
3. Earn your professional status. Demonstrate your expertise through your work rather than claiming to be expert simply because you are deaf.

Recommendations for Agencies

1. Develop clear policies regarding equal access and inclusion. Provide structured opportunities for cross-cultural dialogue and provide support, such as supervision, mentoring, consultation, and mediation. Host a deaf/hearing cross-cultural dialogue workshop onsite once a year or on a bi-yearly basis. Consider building such training into new employee orientation programs.

2. Don't assume that effective communication is happening because an interpreter is in the room. Communication in meetings must work for all parties. Check in with all participants and give people permission to say when communication isn't working for them. Be aware that it is often hard for deaf people to acknowledge, when an interpreter is present, that they still feel left out. Effective communication where two or more language groups are meeting almost always requires skilled management of the communication process so that the pacing gives everyone equal access. Don't make assumptions for employees about what works. Ask them.

3. Discuss audism and hearing privilege openly as well as the postures we have described above. Open respectful communication generally defuses tension, although sometimes people have to be taught more skillful ways of raising concerns. Model a commitment to working through tension. Tension will absolutely be present and should not be avoided. Positively affirm instances of productive cross cultural interactions.

4. Review the physical environment and organizational structure to ensure that hearing privilege is not creating unfair practices within the organization.

Notes

1. The authors wish to express gratitude to Irene W. Leigh, Trudy Suggs, and John Pirone for reviewing an earlier draft of this book chapter.
2. We also hope to model a culturally and linguistically affirmative approach by using appropriate and relevant language. As such, we do our best not to use "the deaf," "hearing impaired," and "deafness," all of which have a negative connation and are associated with the medical model.

References

Andrews J. F., Leigh, I. W., & Weiner, M. T. (2004). *Deaf people: Evolving perspectives from psychology, education, and sociology.* Boston, MA: Allyn and Bacon.

Backenroth, G. (1998). Counselling in order to develop tolerance between hearing people and deaf people in bicultural working groups. *International Journal for the Advancement of Counselling, 20,* 219–229.

Baker-Shenk, C., & Kyle, J. G. (1990). Research with deaf people: Issues and conflicts. *Disability, Handicap, and Society, 5*(1), 65–75.

Benedict, B. S., & Sass-Lehrer, M. (2007). Deaf and hearing partnerships: Ethical and communication considerations. *American Annals of the Deaf, 152*(3), 275–282.

Bowe, F. G., McMahon, B. T., Chang, T., & Louvi, I. (2005). Workplace discrimination, deafness and hearing impairment: The national EEOC ADA research project. *Work, 25*, 19–25.

Bryant, R. (2010, July). *Passport to interpreterhood: Understanding hearing privilege.* Presented to the Registry of Interpreter for the Deaf Region III Conference, Minneapolis, MN.

Corker, M. (1994). *Counselling: The deaf challenge.* London, England: Jessica Kingsley.

Gertz, G. (2008). Dyconscious audism: A theoretical proposition. In I. L. Bauman (Ed.), *Open your eyes: Deaf studies talking* (pp. 219–234). Minneapolis: University of Minnesota Press.

Glickman, N. (1996). *Culturally affirmative psychotherapy with deaf persons.* Mahwah, NJ: Erlbaum.

Glickman, N. (2009). *Cognitive-behavioral therapy for deaf and hearing persons with language and learning challenges.* New York, NY: Routledge.

Hauser, P., Maxwell-McCaw, D., Leigh, I. W., & Gutman, V. (2000). Internship accessibility issues for deaf and hard-of-hearing applicants: No cause for complacency. *Professional Psychology: Research and Practice, 31*, 569–574.

Hoffmeister, R., & Harvey, M. (1996). Is there a psychology of the hearing? In N. Glickman & M. Harvey (Eds.), *Culturally affirmative psychotherapy with deaf person* (pp. 73–97). Mahwah, NJ: Erlbaum.

Humphries, T. (1977). *Communicating Across Cultures (Deaf/Hearing) and Language Learning.* (Unpublished doctoral dissertation). Union Graduate School, Cincinnati, OH.

Jones, L., & Pullen, G. (1992). Cultural differences: Deaf and hearing researchers working together. *Disability, Handicap, and Society, 7*(2), 189–196.

Klein, H., & Kitson, N. (2000). Mental health workers: Deaf-hearing partnerships. In P. Hindley & N. Kitson (Eds.), *Mental health and Deafness* (pp. 285–296). London, England: Whurrs.

Lane, H. (1992). *The mask of benevolence: Disabling the Deaf Community.* New York, NY: Knopf.

Leigh, I. W. (2009). *A lens on deaf identities.* New York, NY: Oxford University Press.

Levine, E. (1960). *The psychology of deafness.* New York, NY: Columbia University Press.

Luft, P. (2000). Communication barriers for deaf employees: Needs assessment and problem-solving strategies. *Work, 14*, 51–59.

Nash, J. E., & Nash, A. (1981). *Deafness in society.* Washington, DC: Lexington Books.

NTID News. (2011, February 11). Televised deaf discrimination offers opportunity for discussion, education. Retrieved from http://www.ntid.rit.edu/news/televised-deaf-discrimination-offers-opportunity-discussion-education#

Moores, D. F. (1996). *Educating the deaf: Psychology, principles, and practices, 4th edition.* Boston, MA: Houghton Mifflin.

Myklebust, H. (1964). *The psychology of deafness.* New York, NY: Grune & Stratton.

Paul, P. V., & Jackson, D. W. (1993). *Toward a psychology of deafness: Theoretical and empirical perspective.* Boston, MA: Allyn & Bacon.

Pollard, R. (1996). Professional psychology and deaf people: The emergence of a discipline. *American Psychologist, 51*, 389–396.

Scheetz, N. A. (1993). *Orientation to deafness.* Boston, MA: Allyn and Bacon.

Scherich, D. L. (1996). Job accommodations in the workplace for persons who are deaf or hard of hearing: Current practices and recommendations. *Journal of Rehabilitation*, 27–35.

Smith, K. L. (2007). The experiences of Deaf counselors in developing their professional identity (doctoral dissertation). *Dissertation Abstracts International, 68*(03), 1964B. (UMI No. 3255229)

Snyder, P. J. (1987). Organizational behavior in the cross-cultural delivery of service: A case example of an agency serving the deaf. *Human Organization, 46*(2), 113–119.

Tuccoli, T. (2008). *Hearing privileges at Gallaudet?* Department of ASL and Deaf Studies, Gallaudet University (Unpublished manuscript).

Vernon, M., & Andrews, J. (1990). *The psychology of deafness: Understanding deaf and hard of hearing people.* New York, NY: Longman Publishing.

Weeks, D. (1992). *The eight essential steps to conflict resolution.* New York, NY: Jeremy P. Tarcher/Putnam.

Welsh, W. A. (1993). Factors influencing career mobility of deaf adults. *The Volta Review, 95*, 329–339.

Yee, T. H. (Ed.). (2011, February 4). Deaf to job discrimination [Television series episode]. In A. Paparella (Producer), *What Would You Do?* New York: ABC News Broadcasting. Retrieved from: http://abc.go.com/watch/what-would-you-do/SH5555951/VD55110104/what-would-you-do-24

3 Sign Language Dysfluency in Some Deaf Persons

Implications for Interpreters and Clinicians Working in Mental Health Settings[1,2]

Neil S. Glickman and Charlene Crump

Introduction

Many deaf persons who come into mental health and rehabilitation programs have significant language problems (Glickman, 2009). Poor skills in the spoken language of the community are common and are a natural consequence of being unable to hear the language. However, the language problems we are referring to are evident in American Sign Language (ASL), usually the best language of these persons. In fact, more than half of the deaf patients served on a specialty psychiatric inpatient unit for deaf people, the Deaf Unit at Westborough State Hospital in Massachusetts, were judged by the communication specialist to have severe language dysfluency in signing (Glickman, 2009). Poor language skills in deaf psychiatric inpatients have been observed in numerous other studies of this group (Altshuler, 1971; Altshuler & Rainer, 1968; Denmark, 1985, 1994; Grinker et al., 1969). Poor language skills are also the first characteristic used to describe the subgroup of deaf persons sometimes called "traditionally underserved" (Dew, 1999; Long, Long, & Ouellette, 1993).

In this chapter, we refer to these language problems using the term "dysfluent." By dysfluent, we mean that these persons are not skilled users of the language. Their communication in the language is unclear or, to the native's "ear," peculiar. They sound or look like persons who have not mastered the language because their language is non-grammatical, non-idiomatic, or odd. They can also sound like people who are confused, who aren't thinking clearly. As we will see, the underlying problem may be that the person has not mastered the language, but it may also be that the person has a form of mental illness or a brain condition which affects their thinking and therefore their language. Mental health clinicians doing psychological evaluations will want to know if a patient uses language in a dysfluent manner, and they will try to understand the underlying reason for it. If they do not know the language of the patient and are working through interpreters, they will draw conclusions based on how the interpreters interpret the dysfluent language. If the interpreters "fix" the dysfluent language, it can impact profoundly the diagnostic conclusions that the clinicians draw (Pollard, 1998a).

The purpose of this chapter is to summarize what we know about dysfluency in sign language use among deaf people and discuss its implications for signed language interpreters and mental health clinicians. We will focus primarily upon the implications of sign language dysfluency for clinical assessment. Treatment is addressed more fully in other chapters of this book and elsewhere (Glickman, 2009). We will begin by reviewing briefly the four main causes of signed language disorders in more depth. This is followed by a literature review and illustration of best practices for interpreters working with language dysfluent consumers in mental health settings including language samples from patients served by the Alabama Department of Mental Health. Best practices include not only familiarity with several interpreting strategies but also making decisions based on the task demands and available resources (Dean & Pollard, 2001, 2005). As certified Deaf interpreters (CDIs) are often brought into situations when deaf consumers are very dysfluent, we also consider the risks and benefits of this practice. Our focus then switches back to discussing some of the implications of sign language dysfluency for clinical assessment and, more briefly, treatment. How can clinicians make sense of what these language problems most likely mean? In particular, what do we know that helps clinicians distinguish a language problem from a thinking problem? Finally, we conclude with a discussion of best practice for interpreter-clinician collaboration. Best practice occurs when both clinician and interpreter are aware of the problem of sign language dysfluency in some deaf people, the various interpreting options, and how to make sense of these language problems. Work with a deaf communication specialist or CDI is increasingly becoming understood to be best practice. Crucially, best practice means that the clinicians and interpreters are skilled collaborators with each other in this challenging interpreting and clinical task (Dean & Pollard, 2005).

Causes of Signed Language Dysfluency in Deaf People

There are some fundamental differences between interpreting for deaf people and interpreting for hearing people who use other spoken languages. A difference that concerns us here is that severe language dysfluency in hearing people, unless they have significant cognitive impairments, is relatively rare. By and large, hearing people learn their native language. If a Vietnamese person comes into a mental health clinic, the clinician can assume that the person speaks some version of Vietnamese or another local language. They may or may not be articulate. It is possible they have a thought disorder effecting how they use language. They will use a particular dialect. But they are likely to be native speakers, with fluent command of some language. The same cannot be assumed when working with deaf persons. Some deaf people are fluent users of their signed language but many others are poor users of this language. In extreme cases, some deaf people are virtually alingual (Schaller, 1991). This wide range of language skill, from native users to alingual people, with all sorts of variations in-between, brings to the signed to spoken interpreting task a degree of complexity that is not found in the work of spoken language interpreters.

In the educational literature on deaf children, when people refer to "language problems," they are usually referring to the well-known difficulties that deaf people have acquiring spoken and written language skills. Relatively little attention has been paid to the difficulties deaf people can have developing native sign language abilities. In this chapter, the latter issue is our concern. The challenge for the interpreter in working with clients who are poor communicators in any language is of a different order of magnitude from interpreting for people who use different languages well.

There are four key reasons why deaf people may become poor communicators in any language. The first reason is that there may be a neurological basis for such language problems. Most of the causes of deafness in children can also cause other neurological, medical or psychological problems (Vernon & Andrews, 1990). The leading causes of deafness have been: prenatal rubella, meningitis, prematurity, complications of Rh factor and genetics. One third of genetic hearing loss is associated with a trait recognizable as a syndrome (e.g., Down Syndrome, Usher Syndrome), and these syndromes can have multiple associated disabilities. The other four leading causes of deafness can all result in developmental delays, cognitive disabilities, and learning problems affecting language. In practice, it is usually difficult to separate out presumed neurological bases for language problems from the environmental causes, especially lack of exposure to ASL.

Deaf children struggling with attention and behavioral problems may be diagnosed with Attention Deficit Hyperactivity Disorder (ADHD), but a deaf child without adequate language is highly likely to show problems with attention and behavior and is therefore vulnerable to misdiagnosis. This misdiagnosis can be motivated in part by the desire to seek a simple solution in medication whereas the real resolution is the provision of an appropriate linguistic environment. Deaf children may also get diagnosed with learning disabilities, but a deaf child without adequate language is highly likely to have difficulty learning. There may or may not be a neurologically based learning disorder, and in the absence of appropriate language input, this may be impossible to determine. It is much easier to assume the problem lies in the brain of the child rather than in the classroom and home environments. Deafness etiologies like prematurity, meningitis, prenatal Rubella, cytomegalovirus (CMV), may predispose the deaf child to learning problems, but even in these cases a lack of appropriate learning environment should be presumed to be the dominant cause. If the etiology of the child's deafness is known, a neurological basis for language and learning problems can be presumed, but even in these cases the most powerful reason for such problems is likely to be the language environment, not the child's brain. One can only be confident that a cause of language disorder is *not* language deprivation when the child has had early and consistent rich exposure to good sign models. This happens in a minority of instances.

One such example of a deaf child of deaf parents, exposed to British Sign Language from birth, with normal intelligence, was recently published (Morgan, Herman, & Woll, 2007). This child used exaggerated gestures and facial expressions to compensate for poor language competence. He used repeated pointing and exaggerated facial expressions rather than grammar. Samples of his language show repetitions of single signs with few grammatical inflections. Using norms available for British signing deaf children, he was found to be more than two years behind in language development. The researchers concluded that his example provides evidence that specific language impairment can exist in deaf signers. They hypothesize that specific language impairment would occur in deaf children with at least the same incidence rate as hearing children; that is 5%–7% of the population. They could only measure this because they had a standardized instrument to use, the British Sign Language Receptive Test, norms, and a deaf child of deaf parents who had full, rich BSL exposure.

A second reason a deaf person may be sign language dysfluent is because of a head or brain injury such as what occurs when people have strokes. This was demonstrated by the first researchers to take sign language dysfluency seriously, Poizner, Klima, and Bellugi, in their research into deaf people affected by aphasias (Klima & Bellugi, 1979; Poizner, Klima, & Belllugi, 1987). An aphasia is an acquired language disorder, usually resulting from lesions to the language relevant areas of the brain. Aphasias can result from strokes, tumors, or closed head injuries. Aphasias in hearing people can result in the inability to comprehend language, form words and name objects, speak in a grammatically correct fashion and be able to read or write. Aphasias may cause persons to invent words, persistently repeat phrases, substitute letters, syllables or words, and alter inflexion, stress and rhythm (prosody). Depending on the location of the lesion, aphasias can manifest in problems such as difficulty narrating a story in an organized, linear fashion, slow output of words, limited vocabulary, inability to access specific nouns, use of the wrong noun or wrong verb, use of a pronoun without an antecedent (saying "he" before establishing who "he" refers to), and inability to express the point of a story (Ash et al., 2006). The research of Poizner, Klima, and Bellugi demonstrated that deaf people who were native signers of ASL, and who experienced strokes, developed sign language aphasias that were comparable to spoken language aphasias in hearing people.

A third cause for sign language dysfluency may be a severe thought disorder associated with a mental illnesses that causes psychosis. Along with hallucinations and delusions, severe mental illness may cause persons to show disorganized thinking, an inability to put together words, signs and thoughts in a coherent way that makes sense. This phenomena is well known in hearing people, but it occurs in deaf people also (Glickman, 2007; Pollard, 1998b). Patients may, for instance, demonstrate *loose associations* where there is only a marginal connection between one idea and the next. They may be unable to think abstractly, to see patterns or relationships, or to generalize as to what things mean. They may be unable to think in logical, cause and effect terms. They may make up new words (*neologisms*) or make connections between words based not on meaning, but on sound or on the physical properties of signs (*clanging*).

Sign language dysfluency related to mental illness was demonstrated by the second researcher to take sign language dysfluency in deaf persons seriously, Alice Thacker in Great Britain. Thacker studied the sign language output of deaf people diagnosed with schizophrenia (1994, 1998). She found examples of deaf persons with schizophrenia demonstrating the same kinds of thinking problems as hearing people with schizophrenia, only manifested in sign language. In particular she found evidence of:

1. The linking of a sign to an English word that sounds similar (Interviewer: YOU SAY WOMAN INSIDE YOU HAVE? MEAN WHICH, BODY OR SOUL? Schizophrenic subject: SOUL (conventional sign) SOLE (pointing to bottom of foot). TWO FEET JUMP IN MY MOUTH.
2. Finger spelling backwards or moving signs backwards; placing signs in the wrong location.
3. Connecting signs based on their properties (handshapes, location, movement) rather than on meaning.
4. Very loose associations; going off topic and not finding one's way back ("derailment").
5. Repeating a sign or sign phrase or theme unnecessarily.
6. Copying the signing of the examiner ("echolalia").
7. Errors in the syntax or grammatical order of signs.

Thacker assumed that the sign language dysfluency she found in deaf persons diagnosed with schizophrenia was due to the thought disorder. She did not address the issue of deaf psychiatric patients who are language dysfluent for other reasons such as inadequate language exposure.

The most well-known and common reason that deaf people may be sign language dysfluent is due to inadequate exposure to signed language during childhood. The problems deaf children have acquiring spoken language is well known, but without adequate exposure to sign language, they can lack native skills in any language, signed or spoken.

Trumbetta, Bonvillian, Siedlecki Jr., and Hasins (2001) also examined dysfluency shown by deaf individuals with schizophrenia. The authors noted that communication deficits may arise from reasons other than mental illness, including language deprivation, etiological complications and the lack of familiarity of clinicians with the deaf population (Trumbetta et al., 2001).

The Deaf Unit at Westborough State Hospital in Massachusetts was, for 23 years, a specialty psychiatric unit for deaf persons with severe emotional and behavioral problems. Research stemming from this unit showed that the majority of deaf persons served there were not fluent users of any language (Black, 2005; Black & Glickman, 2005; Glickman, 2009).[3] Since there is no reason to think the Westborough Deaf Unit was atypical, this is presumably the case in all specialized mental health and rehabilitation programs for deaf people. The literature on "traditionally underserved deaf" bears this out (Bowe, 2004; Dew, 1999; Mathay & LaFayette, 1990) as does most of the literature on inpatient treatment of deaf persons (Glickman, 2009, Chapter 1). A recent study of language skills in among deaf prisoners in the Texas Correctional System also found very high levels of language dysfluency in both spoken and signed languages (Miller, 2004).

Glickman (2008, 2009; Black & Glickman, 2005) presented examples of the kinds of language errors that were commonly seen among deaf persons on the Westborough State Hospital Deaf Unit. These language errors were attributed mainly to language deprivation and not to mental illness although it is reasonable to assume that neurological problems contributed as well. These common errors were:

1. Impoverished vocabulary with many signs used incorrectly. The limited vocabulary is the most obvious form of language dysfluency seen, with some deaf patients communicating only with isolated signs or short sign phrases.
2. Inability to sequence events in time. This often includes a lack of signs and grammatical structures to indicate tense. These persons seem unable to tell any story, using a beginning, middle and end, much less the story of their own life. They jump back and forwards in time without indicating that they are doing so. This deficiency also makes it difficult for them to see cause and effect or to use conditional phrasing (if this, then that.)
3. Spatial disorganization. Inability to use the space around the signer grammatically. For instances, referents are not established and maintained in one part of the spatial field. Sign inflection involving movement through space is absent or inconsistent.
4. Syntax. The topic-comment structure of much ASL is missing. Subjects are not established clearly. Nor are they related appropriately to verbs and objects. Pronouns (like an index finger to establish a person)

may be used without any referent. Often these patients seem to be listing nouns or sometimes verbs without establishing relationships. They make heavy use of sign repetition as a poor substitute for grammar.

5. Mixture of gesture and pantomime with sign. Because their vocabulary is so poor, these persons make frequent use of gesture and pantomime. While competent signers may do this on occasion, usually for emphasis or for creative storytelling, they have the necessary language structure if they choose to use it, while these persons have no alternative but to act things out.

Just as Poizner et al. (1987) demonstrated that aphasias can exist in deaf people by studying the sign language errors of deaf persons who had experienced brain injuries, Thacker demonstrated that thought disorders can exist in deaf persons by examining the sign language errors of deaf persons with schizophrenia. To make their respective points, the researchers had to study deaf persons who had relatively good sign language skills prior to their injury or illness. Both kinds of language errors would be confounded dramatically if the samples of deaf persons included those with the far more common problem of language dysfluency due to language deprivation. With this latter group, one *cannot* say that their previously intact signing abilities suffered as a result of a new condition. Rather, their sign language skills were always impaired (i.e., they have a developmental deficit) and now they have one or more new problems (an aphasia, a severe mental illness), creating language deficit upon language deficit, and probably making it impossible to figure out any single etiology.

The case load from the Deaf psychiatric unit at Westborough State Hospital showed that relatively pure examples (proficient signers who suddenly experience a dramatic loss in signing abilities) were rare. Far more common were deaf patients who, as best staff could determine, have always signed poorly, who now may *also* have a mental illness. In a mental health setting, aphasias related to strokes or other forms of traumatic brain injuries are easier to rule out because there will be other neurological evidence for such events, and there will be a story about a dramatic worsening of language skills following some event. Language deprivation, on the other hand, is widespread in the deaf clinical population. When faced with a patient who demonstrates a severe sign language disorder, the most likely cause will have been language deprivation, and this should be the working default hypothesis for clinicians. However, mental health clinicians should be very interested in such language problems, and should wonder what might be the cause or causes. They would be most likely to wonder whether such language problems reflect mental illness or other forms of brain pathology.

This means that mental health clinicians, working with interpreters, want to know not just what a person says but how he or she says it. They want to know if something is unusual or strange about the way the person uses language, and they will be completely dependent upon interpreters to even know there is a language problem.

Interpreting for Deaf Persons with Language Dysfluency: Literature Review and Core Strategies

There is very little written on the subject of interpreting for deaf persons with language dysfluency. A literature review found 16 publications that mention the problem but only five provide any substantive discussion of the issue (Glickman, 2007; Karlin, 2003; Pollard, 1998a, 1998b; Trumbetta et al., 2001). We were unable to find any research that has been conducted examining the effectiveness of varying interpreter responses to this challenge.

Tracie Karlin (2003) outlines the types of language errors made by deaf persons with schizophrenia, based on Alice Thacker's work (1998), and discusses strategies for interpreting from ASL to English when faced with these errors. She explains that clinicians are often less interested in the specific message the patient communicates than in what the language patterns reveal about the consumer's mental world. She favors, therefore, interpreters commenting on their behavioral observations, when potentially relevant to the purpose of the interview.

When interpreting for a deaf person with an active thought disorder, the clinician may be more interested in how the person thinks, as illustrated by how they use language, than in the message itself. This means the interpreter voicing, "I am Jesus Christ, and I am very smart and can fly" might not be as useful to a clinician as you saying, "he appears to be talking to someone invisible to us. He is telling them, 'I am Jesus Christ. I am very smart and can fly.'"

The RID Standard Practice Paper, "Interpreting in Mental Health Settings," states that "The interpreter can provide information and opinion related to the communication process, but not on the therapeutic process" (RID, 2007). In other words, it is well within the interpreter's role to comment on a person's language and communication abilities, if appropriate to the context, but not to offer an opinion about what language skills and deficits mean clinically.

Robert Pollard has written the most extensively on the subject and examines the interpreting role with dysfluent patients as a part of a mentored curriculum for mental health interpreters, including a section on strategies for interpreting with language dysfluent consumers (Pollard, 1998a). Pollard's curriculum goes into some depth about the interpreting strategies recommended by the Registry of Interpreters for the Deaf in their standard practice paper (RID, 2007). In this chapter, we draw most heavily upon his work.

Pollard identifies four strategies that can be used by mental health interpreters for interpreting dysfluent communication: use of the first person, third person, description and glossing. Each of these strategies can be illustrated with reference to a specific kind of language error.

First person is the strategy interpreters are most used to. This works best when the consumer's language is reasonably clear and intact but the consumer is showing a distinct mood or varying his speed, tone or intensity.

Third person is the strategy of saying "he or she is saying that ..." Sometimes it is better for the interpreter to describe the language of the deaf consumer in this manner. For example, if a deaf consumer is very agitated, it could be disruptive for the interpreter to mimic the same level of agitation. This could make a difficult situation much worse. Using third person strategy, the interpreter could explain in a calm voice, rather than trying to match the intensity and specific word choices used by the consumer, that "the consumer/he is screaming that his siblings have stolen his money left to him by an uncle who passed away recently and now he has no money for food or rent."

The more dysfluent the deaf consumer's language becomes, the more necessary it becomes to use third person and/or to **describe** the consumer's language. Pollard recommends the descriptive strategy any time the interpreter is unsure of logic or meaning and when such a description may be clinically useful.

Pollard gives examples of common forms of language dysfluency and suggestions for how they be interpreted. Some of these are presented here.

A neologism, a made up word, would have no generally understood translation. It can be hard for interpreters and clinicians to be confident that an unrecognized sign is a neologism, rather than a home sign, a regional variant, a gesture, ethnic variant, or even a sign from a different signed language. Additionally, ASL users can form signs in creative and unique ways while still maintaining the signs' meaning. An example of a neologism in sign language provided by Roger Williams, Director of Deaf Services for the South Carolina Department of Mental Health, was given by a consumer who knew that aliens were coming to earth because "computer keypad signed on the nose." This is actually a very sophisticated play on a sign which, outside of an artistic context, suggests a thought disorder, not language deprivation. Faced with an apparent neologism, interpreters probably should describe it and comment on it. "I don't recognize that sign. It appears to be something that the consumer understands, but it is similar to the sign for a "computer keyboard used to input information," but it is placed in an unusual space, on the nose.

In topic derailment, the person changes topics mid-discourse and is unable to stay on point. This is illustrated in the following segment of an interview, audiotaped with a hearing psychiatric patient at Westborough State Hospital.

"I'm just afraid of great things happening. I'm not afraid of little wars. I'm just afraid of the ... I'm afraid of big wars ... and the main problem

I'm having over the last days or weeks or so is who I am. They say I'm a liberal intellectual and I'm a Christian sometimes and it's always a pleasure to be with you. I'm very happy with you doctor. I appreciate all you have done to me. You'll have to excuse my nastiness. It's caused by … I was very dismayed. I prayed for a little bit for a boy this morning from a suburban high school who was gay and who was shot to death by another student, by a straight student. Blew him away, you know?"

First person strategy can work well in the situation described above. In this example, no one would think this person was not a fluent speaker of English. People would recognize his skill in English but note that his thinking appears off in some way. This is usually the case with persons suffering from thought disorders. They do not give the appearance of not being fluent or native users of their language. Rather, they appear to be confused, have strange ideas, or be unable to stay on point. They do not usually, for instance, forget subjects, verbs or objects or inflect verbs incorrectly. More commonly, they are just putting thoughts or ideas together oddly. This is illustrated well in the above example.

This is in striking contrast to many deaf persons who are dysfluent because of sign language deprivation. In extreme cases, their language skills can be so poor that they are incoherent or barely able to communicate an idea, even to native signers. When using first person strategy breaks down, the interpreter can incorporate **third person narrative** and **descriptive** strategies. The descriptive strategy differs in that it refers to commenting on the person's language as well as paralinguistics. When a deaf consumer's language skills are exceptionally poor, the interpreter must rely increasingly on third person, description, and even on the strategy known as **glossing**.

Glossing is sometimes referred to by interpreters as a word for word translation of the source material. More correctly, it is the process of applying a common label for the sake of convenience or expediency (Pantel & Dekang, 2000). For example, a variety of English words (angry, enraged, livid) might all be glossed with the sign ANGRY even though the different shades of meaning are conveyed through how the sign is made. Glossing can be a technique utilized in interpreting especially when the language is very dysfluent or incoherent.

Pollard (1998a) gives the following example which combines glossing with third person and descriptive strategy. The interpreter explains that he is attempting to provide the clinician with individual words or short clauses that as near as possible represent the language sample he is seeing. He says,

> She is saying something about her mother and a devil and something about an argument, but she is not speaking in complete sentences and she is using past tense and present tense in a way that doesn't make sense to me. (p. 95)

Additionally, some of the message that is being signed may be glossed as follows:

> Mother ... went (somewhere) ... devil with red eyes glaring, coming ... (something about) shouting and hitting ... mother was girl a long time ago ... the devil won't won't.... (I missed some here) ... you know the devil ... I'm 50 years old. (p. 95)

ASL and English have very different grammars and literal transliteration from ASL into English, just like such transliteration from other foreign languages into English, gives the appearance of bad English. Glossing is not recommended with persons who are signing well, and must always be used carefully, with explanations, with hearing people who are unfamiliar with ASL.[4] Whenever glossing is done, it inevitably makes the deaf person appear even more language impaired. Glossing may be more acceptable with clinicians who have some familiarity with ASL and who want in certain situations to know specifically the signs that are being used, as much as possible.

Finally, although interpreters use this less frequently, one could cite one more strategy in which the interpreter provides contextual or background information to help clinicians understand a deaf person's statements. For example, if the clinician asks the consumer the question, "who is the president of the United States?" and the person responds "Bobbie Scoggins," the interpreter might add, in the third person, "he gave the name of the person who is/was the president of the National Association of the Deaf." This addition to the interpreting process provides contextual information that will help the clinician evaluate the deaf person's thinking. The clinician could then probe further if he or she wishes. This strategy might be used when an interpreter comments that a person from a signing deaf family who attended a residential school would normally sign much more proficiently that what she or he is observing at that moment.

All these strategies can be summarized by using the familiar children's song, "Jack and Jill." For instance, **first person,** told from the point of view of Jill would be:

> *Jack and I went up a hill to fetch a pail of water. He fell down and broke his crown and I went tumbling after.*

Third person is how the story is normally told.

> *Jack and Jill went up the hill to fetch a pail of water. Jack fell down and broke his crown and Jill came tumbling after.*

Glossing would look something like this:

JACK JILL THEY-TWO-MOVE-UP HILL. JACK FALL ROCK HEAD HIT HURT FINISH. JILL FALL ROLL-DOWN-HILL.

The **narrative** strategy would look like this:

The consumer is telling the story of "Jack and Jill."

In the **descriptive** strategy, comments are added to clarify the person's use of language:

The consumer is telling the story of "Jack and Jill." However, his expression is more stoic than I am used to seeing. Every time he signs Jill's name he adds (as in a side comment) "kill son, kill mother." His left hand is fidgety, not producing language, but moving in a short quick movement.

Finally, although interpreters use this less frequently, the interpreter might provide some relevant background information:

The roots of the story, or poem, of Jack and Jill are in France. Jack and Jill are said to be King Louis XVI—Jack—who was beheaded (lost his crown) followed by his Queen Marie Antoinette— Jill—(who came tumbling after).

While the examples above may appear simplistic in nature, many interpreters participating in supervised mental health practica will often default to a first person simultaneous interpretation when faced with dysfluent language production. Alternative strategies, not yet having been internalized, regularly have to be retaught during supervision.

Interpreters need to be careful to limit their comments to their areas of expertise (RID, 2007). Sometimes clinicians unfamiliar with deaf people and interpreters ask the interpreter to make clinical judgments such as "is he hallucinating?" or "why doesn't she make sense?" As someone who is not trained to make clinical assessments, an appropriate response would be to help the clinician understand the interpreter's function. The interpreter could say, "I'm not trained to make that type of determination. What I can provide you is access to the person's language and also discuss how they are using language."

Interpreter Decision Making: Using the Demand Control Approach to Select Interpreting Strategies

Interpreter methods will vary, depending not only on the cause of the dysfluency, but the setting, goal of the environment and many other factors. The Demand Control schema provides a tool for analyzing the demands of any given interpreting situation and considering the appropriate interpreting choices or controls (Dean & Pollard, 2001, 2005). Language dysfluent deaf consumers present especially difficult demands for interpreters. These demands are compounded when the clinician knows nothing about deaf people and when both parties hold unrealistic expectations for what interpreters can accomplish. The Demand Control schema gives interpreters a way of discussing these challenges and will be drawn upon here in relation to interpreting for language dysfluent deaf persons.

The strategies discussed in the literature review focus primarily on dysfluent language that can occur as a result of mental illness. As noted above, there are other possible causes of language dysfluency in deaf people. The far more common cause is sign language deprivation, and the kinds of language errors that such language deprived persons show are typically different than persons with intact language who develop mental illnesses.

Interpreting choices can include timing. Consecutive interpreting can be useful to the interpreter in mental health settings when working with dysfluent consumers since it allows for a fuller, more accurate understanding of the source language message to be understood before interpreting it into the target language (Russell, 2002). Consecutive interpreting also allows the interpreter time to assess if the language produced is typical or to identify what patterns of language dysfluency are exhibited. It provides the interpreter with the time needed to provide at least some third person description or narrative of dysfluent language if the interpreter so chooses.

While there are many reasons why an interpreter would choose consecutive interpreting, there are times within mental health interpreting when an interpreter might choose to utilize simultaneous interpreting. For example, when a client's signing is "pressured" (that is rapid, virtually non-stop, emphatic, seemingly driven, and difficult to interrupt), the interpreter may be unable to mentally hold on to the message, and consecutive interpreting may not be possible. The interpreter might explain that the message is being signed rapidly and does not contain natural pauses that would allow her to work consecutively and to retain the content of the message. Then, the interpreter may choose to work simultaneously, at least as much as is possible. There may also be times when the consumer is an above average speech reader and is hypervigilant about the interpreter's word choices. In this case, delaying the interpretation or providing commentary on the language might hinder the therapeutic process.

An example of a language sample from a sign language deprived person follows from the Alabama Department of Mental Health. There was no stimulus question and no background to the context provided prior to the person beginning the narrative. Using first person, the interpreted message would sound something like this:

> "P" a person named 'P' you know 'P'? Her Dorm. She's in trouble. I'm mad, I'm mad. Trouble mad. All. Every. No problem. I, umm, umm, zip my lips, umm, me. I calmed down. I enter hear carry out

the trash all day. Fine with me. Can hear people talking, yes, yes. Can hear? Yes. Can hear? I talk a lot, hear, talk a lot. WISNERS(?), the interpreter explains to me all day. I know that they really didn't serve. I work, I'm working. The teacher writes a lot on paper and I write too. … I, table, I will explain about the chairs all over the place. I talk and chat to deaf, hard-of-hearing and deaf people. Deaf people can't hear. I can't hear people at all."

Utilizing third person narrative and descriptive techniques consecutively, the interpreter could offer the following interpretation.

"The consumer, Billy, is discussing a female whose name begins with a 'P' (the name was spelled out, but was unclear). This individual appears to have some association with the dorm. He is stating that the female may be in trouble or has caused some trouble and that he is upset about it. There is some information that I am not understanding. He seems to be telling himself to calm down and to keep quiet about the situation (to zip his lips). He has now switched topics and appears to be talking about carrying out the trash. It is something that he has been involved in all day. He is talking about hearing and repeating the sign for 'hear' several times and stating that he can hear or that someone else can hear. Billy is finger-spelling something, which is not clear, that appears to be a person's name, 'WISNERS.' WISNER seems to be a person in the role of an interpreter who has worked with Billy. He is again talking about work and assuring that he does indeed work. The topic now centers on a school setting including a teacher and writing and placement of chairs. He is discussing talking and mentions deaf, hard-of-hearing, and hearing people (possibly communicating with people of varying hearing loss?) and the fact that deaf people cannot hear."

Clearly, this second interpretation is a vast improvement. It provides a much clearer presentation of the unclear message of the deaf patient. Providing additional descriptive information for the clinician on the way the message is conveyed may be even more helpful.

"The consumer is signing as if the story is urgent. The story frequently jumps from the present to the recent past to his childhood without any indication of shifts in time or topic. Individual names are not spelled out completely. Many words are poorly or incompletely formed and could be representative of a number of meanings. For example, I'm not sure if he means hearing people or that he can hear and the meaning is not clear from the context. Also, I'm not sure if it is an interpreter present or that someone is explaining information to him because the sign is produced almost as a combination of the two signs. There are several times when signs are repeated, and seem to indicate emphasis or clarification. There appears to be an element of disbelief, and possibly frustration, throughout most of the message. There are some signs that I am not familiar with and could possibly be a gesture used with his family or variant of the word."

The third person descriptive and consecutive technique can be less distressing for interpreters because it allows them time to process the content of the message more fully and in a more accurate and coherent manner and to reveal the form of the dysfluency they observe.

There are multiple demands upon the interpreter in this type of situation. Interpreters are likely to consider their control choices, resulting demands and consequences of those decisions. Some of the demands that an interpreter might consider are:

- Interpreters often do not feel comfortable voicing incomplete and incoherent sentences.
- Interpreters may be unsure whether the dysfluency is a fact or whether the problem lies with their own inabilities.
- Interpreters may be concerned about the opinion of the clinician or consumer who may think that the problem lies in the interpreters' lack of sufficient skills.
- Interpreters may be concerned that the clinician may draw inappropriate conclusions about the deaf person's intelligence or over generalize to draw wrong conclusions about limited language and cognitive abilities of deaf people.
- Interpreters often fear that when the deaf person is not presented in the best possible light or the outcome is an undesirable one, that they will be blamed by the deaf person and, by word of mouth, the Deaf community, for their perceived lack of skills or inappropriate attitude.
- Interpreters are taught that it is important to match the register of consumers so that intelligent deaf people sound equally intelligent in translation. But what about the deaf person who is not clear or coherent or intelligent? Interpreters may be uncomfortable matching the register when it reveals the deaf consumer in a less flattering light.

Clearly, it takes a great deal of skill and confidence for an interpreter to know whether the problem lies with their interpretation, the consumers or, for that matter, with incoherent, unskilled or insensitive clinicians. This is one reason why mental health interpreting requires advanced skills.

One of the most important controls is a pre-assignment understanding of the goal and resources of the clinical environment. What is the clinician's goal for the session? Is the clinician primarily concerned with communicating, as in a counseling session, or is the clinician doing a mental status exam where understanding how the consumer uses language is crucial? How experienced is the clinician in working with deaf people and collaborating with interpreters? Can the interpreter obtain a pre-session with the clinician during which time these issues can be explored? These demands shape the interpreter's decision making

Interpreters assessing demands and employing controls continuously analyze and, when necessary, change their interpreting strategy. The interpreter adjusts strategy based on the assessment of the clinicians' prior experience with deaf people and approach to this particular task. The interpreter may also consider other concurrent demands (Dean & Pollard, 2011) such as how much time is available. If little time is available, the interpreter may stick to first person and add brief comments like "this part is unclear" or "I'm unsure what he meant here." When more time is available, especially if there is the possibility of a post-session, the interpreter can obviously offer much more detailed information.

Another pre-assignment control that the interpreter can bring is the knowledge base about language dysfluency. Interpreters may want to seek out training, therefore, on the most common types of language problems, the most common reasons they occur, the assessment of language disorders and the best strategies for interpreting them. While interpreters would want to avoid overly liberal decisions such as stating, "the consumer is psychotic" or "the consumer just produced a neologism," realizing that such phenomena exist is likely to very helpful. Gaining this knowledge can assist interpreters when they realize that sometimes the consumer really isn't clear. This facilitates an effective dialogue with clinicians.

Once the actual interpreting has begun, controls include those presented earlier in this discussion. They may also include making adjustments to interpretation such as signing slower, using less movement, voicing in a way that does not exacerbate an emotionally charged setting, utilizing listing techniques, gesture, pictures, or manipulatives such as toy figures and other visual tools, etc. The controls listed here and presented throughout the article are not exhaustive. Ideally, the clinician will be involved in helping the interpreter make these decisions because then they are working effectively as a team. Both should understand that it falls to the clinician to determine what these language problems mean. Some examples of this decision making process, with the interpreter using different controls, follow:

The setting is the intake assessment and the clinician asks the consumer, "Do you know what day it is today?" The interpreter chooses to sign TODAY WHAT? This interpretation is actually not as clear as the English question. The clinician may be asking the day of the week but the consumer may think the question pertains to the weather. The consumer may, therefore, not respond in the way the clinician expects. Maybe the consumer is psychotic or perhaps he has language or cognitive problems or maybe the question as signed is too vague, as in this example. The interpreter might therefore interpret the question like this: TODAY MONDAY TUESDAY WEDNESDAY WHAT? This is probably more directive and specific than the clinician wanted. The interpreter could also say to the clinician, "I have asked him your question. However, it is very common when using ASL to offer suggestions or further guidance on the type of answer you want, like an example. Would you like me to do so?"

The same question might be asked as part of the morning community meeting. In this case, the group leader is less interested in an assessment of mental status and more interested in orienting patients about the world around them. Knowing this, the interpreter may be more willing to sign TODAY MONDAY TUESDAY WEDNESDAY WHAT? without consulting with the group leader. The environmental situation (i.e., the purpose of this meeting) leads to the interpreter making a different interpreting choice (i.e., using a different control.)

Post-assignment controls include the ability to have a post-session conference with the clinician to discuss the communication and interpreting dynamics that occurred. Interpreters also gain more controls as they learn more about language dysfluency and obtain supervision from experienced mental health interpreters and clinicians.

Another example of dysfluent language follows, this time of a language sample from an interview with a deaf individual who grew up with deaf siblings and attended a state residential school. He suffered a traumatic brain injury from a car accident in his mid-twenties, and his language skills declined significantly after that accident.

Interviewer: YOUR NAME WHAT?[5]
Consumer: J-A-M-E-S-J-O-N-E-S me[6]
Interviewer: LIVE WHERE?
Consumer: live where? T-Y-L-E-R
Interviewer: OLD HOW-MUCH YOU?
Consumer: 17-19-35
Interviewer: SCHOOL WHERE?
Consumer: S-C-O-O-L
Interviewer: WHERE?
Consumer: M-O-N-O-T-Y
Interviewer: NAME MOTHER WHAT?
Consumer: MOTHER J-A-N-E-T N-J-S
Interviewer: FATHER NAME WHAT?
Consumer: FATHER M-C-H-E-L O-J-S
Interviewer: BROTHER SISTER HAVE?
Consumer: BROTHER/SISTER S-E-V-E (taps on forehead)
Interviewer: BROTHER HAVE?
Consumer: HAVE J-O (pause) S-H-A-N-O-N-J-O-S ME, GIRL, (taps on forehead)
Interviewer: YOU ENJOY FUN WHAT?
Consumer: H-I-I-J-U-Y (nods head)

A discussion of some demands and controls in the assignment are listed below.

Demands

- The consumer may not be understanding the interpreter. If that is true, how much should the interpreter alter her language to fit the consumer?
- The consumer is signing unusually slowly. Should the interpreter also slow down to an unnaturally slow speed?
- The consumer has fingerspelled incorrectly. The interpreter knows that it is common for deaf people to misspell English words and names, but this information could be clinically significant. Should the interpreter repeat the names in the target language with the same misspelling or present the names as if they were correctly spelled?
- The consumer's signing is not reflective of what one would expect from a deaf person who has deaf siblings and attended a state residential school. The clinician would probably not know this, but it could be diagnostically significant information. Should the interpreter offer these observations?
- The interpreter has no prior knowledge of the consumer's language skills before the session begins. Should the interpreter arrange for a pre-view meeting?

Pre-Assignment Controls

- The interpreter can ask to review the consumer's chart, including psycho-social background, medical history, diagnosis and current level of stability.
- The interpreter can inquire about the language ability of the consumer, if known.
- The interpreter can ask the clinician if there is anything significant the interpreter should know based on their previous experience.
- The interpreter can go into the therapist's office and explain to the therapist that she will be introducing herself to the consumer and briefly assessing language needs.
- The interpreter can discuss with the prior interpreter or an interpreter who has worked with this consumer before how they perceive the language needs of the consumer.

During Assignment Controls

- The interpreter could use first person simultaneous method of voicing with the inclusion of some descriptive comments.

- The interpreter could utilize first person simultaneous method and spell the names back as they appear.
- The interpreter could voice the fingerspelled names as intended and then meet with the therapist after the session to provide additional information on what was seen during therapy.
- The interpreter could use third person consecutive/narrative and state that "The consumer is responding to the questions normally by copying the last word that you voiced and then appears to be processing the information and providing a response in a slow and awkward manner. Many of the names are not spelled correctly. Most of the responses are on the level of one word to short phrases."

Post-Assignment Controls

- The interpreter can meet with the clinician to explain that the language is not typical for someone with his educational experience and language exposure.
- The interpreter, depending on the goal of the environment and whether his or her assignment will continue beyond this session, could consider use of a certified Deaf interpreter, gestures, pictures, manipulatives, etc., for future appointments.
- The interpreter could continue expanding his or her own fund of knowledge base in working with consumers who are dysfluent by reading articles, taking trainings, etc.

Thus, the interpreter has many options and goes through a complicated decision making process.

Using a Certified Deaf Interpreter or Communication Specialist

When most hearing interpreters are asked how they work with extremely dysfluent consumers, their response is often, "call in a certified deaf interpreter (CDI)." The use of such a communication specialist, typically a deaf individual who has exceptional communication abilities, including in visual gestural communication, is one solution to communicating with deaf people with severe language dysfluency. Both the Deaf Unit at Westborough State Hospital in Massachusetts and the Bailey Deaf Unit at Greil Hospital in Alabama rely heavily upon a staff communication specialist whose many roles include that of intermediary interpreter between staff who do not sign expertly and language dysfluent deaf patients. There are now programs to train and certify deaf relay interpreters and the role of CDI is becoming increasingly recognized (Bienvenue & Colonomos, 1992; Boudreault, 2005; Forestal, 2005).

However, in the spirit of the Demand-Control schema, with every new control, such as the addition of a CDI, there are resulting demands. There may be few individuals qualified to work as a Deaf interpreter or communication specialist, especially outside large populations of the Deaf community or in rural areas. When the same hearing interpreters are questioned about how frequently they actually work with CDIs, the answer is "not often," even in assignments with language dysfluent consumers. There are even fewer CDIs who are trained to work in mental health settings. An example of a communication specialist, acting as a CDI, working with an interpreter, follows:

A forensic psychologist was interviewing a deaf consumer to determine his competency to stand trial. The hearing forensic psychologist asked "Do you know who the judge is and what their role is?" The hearing interpreter signed this for the deaf interpreter, who in turn proceeded with various interpretation attempts. The hearing interpreter provided a narrative interpretation of what was going on for the forensic psychologist explaining: "The interpreter has used signs that are generally accepted in the Deaf Community to ask your question and the consumer was not responsive and looked somewhat confused or unsure. The interpreter then used an expansive technique where he describes the 'man up front with the black robe and a gavel' and the consumer still did not respond in a way that indicated he understood the question. The interpreter is now using a gestural system of describing a television set as a box that you watch and change channels, to which the consumer responded by nodding affirmatively. The interpreter is describing through gesture an old black and white television show, such as *Perry Mason*, where the judge wore a black robe and had a white wig. The consumer nodded affirmatively that he had recognized what the interpreter was explaining. The interpreter then asked using a combination of basic signs and gestures 'Who is he?' 'What does he do? What is his job?' and the consumer shrugged that he did not know."

If the hearing interpreter had chosen to simply wait until the deaf interpreter had completed the interpretation and voiced "no," the psychologist would have no understanding of language skills of the consumer, which is directly relevant to the issue of competence (Solow, 1988; Vernon & Miller, 2001, 2005; Vernon & Raifman, 1997). Most clinicians would want this level of detail about the consumer's language skills and the interpreting process in order to draw appropriate conclusions regarding issues like mental status and competency.

When two interpreters work in tandem, while striving for collaboration, they may struggle over varying opinions regarding the communication process. For example, a hearing psychologist was interviewing a deaf consumer with the aid of a hearing interpreter and a communication specialist/CDI. A question was passed from the psychologist to the interpreter to the CDI, and when the deaf consumer began to respond, the interpreter began to voice the response. However, at that moment, the communication specialist stopped the interpreter and told her, "I will tell you what to voice when I'm done." The deaf interpreter then tells the hearing interpreter to voice a response that the hearing interpreter believes is much clearer than the consumer actually was presenting. The hearing interpreter acquiesced. When asked later why she acquiesced to the CDI, the interpreter responded, "because he (the communication specialist) was deaf."

The dilemma inherent in this situation is that the hearing interpreter and the CDI have information about the language level and processing ability of the consumer that the clinician needs but is unaware of. This disconnect can impact not only the understanding that the clinician has regarding the mental status of the consumer, but also the clinician and consumer's ability to develop a therapeutic relationship. In addition, the hearing interpreter and the CDI disagree about the appropriate interpretation, but the clinician is not aware of their disagreement. This too effects the clinician's assessment of the client's mental status.

While the use of a CDI or communication specialist is highly valued for their language competency, there are important factors to consider in mental health settings. In the same way that naive clinicians imagine that the provision of an interpreter fixes all the communication problems, the provision of a deaf interpreter can allow the hearing interpreter to believe that now "all is good." In reality, language interpretation remains a highly complex process, even when the client is a fluent language user. The interpreter or interpreting team are making complicated choices which can influence the assessments that clinicians make.

Little research or training has been done to address the dynamics of a deaf/hearing interpreter team in mental health settings. Because neither hearing nor deaf interpreters have training in analyzing demands that may occur within this partnership, the controls may not always be appropriate for mental health settings. They may not realize that clinicians are not just interested in communicating. They are interested in understanding how the consumer thinks. An interpreting process that "cleans up" dysfluent language can lead a clinician doing a psychological assessment to draw wrong conclusions. The risk for this is heightened when CDIs are brought in for work with very dysfluent consumers.

Despite the potential challenges that may arise when adding another team member to the process, there are many benefits of using a certified deaf interpreter. The deaf interpreter can help ensure a more accurate understanding of the message, provide balance to any perceived hearing vs. deaf hierarchies, provide clarification to obscure or dysfluent language and allow for linguistic or cultural collaboration to ensure that the best possible determination is made. In addition, the level of skill required to do ASL to English interpreting and the level of skill required to interpret for very dysfluent signers are different. Sometimes the interpreting process won't be successful without the help of someone with the exceptional language and nonverbal communication skills typically possessed by CDIs.

Implications for Clinicians

Clinicians who do not speak the consumer's language are at a huge disadvantage in assessing their strengths, weaknesses, and potential areas of psychopathology. They are also at a huge disadvantage in lacking an appreciation of what is culturally and linguistically normative for these consumers. They should, therefore, be very conservative in drawing diagnostic conclusions.

Clinicians inexperienced with deaf people, using a disability perspective of deaf people, may not realize that the same cross-cultural dynamics apply. Whereas they may know to be careful in drawing diagnostic conclusions when working with, for example, a Vietnamese speaking person, where the language and cultural differences are obvious, they may not realize that they need to be equally cautious, for the same cross-cultural reasons, in working with many deaf consumers. Even if they picked up somewhere that the Deaf Community has a culture, and that ASL is a real language, they are unlikely to be familiar with the huge variation in language abilities among deaf people, the high numbers of deaf persons seen in clinical settings with dysfluent language skills, and the significance of this for assessment and treatment of the person.

Interpreters are also often unprepared for the problem of language dysfluency. Mental health interpreting as a specialization is fairly new, and most interpreters don't have this specialization. They may have never learned how mental illness or other brain pathology can effect language patterns, and may not realize that the clinician most likely wants to know not just what the patient says, but how he or she said it. The combination of clinicians unfamiliar with deaf people and interpreters unfamiliar with mental health interpreting sets the stage for the clinician to make clinical mistakes. Clinicians working with signing deaf people need to be aware of the possibility (in some clinical settings, we can even say *likelihood*), that their clients are not fluent users of a signed language, that these language dysfluencies are sometimes very severe, and that the disparity between the language and *thought worlds* (Namy, 1977; Pollard, 1998b) of hearing, non-signing clinicians and these clients can be immense. Some implications of this follow.

1.   Are the language problems noticed? Because both the clinician and the interpreter can be unprepared for the challenges of work with very language dysfluent persons, there is a good chance that the language problems will be masked by the interpreting process. Interpreters generally understand their role to be to facilitate communication, to make it

happen, and therefore they strive to make sense of the language patterns they see. Deaf interpreters are sometimes brought in when the deaf person is especially dysfluent, and their job can be to make sense of the most dysfluent language, to communicate with the person in any way possible. Clinicians, in turn, are often uncomfortable because they cannot communicate in their native language (Schlesinger & Meadow, 1972), and they also want their clients to make sense if only to allay their own anxiety as clinicians. Deaf people may also work hard to pretend to understand when they don't. The *pull* to mask language problems can come, then, from all sides.

Sometimes interpreters will attempt to explain to clinicians that particular phrases can't be interpreted verbatim. The clinician wants to ask, "how has your mood been in the last two weeks?" The interpreter knows that the client does not know the sign for "mood" and that this question will have to be *unpacked* further, asking about specific moods. The interpreter may also know that this particular client is not skilled in using time references such as "in the last two weeks" and needs to be shown a calendar. The interpreter tries to explain this, but many an impatient, linguistically naïve clinician has brushed off the discussion, insisting that the interpreter just "sign what I say." The interpreter then realizes this is not someone they can educate or collaborate with so they stop discussing the linguistic challenges and allow the clinician to remain in the dark.

Clinicians, therefore, need to be receptive to discussions with interpreters, in pre or post sessions, about the interpreting challenges and process. While interpreters should never comment on mental status, their willingness to discuss language and the interpreting process can be very illuminating. Clinicians should keep in mind that this pertains mainly to work with language dysfluent clients. More linguistically sophisticated deaf persons can speak for themselves, and interpreters will usually be reluctant to do anything, such as talking about their language skills, which may seem to disempower deaf consumers.

2. When both clinician and interpreter are aware of the problem of language dysfluency, and the various interpreting options discussed above, the clinician is left with the challenge of understanding what the dysfluent language means. Clinicians who are new to this problem should err on the side of delaying judgment. It is simply too easy to make a mistake. However, clinicians who are more familiar with this problem can explore the kind of language errors that the consumer makes and at least draw hypotheses about what these may mean.

While our knowledge of the meaning of sign language problems is very elementary, there are some rules of thumb that help. Psychosis does not usually cause a person to lose the ability to form a grammatical sentence. Persons who are psychotic do not forget how to form tense, for instance, or usually omit major parts of speech like nouns and verbs. Generally, most of their grammar is still intact. They will still say, "I sit" and "he sits" and not forget to inflect the verb. Sign language problems such as limited vocabulary, absence of time references or grammatical indicators of tense, and the inability to construct a simple, grammatically correct sentence, are most likely due to sign language deprivation, though there may be an underlying neurological contributor. By contrast, deaf people who are psychotic are more likely to show other kinds of language problems. They are more likely to make bizarre comments (which are still grammatical), to show "loose" thinking, the inability to connect ideas, or to go off on tangents and possibly never get back to the point. They may speak or sign quickly, be difficult to interrupt, or show other non-verbal indicators of distress. People who normally can communicate well with the person will tell you that they are normally clearer. There is usually behavioral evidence of change. The person has stopped sleeping or attending to hygiene and clothing. They are not following their normal daily schedule. They are doing something which is bizarre such as getting up in the middle of the night because they are expecting a visit from a childhood friend at that time, or their comments are bizarre. Language deprivation does not cause someone to think, as one deaf psychiatric patient told the first author, that Osama bin Laden was sending him secret messages. Conclusions regarding psychosis need to be drawn from the total package, and of course possible medical causes have to be ruled out.

It's very helpful to know something about the language history of the person. A deaf person who had signing deaf parents and attended a signing Deaf school is likely, in the absence of major brain pathology, to sign well. Often there are informants available, sometimes including the interpreter, who have known the person for some time and can comment on their prior language skills. A sudden, dramatic decline in language abilities suggests strongly either a head trauma or aphasia or an acute psychotic reaction. Inside Deaf programs, competently signing staff often notice that when clients show deteriorating or changing language skills, this heralds a change in mental status. Usually, the client becomes much less clear, but some clients have been observed to change how they sign, more or less English like, or making some other changes, depending on their mental and emotional state. Signing clinicians who have worked with particular clients for a long time can see these changes in sign language skills just as hearing clinicians can with the speech patterns of familiar clients.

3.   In Deaf mental health care, communication challenges overlap with clinical challenges, and sorting them out can become a major focus of attention. Sometimes communication challenges lead to clinical problems, and addressing the communication problem well can be an effective clinical intervention. This is illustrated by the following case story from the Westborough Deaf Unit that involved the first author.

A patient we'll call Joe was hospitalized on the Deaf Unit after he told staff in his hearing day program and group home that he wanted to kill himself. Joe was mildly developmentally delayed, a graduate of a Deaf residential school, and could use ASL to communicate basic needs. The first author, a hearing, second language user of ASL, thought that Joe's ASL was reasonably good for communicating basic needs. Joe used complete, grammatical sentences, had no trouble telling a clear story, used tense features correctly, etc. He and the rest of the clinical team quickly determined that Joe was not depressed or suicidal. Rather, Joe was not able to articulate his feelings well and to resolve conflicts with other people. He was living and working in environments where most of the people he interacted with signed poorly or not at all. He was very frustrated by this, especially as he had the prior experience, from attending a Deaf residential school, of communicating easily with people around him. Joe was not able to express his frustration well, and the people around him would not be able to understand him if he did. He couldn't say, "I'm frustrated because no one here communicates with me well. I want to be around other deaf people." Instead, he said, "I hate hearing people," and when this didn't get the right response, he upped the ante to "I want to kill myself." That statement got a reaction, though not the one he wanted. It got him hospitalized.

Joe was very adept at pretending to understand people, at giving the "empty nod" when he didn't understand them. It was very likely that the hearing people he interacted with did the same thing, and that they colluded to pretend that everything was fine. It was also very likely that the administrators and case managers who oversaw his living and day program placements wanted to believe that they served him well because they didn't want the expense and hassle of moving him to an out of area Deaf placement. They had a few hearing staff who signed minimally, and they pretended that this was enough for Joe. They made the mistake of thinking that because Joe was not a sophisticated signer, he didn't need to work with sophisticated signers. Just the reverse was true. Joe needed to work with very sophisticated signers who could match his communication abilities and help them develop. No such staff were available. No one was able to communicate even adequately with Joe, much less help develop the psychosocial skills he needed such as the ability to recognize and label his feelings and engage in problem solving strategies. In this dysfunctional, inappropriate communication environment, Joe developed angry and hostile behaviors, made statements, which appeared pathological, about hating hearing people and wanting to die. In the worst case, but all too common scenario, the result of these environmental barriers would be that he'd become diagnosed with a serious mental illness, put on psychiatric medications, and then returned to the same dysfunctional settings. This, alas, is the rule, not the exception, about how hearing people usually respond to deaf persons with similar problems.

In Joe's case, as in the cases of many deaf persons who are referred in psychiatric crisis, the clinical challenges cannot be separated from the communication challenges. Joe reported that he was suicidal because he literally lacked the words to describe his emotions accurately and to use language for problem solving. The linguistically inappropriate environment in which he lived and worked made this problem worse.

This case illustrates how, when working with deaf consumers, attending well to communication dynamics is a core clinical task. It is certainly not something a clinician can be casual about. The clinical problems are very often embedded in the communication challenges, and how expertly the communication challenges are handled can make the difference between the client re-experiencing the same communication challenges in the treatment process, thereby becoming retraumatized, and actually getting assistance.

4.   As explained above, handling communication challenges expertly often means bringing a second, deaf interpreter into the process. In the case of signing clinicians, including deaf ASL users, who do not have a CDI's level of communication skill, it means working alongside of a CDI. This is illustrated by continuing our account of what happened to Joe on the Deaf Unit.

When the hearing signing staff on the Deaf Unit, including the first author, started working with Joe, we thought we were clear and understood each other. But when our deaf communication specialist and other native signers observed our work, they checked in with him about his understanding and exposed the inadequate communication that was occurring with us hearing signers. Joe was so skilled at pretending to understand that he fooled hearing signers with a great deal of experience. The team then developed a treatment plan which had the communication specialist working alongside the hearing psychologist and all other signing staff, including the deaf Social Worker, whenever treatment was conducted.

The treatment plan the team developed was essentially a plan to teach Joe better communication skills. Part of the plan involved having Joe practice telling people that he didn't understand them. With the help of the communication specialist, the inadequate communication was exposed, and Joe's pretense of understanding was interrupted. The communication specialist would challenge Joe, "Did you understand? What did he say?" When Joe couldn't reply, the communication specialist would coach him to say, "I don't understand you. We need help from a better signer." The staff who worked with him then took responsibility for not signing well enough and validated his response. "Thank you for telling me. I didn't realize I wasn't clear. You did a great job of expressing this clearly. Now I understand you better." This was practiced over and over. Joe was also helped to identify feelings (e.g.," I feel frustrated. I feel lonely. I want to be around other deaf people."). As the team worked with Joe over a few weeks, any indication he might have had of depression disappeared. The unit psychiatrist was in fact able to take Joe off of medication.[7] Finally, the Social Worker organized a case conference in which Joe, with the full backing of the team, communicated clearly for the first time with his case manager and program staff. He told them, "I don't want to die. I want to be around deaf people."

In Deaf mental health care, clinicians understand the kinds of language skills and deficits that clients show, and, whether the clinicians themselves sign or not, draw upon the appropriate resources to ensure effective communication. Sometimes this will mean the inclusion of a CDI. However, the purpose of the clinical work matters a great deal. When the purpose is clinical assessment, clinicians need to take special care that the interpreting resources they draw upon are not covering over the language problems a consumer has. Ideally, this is done by talking with the interpreter(s) in pre and post sessions about the interpreting and assessment process, and agreeing upon a strategy for handling dysfluent language. When the purpose is treatment, this is less a concern, but good clinicians always attend not just to what is said, but how it is said, and interpreters need to understand that also.

Conclusions Regarding Best Practices

In this chapter, we've been describing best practice for interpreters and clinicians in mental health settings working with deaf persons with severe language dysfluency. Best practice assumes that clinicians and interpreters are both very familiar with the widely different communication skills that deaf people have, and the frequency with which one encounters deaf persons who are dysfluent in their best language, a signed language. However, it is relatively rare for this to happen. It is far more common for one or both of members of the team to be unprepared for the interpreting and clinical challenges of evaluation and treatment of deaf dysfluent signers. What, then, might be some "rules of thumb" for interpreters and clinicians just becoming aware of this issue?

First, it is important to educate oneself about language dysfluency. For interpreters, this means getting specialized training in mental health interpreting and practicing the strategies for interpreting for language dysfluent consumers. The Mental Health Interpreter Training (MHIT) developed by the Alabama Office of Deaf Services provides such training. Dean and Pollard's Demand-Control approach (2001, 2005) is particularly helpful to guide interpreter decision making and has been incorporated as a part of the aforementioned MHIT. For clinicians, it means pursuing appropriate consultation and supervision regarding evaluation and treatment of deaf persons. For interpreters, it means seeking supervision from an interpreter mentor.

Second, it is important that the interpreter and clinician have pre- and post-sessions with each other in which the language, cultural and clinical issues can be discussed. Interpreters and clinicians need to ask each other whether they are comfortable having this discussion. Clinicians need to be aware that the expertise of interpreters usually extends to language and culture, not to psychology. They need to develop skill in asking interpreters the appropriate questions. Interpreters should recognize that they have the option of not just interpreting but also being a language and culture informant. Interpreters will generally be more comfortable in such a role where it is clear the deaf consumer cannot speak for themselves on the subject.

Third, clinicians who are inexperienced in collaborating with interpreters, who are themselves monolingual and uninformed about language differences, are advised to approach this task with humility. Insisting that the interpreter just "interpret what I say, word for word" reflects gross naiveté about language and marks you as a difficult person to work with. It also puts the interpreters into an impossible bind. They *cannot do it.* Languages don't map upon each other in this simple way. It is much more effective to discuss with the interpreter the interpreting challenges and agree upon some interpretation strategy together.

Fourth, collaboration with certified deaf interpreters is becoming a best practice when working with clients who are dysfluent, but both kinds of interpreters need training in mental health work. They need to understand that clinicians doing diagnostic assessments need to know about the language skills of consumers. They do not usually want the interpreting process to mask the language deficits of clients because language usage is a primary means by which clinicians make inferences about mental processes. Clinicians, especially those who sign already, need the humility to draw upon this additional resource, and everyone needs practice managing this complex process.

The key idea really is collaboration. Clinicians and interpreters are a team of professionals working together. It helps interpreters to understand the reasons for dysfluency and the clinical implications. It helps clinicians to understand the interpreting decision making process when working with dysfluent clients. Best practice must surely be a clinician-interpreter(s) team skilled in responding to this formidable interpreting and clinical challenge.

Notes

1. The authors wish to thank Robert Pollard and Robyn Dean for their helpful review of this manuscript.
2. An earlier version of this chapter was printed in the 2011 *Journal of Interpreting.* The revised version is reprinted here with permission from the *JOI.*
3. See Chapter 1.

4. This could be explained as follows: "I will attempt to provide you with a rough equivalent of the concepts expressed as one possible interpretation. However, the English words that I am presenting are not a complete representation of the signs being conveyed, as single words do not exist in a vacuum and need the structure of the sentence for its complete meaning to be understood."
5. The interviewer's ASL is glossed here to illustrate that the interviewer is not language dysfluent in English. The glossing just makes it appear so.
6. Identifying details have been changed to protect confidentiality.
7. Exposing how such environmental communication problems contribute to the clinical problems of deaf people, *not* diagnosing them but diagnosing the dysfunctional environment, and taking them off of medication, is in fact one of the key functions of a quality Deaf treatment program. See Chapter 1.

References

Altshuler, K. (1971). Studies of the deaf: Relevance to psychiatric theory. *American Journal of Psychiatry, 127*, 1521–1526.

Altshuler, K. Z., & Rainer, J. D. (Eds.). (1968). *Mental health and the deaf: Approaches and prospects*. Washington, DC: U.S. Department of Health, Education and Welfare.

Ash, S., Moore, P., Antani, S., McCrawley, G., Work, M., & Grossman, M. (2006). Trying to tell a tale: Discourse impairments in progressive aphasia and front temporal dementia. *Neurology*, 1405–1413.

Bienvenue, M., & Colonomos, B. (1992). Relay interpreting in the 90's. In L. Swabey (Ed.), *The challenge of the 90's: New standards in interpreter education, Proceedings of the eighth national convention of interpreter trainers* (pp. 69–80). Pomona, CA: Conference of Interpreter Trainers.

Black, P. (2005). *Language dysfluency in the Deaf inpatient population* (Unpublished doctoral dissertation). Fielding University, Santa Barbara, California.

Black, P., & Glickman, N. (2005). Language deprivation in the Deaf inpatient population. *JADARA, 39*(1), 1–28.

Boudreault.P. (2005). Deaf interpreters. In T. Janzen (Ed.), *Topics in sign language interpreting: Theory and practice* (pp. 323–355). Philadelphia, PA: John Benjamins.

Bowe, F. G. (2004). Economics and adults identified as low-functioning Deaf. *Journal of Disability Policy Studies, 15*(1), 43–49.

Dean, R. K., & Pollard, R. Q. (2001). The application of demand-control theory to sign language interpreting: Implications for stress and interpreter training. *Journal of Deaf Studies and Deaf Education, 6*(1), 1–14.

Dean, R. K., & Pollard, R. Q. (2005). Consumers and service effectiveness in interpreting work: A practice profession perspective. In M. Marschark, R. Peterson, & E. Winston (Eds.), *Interpreting and interpreter education: Directions for research and practice* (pp. 259–282). New York, NY: Oxford University Press.

Dean, R. K. & Pollard, R. Q. (2011). The importance, challenges, and outcomes of teaching context-based ethics in interpreting: A demand control schema perspective. *Interpreter and Translator Trainer, 5*(1), 155–182.

Denmark, J. (1985). A study of 250 patients referred to a department of psychiatry for the deaf. *British Journal of Psychiatry, 146*, 282–286.

Denmark, J. (1994). *Deafness and mental health*. London: Jessica Kingsley.

Dew, D. W. (Ed.). (1999). *Serving individuals who are low-functioning deaf*. Washington, DC: The George Washington University Regional Rehabilitation Continuing Education Program.

Forestal, E. (2005). The emerging professionals: Deaf interpreters and their views and experiences in training. In M. Marschark, R. Peterson & E. Winston (Eds.), *Sign language interpreting and interpreter education: Directions for research and practice* (pp. 235–258). New York, NY: Oxford University Press.

Glickman, N. (2007). Do you hear voices?: Problems in assessment of mental status in deaf person with severe language deprivation. *Journal of Deaf Studies and Deaf Education, 12*(2), 127–147.

Glickman, N. (2009). *Cognitive behavioral therapy for deaf and hearing persons with language and learning challenges.* New York, NY: Routledge.

Grinker, R., Vernon, M., Mindel, E., Rothstein, D., Easton, H., Koh, S., Collums , L. (1969). *Psychiatric diagnosis, therapy and research on the psychotic deaf* (No. Research Grant number RD-2407-S). Washington, DC: U.S. Department of Health, Education and Welfare.

Karlin, T. (2003). "Umm, the interpreter didn't understand": Interpreting for individuals with though disorder. *Views, 20*(4), 1–11.

Klima, E., & Bellugi, U. (1979). *The signs of language.* Cambridge, MA: Harvard University Press.

Long, G., Long, N., & Ouellette, S. E. (1993). Service provision issues with traditionally underserved persons who are deaf. In O. M. Welch (Ed.), *Research and practice in deafness: Issues and questions in education, psychology and vocational service provision* (pp. 107–126). Springfield, IL: Charles C. Thomas.

Mathay, G., & LaFayette, R. H. (1990). Low achieving deaf adults: an interview survey of service providers. *Journal of the American Deafness and Rehabilitation Association, 24*(1), 23–32.

Miller, K. R. (2004). Linguistic diversity in a Deaf prison population: Implications for due process. *Journal of Deaf Studies and Deaf Education, 9*(1), 112–119.

Morgan, G., Herman, R., & Woll, B. (2007). Language impairments in sign language: Breakthroughs and puzzles. *Internal Journal of Language and Communication Disorders, 42*(1), 97–105.

Namy, C. (1977). Reflections on the training of simultaneous interpreters: A metalinguistic approach. In D. Gerver & H. W. Sinaiko (Eds.), *Language interpreting and communication* (pp. 22–33). New York, NY:: Plenum.

Pantel, P., & Dekang, L. (2000). *Proceedings of the First Meeting of the North American Chapter of the Association for Computational Linguistics* (pp 78–85). Stroudsburg, PA: Association for Computational Linguistics.

Poizner, H., Klima, E. S., & Belllugi, U. (1987). *What the hands reveal about the brain.* Cambridge, MA: The MIT Press.

Pollard, R. (1998a). *Mental health interpreting: A mentored curriculum* [Videotape and users' guide]. Rochester, NY: University of Rochester School of Medicine.

Pollard, R. (1998b). Psychopathology. In M. Marschark & M. D. Clark (Eds.), *Psychological perspectives on deafness* (Vol. 2, pp. 171–197). Mahwah, NJ: Erlbaum.

RID. (2007). *Interpreting in mental health settings standard practice paper*: Registry of interpreters for the deaf. Alexandria, VA: Author.

Russell, D. L. (2002). *Interpreting in legal contexts: Consecutive and simultaneous interpretation.* Burtonsville, MD: Linstok Press/Sign Media Inc.

Schaller, S. (1991). *A man without words.* Los Angeles: University of California Press.

Schlesinger, H. S., & Meadow, K. P. (1972). *Sound and sign: Childhood deafness and mental health.* Berkeley: California University Press.

Solow, S. N. (1988). Interpreting for minimally linguisticallly competent individuals. *The Court Manager, 3*(2), 18–21.

Thacker, A. (1994). Formal communication disorder: Sign language in deaf people with schizophrenia. *British Journal of Psychiatry, 165,* 818–823.

Thacker, A. (1998). *The manifestation of schizophrenic formal communication disorder in sign language* (Unpublished doctoral dissertation). St. George Hospital Medical School, London, England.

Trumbetta, S., Bonvillian, J., Siedlecki Jr., T., & Hasins, B. (2001). Language-related symptoms in persons with schizophrenia and how deaf persons may manifest these symptoms. *Sign Language Studies, 1*(3), 228–253.

Vernon, M., & Andrews, J. F. (1990). *The psychology of deafness.* New York, NY: Longman.

Vernon, M., & Miller, K. (2001). Linguistic incompetence to stand trial: A unique condition in some deaf defendants. *Journal of Interpretation*, 99–120.

Vernon, M., & Miller, K. (2005). Obstacles faced by deaf people in the criminal justice system. *American Annals of the Deaf, 150*(3), 283–291.

Vernon, M., & Raifman, L. J. (1997). Recognizing and handling problems of incompetent deaf defendants charged with serious offenses. *International Journal of Law and Psychiatry, 20*(3), 373–387.

4 Creating a Culturally Affirmative Continuum of Mental Health Services

The Experiences of Three States[1]

Michael John Gournaris, Steve Hamerdinger, and Roger C. Williams

At 26, Cathy (not her real name) had spent 7 years in and out of state psychiatric hospitals. She had been given a host of diagnostic labels from personality disorder to schizophrenia to mental retardation. Cathy communicated with mental health providers in ways as varied as her diagnosis, from writing to using her speech to the occasional use of an interpreter. Her speech was often very difficult to understand; however, she could be understood through American Sign Language (ASL). In addition, her prognosis was poor. With a long history of mental illness and aggressive behaviors and little support from community and family, she was destined to spend the foreseeable future shuttling in and out of hospitals. However, Cathy now lives in an independent apartment and has not been hospitalized in over a decade. This cure was not the result of some new miracle medication. It occurred because Cathy was fortunate enough to be living in a state with a comprehensive continuum of mental health services for deaf individuals. She is in the process of recovery, still dealing with a serious mental illness and frustrated by being unable to secure employment. But she has a psychiatrist, a case manager, and a clinician with whom she can communicate directly and a community of friends and peers to offer support and assistance. In this chapter, we will explore how those services have been developed and why they can be an effective and efficient solution to what is a serious and persistent challenge in many states.

Mental health services provided to consumers who are deaf in communities throughout America vary widely in quantity and quality depending on which state or city in which the consumer lives. Some deaf consumers have access to excellent specialized programs but, most commonly, deaf consumers are a vastly underserved minority within the larger behavioral health system, if they are served at all. The term "mental health services"[2] will be used as inclusive of the identification, assessment, diagnosis, and treatment of deaf individuals with mental health needs (National Association of the Deaf, 2003).

The deaf people we are addressing throughout this book chapter use ASL or a visual-gestural communication system. Although some deaf individuals have fluency in written English, more commonly they are not fluent English users. These consumers often experience difficulties and frustration when seeking mental health care because the system sees them as merely people who happen not to hear, rather than consumers who are linguistically, culturally, and phenomenologically different from consumers who hear. Consider Cathy, described in the opening paragraphs. The services that she received initially were not effective with her. For example, providers not used to working with deaf consumers did not notice that when she changed from using ASL to sign-supported speech, this was correlated with an increase in psychotic ideation. They did not appreciate why her mother's side of her family, where she had numerous deaf relatives, was more important to her than her father's (even though she had little contact with her mother). She thought that when hearing people were talking, and she could not understand, that they were plotting against her. This paranoia resulted in acts of aggressive behavior, which appeared out of the blue, to hearing staff and peers. All of these additional challenges resulted in Cathy staying in inpatient settings, despite interpreters and "access" being provided to good programs in the community.

Providers often encourage deaf consumers to "lip-read" and speak for themselves to avoid the trouble or expense of getting an interpreter while being oblivious to the fact that communication is not happening (Critchfield, 2006). Communication between a hearing therapist and a deaf individual often does not work well (and certainly nowhere at the level of two individuals communicating in the same language) when both individuals are restricted to lip reading or written English. Typically, mental health providers and other service professionals lack awareness of the language barriers that deaf consumers encounter on a daily basis, or misunderstand them in ways that can have a potentially deleterious effect. They are unaware of how their attempts to make deaf people communicate in English may be re-traumatizing, creating conditions which replay oppressive experiences deaf people have had throughout their lives. The "treatment" begins to resemble the stressors that underline the original problems.

A body of research shows that deaf consumers with mental health issues are less likely to be *appropriately* diagnosed or treated, because many mental health clinicians are not properly trained to work with them (Haskins, 2004; Mathos, Kilbourne, Myers, & Post, 2009; Pollard, 1994). While there is evidence that deaf people are more likely to develop personality and/or adjustment disorders (Gentile & McCarthy, 1973; Graham & Rutter, 1968; Meadow, 1981), they are no more or less likely to develop biological mental illness such as schizophrenia than hearing people (Vernon, 1980). The combination of language and cultural differences, high prevalence rates for behavioral problems, and clinician unfamiliarity with deaf people results in a high probability of misdiagnosis with a psychotic disorder (Vernon & Greenberg, 1999; Glickman, 2009; Pollard, 1998).

It is not uncommon for providers in mental health systems to protest that their services are "accessible." Accessible and appropriate are not the same thing. Appropriate, or as Glickman (2003) called "culturally affirmative" service provision goes beyond the standard of reasonable accommodations. It is a higher standard. As Glickman noted, providing an interpreter or a clinician with some signing skills may meet the letter of the law, but more often than not it creates an "illusion of inclusion" (Glickman & Gulati, 2003, p. 8). The barriers to creating real access for many deaf consumers are much more formidable.

Culturally affirmative mental health treatment for deaf persons means that they receive services from ASL-fluent clinicians working in programs tailored to their particular strengths (Glickman, 2003, 2009) and that these clinicians know when and how to supplement their communication with auxiliary aids, such as gesture, props, drawings, and role playing to enhance communication with deaf consumers and have minimal or no understanding of ASL (or any other language, for that matter).

A special note needs to be taken of a type of communication access provided by deaf interpreters. Deaf interpreters are individuals who have native fluency and have had training and experience in visual-gestural communication. Deaf interpreters specialize in use of gesture, props, drawings, and other tools to enhance communication. They are an important part of service delivery in a culturally affirmative program. The use of deaf interpreters with deaf people with minimal ASL skills are a crucial part of mental health services provided in Alabama and other places, *even when the clinician is a fluent ASL user.*

The Current State of Treatment for Deaf Consumers

While very few consumers with disabilities are well served by the nation's mental health system, deaf consumers have been identified as the most underserved of any disability group (Basil, 2000). Lack of visibility and lack of advocacy are two common reasons the Deaf Community is underserved. Leigh, Powers, Vash, and Nettles (2004) found that both of these reasons are closely correlated to the lack of funding for services and expertise in working with people with disabilities including deaf consumers. Very few insurance networks provide direct outreach to deaf individuals, and insurance case managers are not likely to be aware of the availability of, or the need for, culturally and linguistically affirmative mental health services in their regions (Mathos et al., 2009). Critchfield (2002) notes that insurance provider networks often do not include clinicians who are fluent in ASL even when they live in the same geographic area. Clinicians who are trained in working with consumers who are deaf may not be a member of a particular provider network. Even when that network has no provider with competencies in working with deaf people, the carrier may be unwilling to refer to an out of network provider with such competencies. Thus, the treatment options available to deaf consumers are considerably less and often do not include any clinician who has the language and other competencies needed to work well with them.

Current population estimates indicate that there are approximately 28 million deaf and hard-of-hearing Americans (National Association of the Deaf, 2003) and Dew (1999) concluded that this group represents the largest "physical disability group" in America. Estimates of the number of deaf people (not including hard of hearing) vary widely but a conservative estimate would be 5 million individuals (Steinmetz, 2006). Estimates of how many deaf people use sign language exclusively vary wildly, but 500,000 may be the best estimate possible at this time, given the lack of an accurate count (Mitchell, Young, Bachleda, & Karchmer, 2006). This is consistent with the prevalence rate reported by the Alabama Department of Mental Health, where consistently since mid-2009, 1.8 out of every 1,000 people served by the public system have been deaf (Hamerdinger, 2011).

If we accept estimates of the prevalence of mental illness published by the National Institute of Mental Health (Kessler, Chiu, Demler, & Walters, 2005), 6% of the general population have a severe and persistent mental illness, the admission criterion for most publicly funded mental health services. There would then be 30,000 deaf people with a severe mental illness needing services in ASL. As noted by Kessler et al. (2006), the prevalence of any mental health disorder is 26.2% in the general population. With this figure, it is estimated that approximately 130,000 deaf people living in the United States will require mental health services in ASL. The number of deaf consumers who receive services from specially trained clinicians is only a small fraction of those who actually receive mental health services (Pollard, 1999; Vernon & Andrews, 1990).

In most urban areas within the United States, it is possible to find an ASL interpreter to facilitate communication in general settings. Many of these interpreters would be considered qualified if the only requirement for qualification was the ASL and English competence needed to effectively relay messages between the parties. However, communication in the mental health arena requires much more than language fluency. Having an interpreter involved in very personal and sensitive sessions can seriously inhibit the counseling process. The presence of the third party shifts the interpersonal dynamic of the client/clinician relationship in ways that neither the interpreter nor the clinician may be trained to recognize or address. For example, Gold-Brunson and Lawrence (2002) found that despondent interpreter mood caused significant negative mood changes in deaf clients who participated in the study even when the therapist mood was neutral or cheerful. Harvey (1982, 1989) noted that interpreters may become the object of transference reactions in clients and counter-transference reactions in clinicians. The presence of an interpreter can lead a naïve hearing clinician to imagine that the unique needs of the deaf client have been fully addressed.

While interpreting services can be substantially improved, as evidenced by the work being done in Alabama (described later in this chapter), the use of an interpreter is not a replacement for directly accessible services. Directly accessible services means that the clinician providing the service is able to communicate directly with the client, rather than using an interpreter. For deaf consumers with mental health issues, as well as for their families, language and culture differences continue to pose enormous barriers to use of mental health services.

For half a century, professional organizations, providers in various fields, and the Deaf Community have addressed and advocated for specialized mental health services with trained personnel (National Association of the Deaf [NAD], 2003). NAD (2003) concluded that, as a result of their efforts and those of others in the field, extensive theoretical, policy, and general literature have been developed, distributed, or published on behalf of deaf consumers with mental health needs. This organization created two vital papers in 2003 and 2008 to advocate the mental health needs of deaf people on the national level (NAD 2003, 2008) and most recently released a model "Bill of Rights" for deaf people needing mental health services on the state level (NAD, 2010a, 2010b). In addition, the Americans with Disabilities Act of 1990 and several landmark court cases related to mental health and deaf people have led to the establishment of direct services in certain city limits or regions, but only a few states provide a true continuum of mental health services for this population. Many deaf consumers continue to have limited access to the larger public mental health system. It is imperative for state governments to fund a true statewide coordination of mental health services serving this population and actively recruit existing culturally affirmative mental health providers, from the non-profit and for-profit sectors, to join in a single service continuum ensuring the highest standard of care. The primary objective of this chapter is to compare and contrast the continuum of care for deaf mental health services offered in three American states, gleaning from these experiences lessons for best practice in establishing and running such systems of care.

Statewide Mental Health Models

Throughout the United States there are some excellent local mental health programs and solo practitioners providing deaf people direct access to services. Usually located in large urban areas with high concentrations of deaf people, they are often restricted by funding or host agencies to serving a strictly defined service area. This may be a city, a county, or even a region of several counties. A hearing person living outside the service area of a particular provider would likely be able to find a provider in the area he or she lives. By contrast, deaf persons in need of services living outside the area with a linguistically competent provider will often not receive services.

The low-incidence of deaf people, and the specialized skills required by clinicians working with this population make it impractical for private agencies in areas of low population density to recruit, hire, and maintain adequate staff with a wide range of services for consumers who are deaf. Economic viability is not the only barrier. Even for private agencies serving a population base which would support a single full-time staff member, a lone clinician trying to serve a caseload of deaf consumers faces multiple challenges. The lack of a cross-disciplinary team places that clinician in the situation of trying to single-handedly serve a very heterogeneous population without access to qualified supervision, support, and resources. This leads to higher risks for both the clinician and the consumer. The consumer is at risk for receiving sub-optimal care and the clinician is at risk for burn out, liability problems for working outside of his or her area of expertise, and professional stagnation.

The best way to address these problems is through a statewide delivery system of mental health care. Statewide delivery systems allow the creation of a structure to assist local agencies when they try to serve clients from outside their catchment area. A catchment area is the geographic limitation typically imposed by a funding agency on the area a service agency can serve clients, be it a city, county or some other political restriction. A statewide system can also help to create a team of clinicians across the state to deal with cross-disciplinary issues, and foster peer support and supervision, thereby increasing the appropriateness of the services.

Three different statewide mental health models, those of Minnesota, South Carolina, and Alabama, will be discussed here. These three states do not make any claims that their programs are superior compared to any other program either in the public or private sector. It is, however, our view that working within a state agency gives us a stronger position in defining optimal mental health services for deaf consumers living in our respective states. Working within a state agency also gives state coordinators[3] the authority to write policies and procedures for serving deaf consumers, thereby setting a statewide standard of care, as well as control in distributing grants to private mental health agencies who meet these standards.

Private agencies have some advantages over state agencies. They are less likely to have a unionized workforce and to therefore be limited in meeting the needs of deaf people within the confines of a large collective bargaining agreement. Considerations like seniority, typically very important in union contracts, can work against the recruitment and retention of staff with the specialized skills needed to serve deaf people. Collective bargaining agreements, which serve a large number of mostly hearing workers, can also become obstacles to setting standards, such as for sign language skills, that small Deaf programs may require. If a program wants to prioritize the hiring of deaf employees for a Deaf program, unions will typically oppose this because it would deprive most of their hearing members from the same opportunities to work in these programs. Union officials can argue, just as uninformed administrators can, that sign language skills can be learned quickly on the job.

Private agencies may also be quicker in responding to market conditions, having much more flexibility in personnel decisions. But private agencies are almost never viewed as an "equal" at the table when working with the state mental health departments, especially when they receive grants or funding from the state. They can only affect the treatment programs that they administer and they are highly dependent upon state and federal funding, with its associated mandates, for everything they do. Private vendors typically provide some specific programs or services, such as outpatient treatment or residential programs, and generally do not have the ability to create a full statewide continuum of care.

Minnesota

History

A Deaf services inpatient unit was established at the St. Peter Regional Treatment Center in St. Peter, Minnesota, after four plaintiffs filed a lawsuit in 1984 (*Handel et al. v. Levine et al.,* 1984) for failure to provide adequate inpatient services. The Deaf Unit was in operation for 21 years, from 1985 to 2006. However, in 2006, state officials created the position of Director of Mental Health Program and hired John Gournaris (first author) to restructure services in a way that allows for a larger number of individuals to be served closer to their communities in addition to being cost effective. The Minnesota plan to serve deaf consumers was to create a mobile response team modeled upon the Assertive Community Treatment (ACT) approach. Assertive Community Treatment is generally considered an evidence-based best practice in psychiatric rehabilitation (SAMHSA, 1999). It aims to provide persons with serious mental illness with a local, multi-disciplinary team (psychiatrists, social workers, substance abuse and vocational counselors, nurses, etc.) that can be available to them at all times, preventing the need for more expensive inpatient treatment. The ACT team goes to the consumers, attempting to provide them with what they need, rather than expecting them to go to various programs and fit into that programs' requirements.

While this is a proven model with hearing persons, it is more difficult to implement with deaf persons statewide. Like Wraparound programs, another model that seeks to build a network of support around persons in their home environments, ACT teams are difficult to create when there are not qualified local providers to make up the ACT team. In essence, there are no local service providers to "wrap around" the consumer. Gournaris knew that mental health providers with the specialized skills to work with deaf people did not exist outside the St. Paul/Minneapolis area. He therefore chose to build a service delivery system out of providers who had the specialized skills and have them travel, at the same time expanding the specialized skills offered as more resources became available. In promoting this model, Gournaris is following a basic principal well understood in Deaf mental health care. That is to create centralized Deaf mental health services and have clinicians connected to this service work regionally, getting most of their clinical and administrative supervision from the centralized program office.

The model Gournaris promoted centered on the creation of four regionally based "mental health specialists" with deaf, hard-of-hearing, and deafblind people living in the areas of St. Paul, St. Cloud, Mankato, and Duluth. The mental health specialists have multiple and flexible roles. They provide culturally affirmative mental health services to deaf Minnesotans in all treatment modalities (i.e., individual, couples, family, and sometimes group). They provide expert consultation services to public and private direct care agencies within their regions including advising and educating them to meet to the needs of deaf consumers. The mental health specialists also perform case coordination, aftercare planning, and community placement assistance when working with counties.

Once the new mental health specialists were in place, the Division's outpatient Mental Health Program was able to serve a larger number of deaf consumers (over 1,000% more clients) for 38% less money than were served in the Deaf inpatient unit in St. Peter Regional Treatment Center. In addition, the hospitalizations at the local and state levels were reduced significantly as the program became available statewide for outpatient services. Minnesota statistics revealed that less than 5% of deaf consumers were hospitalized locally between Fiscal Years 2007–2011. As expected, the creation of specialized mental health services statewide decreased the need for the far more expensive state inpatient program.

Model

The Division's Mental Health Program is staffed by mental health specialists, fluent in ASL and experienced in providing direct mental health services to deaf consumers. The program in Minnesota is a stand-alone program that only sees deaf, hard-of-hearing, and deafblind adults for outpatient services (the consumers in prisons and sex offender programs receive treatment separately through state-operated services) and those consumers with minimal mental health issues will qualify for services. The program's scope of services is as follows:

- Crisis Intervention
- Assessment and Stabilization
- Outpatient Therapy
- Telemental Health
- Technical Assistance and Consultation

- Case Coordination
- Aftercare Planning
- Community Placement Assistance

Group Homes

Minnesota has several group homes serving deaf mentally ill adults throughout the state. Very few group homes are deaf-run, like the program in Minneapolis, but many are part of hearing residential programs with some signing staff available. Steps are taken to ensure that deaf consumers are best matched to the group home selected based on individual's needs and the group home's ability to serve them. The Division provides training to the program staff on working with deaf consumers. Even though there is a long waiting list of deaf mentally ill persons needing such residential treatment services, it has been difficult to convince existing programs to expand their services for this group. They key problem, of course, is money. Counties in Minnesota have actually been reducing their reimbursement rates for residential treatment services and vendors do not want to admit persons they cannot serve adequately, much less well.

Grants to Private Vendors

Sometimes state agencies provide services directly. Sometimes they award grants to private vendors to provide particular services. Minnesota does both. The state provides grants to private vendors for additional outpatient treatment, assessment, housing outreach, and a drop-in center for people who are deaf, deaf-blind, hard of hearing, and mentally ill. Consumers can go to the drop-in center for help with specific problems or just to socialize. At this time (2011), virtually all specialized mental health services for deaf children have been provided by vendors receiving money from the state and other sources, not through state programs themselves.

Over the past 7 years, the Division, the Minnesota State Academy for the Deaf (MSAD), and Volunteers of America-Minnesota (VOA) have combined efforts to establish a treatment program that would serve the needs of deaf children and adolescents in Minnesota. All these agencies together fund a program called Deaf/Hard of Hearing Intensive Mental Health Program for Adolescent and Child Treatment or DHH-IMPACT. This program provides three hours of therapy per day, five days a week for each child or adolescent. While intensive, this service is less expensive than residential treatment, and is designed to avoid even more expensive out of state placements. For those students with very severe emotional or behavioral problems, Minnesota has been willing to consider out of state placements.

Programs that depend on state or federal grants are always vulnerable. State run services can be slashed also, but they often have more institutional support making them more resilient. As the 2008–2010 recession hit Minnesota particularly hard, many grants were cut dramatically. Support for highly specialized programs tends to weaken considerably in tough economic times. The economic imperative to save money often drives a mistaken ideological belief that everyone can be served well in mainstreamed programs. At such times, it is especially important to have a position in state government, like a Director of Deaf Mental Health Services, whose job it is to champion such specialized programming.

Chemical Dependency Program

The Minnesota Chemical Dependency Program for Deaf and Hard of Hearing Individuals (MCDPDHH) is an inpatient chemical dependency program located at Fairview Hospital in Minneapolis. This program has been a national resource for deaf persons in recovery since 1989 and is a key part of the continuum of care of mental health services offered for deaf people in Minnesota. Although, this one-of-the-kind substance abuse treatment program is mainly funded by private health plans and is not one of the Division's grantees, collaboration between the Division and MCDPDHH is frequent. People who work and receive services in rehabilitation and clinical programs that serve deaf people find much more of a community with each other and care less about distinctions like public vs. private or even mental health vs. substance abuse. The specialized language and clinical skills tend to trump all other considerations.

Future Goals

It is the Division's goal to establish statewide direct psychiatry and telepsychiatry services to be offered by an ASL-fluent, licensed/board certified psychiatrist skilled in working directly with both children and adults. This concept is modeled after the South Carolina Department of Mental Health, Services for the Deaf and Hard of Hearing. In addition, the Division will continue to explore strategies to launch statewide mental health services for deaf children and adolescents. The biggest barrier to these important initiatives is, again, money. Either the state legislature or other divisions would have to be willing to fund this important service. One of the best arguments we can make, therefore, is that a service like telepsychiatry is both clinically and fiscally effective (Afrin & Critchfield, 1997).

Deaf Minnesotans need better access to the full continuum of mental health services. There is a need for more deaf-run residential services, specialized adult day treatment programs, and deaf-focused partial hospitalization for deaf Minnesotans. While Minnesota has made a beachhead in the statewide mental health service delivery system to date, with a state coordinator and mental health specialists in place as well as grants being distributed, we do not yet have a true continuum of mental health care.

South Carolina

History

In 1988, in response to a Task Force led by representatives from the South Carolina Association of the Deaf and staff from the South Carolina School for the Deaf and the Blind (SCSDB), the South Carolina Department of Mental Health hired a Director for Services to the Deaf and Hard of Hearing. In 1989, the South Carolina Protection and Advocacy for People with Disabilities prepared to file a complaint against the Department of Mental Health for failure to serve deaf consumers. As with much litigation, one individual who was in an inpatient facility was identified and named in the complaint. Not until the impetus of a threatened lawsuit were services established under the leadership of Barry Critchfield, then the Director of Services for the Deaf and Hard of Hearing, Initially, the services were at a single 11-bed inpatient unit at Patrick B. Harris Hospital, in the upstate program of South Carolina. Then an ASL-fluent counselor was hired at each of four mental health centers across the state. In 1994, the McKinney House, a 10-bed Community Residential Care Facility was opened.

Initially, the census at the inpatient unit steadily increased, from an initial 9 inpatients in 1990, to a high of 22 in 1994. With the opening of appropriate community resources, the inpatient census rapidly declined until 2011 when the average census was less than 0.5 (meaning that most days there is no deaf individual on an inpatient basis in the psychiatric facilities). The length of stay has also decreased from an average above 160 days (almost twice as long as for the general population at that time) to an average of 25 days, compared to an average of 28 days for patients who are hearing. This reduction in inpatient stays required outpatient services which were culturally affirmative. While examples abound, attempts by the inpatient team to discharge patients without appropriate community resources were consistently failures. One patient was tried at five different placements with community tenures lasting from 3 weeks to 20 minutes. Once appropriate placements were available, he did not return to the inpatient program.

The outpatient services were consolidated in 2000 and are now being administered and supervised through a single mental health center, even though staff are still stationed in three regional teams throughout the state. This consolidation has allowed for the provision of qualified supervision, and for the supervisors to have middle management support which understands the unique programmatic considerations needed by counselors working with this population. Prior to this consolidation, conflicts and misunderstandings were common between the Deaf Services staff in the field, their hearing supervisors and state level Deaf Services administration. Supervisory staff at a local community mental health center are properly concerned about the services within their catchment area. When

Deaf Services staff had to travel great distances to see consumers in another catchment area, productivity was negatively affected and their ability to see consumers at their "home" center was necessarily reduced. Supervisors, wanting to maintain equity between staff, would expect the same productivity level from Deaf Services staff as from other staff. This would leave staff in the awkward position of either serving hearing consumers at the local center to maintain productivity or serving deaf consumers throughout the larger region and risking possible disciplinary action for lower productivity. There were also questions about why the Deaf Services staff needed to travel to Columbia to meet together as a group once a month when they had weekly staff meetings at their local center.

In 2000, federal block grant funds were identified which enabled the expansion of services to include providing services to children and adolescents with severe emotional disorders.

Model

At the state office of the Department, Roger Williams (third author), the Director of Services for the Deaf and Hard of Hearing, is responsible for overall program direction as well as ensuring that the needs of deaf or hard of hearing consumers are addressed in all Department programs and initiatives. This includes the identification of funding resources and ensuring that the Department policies and procedures reflect the needs of these consumers. Direct services are provided by mental health professionals, fluent in ASL and experienced in providing direct mental health services to deaf consumers, administratively based out of a single mental health center. A half-time psychiatrist provides services to consumers across the state, both in person and through telepsychiatry. A full-time deaf peer support position provides support to deaf consumers across the state. Peer Support Services are still developing in South Carolina but has been well received by consumers and has also provided a way to bring deaf paraprofessionals into the system and provide Medicaid reimbursable services. Two full-time interpreters, both who have completed the Mental Health Interpreter Training program offered by the Office of Deaf Services in Alabama, provide interpreting services for staff and consumers, supplemented by contract interpreting services as needed. The program's scope of services is as follows:

- Crisis Intervention
- Assessment and Stabilization
- Outpatient Therapy
- Telepsychiatry
- Consultation
- Case Management
- Inpatient Services

- Residential Services (both CRCF and supported apartments)
- Aftercare Planning
- Community Placement Assistance

Locations

In order to enhance direct accessibility to mental health services for the deaf and hard of hearing population living in the state of South Carolina, three mental health centers in Simpsonville, Columbia, and Charleston are used as host sites for the regional teams. With these two to four person teams, services are available at any of the 17 mental health centers which reach deaf adults, children, adolescents and their families through a series of satellite offices in all 46 counties of the state. This ensures consumers have direct access to services at the mental health center closest to them. In addition, outpatient services are available for children who attend the residential school for the deaf.

Deaf Psychiatric Unit

As the experience in Minnesota showed, as the community services expanded and residential services were developed, the need for a fully staffed inpatient unit decreased. In 1998, the clinical staff who had been assigned to the inpatient unit at Harris Psychiatric Hospital in Anderson were transferred to the regional outpatient team which serves the upstate region of South Carolina. Starting in 2006, there were no ASL-fluent staff assigned full-time to work within the inpatient psychiatric facilities. As deaf adults or children are admitted to a state psychiatric facility, staff from the community outpatient team provide consultation, direct services, and interpreting services. Because South Carolina has a consolidated public system in which both inpatient and outpatient programs are operated directly by the state mental health agency, it is relatively simple to have this flexibility of staff assignment. This ability to use staff flexibly is very helpful in designing services for deaf people when staff with the requisite skills are hard to find. Although staff productivity inevitably falls when having to serve a consumer in the inpatient unit, a unified program can make that accommodation in the quest for the overall program goal of reducing the length of inpatient stays. For the last 5 years, South Carolina has not had more than one deaf consumer in the facility at any one time, and, in a typical year, there are only deaf consumers in the facility for a third of the year. A new challenge facing South Carolina is to meet the needs of deaf individuals admitted to the sexually violent predator program, which is administered by the Department. As is true for hearing residents of this program, admissions are for extended periods and the number of deaf residents, just two, at present, is too small to justify a comprehensive specialized program. These individuals have specialized treatment needs, in the context of sexual predation, and nationwide there are virtually no clinicians trained in this clinical specialty and fluent in ASL. This makes discharge planning particularly difficult as the Department is prohibited from serving individuals from this program after discharge, unless they also have a severe mental illness.

Residential Programming

South Carolina has one eight-bed residential program which serves exclusively deaf adults who are mentally ill. Residential services are centered on the McKinney House (named for Charlie McKinney, a lifelong advocate for the Deaf Community) in Mauldin which provides a structured living environment for 8 individuals, most commonly as a step-down from the hospital before moving to a more independent setting. The decision to develop a "deaf-only" residential program was not one initially supported by the Mental Health Department's senior administration. Like many individuals not familiar with the Deaf Community, the department Director wanted to integrate deaf consumers into programs in their home community. It took a visit to Chicago to see the Thresholds program and a serendipitous event in which the Director and the Deaf Services staff had a two hour block of time to role play interviewing through an interpreter. He had been asked to present at a conference at Gallaudet University but was scheduled against a well-known deaf presenter. With one exception, the only people who came to his workshop were members of the Deaf Services staff. This rather awkward situation was turned to our advantage as we were able to use the interpreter already present for his workshop to have him attempt to conduct a mental status examination with our staff playing the role of a client. Despite his lengthy clinical experience, he was repeatedly stymied in his efforts to conduct a clinical interview he had performed hundreds if not thousands of times over the years. This frustrating experience was enough to convince him that integrated programming would not be effective.

In addition to the congregate living program, in the same county, as well as in a neighboring county, 12 rent-supported apartment unit complexes are available which provide an alternative for individuals who do not need the more intensive residential program. In South Carolina, we have found that many clients prefer an apartment complex where other deaf clients are in residence. This provides clients with opportunities for peer support with such activities as transportation to food stores and social activities, shared use of videophones and the normative opportunity for interaction with neighbors. This also makes providing case management services easier as we only have to create access with a limited number of landlords and locations. With consumers in other apartment complexes, we often have to repeatedly advocate for visible fire alarms, door bells, and for the landlord to use relay to contact tenants. These dedicated apartments were built with state and federal housing funds and owned by private non-profit community organizations. Having a state level Director for Deaf Services ensures that the needs of the deaf consumers are kept on the table as funding projects and priorities are developed.

Future Goals

For the initial 10 years of the program's operation, the number of deaf children and adolescents served by the program was very small. With the availability of the funding support from the SAMHSA Block grant, the proportion of services to children has steadily increased and is now at 25%. This is still below the Department's overall proportion of services to children (38%) and is a focus of our service enhancement process. Of particular concern in this area is the limited number of children being served who attend mainstreamed educational settings and who make up over 80% of the deaf children in the state but less than 10% of our case-load. To that end, we are working with the South Carolina Department of Education to identify ways to educate public classroom instructors and support personnel.

The services that the Department can provide to children are primarily outpatient services, provided in schools or at our county mental health centers. However, deaf children with more severe emotional and behavioral problems often need highly specialized residential treatment and family support services. South Carolina has a relatively small population, and the numbers of deaf children/adolescents needing this level of programming is small and fluctuates greatly from month to month, making it difficult to identify a stable population to develop appropriate resources. This is an area where the Department hopes to develop collaborative programming with the state school for the deaf as well as existing providers of intensive services to hearing children and adolescents. Because of an uproar over out-of-state placements in the 1990s, South Carolina state agencies will not place a child out-of-state, despite the lack of available options in state.

As broadband and video technology become increasingly available at all of the satellite offices across the state, the Department aims to continue to explore ways to make the most effective use of the limited staff. This may include routine appointments being provided by use of teleconferencing and video access for crisis line calls.

The Department also anticipates seeing an increase in the number and comprehensiveness of Peer Support Services. As a pioneer in the provision of Deaf Peer Support, the Department will continue to explore ways to use this resource that is both beneficial to consumers and financially feasible. Deaf Services Peer Support staff go through the same training required of all Peer Support Specialists but the services they provide tend to focus more on issues related to deaf people and communication than on coping with the mental illness per se. Many of our consumers face the daily challenges that any deaf person faces such as communication barriers or hearing people's lack of sensitivity or understanding when interacting with them; however, their mental illness can make these challenges overwhelming. Peer Support staff can provide "real-world" experience about how to cope with these tasks.

Alabama

History

Alabama's Office of Deaf Services is also the result of litigation. Frustrated by more than 15 years of meetings with the Alabama Department of Mental Health (the Department) without any real change, the Alabama Association of the Deaf decided that action had to be taken. Verna Bailey, the mother of a deaf person living with mental illness, agreed to be the plaintiff of a class action lawsuit and *Bailey v. Sawyer* lawsuit was filed in 1999. The lawsuit was settled in late 2001 (*Verna Bailey v. Kathy Sawyer*, 1999).

Steve Hamerdinger (second author) was hired as director in January 2003, and the first regional office in Birmingham was opened in August of that year. Other regional offices were opened over the next 12 months in Huntsville, Montgomery, and Mobile.

The state originally intended to have community-based services that were entirely contracted to local mental health centers, despite pleas from the Deaf Community in Alabama to make the system entirely state-operated. South Carolina's system, in which all the staff of Deaf services were employed by the state, worked very well in the view of Deaf Community leaders, because staff could be used flexibly and there was little fragmentation of services. This same flexibility in how staff are used is also a strength of the Minnesota model, even though that group is not employed by the state mental health authority. There was significant and justifiable apprehension among Deaf Community leaders that deaf people would face significant hurdles to access if the clinical staff were hired by the community mental health centers where staff were unfamiliar with the treatment needs of deaf people at that time.

The Department of Mental Health in Alabama, like many states, has a series of private, not-for-profit mental health boards and all community mental health services are delivered through contract arrangements with those boards. The Deaf Community preferred the centralized approach of having the regional Deaf Services staff work as employees of the Department, as in South Carolina. This did not match the Department's decentralized and private vendor-based approach. DMH officials were convinced that the community mental health boards would be able to absorb the regional therapists to serve deaf persons with a subsidy to pay part of the salary of the clinician.

Within 12 months, it became obvious that this approach would not work in Alabama due to low population density with resulting small case-loads that did not provide enough billable hours, especially from any single catchment area. Centers were simply not able to hire deaf clinicians and bill enough to cover the costs, even though the Department was subsidizing almost all of the salaries. In a nutshell, Medicaid revenue projections were unrealistic because Medicaid reimbursements were restricted to only licensed clinicians (some Deaf Services clinicians were non-licensed), and many consumers needed far more support services than were authorized by either Medicare or Medicaid. Clinicians working with deaf people are used to providing a lot of "catch up" services and teaching that are not, strictly speaking "clinical services" but are necessary to level the playing field for deaf consumers. Clinicians who serve deaf consumers often assume multiple roles beyond that of therapist. This can be a problem when these services are not "billable" and the clinician has to meet strict productivity expectations.

It was not intended in the original design that the Department would pay the entire salary of the clinicians to work with deaf consumers. Nevertheless, the subsidy was set high enough to be roughly equal to the yearly pay of a licensed counselor in an average community program. The centers in Alabama were then expected to make up the difference between the subsidy and the combined cost of fringes, overhead and differential pay needed to recruit specialized clinicians. Centers generally did not use the subsidy to create a nationally competitive salary for the deaf clinicians' since that would have made their pay higher than the hearing clinicians and even some of the clinical directors. The centers were then in a bind. If the salaries were high enough to attract qualified applicants to work with deaf people, the staff not working with deaf people would revolt. If they did not set the salaries high enough, they would not be able to find applicants. During that first year, there was never a time when all four regional offices in Alabama were filled. Applicants were not interested in applying for positions that were being advertised at as much as 40% below what they could earn elsewhere with the same training and experience.

Nor were salary issues the only problem with the arrangement. Other questions remained. How would overhead costs be covered? Who paid for the environmental accommodations? What about interpreter costs for the clinician, if he or she happened to be deaf? What about the tendency for deaf consumer to require significantly more time and services than hearing consumers would?

Finally, the centers balked at covering costs for the clinicians to travel to other mental health centers in the regions. There were two reasons for this. First, if the subsidy did not cover the whole salary of the clinician, how would they recover the cost for travel? But more important was the issue of ownership. If the clinician worked out of mental health center A, and traveled to work with a consumer at mental health center B, who "owned" the consumer? If mental health center B did, mental health center A would not be able to bill for services and thus not able to cover the costs. If mental health center A did, where was the chart held? What about restrictions on where services could be provided under state Medicaid rules? And how did the centers recover the "lost time" spent on the road?

There was tremendous pressure to increase revenue and some centers experimented with assigning hearing consumers to the deaf clinicians. Not only did this result in increased interpreter costs and active resistance by the hearing consumers, it led to staff dissatisfaction and resignation of several clinicians.

Another problem was the isolation of the deaf clinical staff. They were not just geographically isolated, but were organizationally orphaned as well. Staff felt as if they "belonged" to neither the Office of Deaf Services, who was indirectly paying them, or to the mental health centers, which had control of their schedules and working conditions.

By late 2004, the centers which had regional Deaf Services Offices were in active revolt. They basically demanded that the Department of Mental Health either increase the contract amounts by an unsustainable amount—to the point where it was actually cheaper to make them state employees—or allow the centers to hire hearing clinicians in the positions reserved for clinicians who specialize in working with deaf individuals in order to keep the case loads high. While the Department could have raised the contract amounts, the other issues, such as isolation, working conditions and so on, had convinced the Department to make the Deaf Services staff state employees. By mid-2005, this process was completed.

The Office of Deaf Services (the Office) works with people who have severe and persistent mental illness. At the time of this writing, there are no specialized services for deaf people who have substance abuse problems only. They are served by another division of the Department. People with dual substance abuse and mental illness presentations are often served by Deaf Services, especially if the mental illness is clearly primary.

Model

The regional staff are all employees of the Office and the group homes are privately operated under contract from the Department. In addition, the inpatient unit is state-operated and all staff are state employees.

The program's scope of services is as follows:

- Crisis Intervention
- Assessment and Stabilization
- Inpatient treatment
- Outpatient Therapy
- Communication assessments
- Psychological Evaluation
- Telemental Health
- Technical Assistance and Consultation

- Case management
- Substance abuse referral and assistance, Co-occurring disorders therapy
- Community Placement Assistance

One limitation of the scope of services is that only people with severe mental illness are eligible for services through the Office. Although people with co-occurring disorders are served by the Office, severe mental illness still must be primary. This limitation is a function of both the *Bailey* settlement and structure of the Department of Mental Health.

Regionally Based Therapists

The heart of the Office of Deaf Services is a network of regionally based therapists (clinicians) who specialize in working with deaf people. Based in community mental health centers, but employed by the Office, these clinicians provide linguistically and culturally appropriate services. They are also sources of technical assistance and consultation for community mental health centers. They work in the centers through a contract, perhaps better understood as a memorandum of agreement, through which the clinicians "work for the centers" while they are on site. This solved the unanticipated problem of "who owned the chart." The agreement also addressed liability questions. The contract is with the Office, not with the individual clinicians. This has several positive consequences. A center with a contract is not limited to using only the regional clinician in their area. They can request any clinician from the Office, allowing more consumer choice than would otherwise be possible. What this means, is that while the regional clinicians are based in one of four mental health centers around the state, their clinical skill are accessible to everyone in the state. A natural outgrowth of this arrangement is the creation of a statewide "catchment" area for deaf consumers. All mental health centers are linked by videoconferencing equipment so catchment area boundaries are administrative only. A deaf person anywhere in Alabama has the ability to receive direct services from any of the clinicians on staff with Deaf Services through videoconferencing if they are not local.

The Bailey Deaf In-Patient Unit

The Bailey Deaf Unit (the Unit) is located within Greil Memorial Psychiatric Hospital in Montgomery. It has 10 beds, with two beds designated as statewide crisis beds. The Unit is designed to be a culturally affirmative program with signing staff that are trained to work with people who are mentally ill and deaf. The Unit is also the locus of the statewide Communication Access Team, having both Qualified Mental Health Interpreters and Certified Deaf Interpreters on staff.

All deaf consumers in state operated facilities have been transferred to the Unit as of the spring of 2009. For a variety of reasons this transition was challenging. Greil is considered an acute psychiatric facility and, as the Unit is embedded there, it was assumed by the hospital administration that the Unit would also be acute care only. This created a perceived barrier to moving deaf consumers who were in need of "long-term" care. It also was a barrier to moving forensic consumers to the program.

In both cases, issues related to consumer rights in acute care versus long-term care were in conflict. For example, acute care programs are generally not set up to handle things like shopping for clothes or getting haircuts, both things that long-term care programs handle through various types of passes and levels of freedom. There was, and still is, a justified concern about "length of stay" and how having 10 beds that are functionally, if not definitionally, long-term bed affects the facility's average length of stay.

Consumers who are referred to the Unit often lack an appropriate place to which they can be discharged. While there are some beds in programs that are linguistically appropriate and culturally affirmative, the demand is greater than the supply. Perhaps more correctly, those remaining in the Unit are long-term in-patient care patients, not acute care, which was what the Unit was designed to be. People filling beds in the Unit because there is no place for them to go block others who need care from coming in.

The final, and on-going, challenge to establishing the Unit was staffing. There has been constant tension between the need for linguistically competent staff and the ability to fit into the hospital's organizational structure. One of the most interesting battles was over the qualifications of the direct care staff. The hospital administration felt a need to have people who were able to pass the merit system (civil service) examination for Mental Health Workers and still have the sign language skills needed for this deaf program. The problem they found was no one who was fluent enough in ASL to pass the set standard, which was Intermediate Plus or better on the Sign Language Proficiency Interview, was willing to work for the amount of money being offered for entry level people (barely above minimum wage). They also had to pass the merit system examination. Those who could pass the merit system examination and were willing to work for the wage set were unable to sign or if they could, could only do so at survival levels. Raising the level at which people were brought in would have created an unacceptable pay inequity where a person with less experience in the same classification could be paid much higher than a veteran already working on the floor. The only solution to this was setting up a new classification for "Deaf Care Worker," where the pay rate could be set high enough to attract people. Eventually this was the route chosen.

These barriers, real and perceived, were slowly overcome, and at the time of this writing, there are no deaf consumers in any state operated facility other than the Unit at Greil.

Small Group Homes

The *Bailey* settlement called for the establishment of group homes for deaf consumers. This effort began very soon after the Deaf Services was established. The state settled on a de-centralized model, rather than putting all the beds in one location. This model was chosen in light of the deinstitutionalization effort nationally.

Located in Birmingham and Mobile, Alabama's residential services are made up of a series of three-person group homes and independent supported living slots. The group homes serve as "intermediate care" options, helping people who are ready to leave the Unit, but not ready to live independently in the community. Admission to these homes is at the discretion of the operator.

Recently, the pressure from the Deaf Community protesting linguistically inaccessible placements and impetus from *Olmsted*[4] led the Division of Intellectual Disabilities to open a four-bed home for deaf consumers who have cognitive/intellectual disabilities. The intent of this project was to create a place for deaf people who needed a high level of supervision and support in order to be able to live outside the Partlow Developmental Center, a state-run institution for people with severe intellectual disabilities, which was going through a series of downsizing moves in preparation for closing. Most of the deaf residents have learning and language challenges and they met the clinical criteria for having an intellectual disability.

The establishment of a core of group homes and independent supported living slots in Birmingham has created a critical mass of deaf consumers that has encouraged the local mental health authority there to hire signing clinicians outside of the Office. This program, established in the spring of 2010, operates independently of the Office but is governed by the same standards of care that the staff persons at the Office follow. Clinicians are expected to have Advanced Plus or better ratings in the SLPI and must have on-going training in treating deaf people with mental illness. Money for that program comes from a contract arrangement with the Division of Mental Illness, Deaf Services and billing Medicaid or Medicare where appropriate.

Clinical Training

The Department believes that training interpreters without concurrently training consumers and clinicians will not be effective. A clinical/community education component was set up as a companion piece to the mental health training piece. Noteworthy activities include:

- Educational programs for deaf and hard-of-hearing people about mental illness and substance abuse, emphasizing the potential for recovery.

- Training for facilities and providers to help them understand the importance of culturally and linguistically appropriate services.
- Intense and focused training for clinicians who work with deaf consumers.

Mental Health Interpreter Training

Recognizing that there are not enough, nor is it likely that there will ever be, ASL-fluent clinicians to meet the need, Deaf Services began looking at improving the skills of interpreters working in mental health. Alabama has codified a definition of "qualified mental health interpreter" in the Code of Alabama (§580-3-24) in an attempt to set a floor on what it means to be a "qualified interpreter" in the context of mental health. This, in turn, led to recognizing the need for specialized training for interpreters to help them become qualified.

The heart of this effort, the annual 40-hour Interpreter Institute,[5] has become internationally recognized as the best training of its kind and has been attended by participants from 35 states and the United Kingdom. But that is only part of the effort. The Office is heavily involved in the interpreter training program at Troy University as well. In addition to funding several stipends for students, the Office serves as a site for internships and externships. In addition, the Office offers training for Deaf Interpreters, both at the Institute and separately during the year.

A major focus of this effort is to understand how language deprivation and dysfluency impact clinical effectiveness. It is becoming increasingly clear through the work of the Communication Access Team that mere knowledge of ASL is insufficient to assure effective communication with severely dysfluent consumers. The Office has developed several protocols related to use of hearing interpreter/deaf interpreter teams for assessments not done by clinical staff at the Office. In the Bailey Deaf Unit, assessments by ASL fluent clinicians always include the Unit Communication Specialist who is also both a Certified Deaf Interpreter and a Qualified Mental Health Interpreter candidate.

These training efforts are supplemented with cross-discipline training for clinicians and interpreters together. The idea behind that effort is to take a particular topic, say for example, late onset psychiatric symptoms in people who have Congenital Rubella Syndrome, and discuss it in a roundtable format using training teams of interpreters and clinicians are knowledgeable in the subject matter.

The array of specialized services in Alabama has resulted in several notable outcomes. There are no deaf people in any long-term care facility except for the Bailey Deaf Unit or medical nursing facilities. The Office also has active oversight in the care and treatment of all deaf consumers served in the community, whether they are receiving direct services from Office clinicians or not. This has also led to accurate demographic information and better diagnostic profiles.

Future Goals

The Office hopes to expand the number of community residential options, including number of beds and types of beds, increase the use of telemental health services, and improve options for people with substance abuse issues who do not have co-occurring mental illnesses. As with other states, the biggest barrier to expanding services is funding. Alabama also has the goal of overcoming the severe shortage of ASL-fluent professionals and para-professionals to fill positions if they were created.

State Model Comparisons

In the three statewide mental health models described above, there are important similarities and differences. Funding mechanisms in each and how each state delivers mental health services are different. The models described in this chapter are examples intended to give states ideas that can be adapted or modified to best fit their funding and governance system.

Similarities

There are several important similarities between the models presented by Minnesota, South Carolina, and Alabama. The experiences of these three states identify some "best practices" in setting up statewide mental health services for deaf consumers.

Reason for Establishment

One striking similarity between these three statewide mental health models is that all were launched by litigation. In each state, there had been years, if not decades, of advocacy to establish appropriate services. Armed with Section 504 of the Rehabilitation Act of 1973 (29 U.S.C. § 794) and Title II of the Americans with Disabilities Act (42 U.S.C. §§ 12101 et seq.), study groups were formed and needs assessments were conducted in each state. Repeated meetings were held with representatives of the state mental health authority and assurances given that the needs of deaf consumers would be met. However, litigation, or, as in South Carolina, the clear intent to file litigation, was required before actual action was taken in terms of hiring staff and committing funds. Absent the "big stick" of court involvement, several states have established pilot or model programs, only to have them fade away when key personnel change or budgetary constraints make funding "optional" programs untenable. It may seem inappropriate to argue that the threat or reality of litigation is a best practice, but the reality has often been that nothing short of this has moved states to create appropriate programs.

Regionally Based Mental Health Services

Another important similarity between the three states is that the mental health services are regionally based with staff located in areas with the largest concentrations of deaf people. In doing this, the clinician is assigned to a specific region and travel within the region. This person reports, at least partially, to a supervisor who is located centrally, usually the statewide coordinator or Director of Deaf Services. Regionally based teams allow qualified supervision by a centrally located supervisor knowledgeable in the unique needs of serving deaf consumers. This is critical in a specialization where clinicians are expected to serve a diverse client mix and, given the newness of the field, are likely to be new clinicians with limited experience.

The use of regional teams also provides an increased likelihood that staff who are deaf themselves will be recruited, hired and retained. Core ASL-fluent clinical staff are state employees in all three states, which is attractive to new employees who like the security of state jobs. As was shown in the South Carolina example, having a comprehensive statewide system can also facilitate a change from an inpatient program to an outpatient program as staff can be used flexibly as consumer needs dictate and not be constrained by the service limits placed on smaller private agencies.

Other significant similarities with all three programs are that mental health services are being provided directly to deaf consumers, not through interpreters, and that all professionals are under the direction of a state coordinator in each state. The presence of a state-level position provides a visibility and an institutional presence that cannot be duplicated by an agency serving a smaller target population or geographic area. Whether the state provides the services directly or contracts out for service delivery, the statutory responsibility for mental health services in the public sector rests with the state mental health authority. The job specifications of the state coordinators in all three states require that they be clinically trained and have significant experience in providing services to deaf consumers. This has ensured that, as policies and procedures are developed, they are based in the actual service needs of the consumers, not just what is bureaucratically most feasible. It cannot be emphasized enough that it is not a good idea to have a person who has no experience in mental health or working with deaf people in this role no matter how proven the leadership skills of this person may be. Both having the experience working with deaf consumers and being an effective leader in a bureaucracy are necessary. It is crucial that this is not a political appointee but rather someone who is genuinely qualified to do this work. The wrong person in such a vital role could easily doom the efforts of setting up a statewide mental health delivery system.

Organization of Services

While the Minnesota model appears to be the most "Deaf-centric" of three models presented here, due to the mental health services being built into regional offices of Deaf and Hard of Hearing Services Division (as opposed to the Department of Mental Health), this model may not work well for other states that view deaf consumers as a low priority or have no regional offices. The South Carolina model appears to be the most effective because it has wider continuum of services that are intertwined within the state mental health delivery system and a strong 20-plus year record track of successful mental health services for deaf consumers. In part, this is because in South Carolina, all public mental health services are provided directly by the state mental health authority. This eliminates the need to work with the patchwork of local agencies more typical when the state system contracts with private vendors. In addition, South Carolina may have more deaf specialized services simply because it has survived the test of time. With its 20-plus year history, South Carolina has been able to do more than the relatively new services in Minnesota and Alabama. South Carolina has so far also gone against a disturbing trend which is for quality services to be established but then to deteriorate over time.

Alabama is a hybrid model that, structurally, is like South Carolina but shares important similarities with Minnesota. In particular Alabama and Minnesota have similar funding streams, i.e. direct appropriation of state dollars rather than Medicaid/Medicare. Please refer to Table 4.1 for a summary of state model similarities.

Table 4.1 State Model Comparison: Similarities

	Minnesota	*South Carolina*	*Alabama*
Reason for Establishment	Initially established by lawsuit to create an inpatient unit for Deaf people; evolved to a statewide outpatient program	Established by threat of a lawsuit to create statewide outpatient and inpatient programs	Established by lawsuit to create statewide outpatient and inpatient programs
Service Locations	Services regionally based in 7 locations	Services regionally based in 3 locations	Services regionally based in 4 locations
Type of Services	Direct mental health services	Direct mental health services	Direct mental health services
Employing Agency of staff	ASL-fluent MH professionals employed by the state	ASL-fluent MH professionals employed by the state	ASL-fluent MH professionals employed by the state
Qualifications of State Coordinator	State Coordinator is clinically trained (as required by job specifications)	State Coordinator is clinically trained (as required by job specifications)	State Coordinator is clinically trained (as required by job specifications)

Differences

Public versus Private Funding of Services

The differences between the state models begin with how each state integrates public versus private services. The next difference is in how services are organized over regions of a state, the catchment area problem. Then there is the question of standards of care: who is eligible for services. Eligibility is often determined by which agency a service is located in, especially whether or not it is located in the state mental health agency (SMHA). Standards of care also relate to who is qualified to provide services.

There are pros and cons to operating state funded verses private contracted services. One advantage of state funded services is that the program can operate (up to a point) at a loss. This allows for attention to be given to small, isolated areas that could not be served if there was pressure to cover expenses. This flexibility comes at a price. In most states, the SMHA cannot bill Medicaid/Medicare directly for outpatient services. Most states contract instead with public or private agencies to provide billable services. Second, state governments are typically not nimble at adapting to a changing marketplace. In economic downturns, as the United States is experiencing in 2008–2011, states react by instituting broad-based hiring freezes that disproportionally impact small programs. Alabama, for example, has clinical positions it cannot fill due to statewide hiring freezes, negatively impacting the ability to deliver services to deaf persons. Private providers can maintain flexibility to expand and contract their programs to fit economic realities. This is an advantage. They are, nevertheless, faced with incredible pressure to "bill or die," a huge disadvantage.

It is difficult to make a private system of mental health services for deaf people profitable because the incidence is too low to justify the additional costs. It usually costs more to provide services to deaf consumers than those who are hearing because there is usually the need for additional services, which are often non-billable, such as greater travel costs, meetings to gather information and coordinate these additional services. The reimbursement mechanisms do not recognize that increased cost. In most places, for private vendors to succeed at serving deaf clients, they will need grants to supplement income coming from billable services. Most states have a public-private partnership of some kind. This is true in Minnesota and Alabama. The state can set standards and provide funding to private vendors while overseeing their compliance with the standards. Provided the state has the right synergy of factors (a qualified state coordinator; qualified clinical, interpreting and paraprofessional staff; interested and culturally attuned vendors, sufficient numbers of clients), this can work well.

Solving the Catchment Area Problem

Deaf services are always plagued by artificial boundaries that limit flexibility. Because there is both a small number of eligible clients and qualified staff, programs work best when they can use staff flexibly to serve a large geographic area. The catchment area problem is notorious. States divide service delivery into geographic regions and fund accordingly. This places great pressure on regions to only serve clients in their region and to resist sending clients out of region. A state can have numerous catchment areas, with one or two deaf persons in each area needing a residential program. No region itself has enough clients to create a program but collectively they do. Private vendors also usually limit their services to a smaller geographic area.

In Alabama, the catchment area problem was solved by declaring (in administrative regulations) that the entire state was the catchment area for deaf people. In South Carolina, since each mental health center is a state-operated program, services to the deaf are provided at every location. When staff can serve an entire state, they will have to travel (a disadvantage) but they can be supervised centrally by clinicians with the appropriate training (an advantage). Unless the catchment area problem is addressed administratively, services will likely be limited to large urban areas at the expense of rural areas.

Standards of Care

States have different standards of care for who is eligible to receive and provide services. Another artificial boundary is made when services are limited to persons with severe mental illness. This occurs when services are located within the state mental health agency because these agencies are mandated to serve only persons with severe mental illness. They are not mandated to serve the vast majority of deaf people who have mental health needs but are not severely mentally ill. This means that the SMHA may hire qualified clinicians who may be the only clinicians prepared to work with deaf consumers in an area, but who will be unable to see clients who are not considered severely mentally ill. This is a problem in South Carolina and Alabama but not in Minnesota.

In the authors' experience, there are more pros than cons to operating a mental health program serving deaf consumers within the SMHA, as opposed to a state agency serving deaf people. The SMHA has the legal obligation to provide services to individuals who have a mental illness, and has the resources (by contract or directly) in terms of psychiatric coverage and local clinic facilities. They also have a statewide responsibility, not just a local or regional focus. This is not, however, an absolutely necessity. For example, the Minnesota model is operated outside of the SMHA; however, the Minnesota model serves the entire state and has the authority to create and distribute mental health grants to the private sector and determine the standards of care. Although Minnesota's program (Deaf and Hard of Hearing Services Division) is not housed within the Adult Mental Health Division, both divisions are under the Minnesota Department of Human Services and they work jointly as needed.

While it is our view that the statewide mental health services continuum should be operated by a state agency (regardless if the agency is within the SMHA or not), we acknowledge that it is entirely possible that statewide mental health programs are operated outside the state agency. For example, the mental health program in Nebraska is housed within the Nebraska Commission for the Deaf and Hard of Hearing[6] and Kansas' statewide services are provided through the Johnson County Mental Health Center in Olathe, Kansas[7] (S. Dennis, personal communication, April 16, 2009). These programs are usually funded through grants and fee-for-service billing system. Their ability to survive when grant funding ends may be always a question. Where a statewide mental health program serving deaf consumers is operated depends largely on where it would fit best, both financially and politically within a state system.

Standards of care also determine who is qualified to provide services. It sets a "floor" for the quality of these services. Most importantly, it may define "ASL-fluent" in terms of a specific score on a nationally recognized assessment of ASL such as the Sign Language Proficiency Interview: ASL (SLPI: ASL). This is considered especially important in light of increasing evidence that overcoming barriers caused by language deprivation and dysfluency is critical to clinical effectiveness (Glickman, 2009). These standards are enormously helpful whenever services are threatened with cuts, or new administrators are brought on who think that deaf people can communicate by lip-reading and that all signing is "good enough." They are also helpful whenever administrators decide they need staff who are more "flexible," (often a euphemism for hiring hearing clinicians who "sign" over native signing deaf clinicians). A primary task of any state coordinator should be to establish statewide standards for language skills in Deaf services. Precedents have been set in all three states discussed here.

Clinical Supervision

In terms of clinical supervision, the three states operate differently. In Minnesota, the state coordinator has the sole responsibility of providing clinical supervision to the Mental Health Specialists employed within the program. Therefore all client charts are owned by its Division. In South Carolina, clinical supervision is provided by the regional supervisors and then the program manager with the Director of Services for the Deaf and Hard of Hearing. Local mental health center staff are available to provide consultation or support around a specific need (for example, locating a local resource or dealing with an unusual presenting problem). In

Alabama, shared supervision is provided by both clinical directors within the local mental health centers and the state coordinator, similar to how South Carolina does it. Alabama regional clinicians often collaborate with local mental health center staff to share expertise when working with consumers who have complex treatment needs.

Insurance Reimbursement

Billing Medicaid/Medicare for services is a standard practice in mental health for hearing consumers. It is not necessarily so for programs serving deaf consumers. South Carolina bills for services because all of the public mental health providers in the state are state employees, and the Medicaid/Medicare reimbursement system and state mental health agencies are intertwined. However, the program in Alabama does not bill for services, because most deaf consumers are on Medicare (not Medicaid) and billing for services would require hiring physicians, PhD-level psychologists or licensed clinical social workers to provide services, both of which are in woefully short supply. This reduces the applicant pool for positions and historically has had a disparate impact on the ability of the system to hire clinicians who are themselves deaf. Alabama and Minnesota decided to fund clinical services with state dollars. Both Alabama and Minnesota do, however, bill for residential services when possible.

Mental Health Services for Children and Adolescents

Mental health services for deaf children and adolescents are available in Minnesota through grants and private practice. Virtually all of the providers for this population are located in the Twin Cities, but some provide services via videoconferencing. Some providers travel to various sites outside the Twin Cities, but the frequency of services provided are often limited due to travel time. A day intensive treatment program (DHH-IMPACT) has recently opened its doors for deaf children. This program is located at the state's school for the deaf in Faribault. More recently, Minnesota brought back its psychological assessment program for deaf, hard-of-hearing, and deafblind children living in Greater Minnesota through a grant.

South Carolina has direct outpatient services for deaf children and adolescents throughout the state, as well as inpatient services in a program for hearing children using interpreters and Deaf Services staff for consultation. Services are also available at the South Carolina School for the Deaf and Blind. Referrals for children and family services often come from local school districts.

Alabama does not generally have direct services for children and adolescents at the time of this writing. However, regional therapists working within Deaf Services can work with children and their families if they are consumers of services at their local mental health centers.

Mental Health Interpreting

Mental health interpreters are an important component to any behavioral health system. Alabama is the only state in the country where the state code defines qualified mental health interpreters, including restrictions on some certification levels. They are also the only state that has a specialized certification for interpreters who want to work in mental health interpreting. To help interpreters earn this certification, Alabama established the Mental Health Interpreter Training project (MHIT), a 40-hour intensive training solely on mental health interpreting. The training is open to interpreters from any state who are interested in obtaining a formal certification in mental health interpreting. Interpreter services in all three states are provided by a mix of staff and contract interpreters. In Alabama and South Carolina, these contract interpreters supplement the staff interpreters and the cost of interpreting services is borne by the state office. The Registry of Interpreters for the Deaf (RID) certification is a requirement to be a provider of interpreting services in both. Alabama also has a licensure law and interpreters in mental health settings are required to be licensed. Neither Minnesota nor South Carolina has a specific state code defining qualified mental health interpreters. In Minnesota, certification from the RID is strongly encouraged but not required. For a complete summary of state model differences, please refer to Table 4.2.

Establishing and Advocating Mental Health Services in Your State

The development of a statewide mental health delivery system serving deaf consumers requires public and private providers, stakeholders, and the Deaf Community in the respective states to work together cohesively. The National Association of the Deaf (NAD) created a position paper in 2003 (National Association of the Deaf, 2003), a supplemental paper in 2008 (National Association of the Deaf, 2008), and the Model Mental Health for Deaf and Hard of Hearing Individuals Bill of Rights Act in 2010 (National Association of the Deaf, 2010a). These documents offer excellent recommendations for states to adopt, from which many ideas are borrowed and illustrated below.

The following developments will foster the creation of culturally affirmative mental health continuum in your home state and they are not necessarily to be followed in exact order.

Advocacy Efforts

Setting up a continuum of mental health services will require the coordination of key stakeholders. It is important to create a task force which can function as an advisory council to the state mental health authority, the

Table 4.2 State Model Comparisons: Differences

Location	Minnesota	South Carolina	Alabama
	Department of Human Services-Deaf & Hard of Hearing Services Division (DHHSD)	Department of Mental Health (DMH)-Office of Services for the Deaf and Hard of Hearing	Department of Mental Health-Mental Illness Division (DMH)-Office of Deaf Services
Standards of Care	a) Stand alone, no client criteria for outpatient services b) Well-coordinated with other culturally and affirmative providers (grantees and private practice) c) Has ASL fluency requirements. Uses a proficiency test for fluency measure	a) Follows South Carolina DMH's existing standards of care for all DMH consumers b) Has ASL fluency requirements. Uses a proficiency test for fluency measure	a) Alabama DMH has specific standards of care for D/HH people in state code as part of community program standards Sets a "floor" b) Code specifies ASL fluency requirements for staff providing direct services using SLPI: ASL
Clinical Supervision	State Coordinator	a) Shared: Administrative Supervision provided by local authorities b) Clinical supervision provided by clinicians who are fluent in ASL and knowledgeable about deaf people c) Services of an ASL-fluent psychiatrist	Shared: State Coordinator for practice and overall theory, clinical directors of MH Centers for individual cases
Employment	a) MH Specialists are employed by DHHSD b) Grant-based programs employ their own MH staff c) Some are in private practice	All staff are employed by DMH	a) Most clinical staff are employed by DMH-Office of Deaf Services b) Community residential staff are employed by CMHCs
Client Chart Ownership	DHHSD	Local MH centers	Local MH centers

Location	Minnesota	South Carolina	Alabama
Insurance Reimbursement	The program is funded by the state and does not bill for services	South Carolina bills for services because all of the public MH providers in the state are state employees; therefore Medicaid/Medicare reimbursement and state MH agencies are intertwined by default	The program no longer bills for services because most of their deaf consumers are on Medicare (not Medicaid) and would only allow payment for services provided by physicians or Ph.D. level psychologists. The program is entirely funded by state dollars
Funding	Any funding left will be swept to the State's General Fund at end of fiscal year	No appropriated funds may be carried over to the next fiscal year. Medicaid revenue is ongoing as services are provided	Funding can carry over to the next fiscal year at the discretion of the Governor
Children MH Services	a) Has direct services for children through grants b) General MH services are mostly located in the Twin Cities, some receive services via telehealth in Greater MN c) Assessment services are for Greater MN only d) Children's MH Task Force established e) Intensive treatment program recently established at MN Academy for the Deaf	a) Has direct services for children b) Services at SC School for the Deaf and Blind c) Local school-based services in districts d) Child and family services as referred from local schools	a) No direct services for children at this time b) Regional therapists can work with children who are consumers of MH Centers in collaboration with DMH Office of Children's Services
Interpreters	a) No specific state code defining qualified MH interpreters, but RID certification is encouraged b) Training in MH interpreting are given often through DHHSD grants	a) Interpreting contracts throughout the system as needed b) MHIT training provided by Alabama as available	a) State code defines qualified MH interpreter including restrictions on some certification levels b) Has certifications for MH interpreters c) Mental Health Interpreter Training (MHIT) is internationally recognized

state department of Deaf Services, or to a similar state agency that shares common goals. It can also be an advocacy force if the state system is not responsive. The task force must consist of deaf consumers and family members who are familiar with mental health services and state government. It is important to note that the involvement of unprepared consumers (and those with minimal language skills) is often not helpful. Additionally, active involvement of the state Commission of Deaf and Hard of Hearing or Association of the Deaf, or both, has been demonstrated to be an effective element, as it was for Minnesota. The involvement of the Commission of Deaf, DeafBlind and Hard of Hearing Minnesotans have helped to reduce the severity of funding cuts made to the mental health grants in Minnesota as they lobbied hard in behalf of the Deaf and Hard of Hearing Services Division. In addition, enlistment of the public and private offices of consumer affairs and community-based organizations within the state such as those from counties and Deaf-run agencies will promote a broad selection of members for the task force and support from more members of the community.

States should consider the example of Massachusetts in 1986 when advocacy efforts from a large coalition of Deaf Community and specialized providers succeeded in getting the state to set up a variety of programs including the Commission for the Deaf and Hard of Hearing, the Westborough State Hospital Deaf Unit as well as expanding Independent Living Services (ILS) programs and interpreting referral services. This was done without a threat of a lawsuit, although years later the threat of litigation helped to expand and to maintain these services within the state. It is also important for the advocates to collect data and make the case for services based on actual clients in need. State officials always want to know numbers even if they are estimates. Identifying real cases to build advocacy around is of paramount importance.

The Commission of Deaf, DeafBlind and Hard of Hearing Minnesotans developed a self-study online course[8] in October 2010 with six modules designed to help people advocate for positive changes in public policies that impact people who are deaf, deafblind, and hard of hearing in any state. This online resource is in both English and ASL. It is particularly useful for professionals, advocates, parents, direct care workers, and service providers to (a) understand how public policy is made and who makes it; (b) understand the advocacy process and apply it to one's situation; (c) tell one's story in writing and in person; (d) know how to identify the policy makers who can help bring about the changes needed; (e) write effective letters and e-mails; (f) give effective testimony and answer questions; and (g) work with others to address community issues. Using these online modules as guidelines is likely to be useful in building efforts to advocate for the development of a statewide mental health delivery system in your home state.

Data Collection, Legal, Action Plans, and Statutes

It is important for states (i.e., deaf state associations or commissions) to set up a Task Force to start collecting data in preparation to argue their positions why statewide mental health services are necessary in their home states. The data collection should be guided by these questions: How many deaf people need mental health services? What are currently available mental health services in the state? What are the gaps in services? What are the funding sources for such services? What are the recommendations in setting a statewide mental health delivery system for deaf consumers? It is also imperative to thoroughly review the ADA laws and landmark court cases that have led to the creation of culturally affirmative mental health care for people who are deaf (e.g., *Handel et al. v. Levine et al.*, 1984; *Jean DeVinney v. Maine Medical Center*, 1998; *Tugg v. Towey*, 1994; *Verna Bailey v. Kathy Sawyer*, 1999). Reviewing these cases would be helpful for the Task Force, advisory council, or the key stakeholders to help the state mental health authority understand that specialized mental health services can be formed without requiring legal action. In addition, evaluating other states' recent action plans for direct mental health services can offer additional ideas for a multitude of services. Two plans that have been described in a very detailed manner are the plans for Missouri (Critchfield, 2006) and Colorado (Center for Systems Integration, 2008), although these states' action plans have not been fully achieved at the time of this writing (2011).

As noted earlier, while it is feasible for a state to develop services without litigation, as it was for Massachusetts, this is the exception, not the rule. Public mental health agencies will always be under financial constraints and faced with multiple demands from consumer populations. Without litigation, it has been difficult to convince funding agencies that services for deaf consumers is not just an option to be provided when funding is available but a basic question of access and human rights. The threat or reality of litigation will usually be needed. Many services, which were established without litigation, were eliminated or phased out through attrition once the initial impetus for establishment passed and budgets became tighter. While civil rights complaints might not be the first step in attempting to advocate for services, they are usually a necessary element in making the transition from talking about services to actually taking the concrete steps of hiring staff and developing programs. In all three states, these lawsuits have been brought, or threatened, on behalf of individuals in inpatient facilities without access to the treatment program. At the present time, there are three other states where members of the Deaf community are pursuing litigation (Bluestein, 2010; Disability Rights Network of Pennsylvania, 2010; Patrick, 2010).

Finally, reviewing and adopting similar department policies or statutes as mandated in both South Carolina (Directive No. 839-03)[9] and

Alabama (Administrative Code Chapter 580-2-9)[10] in providing culturally and linguistically affirmative mental health services to deaf and hard-of-hearing people, is likely to give Deaf Communities a powerful position in making sure that their home states are held accountable for the provision of these specialized services. Oftentimes, there are state policies that emphasize the importance of language access, cultural accommodation, and inclusion, but, these state policies don't usually call for the standard of culturally affirmative treatment which, as stated above, is higher than that required by federal law.

State Coordinator

The creation of a state coordinator position (often called the state director) within the appropriate state department to establish and maintain the mental health continuum serving deaf consumers would be the next step. An ideal state coordinator would be clinically trained, have the ability to supervise staff responsible for the statewide delivery of mental health services, have clinical experience providing direct services to individuals who are deaf and have a mental illness, and have competency in ASL. This person should have the authority to establish standards of care for personnel and programs serving deaf consumers in the state. In addition, a state coordinator also should be skilled in providing consultation and technical assistance to providers at the inpatient facilities and group homes. If the state coordinator has the authority to create and distribute mental health grants to the private sectors, this person should have the ability to skillfully evaluate each grantees' outcome data. In addition, the state coordinator must have a comprehensive knowledge of the regulatory aspects of state and federal policies related mental health services. With this experience, the state coordinator can either create programs or integrate within the existing service delivery system in the state, thus creating a service continuum.

Mental Health Continuum of Services

Several states began with a psychiatric inpatient unit serving individuals who are deaf only to phase it out as outpatient mental health services are established in the community. The mental health services in the community in several states may never have been created if not for the inpatient Deaf unit. The Deaf units became a place where deaf individuals were referred, and when they could not be discharged without culturally affirmative community programs, the need for these programs and services became clear. The Deaf unit within a state hospital often has a power base or a visibility within the State Department that forces attention on the special needs and abilities of deaf consumers. Deaf Units can also bring together and create treatment resources for deaf consumers. If a Deaf Unit is subsequently closed, it helps if staff can be moved into community positions. This occurs most easily if the inpatient and community programs are all in the public sector.

If states seek to create a statewide mental health delivery system today, creating an inpatient Deaf unit first is not absolutely necessary. In Minnesota, South Carolina, and Alabama, as the outpatient mental health services and residential services expanded, the need for a fully staffed inpatient Deaf unit decreased significantly. Glickman (Chapter 1, this volume) reports this is the case in Massachusetts also. Since the creation of community-based residential and case management/counseling resources, both Minnesota and South Carolina have not had more than one deaf consumer in the unit at any one time, and in a typical year, less than four individuals have been admitted for care.

At their best, specialty Deaf inpatient units are places where deaf people with severe emotional or behavioral problems can get expert evaluations, have medication prescribed and managed properly (quite often this means decreasing or simplifying medication regimens), and be assisted with behavior to the point that they can live safely in a less restrictive setting. In practice, many of the persons served by Deaf inpatient units are there because they pose a severe threat to themselves or the community and because there are not community programs that can address adequately their needs. Some of these persons are on forensic commitments. Even when there are quality Deaf residential treatment programs, some persons still pose safety challenges that tax the resources of even the best community settings.

Because state funds are always tight, we believe, and the experiences of our three states have shown, that larger numbers of deaf people are served best by devoting scarce dollars to community programs rather than inpatient units. The best system of care is one where regionally based clinicians who work with deaf people can be used flexibly, working both inpatient and outpatient as the need arises. This is the case in South Carolina and is made possible by the fact that all mental health providers work for the state. Ideally, those who are expert in work with deaf people could work actively alongside inpatient providers doing the work of assessment, treatment, and disposition. For the small numbers of deaf persons who do need highly restrictive settings for longer terms, the best option is probably the referral to state or national programs that are available.

While the services of the state mental health authority or department generally target the severely mentally ill as in both South Carolina and Alabama, it is Minnesota's experience that being able to serve any deaf consumer makes the program more acceptable to the state legislature, organizations, providers, and the public. This is partly because the number of persons served will be much larger. Regionally based clinicians, who are also few in numbers, will be able to serve a larger number and diversity of clientele.

Organizing deaf mental health services this way relates to a fundamental principal of setting up culturally affirmative mental health services: serve as many deaf people as possible through one centralized program; eliminate artificial barriers to service provision such as the restrictions to catchment areas, particular insurance plans or through eligibility (serving only those who are severely mentally ill). There are too few consumers and specialists to do this work well unless the program casts a broad net, even though this means both consumers and staff may have to travel to get appropriate care.

Video technology can extend the reach of deaf mental health services to less populated areas, reducing the need for travel. With the explosion of video relay services in the first decade of the 21st century, deaf people today have become much more comfortable using videoconferencing equipment to communicate as well as obtaining mental health treatment through this medium (Gournaris, 2009).

Outcome Studies

Once the statewide mental health service delivery system is in place, the state coordinator should gather outcome data, demonstrating the relative effectiveness of these culturally affirmative approaches. The absence of good outcome data has made advocacy efforts more difficult. Outcome data will help establish an objective basis for drawing conclusions about best treatment practices with deaf people.

One form of outcome data is consumer satisfaction. Another is a measure of percentage of client goals met. Minnesota was able to collect this data from its consumers. A recent audit of all treatment plans formulated by program staff in the past 4 years revealed that most of the goals developed for deaf consumers have either been achieved or are in good progress. Program statistics show that deaf consumers in Minnesota programs fully accomplish their goals 81% of the time.

The Minnesota Division sent out 113 consumer satisfaction surveys in Fiscal Year 2011 and 57 surveys were returned with an approximate 50% response rate. The survey consisted of 14 questions asking consumers to rate the mental health services that they have received. The program received an overall score of 4.63 (out of 5), ranging from 4.47 to 4.84 for each question. These scores indicate that consumers in Minnesota who have received services from the Mental Health Program are highly satisfied.

The ideal study would compare goal achievement and consumer satisfaction before and after the development of specialized mental health services. Other outcome data has to do with costs including utilization of inpatient stays, the most expensive service. Both Minnesota and South Carolina were able to demonstrate that they served a larger number of deaf people better by focusing resources on specialized community treatment programs and not inpatient units.

What Has Not Worked

No review of systems that are working would be complete without at least a cursory review of the "white crosses" in our field, programs which have been started with the best of intentions and with well-qualified staff but which have not survived. While individually these programs did not continue for reasons that are as unique as the program themselves, there are some consistent problems which confounded them all:

1. Programs overestimate the numbers of individuals who will present for services. This is a combination of using inflated estimates of the number of deaf individuals in a given catchment area and unrealistic estimates of the percentage of individuals who will seek those services. For example, some programs have used the number of individuals who have a hearing loss (approximately 6%), far exceeding the number of deaf individuals who will seek specialized services. Other programs have based service estimates on the assumption that 100% of individuals who need services will seek such services, as unlikely for deaf individuals as it is for the population as a whole.
2. The ways in which services for the larger population are divided up (e.g., by catchment area, insurance provider, or eligibility criteria; even the well-worn distinction between mental health and substance abuse treatment) interferes with the establishment of culturally affirmative treatment resources for deaf people. When Deaf programs follow these same restrictive guidelines, they inevitably serve too few deaf consumers to attract trained specialists and justify the additional expenses. Again, the lesson in serving deaf consumers is to cast the net broadly.
3. A failure to be Deaf-centric in program design and staffing. Programs may try to serve deaf individuals as "hearing people who don't hear" resulting in losing credibility in Deaf Community and deaf people not wanting to refer anyone to that program because they do not want community members to have a negative experience. As with other cultural and language minorities, programs that serve deaf people must achieve cross-cultural legitimacy to be successful. The Deaf Community and their affiliated organizations are known for being extremely selective of who they view as credible. Working strictly from a medical model of deafness is a sure fire way to guarantee that deaf people will show no interest in a program. Glickman (Chapter 1, this volume) extends this argument to say that treatment programs which serve deaf people strictly from a medical model of *mental illness* (as opposed

to a skill building rehabilitation/recovery model) also fail to serve many deaf people appropriately.

4. A lack of institutional support and integration with state mental health systems. Regardless of the approach used, there needs to be a close relationship with the larger mental health delivery system, preferably within the state structure. This is the potential major disadvantage of locating programs outside of the state mental health authority, as in Minnesota. As many chapters in this volume illustrate, cultural competence does not guarantee clinical competence. Deaf treatment resources which are well integrated with the larger network of service programs will have the greatest chance of adapting best practices for deaf consumers and of surviving the ups and downs in the economy.

Conclusion

We begin with the belief that deaf consumers have an equal right to access a wide range of appropriate mental health services in their preferred language, from mental health professionals or providers who are culturally and linguistically competent. However, for most deaf people this is but a dream. The authors' ongoing professional networking on the national level indicates that there are few statewide mental health programs, an impression reinforced by the Mental Health Directory maintained by Gallaudet University.[11]

In this chapter, we have drawn on the experiences of Minnesota, South Carolina, and Alabama to identify best practices in the development of statewide continua of mental health care for deaf persons. The key points we have stressed are:

1. Most programs have been created through a combination of advocacy, the threat or reality of litigation, the presentation of realistic data including stories about particular consumers in need, and the ability to convince key personnel in state government or private non-profit agencies to develop such services.

2. A key first step is the creation of the position of state coordinator for culturally affirmative mental health services, the hiring of a qualified person, and the empowering of that person to move the state to create additional services.

3. The best service delivery system will have central coordination and regional offices with mental health specialists who are able to communicate directly with clients and then travel within particular regions. There is typically shared supervision of regional specialists between the State Coordinator and the local region or office.

4. Specialized inpatient units have often been a first service created. They have advantages and disadvantages. In most states, they tend to be dismantled once an appropriate community continuum of care,

especially residential treatment programs, is created. A strong community-based program will decrease the expenses associated with an inpatient level of care.

5. When creating a statewide continuum of care, major efforts are always directed towards overcoming artificial barriers (catchment areas, insurance restrictions, eligibility requirement restrictions, etc.) so that the maximum number of deaf persons can be served in the equivalent of some "center of excellence." Centralization and coordination of services works better that small local resources when serving a population, like deaf people, with small numbers yet highly specialized needs.

6. There is no one formula for the mix of public and private treatment resources within a state, but generally speaking the state, through the efforts of the State Coordinator, should, at a minimum, establish and oversee standards of care. This should include objective measures of sign language competency in program personnel. In most cases, when private vendors are used, state grants have to supplement third party payments because Deaf programs inevitably serve smaller case loads, spend longer amounts of time per each case, and do a great deal of collateral work outside the billable hour. There are also additional expenses associated with interpreters, including deaf interpreters.

7. Mental health and rehabilitation programs that serve deaf consumers must work to achieve cross-cultural legitimacy with the Deaf Community to be effective.

In most states, there are individuals like Cathy, locked in a revolving door of hospitalizations without communication and inadequate care in a community that fails to appreciate being deaf is more than simply the inability to hear. Whether as prudent taxpayers or strident advocates, we owe it to those we serve to not accept an interpreter as sufficient for access. The experiences in Minnesota, South Carolina, and Alabama show that culturally appropriate, linguistically accessible services are both possible and affordable, given creativity, specialized skills, and motivation to serve deaf consumers as they would want to be served.

Notes

1. From "Promising Practices of Statewide Mental Health Models Serving Consumers who are Deaf: How to Advocate For your Model in Your Home State," by M. J. Gournaris, S. Hamerdinger, & R. C. Williams, 2010, *Journal of the American Deafness & Rehabilitation Association, 43*(3), pp. 152–182. Copyright (2010) by JADARA. Adapted with permission.

2. The term also includes services funded by public and private sources and inpatient, outpatient, and residential care.

3. In some states the term director is used, in some states coordinators. We use the term in this article to denote the person ultimately responsible for mental health services to deaf people in that particular state.
4. Olmstead V. L. C. (98-536) 527 U.S. 581 (1999) 138 F.3d 893 A 1999 Supreme Court decision ruling that the Georgia State Commissioner of Human Resources discriminated against two women with mental illness and Developmental Disabilities under Title II of the Americans with Disabilities Act (ADA, 1990). The decision held that the women had the right to receive care in the most integrated setting appropriate and that their unnecessary institutionalization was discriminatory and violated the ADA.
5. Retrieved from http://mhit.org
6. Retrieved from http://www.ncdhh.ne.gov/mh_services.html
7. Retrieved from http://mentalhealth.jocogov.org/special.htm
8. Retrieved from http://www.mncdhh.org/makingyour case/. Click "My Syllabus" to view the modules
9. Retrieved from www.state.sc.us/dmh/directives/839-03.htm
10. Retrieved from www.alabamaadministrativecode.state.al.us/docs/mhlth/McWord 580-2-9.pdf
11. Retrieved from http://research.gallaudet.edu/resources/mhd

References

Afrin, J., & Critchfield, B. (1997). Low-cost telepsychiatry for the deaf in South Carolina. *Journal of American Medical Informatics Association, 4*(2), 102–111.
Bluestein, G. (2010, March 4). Deaf residents challenge Georgia's mental health policy. *The Cherokee Tribune.* Retrieved from http://www.cherokeetribune.com
Basil, R. N. (2000). Providing mental health services to the deaf community. In L. Vandecreek & T. L. Jackson (Eds.), *Innovations in clinical practice: A source book* (Vol. 18, pp. 369–381). Sarasota, FL: Professional Resource Press/Professional Resource Exchange, Inc.
Center for Systems Integration (2008). *Deaf and hard of hearing mental health and substance abuse action plan.* Denver: Colorado Department of Human Services, Colorado Commission for the Deaf and Hard of Hearing.
Critchfield, A. B. (2002). *Meeting the mental health needs of persons who are deaf.* Alexandria, VA: National Technical Assistance Center for State Mental Health Planning.
Critchfield, A. B. (2006). *Revisiting the dream: Proposing a comprehensive treatment model for deaf, deaf/blind and hard of hearing people who have psychiatric disorders, mental retardation and substance abuse disorders.* Jefferson City: Office of Services to Deaf and Hard of Hearing People, Missouri Department of Mental Health.
Dew, D. W. (1999). *Serving individuals who are low-functioning deaf: Report from the study group, 25th Institute on Rehabilitation Issues.* Washington, DC: George Washington University.
Disability Rights Network of Pennsylvania files class action lawsuit against DPW. (2010, April 30). *The Medical News.* Retrieved from http://www.news-medical.net/news/20100430/Disability-Rights-Network-of-Pennsylvania-files-class-action-lawsuit-against-DPW.aspx
Gentile, A., & McCarthy, B. (1973). *Additional handicapping conditions among hearing impaired students, United States, 1971–1972.* Washington, DC: Gallaudet College.

Gold-Brunson, J., & Lawrence, S. P. (2002). Impact of sign language interpreter and therapist moods on deaf recipient mood. *Professional Psychology: Research and Practice, 33*(6), 576–580.

Gournaris, M. J. (2009). Preparation for the delivery of telemental health services with individuals who are deaf: Informed consent and provider procedure guidelines. *Journal of the American Deafness & Rehabilitation Association, 43*(1), 34–51.

Graham, P., & Rutter, M. (1968). Organic brain dysfunction and child psychiatric disorder. *British Medical Journal, 3*, 695–700.

Glickman, N. (2003). Culturally affirmative mental health treatment for Deaf people: What it look like and why it is essential. In N. Glickman & S. Gulati (Eds.), *Mental health care of deaf people: A culturally affirmative approach* (pp. 1–32). Mahwah, NJ: Erlbaum.

Glickman, N. (2009). *Cognitive-behavioral therapy for deaf and hearing persons with language and Learning Challenges.* New York, NY: Routledge.

Glickman, N., & Gulati, S. (2003). *Mental health care of deaf people: A culturally affirmative approach.* Mahwah, NJ: Erlbaum.

Hamerdinger, S. (2011). *Hearing status of community program population: Dec 2011.* Montgomery: Alabama Department of Mental Health Office of Deaf Services.

Handel et al v. Levine et al, File 468475 (Ramsey County District Court 1984).

Harvey, M. (1982). The influence and utilization of an interpreter for deaf persons in family therapy. *American Annals of the Deaf, 127*(7), 821–827.

Harvey, M. (1989). *Psychotherapy with deaf and hard of hearing persons: A systemic model.* Hillsdale, NJ: Erlbaum.

Haskins, B. (2004). Serving deaf adults psychiatric inpatients. *Psychiatric Services, 55*(4), 439–441.

Janet DeVinney, Plaintiff and the United States of America, Plaintiff-Intervenor v. Maine Medical Center, Defendant — Consent Decree, Civil No. 97-276-P-C (U.S. District Court, District of Maine 1998).

Kessler, R. C., Chiu, W. T., Colpe, L., Demler, O., Merikangas, K. R., Walters, E. E., Wang, P. S. (2006). The prevalence and correlates of serious mental illness (SMI) in the National Comorbidity Survey Replication (NCS-R). In R. W. Manderscheid & J. T. Berry (Eds.), *Mental health, United States, 2004* (pp. 134–148). Rockville, MD: Substance Abuse and Mental Health Services Administration.

Kessler, R. C., Chiu, W. T., Demler, O., & Walters, E. E. (2005). Prevalence, severity, and comorbidity of twelve-month DSM-IV disorders in the National Comorbidity Survey Replication (NCS-R). *Archives of General Psychiatry, 62*(6), 617–627.

Leigh, I. W., Powers, L., Vash, C., & Nettles, R. (2004). Survey of psychological services to clients with disabilities: The need for awareness. *Rehabilitation Psychology, 49*(1), 48–54.

Mathos, K. K., Kilbourne, A. M., Myers, R., & Post, E. P. (2009). Disparities in mental health services for persons who are deaf: Advancing research towards action. *Journal of the American Deafness & Rehabilitation Association, 42*(3), 152–166.

Meadow, K. P. (1981). Studies of behaviour problems of deaf children. In L. Stein, E. Mindel & T. Jabaley (Eds.), *Deafness and mental health* (pp. 3–22). New York, NY: Grune and Stratton.

Mitchell, R. E., Young, T. A., Bachleda, B., & Karchmer, M. A. (2006). How many people use ASL in the United States? Why estimates need updating. *Sign Language Studies, 6*(3), 306–335.

National Association of the Deaf. (2003). Position statement on mental health services. Retrieved from http://www.nad.org/issues/health-care/mental-health-services/position-statement

National Association of the Deaf. (2008). Position statement supplement: Culturally affirmative and linguistically accessible services. Retrieved from http://www.nad.org/issues/health-care/mental-health-services/position-statement-supplement

National Association of the Deaf. (2010a). Model mental health for deaf and hard of hearing individuals bill of rights act. Retrieved from http://www.nad.org/issues/health-care/mental-health-services/model-mental-health-deaf-and-hard-hearing-individuals-bil-0

National Association of the Deaf (2010b). Promoting a bill of rights to ensure appropriate direct mental health services for individuals who are deaf or hard of hearing. Retrieved from http://www.nad.org/issues/health-care/mental-health-services/promoting-bill-rights-ensure-appropriate-direct-mental-hea

Patrick, R. (2010, April 27). Advocates for deaf sue state over mental health care. *St. Louis Post-Dispatch.* Retrieved from http://www.stltoday.com

Pollard, R. Q. (1994). Public mental health service and diagnostic trends regarding individuals who are deaf or hard of hearing. *Rehabilitation Psychology, 39*(3), 147–160.

Pollard, R. (1998). Psychopathology. In M. Marschark & M. D. Clark (Eds.), *Psychological perspectives on deafness* (Vol. 2, pp. 171–197). Mahwah, NJ: Erlbaum.

Pollard, R. Q. (1999). Psychological services to deaf individuals via teleconferencing (Unpublished manuscript). University of Rochester Medical Center, Rochester, NY.

Steinmetz, E. (2006). *Americans with disabilities: 2002* (No. P70-107). Washington, DC: U.S. Census Bureau.

SAMHSA. (1999). *Assertive Community Treatment (ACT), An evidence-based practice kit* [CD-ROM/DVD version ed.]. Rockville, MD: SAMHSA.

Tugg v. Towey, 864 F. Supp. 1201 (U.S. District Court, S.D. Fla., Miami Division 1994).

Verna Bailey v. Kathy Sawyer, Civil Action No. 99-A-1321-N (U.S. District Court, M.D. Ala. 1999).

Vernon, M. (1980). Perspectives of deafness and mental health. *Journal of Rehabilitation of the Deaf,* (13), 9–14.

Vernon, M., & Andrews, J. F. (1990). *The psychology of deafness:understanding deaf and hard-of-hearing people.* White Plains, NY: Longman.

Vernon, M., & Greenberg, S. F. (1999). Violence in Deaf and hard of hearing people: A review of the literature. *Aggression and Violent Behavior, 4*(3), 259–272.

5 Creating Culturally and Clinically Competent Deaf Residential Treatment Programs[1]

Neil S. Glickman and Wendy Heines

Introduction

After a 1-year stay in a Deaf psychiatric inpatient unit, Juan was finally discharged. Juan has Schizoaffective disorder. He has periods of depression and psychotic symptoms like auditory hallucinations[2] and extreme cognitive disorganization. Juan also has a trauma history. He was sexually and physically abused as a child and adolescent. He had immigrated with his mother to the United States when he was 9, a major life disruption which no one had been able to explain to him or discuss. Juan has functional sign language skills in ASL. Good ASL signers can communicate reasonably well with him. Users of Sign English might as well be speaking Greek. During his inpatient stay, Juan learned some basic coping skills such as the "red, yellow, green" (Glickman, 2009) skill, giving himself a time out, deep breathing, and use of a rocking chair while sitting under a weighted blanket. He is not as explosive as he was on admission. Medication has helped his mood stabilize and his mind clear, and he was now able to discuss simple plans for next steps in his life.

To stabilize his mood and psychosis, Juan needed about a month inpatient stay in a program where staff could communicate with him. To learn basic coping skills, he needed about a 6-month stay in this program as no one had taught him any of these simple skills before. Juan could not discuss his traumatic experiences. He lacked both the language skills and emotional stability, and staff focused on helping him calm and soothe himself. However, the main reason for the 1-year hospital stay was difficulty finding a community placement for him. Juan was homeless. He had lived in a hearing group home for a few months where his psychosis got worse without staff knowing it. Staff did see his more explosive behaviors, and it was these that got him hospitalized. They could not communicate with him over what might be bothering him. Previously, he had one specialized treatment resource, a counselor who signed in Pidgin Sign English. They didn't communicate well, and Juan stopped attending after a few sessions. He had been offered psychiatry appointments with an interpreter. The psychiatrist spent the whole 15-minute appointment typing on her laptop, barely making eye contact before giving the staff medication prescriptions. Juan didn't like her because she wouldn't look at him and he didn't understand what she, or the interpreter, were saying. The staff gave him the medication, but Juan didn't understand what he was taking or why or what the possible side effects were. When later he developed some painful muscle cramps, he didn't know they were medication related and couldn't communicate his experience to the staff. This all culminated in any angry outburst in which he threw a chair and pushed and punched a staff person after that staff person mouthed and gestured that he should clean his room.

Juan had lived in a rural part of the state where there were no Deaf residential treatment services. There was a Deaf group home in the more urban part of the state, but it was outside of the "catchment area" in which Juan was served.[3] The main reason for the delay was the difficulty getting approval for an out of area placement. The director of the Department of Mental Health (DMH) area office out of which Juan was served finally agreed because the hearing placement tried first did not work and because Juan was fortunate enough to have advocates who could explain why he needed this specialized service.

Now Juan would be placed, finally, in a Deaf group home. He would have access to some long-term psychiatric rehabilitation provided the program could adapt best practices so that they worked for Juan. He had a great number of treatment needs. He knew next to nothing about psychiatric medication. His independent living skills (food preparation, money management, using public transportation, getting and holding a job) were very poor. He still had an explosive temper and needed sustained quality treatment to solidify and strengthen the coping skills he learned in the hospital. His interpersonal skills were poor and he frequently got himself in arguments, and sometimes fights, with peers. He had experienced multiple kinds of trauma which he had very limited capacity to process. Overlaying all of this were barely adequate communication skills in ASL and enormous psychosocial deficits, and the fact that Juan was so disempowered that he did not have any sense of how he could do things to improve his own life. Juan was 25, but emotionally he was somewhere between 5 and 8 years old.

To serve Juan well, the program needs specialization that went well beyond having signing staff. Nothing could be done without staff who sign not just adequately, but expertly, but then the program staff needed to be prepared to work clinically with Juan. What does a residential program, where staff are both culturally and clinically prepared for clients like Juan, look like?

There are two fundamental dimensions to creating treatment approaches for deaf persons. The first is cultural and the second is clinical. Both dimensions require a great deal of specialized expertise, and it is rare to find everything one needs in one treatment program. The authors of this chapter have been administrators and clinicians in such programs.

In this chapter, we will draw upon our experiences in these programs to describe the cultural and clinical challenges to creation of such programs. We address here the fundamental question at the heart of this book; what exactly is different about Deaf mental health care, but focus our discussion on community-based residential treatment programs.

The Cultural Challenges

In the Spring of 2010, I (Neil) ended 17 years of working in a Deaf inpatient unit and joined a private-non-profit organization called Advocates, Inc., in Framingham, Massachusetts. Advocates already had a strong Deaf psychiatric rehabilitation program that included, at the time, seven Deaf residential treatment settings. Their culturally affirmative attitude was reflected in the agency's mission statement, as posted on their website:

> *Advocates, Inc. believes that the best way to effectively serve Deaf clients and to become an "employer of choice" for Deaf professionals and paraprofessionals is to honor the culture and values of the Deaf community. Advocates achieves this by carefully attending to 4 key components of the workplace: providing a* **culturally competent environment;** **employing Deaf professionals and paraprofessionals in Deaf programs** *as well as in key leadership positions; maximizing communication access across the organization; and offering a* **comprehensive training** *curriculum.*

Though I am hearing, this mission statement and approach appealed to me. I accepted a part-time position, sharing the role of Clinical Director with a deaf colleague.

At the time of my hire, there was a lot of discussion occurring between the deaf leadership team and the Human Relations team about how the orientation and training programs offered were not "Deaf friendly." Interpreters were always provided, and the interpreters at Advocates were all exceptionally skilled, but still the deaf staff felt that the trainings were not conducted in a Deaf friendly way. Their complaints had to do with how information was organized and presented; the heavy reliance upon dense English language Power Point slides, often containing acronyms and technical jargon, and reading materials. They had to do with a training style that was sometimes too much lecture and not enough discussion, where multiple policies and procedures were reviewed, one after the other. They had to do with frustration that there weren't any deaf staff in the Human Relations department who could provide trainings in ASL. It didn't seem to matter that information was presented with skillful interpreters present. Much of the information just went in one eye and out the other. Despite the best of intentions, the deaf staff were not getting the same quality training as the hearing staff.

I was familiar with these problems from my years managing the Westborough Deaf Unit. We had exactly the same problems there. We hired deaf staff who consistently complained about how boring and unhelpful the new employee orientation procedure was (hearing staff complained about this also). We had a constant stream of new policies and procedures to train staff on and sometimes very little time to do the training. Sometimes staff would be asked to read a policy in a manual or on line and then sign off on it. Of course, this was an atrocious way to develop knowledge and skills in any staff person who couldn't read at a college level (and there were many such hearing staff, including the large number of English second language users who were immigrants from other countries). The fact was that English literacy at a high school level was needed even for direct care positions, and many staff, deaf and hearing, read and wrote English poorly. In Deaf services, this problem of poor English literacy is widespread, and it is chief among complaints that hearing employers often have with some deaf staff.

In a previous work (Glickman, 2009), I had written about efforts that were made in other places to make counseling and teaching more "Deaf friendly." I cited in particular the ground-breaking research of the Deaf Wellness Center (DWC) in Rochester, New York (O'Hearn, Pollard, & Hayes, 2010; Pollard, Dean, O'Hearn, & Hayes, 2009). From the DWC work, the efforts of my Westborough State Hospital team to adapt Cognitive Behavioral Therapy for deaf patients and the work of other people, I had come up with a list of ways to adapt the trainings to make them more Deaf friendly. These strategies are presented later in this chapter.

When I joined Advocates, I saw this discussion of how to improve our training program for staff going on, and I rushed to join it. There was an email stream going back and forth between the deaf and Human Resource (HR) leadership teams. I jumped in with a fairly long email presenting some of the research and insights of the DWC team and others on how to improve training for deaf staff. I thought I was being helpful, but I was making a huge cultural mistake.

My intention was to validate the concerns raised by deaf staff about the training programs not being Deaf friendly and to offer some concrete suggestions for improvement. To my astonishment, the reaction of my deaf colleagues to my comments was universally negative. They objected strongly to what they saw as my academic discourse style (i.e., a lengthy, technical email that was hard to understand) and to what they saw as me presenting myself as an expert on all things deaf. They perceived I was taking over the conversation, speaking for them. I had exactly the opposite reaction from the hearing HR colleagues. They welcomed my input and invited me to head a work group to refashion our training program. The reaction of the hearing HR staff validated the perception of the deaf staff that I was, in fact, stepping in to speak for them. Here I was, a new hearing employee at Advocates (no matter my previous work experience), appointed to one of two leadership positions in Deaf services over a large group of mostly deaf staff, jumping in to speak, as a presumed expert, about how to fashion training programs for deaf people. They believed that, once again, a hearing person would be speaking for deaf people and that their own voices would be silenced. I think they were particularly sensitive to this because Advocates had already become a place where deaf people had a strong voice. They were in leadership positions. Compared to many other agencies, Advocates was a great place for deaf people to work. They feared losing all that; and in fairness, they had good reason to fear. The reality is that most of the time hearing people get involved, we do take over, and deaf voices *are* pushed aside. Even when hearing people intend to empower deaf people, we can still push them aside. How were the deaf staff to know this wouldn't happen again?

Something very similar happened at Deaf Services Center (DSC) outside Philadelphia. When I (Wendy) accepted the challenge of administering DSC, I intended to make it a Deaf-centered place for consumers, staff, and family members alike. As a deaf person, I felt a personal and professional commitment to this. To a large extent, this mission of creating a culturally affirmative treatment setting has been achieved. The majority of our staff are deaf, and most of the hearing people we've hired, including a psychiatrist who had worked for us for years, sign well. When we've had to hire professionals such as nurses, additional psychiatrists, and quality management people where there were no deaf or signing applicants, we looked for and found people who are humble, open minded, respectful of diversity, and willing to step outside their comfort zone. In fact, this setting is so Deaf-friendly that I believe cross-cultural conflicts are relatively rare.

Rare, but not unknown.

We have had to hire hearing people without signing skills or prior experience with deaf people. Even when they have the personal qualities we look for, they inevitably make cultural mistakes. One example occurred when we were asked to set up a statewide "warmline" for deaf people. A warmline is a phone in support service staffed by certified peer specialists. It is different than a "hotline" in that it is not meant for crisis situations but rather to be a resource for people who just need to talk. To establish this service, we first had to find an agency that provided training. This was actually quite difficult, as there were few agencies providing this new service. After finding an agency, we needed to demonstrate that providing interpreters during the training would not interfere with the training the hearing people were receiving. We paid a large fee for our deaf peer specialists and deaf managers to attend and we also paid for interpreters.

The only staff person in the agency who had prior experience with using peer specialists to staff a warmline was a new administrator. She was a hearing person, a beginning signer, who was hired because she brought other essential skills to the agency. I as C.E.O. and the other deaf managers all decided for her to attend the training because her future role would be to consult to the deaf managers on supervising the deaf peer specialists who do the warmline work.

Early in the training, a problem emerged; actually, a classic cross-cultural conflict. Part of the certification process for warmline training was for the peer specialists to be supervised working on the county's warmline calls. Our deaf peer specialists needed this experience also, but they would need to work with interpreters in phone calls with hearing clients. The director of the training balked at this prospect. She believed the interpreter time lag would jeopardize the effectiveness of the warmline calls, and she wouldn't permit the deaf trainees to have this experience. Without this training experience, our deaf trainees could never become certified to do the work. The crisis came to a head at a concluding session when the administrator of the training handed out certificates to the hearing participants but not to the deaf participants. She told the group that the deaf participants could not get the certificate.

This discriminatory situation naturally upset us. The hearing manager in our program, who attended to assist our deaf staff in setting up this service, then made a serious cultural blunder. At this emotional last meeting, she took the role of spokesperson for the agency on this problem. Rather than advocate against the discrimination, she tried to mediate between the parties. All the deaf staff viewed her assumption of a spokesperson role and her attempt at neutrality to actually be support for the discriminatory practice. They objected vigorously to this new hearing person stepping in to speak for them and then taking a position that actually tolerated the discriminatory practice.

Fortunately, this hearing staff person did have the personal qualities we looked for so that when we were able to address the issue with her, she recognized her error and apologized to everyone. She had the wisdom to assume the humility the situation called for.

It is so easy for hearing people to take over. Even people, like the first author, who should know better, make this mistake. On the other hand, being deaf is no guarantee of being wise or of having the knowledge and skills needed in different roles. There are multiple skills needed for clinical and administrative positions, and one can't always find all the skills one needs in the same person. Quite often there are no deaf or signing candidates who have other skills vital to the organization. How then will the program balance all these needs? The challenge is complex and ripe for cross-cultural conflict.

Other questions emerge from the staff and program development challenges: Will a nominally Deaf program truly emerge out of a Deaf perspective or will it be yet another example of a hearing run program with a few token deaf staff? Who is qualified to work in these programs? Even more crucially, who is qualified to administer them? How do we weigh the importance of whether or not someone is deaf; and if we consider that vitally important, how much weight do we place on whether they are culturally Deaf? How much weight should be placed on sign language skills as opposed to other skills? What if the person has superb ASL skills and work habits but poor English literacy? How much weight should we place on clinical experience and credentials, on demonstrated leadership abilities? How is power distributed between deaf and hearing staff in the program? Are there deaf people in leadership positions? How are the complicated communication dynamics between deaf and hearing people managed? Is there a career ladder for deaf staff in this organization or is there a "glass ceiling?" Does the program ensure that a culturally Deaf vantage point is weighed in key decisions? How does a program attempt to balance cultural and clinical expertise?

These questions are difficult because deaf and hearing people often answer them differently. We don't know of any Deaf school or treatment program that does not struggle with these questions. How well these questions are addressed in the work and treatment environment often make or break programs. When they are handled unskillfully, deaf people give up on a program, and it loses any cross-cultural legitimacy. When they are handled well, this still does not insure a clinically competent program. *Cultural competency is the necessary, but not sufficient, condition for Deaf schools and treatment programs.*

Deaf hearing cross-cultural conflicts are actually fairly predictable.[4] With enough experience, one can observe that certain themes almost always emerge. We're addressing here the common beliefs and perspectives of hearing people who have had some sustained contact with deaf people, and who value signing, not the hearing people who are committed oralists, who are trying to cure deafness through medical interventions, or who think that deaf people should speechread them. Based on our experience with many programs, we could represent these conflicts in an imaginary dialogue between a hearing and deaf administrator of two Deaf programs. This imaginary, but reasonably representative hearing administrator who was brought in to run a Deaf program does not sign or have much prior knowledge of deaf people. He recognizes that he has to hire deaf people and that sign language is important. He commits to taking sign language classes and believes that should satisfy the concerns of his deaf staff. The imaginary but reasonably representative deaf administrator here tries to help the hearing administrator move beyond commonly voiced complaints about deaf staff. She articulates a Deaf-centric vision for the program.

Hearing Administrator:

We want to hire deaf people. We work hard to recruit, train and promote qualified deaf people. But the key word is "qualified." We are not going to hire people just because they are deaf, and we are certainly not going to put people in key clinical or administrative roles unless they have appropriate training, experiences, and credentials. We hire people based on ability, not cultural identity, ethnicity, race or any other status factor. To behave otherwise is discrimination.

In fact, our experience hiring deaf people has been very mixed. As much as we strive to hire deaf people, we've had some problems with some deaf staff over the years, and this has led us to want more from deaf applicants. This is difficult to talk about without deaf people accusing us of being prejudiced. One of the big areas of difficulty we have faced was with anything involving record keeping. Most of our positions are paraprofessional (direct care workers) where it is not necessary to have a college degree. However, it really is necessary to be able to read well enough to understand written communications, policies, procedures and it is necessary to be able to write well enough to complete shift notes and treatment plans and to communicate observations and concerns to other people in writing. This is not a matter of "just paper work." Some of our deaf staff have difficulty appreciating that programs can live or die based on documentation.

Even more importantly, poor documentation can result in dangerously poor treatment. For instance, staff in a residential program need to be able to follow written procedures for administration of medications and other medical treatments. Without proper documentation, we won't know such basic issues as whether or not clients received medication as ordered. All of our clients have treatment plans. The agencies that fund us expect us to be able to demonstrate that our staff understand and follow the treatment plans. Often we have to collect data to prove this. Staff who can't read or write well are usually unprepared to carry out such crucial documentation responsibilities. Hearing people can have these problems also, but basic literacy problems seem to be common in our deaf staff without college degrees, and we have an awfully difficult time training staff and overcoming this problem. In some cases, the documentation problems have been so severe that we lost, or nearly lost, accreditation and funding.

We understand that signing is crucial. We want staff who can communicate with clients. But we don't see evidence that just being deaf makes you especially compassionate or insures you work well with clients. We don't see any clear correlation between being deaf and having clinical skill or professionalism. We've had deaf staff who had excellent ASL skills but were neither compassionate nor competent nor professional in their work behaviors. When persons like these "play the Deaf card," arguing that being deaf means they should have some special status, we get very annoyed. They seem entitled. They are actually asking us to discriminate against hearing people and give them preference regardless of their demonstrated abilities. Fundamentally, all of us need to demonstrate that we are compassionate, competent, and professional. We don't need to be told to hire and promote deaf people with these qualities. Any employee with these qualities will be valued, but it is especially exciting to find deaf staff with these qualities. Our advice to deaf applicants is this: Don't make an issue of being deaf. Instead, do the work well. That's what will advance you in the organization.

Deaf Administrator:

This program is designed to serve deaf people, yet virtually all the leadership staff are hearing. The one or two deaf people you promote often act as tokens and aren't culturally Deaf people. The key leadership people say they support a signing environment, but they don't sign well, and they wouldn't know a good signer from a poor signer. They don't recognize just how much skill it takes to communicate with some deaf clients. They think anyone can do it. You hearing people always value credentials first. We deaf people value communication first. Without people who can communicate well with the clients, nothing will get done around here. No one will get treatment. No one will recover. You don't recognize the skills deaf people bring to this job and not just communication skills. You don't appreciate that this is not really about Deaf culture as some abstraction. It is about the bone-deep level of empathy that deaf people bring to work with other deaf people and our ability to challenge each other, in a way that a hearing person can't, to rise above expectations that have been set for us. Ironically, it is hearing people who see us as "the deaf." We see beyond the hearing loss to people who are full human beings.

When you say you have concerns about the English literacy of some deaf staff, but don't have the same concerns about the signing abilities of some hearing staff, you *are* being prejudiced. You are selectively highlighting the weaknesses of some deaf staff while not raising comparable concerns about some hearing staff. Both English and ASL skills are essential. But if you make allowances for hearing people, like yourself, who have no signing ability, and then do not hire deaf people if they are less than native users of English, this is discrimination, no matter what your intentions. If you are going to make your personnel decisions purely on the basis of ability, then you need to consider *all* the relevant abilities, not just those that favor hearing people. By this criteria, you are unqualified to hold your position.

You say your experience hiring deaf people has been mixed. I would assume that your experience hiring hearing people has also been mixed. Why would you generalize from this experience about deaf people but not about hearing people?

Like all people who hold power, you imagine yourself to be neutral and objective. You don't see your own biases. You say that deaf people with the right set of abilities will naturally advance, but why does this happen so rarely? Whenever there is a promotional opportunity, the bias is always in favor of the hearing candidate. Why is this the case? Because you don't perceive what deaf applicants bring to the table. You assume, for instance, that anyone who signs is a good signer. You think that any signing is "good enough." You never make the comparable mistake of thinking that any level of English skills is good enough. Indeed, when it comes to English ability, you become very fussy. With regard to signing ability, any level is good enough.

You argue that you should hire the most qualified candidate. You base qualifications largely on credentials and prior work experience but you don't see how this systematically biases you against deaf applicants. Hearing people usually have better resumes because they've had training and work opportunities that are not available to deaf people. This is especially true when it comes to leadership positions. How are deaf people to get leadership experience when even in so called Deaf programs we're denied leadership roles, often on the basis of not having prior experience? At some point, everyone needs their first leadership experience. Why are the standards for deaf people higher than those for hearing people?

We think that Deaf programs have a particular responsibility to be respectful of deaf people and Deaf Culture. How can you claim to be teaching, counseling or helping deaf people when you still have an underlying paternalistic, controlling and oppressive attitude? How effective would a treatment program be for, say, Hispanic Americans, if the administrators and staff were English speaking Anglos? It is the same for us. In programs that serve minority persons, strong affirmative action on the part of employers is essential. This is not just to remedy past discrimination. It is to ensure that the program meets the needs of the minority community.

We object when hearing people are assumed to be experts on deaf people and are given the opportunity to speak for and about deaf people. Why don't you ask us? We object when yet another hearing person, who signs badly and knows little about deaf people, is brought in to manage the program, manage us, and then presumes to speak for us. I know you don't want to hear this, but we see the same oppression happening here, in your "Deaf program," as occurs everywhere else in the hearing world. The idea that you can provide effective therapy for deaf people while simultaneously disrespecting and disempowering us is absurd.

Hearing Administrator:

You know I become very frustrated when every issue is cast in deaf vs. hearing terms. We truly want to hire and promote deaf people but when we are faced with any personnel decision, we must select the candidate who has the most to offer the organization. There have been times when we did not select the deaf candidate for very sound reasons, and the next thing we know we are accused of being prejudiced. When we have promotional opportunities especially for leadership positions, we are not just looking at credentials, though they are important. We are looking for people who have made a demonstrated commitment to this organization, who have exceptionally strong work ethics, who are wholly dedicated to quality patient care, and who will go the extra mile to be sure the organization meets its' goals. When we find these qualities in deaf staff, we are delighted, but frankly we don't always find them, just as we don't always find them in hearing staff. The point is the work and personal qualities, not whether you are deaf, hearing, White, Black, Christian, or any other attribute other than ability to excel in the job. It's you who are arguing for discrimination because you want us to privilege whether a person is deaf over whether they can do the job. It's very annoying to be accused of discrimination when you do not have, in a particular situation, a suitably qualified deaf candidate.

Here's another example. People who get fired from a program, whether they are deaf or hearing, rarely blame themselves. They claim unfair treatment. When we've had to fire a deaf person, the next thing we hear is that they are badmouthing us in the Deaf community, making unfair statements about how oppressive the agency is. They do this even when they were fired for being chronically late, for gross incompetence, even for neglecting or abusing clients. We, of course, can never comment on the reasons for their termination. Similarly, every time there is a promotional opportunity, the deaf people here seem to feel they are entitled to it, regardless of work performance and skills. Some deaf people whose work was not particularly strong nonetheless expected promotions because they were deaf or because they signed better than the other applicants. The deaf staff sometimes act as if effective communication and strong deaf representation are the only things that matter. If we hire and promote people without all the needed skills, the program will fail and everyone will lose their jobs. Even more importantly, clients may be hurt. Assuring quality care must always be our chief consideration, not the political agenda of the Deaf community.

Deaf Administrator:

Why do you write off our concerns as just a political agenda? We are just as concerned about quality client care, and we advocate for effective communication because we know how essential that is to quality client care. Hearing people rarely understand just how important good communication is to deaf people. They don't understand how many of our problems stem from communication barriers and they rarely understand how therapeutic it can be just to be treated in an environment where you are understood. And when you've gone through your entire life facing situation after situation where hearing people speak for you, decide for you, evaluate your qualities and find them wanting, and subject you to endless discriminatory and prejudicial practices, well, yes, you get sensitive to these issues.

The issue is larger than how every personnel decision is made. Your organization employs deaf staff, but the deaf people who work there feel they have no voice in the place. You administrators can talk a good game, but you don't seek out the opinions of your deaf staff. You don't listen to them. Often deaf people can't even persuade hearing people who know how to sign to do so when around deaf people. They are always "forgetting" and then are very sorry. At important meetings and events, hearing people also "forget" to schedule interpreters. Even when interpreters are there, administrators think that means all is well. They still dominate the conversation and it is very hard to get a word in edgewise. The administrators have an interpreter in the room, but that doesn't mean they solicit our input or listen.

What does it really mean to have accessible communication? You think it is just about having an interpreter in the room. It is really about having direct communication with people who know your language, about having the pace and flow of timing of communication exchanges being something you can join easily. It includes how seating is arranged, the lighting, taking eye breaks, etc. If you really want deaf people to be included in the decision making, there needs to be, at a minimum, deaf management of the communication exchange. You need only attend one meeting occurring in ASL among deaf people, with you the only hearing participant, with an interpreter there, and you will understand just how well we can communicate, and how disempowering it feels to be the language minority. Try it.

Hearing Administrator:

We can improve in this area. The hearing new signers here are all taking sign language classes and studying Deaf culture. We have a Deaf awareness committee and promote sensitivity to Deaf culture. We invest heavily in staff development. But we have a treatment program to run. We have accreditation standards to meet. We have to maintain the funding flow to this organization. We need to demonstrate that we are meeting the standard of care for treatment in our field. We have to maintain a safe and clinically effective treatment environment. We need to ask our deaf staff to put as much energy into these considerations as they do into whether or not we sign or what the deaf representation is in a particular group or committee.

Deaf Administrator:

You know, if deaf people did not have to spend so much time trying to ensure that Deaf treatment programs are culturally attuned to the needs of deaf people, we would have much more time freed up to actually do our jobs. Do you know how much energy we must put into fighting the system to get a real voice for deaf people? That's not something you have to think about. You have the privileges that go along with power, and these privileges include the ease with which you step into the role of speaking about and for deaf people. The energy we spend educating you could certainly be spent more productively on client care. It would be awfully nice if you didn't need all this education and if power were distributed more fairly without this struggle. You want us to be fully committed to this organization. That would be much easier for us if we saw the organization fully committed to us.

Please remember that you hearing people can leave this job, this agency, and go on to do other work. You can put your years of work for Deaf services, your claims to fluency in sign language, down on your resume, and use that as a step up the ladder of your career path. Other hearing people will think you are wonderful because you spent years helping "the deaf." For you, this can be a phase. For us, it is our life. This means we often bring a much higher level of energy and commitment to this work, and if you can tap into that energy and commitment, the payoff for the agency can be enormous.

You have all these concerns about our abilities, but you don't put anywhere that level of concern into making sure that your orientation and training programs really work for us or to getting us the quality supervision that we need. You think you can sit us down in front of a training manual or place an interpreter in an orientation session, and suddenly all is good. If you had ever seen and understood what it looks like when deaf people train other deaf people, you'd have a whole new perspective on our abilities. Nor do you put any energy into considering creative adaptations in how documentation is done. Why not work with us to explore innovations in that area? We understand the importance of reading and writing, but we could do a lot better with policies and procedures if the orientation and training programs were led by someone who uses our language.

Hearing Administrator:

Fair enough. We can take on projects like this as our resources allow. All these innovations are extremely expensive. As our Deaf services improve in quality, and bring in new revenue, we'll be in a better position to make additional accommodations, like hiring a deaf trainer for our HR department. Do you ever ask yourself what is the return to the agency for all this investment in Deaf services? Do you know how much money we pour into communication accessibility? We spend huge amounts of our personal time learning the language and struggling to be culturally sensitive. In return, we get a lot of criticism. Sometimes, frankly, Deaf services can feel like one colossal headache.

Deaf Administrator:

Fair enough. We may not always appreciate that this can be difficult and expensive on your end. We appreciate these personal and organizational efforts. We want you to understand that we also value compassion, clinical skills, and professional behavior. What frustrates deaf staff enormously is that we are usually extremely invested in the agency demonstrating good work. We know what it is like, as deaf people, to receive poor schooling and treatment. We want the next generation to get better than we got. On a practical level, we don't have the job and educational opportunities that hearing people have. We need to see this agency succeed and we need to be part of that success. We also want the same opportunities to develop the professional skills needed to do more advanced jobs that hearing people have in abundance. If we can't get these experiences in an agency which claims to be dedicated to empowering deaf people, then where on Earth will we get them?

Deaf treatment programs occupy this cross-cultural ground. Variations on these themes are almost always occurring although if there is no venue for dialogue, they are hidden. They play out in unproductive griping, passive aggressive work avoidance, and cross-cultural conflicts that are treated as personality conflicts. Fairly or not, programs that don't handle such conflicts well *do* get a reputation in the Deaf community as oppressive. On the other hand, these cross-cultural *tensions* can be a source of creativity, energy and program dynamism when handled well.

Deaf treatment programs must, at a minimum, have some venue for cross-cultural dialogue, some safe place and procedure for such perspectives to be aired. A dialectical perspective, in which both cultural and clinical competence are actively pursued, must be *lived* by program personnel. We attempt to represent that in the next discussion about developing clinically competent programs.

In addition, cultural and clinical competence are not discrete domains. Part of what makes a treatment program clinically appropriate for deaf persons is the culturally affirmative treatment environment and the presence of staff with all the skills needed. Certainly without this cultural competence, a program can't be clinically competent, no matter the clinical skills of staff.

The remainder of this chapter addresses specialized clinical competencies in Deaf residential programs. It addresses the question of how we adapt best practices in psychiatric rehabilitation so that they work with deaf clientele. All of the discussion which follows assumes a culturally affirmative treatment setting. In a hearing setting, where staff can't communicate directly with clients,[5] and don't know what they don't know about deaf people, this kind of clinically competent treatment can't be provided.

The Clinical Challenges

The clinical work done in Deaf residential treatment programs also must be adapted to fit the population. The main rehabilitation focus is on the development of relevant psychosocial skills (coping, conflict resolution, problem solving, communication, independent living, etc.). All these objectives are secondary to the larger goal of creating in clients the belief that they can do things to reach personal goals; that they are effective in dealing with the world. Conducting the work in sign language is just the first step, and non-signing programs have difficulty getting beyond the communication barriers to active treatment. In the remainder of this chapter, we discuss adaptations to best practices in residential treatment that work with many deaf persons who are in such programs because of challenges related to communication, mental illness, or psychosocial development. We focus not on "average" deaf people, but on the subgroup of deaf people, with language, learning and behavioral challenges, who are most likely to be clients of such programs (Glickman, 2009).

Pretreatment Challenges

Juan, the person described at the start of this chapter, arrived at his Deaf group home. He was delighted to be out of the hospital, to be in a place with other deaf people who signed, and to have his own room, which he proudly painted and decorated. Juan was not hallucinating. His thinking seemed clear and organized, and he reported he was happy. However, some of the behavioral problems that got Juan hospitalized soon appeared in the group home. It began when one of the female staff who worked in the program became alarmed when she found Juan hovering around her quite often, leering at her in a sexual way, and asking her personal questions. He came in one day without a shirt on asking her to look at his muscles and signing in a provocative way about his body. On another occasion he told her that his penis hurt and he asked her to look at it. She informed her supervisor and a series of meetings were held with Juan, expressing concerns regarding these behaviors and setting some limits. However, Juan laughed off these concerns, continued to follow her around and leer, and then, apparently to get her attention, appeared to faint in front of her. He was referred for counseling but he didn't see his behaviors as a problem. The counselor, who is deaf and a competent signer, tried his best to engage him, but communication between these two deaf signing people was also poor. Juan didn't get the point of counseling. He just wanted a girlfriend. Soon, Juan found himself in arguments and fights with his housemates. He had difficulty sharing the television. He took other people's food. He wouldn't assist with the chores. When others teased or confronted him, he became aggressive, forgetting the "red, yellow, green" skills he had practiced in the hospital. Staff saw that Juan had an "anger problem" and a problem with inappropriate sexual behaviors. They tried to engage him in discussions around these problems but Juan either didn't understand or didn't agree. He always saw the other person as at fault and seemed to have no ability to take the feelings and perspectives of other people. Within a short amount of time, he was making both his housemates and staff uncomfortable, and staff started saying he hadn't been ready for discharge from the hospital. In fact, he was ready, in that his mood and psychosis had stabilized, and what staff faced now were the lifelong communication and developmental deficits that would be the real focus of treatment efforts. However, these behaviors were problems for staff and for his housemates, not for Juan, who was always innocent, always the victim in his own eyes.

These are pretreatment problems. Psychiatric rehabilitation, mental health treatment in general, and psychotherapy in particular, are collaborative processes. They can only begin when the client and treatment provider(s) develop a shared understanding of, and commitment to, a specific set of treatment goals and methods. The client must be informed and consenting. Most of what we know about effective mental health care and psychiatric rehabilitation assumes this condition is in place. This is true in residential treatment just as it is in outpatient psychotherapy. A primary goal of treatment, or of psychiatric rehabilitation efforts, is to promote in the persons served a belief in their own ability to change their lives for the better, and then to join with them, collaboratively, in pursuing these shared goals.

But this condition is often not in place for many of the persons we seek to serve. While this is frequently true for hearing persons, deaf persons sometimes have additional burdens related to fund of information gaps which result in their having no model or schema of the treatment, rehabilitation or recovery process. They appear resistant to change, not ready for it, or they don't understand or agree with the treatment process and goals. The problem is often that the treatment process was never explained to them in a way they could understand and find relevant. They may have also not experienced work with educational or mental health professionals as empowering, and are inclined to expect more of the same communication difficulties and mistreatment. Deaf recipients of mental health care and hearing providers often live in different thought or conceptual worlds. They lack a shared understanding of the treatment or recovery process, a deeper problem than just using different languages. This lack of client readiness is referred to here as a pretreatment problem.

Broadly speaking, pretreatment refers to the lack of readiness or willingness to participate in a formal treatment process. This pretreatment problem has been discussed in many places but usually is called by another name. For instance, anti-stigma campaigns, such as those put on by the National Alliance for the Mentally Ill (NAMI) and state departments of mental health, are a form of pretreatment work. They are based on the assumption that people do not participate in mental health treatment because they are embarrassed by the stigma of mental illness. Stories of prominent people who had disorders like Depression and Bipolar Disorder are designed to normalize this experience and to dispel the notion that participating in treatment means you are "crazy."

Such anti-stigma campaigns are a form of psychoeducation, the most common approach to pretreatment. Clinicians educate consumers about mental health and mental illness and about the treatment or recovery process. Movies and television shows that depict people with mental illness getting better in mental health care can be used for this purpose. If TV arch-gangster Tony Soprano can see a psychotherapist for treatment of his anxiety disorder, surely the process can't be that strange or abnormal.

Mental illness holds the same stigma for people in the Deaf community as it does for hearing people (Steinberg, Loew, & Sullivan, 1999). The small, intimate nature of the Deaf community makes concerns about protecting confidentiality vitally important, and people don't want to be known as someone who is crazy. They also have one other concern. Many deaf rehabilitation clients are concerned not just about being considered crazy but also about being considered "low functioning," a more familiar stigma to deaf people. They resist efforts to engage them in programs that they see as designed for "low functioning" deaf people Accordingly, they are anxious to demonstrate that they are "high functioning," and this can mean not accepting anything that resembles the role of being a recipient of care.

The cultural barriers for minority or non-Western people making use of mental health care are widely noted and are given as one reason clinicians need to develop multicultural competencies (Sue & Sue, 2008), another pretreatment strategy. Culturally affirmative treatment approaches for language and cultural minorities often includes making adaptations that go well beyond the provision of interpreters. For instance, in a psychiatric inpatient program for Hispanic Americans described by Dolgin, Salazar, and Cruz (1987), staff developed a "pretherapy" program to educate their consumers about mental illness. They also conceptualized treatment in ways that were more culturally affirmative. Treatment groups for Hispanic men were called "macho groups" and for women were called "nuestras cuerpas, nuestras vidas" (our bodies, our lives). Cultural identity groups were developed to help Hispanic consumers consider the special cultural and identity challenges they face. These are both pretreatment and treatment interventions. The process of preparing consumers for mental health care often segues easily into the care itself.

In Linehan's Dialectical Behavior Therapy (DBT), there is an early phase of work called "pre-commitment" in which the DBT treatment approach is explained. The consumer is told, in effect, "this is how we do treatment here. If you decide to stay, this is the way we work. If you want some other kind of treatment, we will make a referral" (Linehan, 1993a).

Hanna has developed a pretreatment approach he calls the "precursors model," designed for "difficult clients" (Hanna, 2002). Hanna addresses psychological factors that affect a person's readiness to change. These include developing a sense of the necessity for change, a willingness to experience anxiety or difficulty, cultivating self-awareness, the ability to tolerate confrontation of problems, an increasing effort or will towards change, and building hope and developing social support for change. Hanna's book includes a scale for measuring these variables and a description of treatment interventions designed to address them.

Probably the most well-known, explicitly pretreatment approach is Motivational Interviewing, developed by Rollnick and Miller (Rollnick, Miller, & Butler, 2008). Motivational Interviewing is designed for clients who are ambivalent about change. It is a style of interviewing in which counselors first help clients articulate their ambivalence about changing and then "pull" for clients to articulate why change is needed. For instance, a client expresses the pros and cons of not drinking, but the counselor asks questions that encourage the client to elaborate on the reasons for abstinence.

Staff at the Center for Psychiatric Rehabilitation at Boston University developed a training module for helping consumers develop "rehabilitation readiness" (Cohen & Mynks, 1993). Their work focused on people with severe psychiatric disabilities like schizophrenia. The rehabilitation readiness module assumes that the main reasons consumers may not be ready for psychiatric rehabilitation are: (a) They are not unsatisfied enough with their current life situation to see a need for change. (b) They are not ready to make commitments to lifestyle or behavioral changes, usually because they don't believe they are capable of successfully making the change. (c) They are not ready to form a close personal connection with another person and use that connection to support them through the process of recovery. (d). They lack enough self-awareness to identify problems in themselves that they need help with. (e) They lack awareness about how environmental changes can help them function better in the world.

The rehabilitation readiness model shares a number of points with the precursors model of Hanna. The psychiatric rehabilitation professional assesses which factors are behind a client's lack of readiness and then selects from a variety of treatment strategies designed to overcome that barrier. For example, if the main barrier to rehabilitation readiness is that the consumer does not see a need for change, the practitioner may use Motivational Interviewing to help the consumer appreciate the benefits to involvement in rehabilitation efforts. The practitioner may also encourage the consumer to talk with other consumers who have had similar experiences, to read relevant literature or to attend peer led recovery activities.

Deaf people may have all of these reasons for lack of rehabilitation readiness, but there are often other factors more unique to their experience. The most frequently cited reason deaf people resist mental health or rehabilitation efforts is because of communication barriers. Most services are not linguistically accessible to them. Even when an interpreter or a signing counselor is provided, deaf people usually do not expect that these services will be accessible and rush to make use of them (Sussman & Brauer, 1999). The language barrier is obvious. Juan was not able to understand most treatment activities that were offered with interpreters although he did benefit when a certified Deaf interpreter was provided. He didn't communicate well with his deaf signing counselor who signed in a more English like manner that went right over his head. When care was made to ensure the right communication resources were used, Juan could be included, but it is only within Deaf treatment programs that people would know what these right communication resources look like.

When we work with people, deaf or hearing, who have a very limited understanding of the rehabilitation or treatment process, our pretreatment work must include providing them a simple, clear and compelling map or schema of this process. Within the field of psychiatric rehabilitation, the idea of "recovery" has assumed central place as a key organizing concept (Anthony, 2007). Using the recovery model, the whole idea of "treatment" or "pretreatment" is a problem, because these are understood as medical terms, as referring to what staff do to patients or clients, when the real road to health is about helping people become self-determining. Within this framework, it is much more important to talk to "persons served" about what they want in their lives and help them join a community. We make the effort to stop trying to fix people by applying treatments, no matter how collaborative, and instead struggle to join with them around their own desires and goals. Respecting them, moving to support them in their goals, is what creates the therapeutic alliance.

Within Advocates, at the time of this writing, we are working to integrate a recovery model into Deaf services. It is not an easy match, and one problem remains that of searching for a common language. Narrowly understood as "recovery from addiction or mental illness," many deaf persons don't relate easily to this framework. Juan certainly didn't. They see themselves as deaf persons struggling against communication barriers much more than they do persons struggling from mental illnesses or even addictions. Many of the persons we serve, even those who have been diagnosed with major mental illnesses, have developmental disabilities, cognitive and language problems. These are lifelong problems that don't necessarily resolve and it is harder to talk about recovery from these kinds of challenges.

There is a growing "Recovery Community" in Massachusetts, consisting of persons who were diagnosed with mental illnesses, many of whom see themselves as having been victimized by the mental health system, who now see themselves taking back control of their lives from this oppressive mental health system. They see peer self-help efforts as much more important than interventions from mental health professionals. These peer-run organizations have made very active outreach to the Deaf community in Massachusetts, and a small number of pioneering deaf peer recovery specialists have been trained and, at Advocates and in the state Department of Mental Health, hired to work with deaf persons in our program. Deaf peer specialists are also employed by Deaf Services Center.

We expect this new model of recovery to grow, but the same communication barriers that exist in the mental health system for deaf people exist in the recovery movement. Even our deaf staff and deaf recovery specialist have trouble getting Juan and other deaf persons we serve to recovery events. Recovery organizations provide interpreters for events and do active outreach, but when we do get our deaf consumers to the events, many still don't understand or relate to the presentations made. Many don't want to go simply because they see it as a hearing event. We struggle to convince them to go, and when they do, they experience the same alienation from hearing run activities that they have experienced elsewhere in their lives. To them, this is still hearing people talking a different language. They don't easily see shared experiences in the mental health system, or shared efforts to define their own lives, as something they have in common. The more these events can assume a Deaf focus, the more successful they will be, but it is not easy for the courageous pioneers trying to make this happen.

Understanding "recovery" more broadly, it is about assuming control over one's life, becoming self-determining, and forming connections to larger communities. This goal is appropriate for anyone, but this language may still be problematic. The best language we have found so far for joining with our clients in a shared therapeutic endeavor is to discuss skills. As shown below, we can often get at the larger goal, helping people feel they can affect their own fate, by helping them notice skills they use. Using the language of skills, of course presented in the language of sign, is a more accessible pretreatment strategy for engaging many deaf persons served.

Skill Development 1:
Notice and Label Skills Clients Already Use

The single most powerful way to develop skills informally, and to pull clients into the treatment process, is to notice and label skills that clients already have. Embracing this strategy also moves programs from being problem centered to being strength based, something essential for engaging consumers. When the main reason clients are pretreatment is that they lack a conceptual map or schema for the treatment process, talking to them about the skills they already have begins to give them this schema. After staff talk with clients about skills they already have, it is a relatively small step to ask them what additional skills they would like to develop. From there, staff can help construct a "story" about their developing abilities, their capacity for directing their own lives. The skill-based work pulls them into the world of recovery.

While most skill building programs consist of teaching strategies for particular psychosocial skills, it is striking how much can be accomplished informally just by talking to people about skills they already have. To glean the most therapeutic benefit from this strategy, programs need to create cultures based on the idea of skill building. Every conversation with clients regarding treatment goals is framed in terms of skills. The goal is to provide a common language for the treatment process. Of course, with deaf signing people, this all needs to occur in sign language.

Staff need to be introduced to the skills vocabulary and framework alongside of clients. With both staff and clients, formal and informal methods can be used. Formal methods include workshops and training sessions where the concepts are taught. Formal instruction works best with clients who are already "in treatment" or with staff who understand their role as skill coaches. Informal methods include conversations at staff meetings and casual interactions. Leadership introduces a strength-based focus, and the skill vocabulary, by observing and labeling common skills that clients and staff already use. It is rare for people to resist when they are being told what they are doing well, and this is often a non-threatening way to open the door to discussions of what they could do better.

It is important for staff to appreciate that we need to think about skills *developmentally*. That is, we can't have some rigid notion of what constitutes a coping skill. We can't insist that only advanced skills like mindfulness meditation or perspective taking count. The lack of a developmental approach to skill training is probably the greatest weakness of dialectical behavior therapy, one of the most widely used skill development programs. We have to be able to see skills that clients use consistent with their own developmental level. When working with language and learning challenged clients, the skills we notice are often sensori-movement (Trikakis, Curci, & Strom, 2003). The skills might be rocking in a comfortable chair, taking a warm bath, going for a walk, playing with a dog, or watching the fish in an aquarium. While DBT includes skills for "self-soothing," they are a relatively small part of the overall program, and with these particular consumers, either sensory-movement or distraction skills may make up the bulk of their coping skills repertoire.

I (Neil) recall working with a Westborough State Hospital Deaf Unit patient around basic coping skills. This patient was a student at a residential school and returned to the school for a few days on a pass. When I spoke with the social worker at the school about how he was doing, she replied that he was doing well. He had no blow-ups at all, but "he wasn't using his coping skills." This social worker missed the point. She must have had some sophisticated idea about what coping skills were. For instance, if the student wasn't doing yoga, he wasn't using his skills. But because the student had been safe for several days, he must have, by definition, been using his coping skills. The therapeutic challenge was to find out what he *did* do and then to label *those behaviors* as his coping skills. If she understood this, she would have responded that he kept himself safe by using WATCH TELEVISION SKILLS, PLAYING GAME SKILLS, or TALKING TO FRIENDS SKILLS.[6] More importantly, she would have told him that, praised him, and then tried to engage him in a discussion of how he could use even more skills.

This developmental approach to skill development is utilized at Boys Town in Nebraska (Volz, Snyder, & Sterba, 2009). The Boys Town method of treatment for youth with mental health disorders places heavy emphasis upon social skill development. They have developed a very elaborate curriculum for skill training, which takes into account the deficits commonly associated with each kind of psychiatric disorder. Skill sets are broken down into basic, intermediate, advanced, and complex skills. For example, in work with youth with anxiety disorders, basic skills include disagreeing appropriately and talking with others. Intermediate skills include accepting decisions of authority and asking for help. Advanced skills include analyzing social situations and compromising. Complex skills include assessing one's own abilities, using self-monitoring, and self-reflection.

The Boys Town developmental model helps clinicians appreciate how many simple daily behaviors (turn taking while talking, listening without interrupting, asking questions) can be conceptualized as skills. This developmental framework is essential if staff are going to be able to identify skills in clients who may be behaving very badly.

In one instance, for example, staff told a deaf, developmentally delayed client that he had his annual Individual Service Plan (ISP) meeting at his case manager's office that day. For some reason that wasn't clear, the client became very agitated. He stormed around the program yelling, giving everyone the finger, and threw a few objects around before he took himself outside to smoke and calm down. He accompanied staff to the case manager's office and, though grumpy, sat in the meeting watching the deaf interpreter brought in for him. Suddenly, he stood up in a huff, made a dramatic gesture of annoyance, and left the room. He put his newly acquired identification card, which he was proud of, on the table along with a few dollars. He seemed to be communicating through this gesture, "Here!, I'm through with you all!" Staff had a strong hunch he would be returning but no one could be sure.

His abrupt departure could be viewed as a weakness or a strength. After a short discussion, the staff decided to treat it as strength. When he returned, staff made strength-based observations to him. They pointed out that he had noticed he was upset and gave himself a time out to calm down. He made no threats or insulting gestures. He didn't give anyone the finger as was his way. He just left the room. This actually represented an improvement in behavior for him. Certainly it was improvement over the morning meeting when he was far more aggressive. After noting these skills, the group applauded him.

It is rare that this kind of strength-based intervention doesn't have a dramatic positive impact. In this instance, the client, who moments before was very unhappy, smiled broadly and became fully engaged in the rest of the meeting. His full engagement included willingness to participate in some problem solving over how to handle a disagreement with a staff person. At the end of the meeting, staff had even more skills to comment on (i.e., listening, taking turns talking, offering suggestions, accepting, negotiating, compromising) and a plan for him to meet with the staff person in question to iron out their differences. At that point, they could also ask him how, when he is upset, he can show even more skill than leaving the room. It's not hard for many clients to then answer by saying what they just did: talk, listen, stay safe, discuss, etc. This could even be role played at that moment.

Staff meetings can be used to introduce the skill framework. For instance, at one such meeting, staff were asked to identify success stories and then label the skills used in each story. This exercise yielded the following list:

- Clients agreed to clean the bathroom. They used various cleaning skills but also skills involving negotiating, cooperating, caring for their environment, respecting each other.
- A client who was staying in her room excessively finally came out and starting talking with staff. She used COMMUNICATE and SOCIALIZE skills and the staff used ENCOURAGE, WELCOME and COACH skills.
- A client is becoming more independent in administering his own medications. Today, he came to the staff for medicine at the right time, without a prompt, and could name the medicine and say what it was for. He used KNOW TIME TAKE-MEDICINE SKILL and MEDICINE NAME SKILL.
- A client who normally refuses to help with the cooking today made a hamburger for himself. He used HAMBURGER COOK SKILL. With a prompt, he also used COOPERATE and PAN CLEAN skills.
- A client contacted his counselor to say he wasn't able to come to her appointment today. She used RESPONSIBLE SKILL and CALL COUNSELOR INDEPENDENT SKILL.
- A client who was angry at a staff person was able to express his anger without becoming threatening or aggressive. He used EXPRESS FEELINGS SAFE SKILL as well as LISTEN SKILL for the response of the staff.
- A client who had been disruptive on a previous occasion while driving in the staff car told the staff person that he will be safe in the car,

not touch things, and not bother the driver. He followed through on these RESPECT STAFF CAR SKILL. He also, to the astonishment of the staff person, used SAY THANK YOU SKILL after being dropped off at his day program.

- A client who had been expecting staff to clean his laundry for him agreed to bring the laundry basket downstairs to the washing machine, put the clothing in the machine, and follow staff directions regarding putting in detergent and setting the dial. Each skill could be named individually or collectively they could be called LAUNDRY SKILL.

Meetings involving clients, such as house or community meetings, are great opportunities to help clients notice and label their own skills. For instance, at a house meeting, the house manager leads the clients in a discussion of planning for a birthday party. In the course of this meeting, the clients decided who to invite, created a menu, and planned some activities. During this meeting, they had several disagreements to overcome. They disagreed over the menu, but finally decided that the person whose birthday it was could decide. The house manager did need to guide these negotiations, but at the end of the meeting, she gave the clients credit for the meeting going well, asking them to name the skills they used. Having already been introduced to the skills vocabulary, several answered LISTEN, TAKE-TURNS, TALK, AGREE (i.e., negotiate) SKILL. The manager acknowledged these and also pointed out where they had disagreed and solved the disagreement. They listened to each other, compromised and decided to let the birthday person decide. The others used LET OTHER PERSON DECIDE SKILL, one of the CONFLICT SOLVE SKILLs they knew about. They all used EXPRESS FEELING SAFE SKILL.

At another meeting, a client who tends to be inpatient and to react angrily when he doesn't understand something, sits through a much longer meeting than he has previously done. At one point, he signs, EXCUSE-ME, DON'T-UNDERSTAND, CLEAR EXPLAIN AGAIN PLEASE. At the end of the meeting, the staff gave him feedback about the skills he just used which included paying attention for a long time, joining the discussion, taking turns, listening, noticing he wasn't understanding and asking appropriately for clarification. This was enough to make the client beam with pride when he might otherwise have felt inadequate for not understanding the full discussion. Staff noticing the skills he did use also contributed to the construction of a shared story about his developing abilities.

To someone unfamiliar with these persons, this approach may seem paternalistic, similar to how one would respond to a young child. Staff need to match the language they use to the language and cognitive sophistication of each client, but with many of the deaf persons we serve, this is the right language, and the persons experience the positive feedback they get as empowering and respectful *when it is offered in that spirit.*

With clients who have severe behavioral disorders, a treatment goal can be developing skills to express feelings, handle disagreements, and accept limits while staying safe. Whenever clinicians have conversations with such clients in which any of these skills are actually used, it is crucial to point it out. "Did you notice what just happened? You asked to go to the mall. I had to say no, not now. You complained but you stayed safe. We negotiated to do it later. You used "EXPRESS FEELING SAFE" skills. What other skills did you just use?"

These activities are so common place that once staff and clients get the idea, it becomes easy to notice and label skills happening all the time. With encouragement from program leadership, this language and style of interacting alone creates strength-based programs. It fosters positive relationships with clients. It introduces the skill language that will be used to handle the other treatment challenges. In a short amount of time, staff are in the position to say, "what skills can we use here?" All of this occurs outside of anything officially labeled as therapy such as what occurs in formal day treatment groups. However, it creates a useful schema of what therapy is (learning skills), and therefore sets the stage for getting clients into formal therapy. This work of identifying skills clients already have can be considered both pretreatment and treatment.

Once staff grasp the basis of this strength-based work, and understand how to view skills developmentally, it is astonishing how many problem situations can become opportunities to build upon skills already there. Staff move from being supervisors of clients to skill coaches, and the therapeutic value of residential treatment takes off.

Staff engaged Juan and many others by using this strategy. Staff knew that Juan would not be ready and able to discuss skills he needed to develop until he experienced how staff recognized and applauded the skills he already had. Thus, while some limit setting around sexual behaviors had to be set, the focus for staff became the pretreatment strategy of noticing and labeling skills Juan already showed. These included independent living skills (he kept his body, his room, and his clothing very clean) and, even more importantly, every instance of successful coping with a stress and dealing with other people. His aggressive episodes aside, Juan was friendly and sociable much of the time, and this gave staff opportunities to notice and comment when he used skills like helping, supporting, listening, being kind, and cooperating. They applauded him for his willingness to sit with them and discuss a problem. When they did express concerns, it was mostly in the form of out loud worrying. Telling people we are worried about their ability to reach their goals can be a useful intervention. Staff didn't want Juan to get in trouble, be arrested by the police, or sent back to the hospital. They knew he wanted to be more independent. If he touches someone's body without their permission in a sexual way, what could happen? If he hits people and breaks things, like before, what could happen? Is this what he wanted? What could he and we do to help?

Over time, this style of relating with Juan strengthened the relationships he had with staff and brought him to the point that he could, with guidance, set with us goals for skill development. Over time, he entered into a treatment relationship.

Skill Development 2: Formal Skill Instruction, But Adapted for Deaf Learners

Most approaches to skill development used in mental health and rehabilitation programs are formal and didactic. They consist of skill training groups in officially designated treatment settings like day treatment or partial hospitalization programs. They are often broken down into treatment modules which in turn are broken down into various skills. The DBT modules consist of mindfulness, distress tolerance, emotional self-regulation, and interpersonal effectiveness (Linehan, 1993b). The Boston University modules consist of rehabilitation readiness (an approach to pretreatment), goal setting, functional assessment, direct skills teaching, and case management. The modules from the UCLA Center consist of medication management, symptom management, recreation for leisure, basic conversation, community re-entry, job seeking, and workplace fundamentals. Each module is composed of many skills, and each program includes instructions for teaching the skills.

The Cognitive Behavioral Therapy paradigm has yielded a plethora of workbooks and training programs. Sometimes they are oriented around skills (e.g., coping skills, social skills, communication skills, relapse prevention skills) and sometimes around disorders. For example, Bellack and colleagues have a step by step guide for social skills training for persons with schizophrenia that is widely applicable to people with other psychiatric disorders (Bellack, Mueser, Gingerich, & Agresta, 1997). Boys Town has developed social skills training programs for youth with emotional and behavioral problems (Volz et al., 2009). New Harbinger Press specializes in workbooks for just about every psychiatric issue. One need only go to their website, type in Cognitive Behavioral Treatment for (fill in the problem) to get a library of practical treatment manuals designed to teach skills for symptom management and recovery.

A frequently referenced evidenced-based practice used in psychiatric rehabilitation programs today is Illness Management and Recovery (IMR; SAMHSA, 2009). IMR consists of 10 treatment modules usually taught in groups. These modules present the topics that should be part of any competent psychiatric rehabilitation program: (a) Strategies for recovery, (b) psychoeducation about mental illness, (c) the stress-vulnerability model and implications for treatment, (d) strategies and skills to build social support, (e) psychoeducation regarding medications, (f) drug and alcohol abuse, (g) reducing relapses, (h) coping skills and stress management, (i) symptom and problem management, (j) getting your needs met in the mental health system. When we evaluate treatment programs for persons with severe mental illness, we would look to see how well these topics are addressed.

There are many ways to cover these topics, but this work is usually done in group settings that are part of a day treatment program. In these group settings, one imparts information and teaches skills. There is a great deal of overlap between different curricula on the topics covered. For instance, coping skills, stress and symptom management, relapse prevention, psychoeducation, and becoming an informed consumer are almost always covered, and it is hard to argue convincingly that one treatment program is superior to another. More important is a developing consensus as to what "best practice" in psychiatric rehabilitation looks like. Best practice certainly involves drawing upon client strengths, eliciting informed engagement (pretreatment) through all the approaches discussed above, partnering in a collaborative manner, and developing the skill sets relevant to symptom mastery, healthy living, recovery and pursuit of one's life goals. Best practice also involves providing the environmental supports and resources to accomplish these goals, which in the case of work with deaf persons must include culturally affirmative treatment settings with suitably trained staff.

Best practice can also be summarized in terms of the components and method of skill training. From studying various approaches, we would summarize these as involving these steps:

- Explain (break skill down into components) the skill
- Model it
- Practice and role play
- Give feedback, noting what the client does well
- Practice again in varied, real life circumstances
- Reinforce progress
  To these basic steps, we'd add one more that Meichenbaum and Biemiller (1998) have long stressed:
- Have the client teach the skill to someone else

At Deaf Services Center, adaptation of existing approaches is the rule. DSC offers formal skill training groups on topics like coping skills and anger management, but no one established approach is used. DBT has influenced the group treatment at DSC partial hospitalization program, as it did the group treatment at the Westborough Deaf Unit, but the adaptations are so extensive that one can't fairly call them DBT. A highly specialized version of cognitive behavioral therapy is a better descriptor.

For example, in some DSC groups, the DBT concept of mindfulness is taught. Clients are coached to slow down, pay attention to their sensory experiences, and avoid judgments and interpretations of these experiences. Experiences with food, where one is coached to smell, taste, feel, and swallow very slowly, are helpful. Sound-based stimuli (close your eyes and listen to a tape) can't be used. Some clients can do guided visualizations (detailed sensory-based visualizations of safe or peaceful places) and art/drawing is often used as an aid in such visualizations. Others can do progressive muscle relaxation. Many can learn and use diaphragmatic breathing. All of this is compatible with the DBT mindfulness module, but most of that module isn't formally used.

In most of these DSC treatment groups, complex and abstract explanations are avoided. Many clients cannot work with hypothetical situations (i.e., imagine what you would do if …). Many have difficulty working with time lines, projecting themselves into the future to imagine coping with some anticipated trigger or stressor (key elements of relapse prevention work). They have difficulty remembering and following multi-step instructions. A didactic lecture format, such as one finds in DBT, will lose most of the participants within minutes.

At DSC, as at Advocates and in the Deaf Unit at Westborough, formal groups target the population of language and learning challenged deaf consumers who are the majority of consumers. In all these programs, the formal groups share these qualities:

1. Continual adjustment for consumers at varying levels of language skill and cognitive sophistication. Groups are generally conducted in ASL, but the language used varies considerably based on who is involved.
2. Close attention to language and whether or not consumers understand. Frequent check-ins to ask variations of "am I clear?"
3. An action format is emphasized over discussion. Almost all groups involve role play. It often works best for the activity to come first, the discussion second. This is the reverse of the usual (hearing) order of presentation.
4. Therapeutic games and stories are incorporated.
5. Awareness that many clients have these gaps in their fund of information. Therefore, considerable time is spent explaining key concepts and establishing ways to sign them. Pretreatment educational and motivational strategies take up more of the time. The pace of instruction is considerably slower.
6. Heavy reliance on visual aids. DSC, like many other programs, has made use of the visual aids developed by Michael Krajnak on the Westborough Deaf Unit (Glickman, 2009). Clip art is also used. Clients are also encouraged to draw their own pictorial tools.
7. Coping skills are emphasized. This is because many of these clients have significant behavioral problems, and minimizing violence is a

core preoccupation of staff. It is also because coping skills have broad applicability to a wide range of clinical problems.

On the Westborough Deaf Unit, coping skills were a long standing focus of treatment. The first author led hundreds of coping skills groups there and elsewhere, and over time learned how to structure the groups to make them more "Deaf friendly." In his early years, the groups usually began by trying to help clients understand the definition of coping skills. The leader began roughly as follows:

> *Coping skills are strategies people use to regulate emotional states and man-age environmental stressors. All human beings need coping skills because life is filled with stressors and with unpleasant experiences. Indeed, the true measure of psychological health is not how happy and content one feels, but how well one manages the unpleasant emotional states (anger, sadness, anxiety) which are a natural part of the human condition. Some examples of coping skills are deep breathing, exercise and positive self-talk. What are your coping skills?*

With more experience, and the guidance of many talented deaf clini-cians and paraprofessionals, he made a significant shift in how he intro-duced the concept and structured the group. The newer, more effective groups, began roughly as follows:

> *When I am sad, I do a number of things to feel better. I seek out friends to talk to. I go to my yoga class. I play with my dog Baxter who never tires of my attention. When I am angry, I need to go to my room, to stay away from people, until I am calm. Sometimes I'll sit and meditate but other times I'll just distract myself by surfing the internet. Eventually, I calm down, and I can deal with people again. These are some of my coping skills. Everyone has coping skills. When people have many coping skills, they can stay calm and in control no matter what happens to them, no matter what they feel. This makes them more psychologically healthy. What are your coping skills?*

The first kind of discourse, which goes from abstract principal to spe-cific example, is very common among English speakers, especially those, like mental health professionals, who have graduate school education. The second kind of discourse, which goes from specific examples to abstract principals, is more common among ASL users, especially those, like most deaf psychiatric rehabilitation clients, who have not had college educa-tion and have limited English literacy. Neither kind of discourse is supe-rior to the other. One is not abstract while the other is concrete. Rather, they organize information differently. In general, a discourse style that runs from specific to general works better with ASL using deaf residential treatment clients. This is, the first author believes, partly because of the structure of ASL, its tendency to build abstract categories out of lists of specific examples (Klima & Bellugi, 1979). With some thought, classes and treatment groups can be organized around this principal.

Building on specific examples means drawing upon stories. To make skills groups work for deaf rehabilitation clients, they must begin, and be filled with, stories. If the group members are already engaged, the counselor asks variants of: "Tell me what happened to you this week that was difficult? How did you feel? What did you do?" The counselor solicits stories. If it is a new group or the members are not engaged, the counselor may need to begin by presenting stories. On the Westborough Deaf Unit, we often did this by having clients pick cards which depicted situations that elicited stress. For instance, a card shows a person putting money into a vending machine but not getting the candy or soda (see Figure 5.1). With Deaf clients who have language or cognitive impairments, the stories must often be acted out. Someone role plays the person putting in the money. Another person role plays the vending machine withholding

Figure 5.1 A coping skill situation card.

the item. In addition to being fun, clients are challenged to demonstrate the coping skills in the moment, and only after this are they invited to talk about them.

The focus on examples and stories is one way Deaf friendly treatment groups are organized differently. A second way is through heavy reliance upon role playing. A third, the most obvious, is that the discourse occurs in ASL. A fourth difference is that the teaching style is more interactive, with the leader paying close attention to whether or not the members are understanding. This may involve frequent check-ins ("Am I clear?") and a willingness to rephrase differently rather than just repeat oneself. A fifth difference is that the group leader is more likely to know what kind of information the participants already have, and to fill in gaps in the participant's knowledge. Finally, of course, there is the reluctance to use English-based materials and a preference for visual or pictorial aids (O'Hearn, Pollard, & Haynes, 2010; Pollard, Dean, O'Hearn, & Hayes, 2009).

It is a mistake to assume that this Deaf treatment approach is more "concrete" or "simple" In both cases, abstract principals like "coping skills" are being taught. The information is just organized differently. As a second language user of ASL, I (first author) find this Deaf way of working far more difficult. I'd much rather stay afloat in the abstract world of definitions and principals then trudge through the muddy ground of examples from everyday life. I find it much easier to teach people who have a fund of basic cultural information similar to my own. But I have gotten better at this trudging, at adapting treatment for different style learners, and I've seen my groups become much more successful as I've done so. And, in a strange paradox, I've also discovered that this "Deaf" way of teaching; going from specific to general, using stories, acting things out, also works better with many of the hearing consumers in treatment programs.

Many of the persons in the Advocates group homes were patients at one time on the Westborough Deaf Unit and in that setting were introduced to the treatment focus on coping and conflict resolution skills. One way this skill building approach was brought to Advocates was by offering to hire clients to meet weekly to develop films to teach coping and other skills to other deaf people. Clients were paid to attend this weekly meeting which at the time of this writing has been occurring for over 5 years. Two DVDs were produced, one demonstrating coping skills and the other demonstrating conflict solving skills, and the group leadership (that is, the clients) has made formal presentations of this approach at the local school for the deaf and at state and national psychiatric rehabilitation conferences. Over time, group membership has changed, but the weekly meetings in which various skills are practiced have laid the foundation for the use of a skill-based strategy whenever problems occur in the program. Juan and many others have been involved in these groups. Clients are paid to attend, which no doubt influences their motivation, but the payoff in creating a skill-based culture, in decreasing incidents of unsafe behaviors, and in building stories about client abilities, are well worth the modest financial investment. Now, every time there is a behavioral problem, staff and clients know that we will review it, discuss the skills that should have been used, practice, try again, and applaud success.

Skill Development 3: Collaborative Problem Solving

While formal group work in skill development is the most widely used approach in psychiatric rehabilitation, it should not be relied upon as the sole or even primary method in residential treatment. That is because formal classroom like skill instruction assumes engaged, motivated clients who also are ready and able to learn, and a great deal of pretreatment work usually has to be done to get persons to this point. It's also because it is fairly uncommon to have deaf friendly treatment groups, organized as described above, available. When signing residential treatment facilities are available, there is a great deal that can be accomplished informally, in the residence, when staff are properly trained. Residential treatment provides countless opportunities for teaching moments that are especially valuable with clients who are pretreatment, and don't yet make good use of structured treatment opportunities. One strategy that draws heavily upon such teaching moments is "collaborative problem solving."

Collaborative problem solving (Greene & Ablon, 2006) is a method of conflict resolution developed by Ross Greene and Associates for treatment of "explosive" children and their families. There are several reasons why CPS is relevant to deaf psychiatric rehabilitation.

1. Consistent with other skill building approaches, Greene argues that the reasons children (and by extension, adult clients) have behavioral problems is that they lack the relevant psychosocial skills. This is a direct contrast to the older behavioral therapy model which attributed the problem to motivational deficits. Greene finds common "pathways" to explosive behavior in varying types of skill deficits. These are skill deficits in rational thinking (executive skills), cognitive flexibility (overly rigid thinkers), language processing, coping (regulating emotions), and social skills. These kinds of skill deficits are very common in deaf and hearing psychiatric rehabilitation clients.
2. Greene places emphasis upon training parents, teachers and mental health counselors to adopt a flexible problem-solving style so that *they* can teach relevant skills to their children, students, and clients. Greene stresses the importance of avoiding authoritarian limit setting in favor of a collaborative problem-solving style. He teaches parents, teachers, and counselors the importance of leading with empathy, not limits, and then inviting their children, students, and clients to work with them towards mutually satisfactory solutions. This respectful

and empowering style of interaction is encouraged in psychiatric rehabilitation. It is consistent with efforts to teach staff to work from a "one down" perspective in which they invite, rather than direct, clients to work with them. This respectful style of interaction is also good pretreatment work as it elicits client engagement much more effectively than the use of authority, rules, and limits.

3. This is an informal skill building approach which usually occurs in unstructured, everyday life situations, not in formal class rooms or officially designated skill building groups. There is no formal curriculum of designated skills to master. This matters a great deal as we have many clients who won't attend anything labeled "therapy." Collaborative problem solving is an approach to treatment in which clients are invited to solve all the daily conflicts that come along naturally. When staff are trained in this method, every problem that comes along becomes an opportunity for skill building. Each problem is shared with clients, and staff request their help in coming up with mutually acceptable solutions.

4. Sometimes there is very little connection between what happens in formal day treatment and what happens in the residential component of a program. Clients may be taught coping skills in the former setting while no one is helping them apply these skills in their real lives. These are lost therapeutic opportunities. When collaborative problem solving informs a family environment, classroom, hospital unit, or group home, this gap can be overcome.

Greene lists language skill deficits as a factor in the difficulty his clients have with problem solving. He is referring to hearing people, not to the much more severe language deficits that go along with the language deprivation that deaf children commonly face. Language deprived children tend to grow up in families and schools where there is little attempt made to teach language-based problem solving. They grow up in worlds driven by rules, not skills. This is all the more reason why it is essential to build Deaf treatment environments around strategies to help clients develop skills. Authoritarian treatment environments, geared towards getting students or clients to comply with rules, may even elicit the explosive behaviors they are trying to prevent. Sometimes, staff (deaf and hearing) who grew up without good problem-solving skills also need to be coached before they can be called upon to coach others in these skills.

A client named Bob refuses to go to the day treatment program, called "day hab," where some skill building groups are offered. He becomes angry and throws a chair. He screams, gestures angrily, and then storms off to his room.

In collaborative problem solving, staff respond to this in one of two ways. The preferred way is proactive. The counselor *anticipates* the problem before it occurs and *invites* the client to develop a plan to prevent the problem. This is actually a variant of relapse prevention work. The less preferred way is responding in the middle of a crisis. This is when the client is already upset, and the staff person tries to engage him in problem solving at that moment. Greene recognizes that it is much easier to solve a problem and develop skills before a crisis happens than in the midst of one. It would be better to discuss with Bob his concerns regarding day hab and to problem solve them in advance to avoid this crisis.

Either way, the key staff skill is empathy. The staff person says, "You are refusing to go to day hab. What's up?" The staff person does not try to solve a problem without understanding the client's perspective. "Oh, you are bored there. Oh, there is nothing to do. You don't like this staff person. It is more fun to stay at home." The client, at this time, is also using "EXPRESS FEELING SAFE SKILLS." They may well be using other conversational and social skills that are worth noting.

The second step of collaborative problem solving is defining the problem. In this step, both the staff concern and the client concern are put on the table. Finally, the client is invited to come up with solutions that work for everyone. The staff person says, "I understand you don't want to go to day hab. It is boring and there isn't much to do there. But we have a problem. We don't have staff to stay with you at home during the day. Are you willing to try with me to come up with some solutions?" This particular problem is difficult to solve because it probably requires more resources, either staffing at home or at the day program. The client here was helped to talk to day program staff about ways to make their program more interesting to him.

Another deaf language and learning challenged consumer in a group home has made great improvements in his independent living skills. He no longer tantrums like he used to. He participates in cooking and chores around the house. He manages well a small allowance he gets from his mother. The biggest challenge he has now is to convince his very overprotective mother and equally controlling agency case manager that he no longer needs a guardian of person. Prior discussions with both mother and case manager have not gone well, and this has been as much due to their lack of problem-solving skills as his. They stubbornly insisted that he needs this "help," and he responded by becoming angry, abusive, and threatening, which convinced them further that he wasn't ready for more independence. His program staff use collaborative problem solving to prepare him for an upcoming case conference in which he, and they, will again raise the issue of not wanting a guardian. Staff began by empathizing,

> You've improved a lot. You don't blow up like before. You clean your room and the house. You cook your meals. You shop with staff. When you are angry with staff, you talk to us and you listen. You don't want your mother to be your guardian any more. You think she treats you like a baby. You feel ready for more independence. We agree, and we

will help you, but we have to use skill in talking to your mother and case manager. Can we make a plan and practice it here?

The staff then helped the client understand why his mother and case manager may be reluctant to agree (he hasn't always behaved so well in the past). They stress the importance of him showing calm behavior in the meeting. They help him practice telling them what he wants and why. They also help him practice staying calm (using coping skills) as staff, acting in the roles of mother and case manager, argue back with him. Staff explain that agency procedures ensure he can get a new evaluation of his need for a guardianship, and that they will insist on this, though they can't guarantee the outcome. If he stays calm and clearly states his case, it will help him win what he wants.

The staff help the client develop many coping and interpersonal skills here. They help him express his feelings, argue his position, see the point of view of another person, listen, negotiate, stay calm while others disagree, not respond to emotional triggers, etc. Ideally, his mother and case manager would do the same thing, but in this case it is the staff teaching the client how to be more skillful with them. The staff also point out to him all the skills he has just used. This isn't a formal part of collaborative problem solving but it strengthens the skills to give them a name. It also strengthens the "I can do it story" to point out to clients what skills they just used. This skill training is done proactively, in anticipation of the meeting, and the client is also coached again just before the meeting. It is done informally, during a casual meeting in the group home, so the client doesn't even realize he just had a counseling session. In the meeting with parents and case manager later, the client, with staff support, was able to demonstrate the skills he practiced, and to their surprise his mother and case manager responded well. They agreed that he has made improvements and to the process of re-evaluation of his need for a personal guardian.

Samuel is another client with a history of aggressive behaviors that have resulted in many involuntary psychiatric hospitalizations. He receives outreach services in an apartment he shares with one roommate. The fire alarms inside his apartment are connected to the local fire department, and, over a period of several months, there were numerous incidents where he set off the alarms while cooking. This meant that the fire department trucks were dispatched to his residence. This happened so many times that the fire department threatened to fine the program. Staff were apprehensive about discussing the problem with Samuel because he often became aggressive when confronted with something he did wrong. They knew they may have to supervise Samuel more closely, or restrict his access to his stove, and both of these outcomes would likely trigger an explosion. The first time the team raised the fire alarm problem with Samuel, he became defensive and hostile and blamed his roommate. The team couldn't let it go. There were real issues of safety at stake as well as the likelihood of a hefty fine from the fire department.

The treatment team understood they had to make this Samuel's problem, not just theirs. They decided on a collaborative problem-solving approach. They empathized with Samuel's feelings (he didn't like being bossed around; he wanted to be independent) and then identified the problem they had to share together. Samuel's goal was to stay in his apartment. The team shared this goal but it had to be based on Samuel showing safe cooking skills. Samuel insisted he could be safe. They negotiated a plan in which Samuel could demonstrate his safety. If the fire department came to his apartment one more time due to smoke or fire, the knobs from his stove would be removed. He would have to ask staff for the knobs when he was ready to cook and they would supervise him. This seemed like a good plan until one night when staff came into his apartment, found it smoky, with the auditory alarm (precursor to the visual alarm) already going off. The windows were opened quickly before the visual alarm triggered the fire department to come. This incident happened on a weekend. Staff followed the plan of removing the stove knobs even though, as Samuel protested vigorously, the fire trucks had not actually come to his apartment. Technically, the conditions for removal of the knobs had not been met, and Samuel insisted on this concrete, literal interpretation of the contract. To his credit, Samuel was able to stay calm and wait until Monday to discuss the plan with the clinical staff.

On Monday, Samuel participated very well in a collaborative problem-solving session. He stated calmly that the fire trucks had never actually arrived so he shouldn't have to lose the knobs to the stove. Staff pointed out that the apartment was smoky, the auditory alarm had already gone off, and it was just good luck that the staff arrived to open the windows in time. Together they negotiated a plan. Staff would, on a temporary basis, hold on to the knobs and supervise him while he cooked. This would be time limited. If there were no more incidents for a period of time, the knobs would be returned. If there was another incident, the knobs would remain off for a longer period. Samuel stayed cool through this negotiation which enabled staff to point out to him the coping and conflict resolution skills he just used.

Many clients accept this practical, in the moment skill training even when they won't go to formal treatment groups. Staff can use collaborative problem solving whenever they can anticipate clients facing challenges. For instance, staff knows that a client named Fred really wants to go to visit the train station tomorrow and that he is likely to have a meltdown if the trip is abruptly cancelled. They also know that there is a good chance the trip will be cancelled due to staffing limitations. Looking ahead, they invite Fred to discuss the problem. It is helpful to begin with a one down, "can we talk about this?" request.

"Fred, we have a possible problem and we need your help. Can we talk about it?"

After Fred agrees to talk, staff take the lead with empathy.

"We know you love to visit the train station. It is very important to you. You love to watch the trains and ride them. We want to take you there."

Staff then define the problem and invite his participation in solving it.

"But we may have a problem. We need your help to solve the problem. What will we do if there is only one staff person on tomorrow afternoon? You know sometimes staff call out sick. We need to take care of all the clients in the house, all five of you, and we can't do that, and go to the train station, with only one staff person. Do you have any ideas?"

Of course, it is possible that Fred will have a meltdown just talking about the problem. If that is the case, he'd certainly have one when actually faced with an abrupt cancellation. But very often clients can participate in this kind of problem solving, coming up with possible solutions. In this case, Fred suggested they try again the next day. If Fred can suggest that, and also participate reasonably well in the problem-solving conversations, staff will have many examples of his conflict solving skills to comment upon (listening, expressing himself safely, considering different options, brainstorming solutions, accepting if he can't get something he wants, etc.). Staff commenting upon all the skills they just helped the client develop also opens up ways to encourage the client to learn even more skills such as by attending the formal skill training groups offered or addressing this formally in the clients' individual counseling.

There are times when a one-up, limit setting stance may be called for. Some of the times when this may be preferable are:

1. When immediate safety is at stake and behavior is non-negotiable;
2. When, for personal or cultural reasons, the client expects and wants the staff to be the authority;
3. When clients are sociopathic and interpret negotiation as weakness on the part of staff;
4. When clients show extreme "therapy interfering behaviors" that are non-negotiable (e.g., calling the therapist in the middle of the night for minor reasons, skipping appointments but calling in between appointments in crisis);
5. With very severely impaired clients who are unable to manage the anxiety related to decision making.

A collaborative problem-solving approach should be the default stance of program staff with most clients. Generally speaking, it will reduce violence, engage clients, and give them opportunities to develop skills. It will also foster better relationships with staff and make the treatment setting a more rewarding place to work and receive care.

Skill Building 4: Using Clients as Helpers and Teachers

Persons can be pretreatment because they are tired of being acted upon, of being the recipients of care, a position they regard as stigmatizing and weak. Even when they have had very little experience of being in control of their lives, they still strive for it. Staff can solicit their involvement and give them the experience of greater autonomy by taking a "one-down" stance on most matters. A one-down stance occurs when staff take the position of not knowing, of recognizing the authority of someone else, of needing help and requesting assistance. A simple one-down stance is just to say, "Can you help me?"

Whenever possible, it is powerful to put clients into the helper or teacher role. One reason the Advocates skill group has lasted for many years is that it operates from such a stance. Clients are invited to a group which is defined as a job (i.e., developing skills to help others) and paid for their time. The most competent members of that group do become skill teachers. Some have presented this material at conferences and at the local Deaf school. Some are included in a second "leadership" group in which they are trained to become co-facilitators of the larger group. The leader is always taking the stance, "I can't do this without you. I appreciate you helping me." This trainer model has also paid rich dividends because once people see themselves as capable of using skills; indeed, of teaching skills, it is far easier to get them to use the skills when they need them.

Staff rotate in and out of the groups and attend other trainings on skill development strategies. Staff need to have the same skill vocabulary and help clients make the connection between the group sessions one evening per week and what happens in their lives every day. Staff skills develop as they come to function less as supervisors and more as skill coaches. When a new problem occurs, staff learn to begin addressing it by asking for help from clients. "We have a problem. We need your help. Can we discuss this and use our skills now to solve the problem?"

For example, one of the group leaders, David, has a tendency to pressure other clients into giving him cigarettes. He is big and can be intimidating. Other clients have a hard time saying no to him, but resent his high pressure tactics. One day, several of the other clients announced that they didn't want David to come to their house any more. Since the group meetings were held in their house, that meant he would be barred from participating in any capacity with the group and he would also be cut off from half of his peers.

Staff followed these steps to solve the problem:

> Staff approached David in a one-down manner, expressing concern, and asking for his help to solve a problem. They reminded him of the conflict solving skills he had learned and asked him whether he would be willing to use them now. He said he would.

Staff then explained that several of his peers had complained about him pressuring them to give him cigarettes. They were angry with him and did not want him to come to their house any more. Staff were worried that he would lose these friends. Would he be willing to use his skills to help solve the conflict with his peers?

David at first needed some encouragement. He became depressed, obsessed for a while about how everyone hated him, but eventually agreed to a meeting with his peers. David also agreed to have the peers that, with him, were in the leadership group act as mediators for the conflict with the other clients.

The most difficult part was getting one of the clients who had complained most loudly about David to agree to meet with him for a conflict solving session. However, the norm for using skills to solve problems had been established and eventually he agreed.

The large session was set with David, the peers who complained about him, his peers from the leadership team, and a few staff. The rest was fairly easy. David was already prepared to listen, not interrupt, and accept the request that he not ask for cigarettes any more. He knew this procedure from the group. The others were coached to use good communication skills like "I statements" just as they had practiced in the group. In a short time, the resolution was found, and clients and staff could all notice and label the conflict solving skills used in the group.

Samuel, the client discussed in the previous section who had the problem with not cooking safely, had a bigger problem with his explosive temper. His temper had gotten him hospitalized numerous times and kicked out of various programs. Samuel really started to make gains on his behaviors when he was asked to help another client with *her* explosive behaviors. This other client became furious with staff, screaming, cursing, and throwing objects, whenever they didn't do what she wanted. Samuel was asked to teach this other client, and he was amazingly effective, far more so than staff had been. His effectiveness teaching her also provided evidence which he couldn't refute that he had the skills also, and this contributed to the construction of a new story, about his abilities, and an improvement in his behaviors so they matched better this new strength-based story.

Additional examples are those of Jake and Terrence, two young men with substantial histories of aggressive behaviors. One day, Jake was struggling with increased irritability and mood swings because he had stopped taking his medication. Jake attempted to introduce himself to a new peer, Michael (who also has a history of aggression and threats and who had recently started the program). Michael made a face and signed DON'T-WANT. Jake felt insulted and angry. He approached Michael, making threatening statements and grabbed Michael's crotch.

At this point, the program director who was across the hall entered the room in response to the disturbance. Jake was yelling at Michael and saying that he was going to beat him up. The two were about 5 feet apart, and Jake was approaching Michael in a menacing manner. The program director placed herself between the two. She signed STOP and OUTSIDE to Jake. He didn't respond to her prompts. At this point Michael, who has limited mobility, was struggling to get up and was yelling and signing back at Jake, "I'm not afraid of you" and urging him on. Jake began moving to come around the table toward Michael from the other direction. The program director moved herself in between the two men again, and continued to sign STOP, OUTSIDE. Other staff entered the room, and another female staff encouraged Michael to leave the room with her.

Terrence was present in the room as this was occurring and was trying to support Jake in calming down. Although Jake was not listening to any of the staff who were present, he did respond to Terrence's prompts. Terrence touched Jake lightly on the shoulder and signed OUTSIDE CALM-DOWN just as the program director had, but with much more success. Jake was still agitated and yelling but he signed FINE to Terrence and began to move toward the exit, yelling threats as he went. Michael continued to yell and sign threats back.

Once Terrence left the room, Michael agreed to go with the female staff to talk about what happened. The program director went outside to see how Jake was. At that point Jake was outside with Terrence and two male staff. He was smoking a cigarette and said he was going to calm down. Jake was thinking about what happened but when he thought about Michael's behavior he became agitated again. Terrence noted that he gets angry too and he understood how Jake felt. Terrence offered Jake a prompt to LET-GO so that he could CALM-DOWN instead of getting more upset. He pointed out that Michael had his own problems. Jake said, "I know. I have to control myself. I know that I can." The program director praised Jake for taking control by choosing to leave the room and going outside to give himself a chance to calm down. She praised and thanked Terrence for stepping up to support his friend. She noted that it was Terrence who was able to help Jake to make the decision to leave the room. Terrence flashed a bright smile and signed YOU-ARE-WELCOME.

Staff then seized upon the opportunity to build upon these examples of client helping skills. They praised Terrence for his ability to recognize the skills that his friend Jake had needed, the WALK-AWAY, CALM-DOWN, AND LET-GO skills. Terrence was showing good ability to recognize the need for other people to use these skills but struggled to apply them himself when he needed them. Often, when staff prompted Terrence to use his skills, this would escalate his anger. This might happen because staff slipped back into a "one-up" stance, telling Terrence what to do, and offering a superficial USE YOUR SKILLS prompt which, done in this manner, is no more helpful than telling someone to "cheer up." Terrence appeared insulted at those moments and responded that I KNOW and I NOT STUPID. Staff were more effective when they moved back into the one-down stance, *wondering* aloud why Terrence was so skillful at helping others but struggled so much with helping himself. Staff repeatedly pointed out how well he intervened with Jake. They showed a puzzled expression, said they were stuck and asked for his help. Terrence was then able to identify a few staff and members from whom he felt more comfortable receiving prompts to use his skills. Staff agreed to try to have those staff/members offer supports whenever possible. When Terrence became upset and agitated, his preferred staff offered prompts, and he was much better able to accept them and practice BREATHE and WALK-AWAY skills himself. Here staff were using collaborative problem solving as well as drawing upon Terrence's abilities as a helper.

Staff was also encouraging Terrence to join a domestic violence group, but he was very hesitant to go. Staff used the situation with Jake to support Terrence's positive recovery story, underscoring that he was a smart man who could identify skills. Staff met with Terrence when he was calm and asked him to grade his performance in managing his anger effectively[7]. Surprisingly, Terrence gave himself a "C." He noted some things he was able to handle well and some things he still needed to work on. Staff asked Terrence if he was satisfied with that grade. Terrence said that he wasn't. Terrence then agreed to give the domestic violence class a try. Since Terrence had shown himself to be able to teach and support his peers in using skills with Jake and others, staff asked Terrence if he would be willing to work with staff to teach skills he learned in domestic violence group here as well. Terrence loved that idea and said he would like to be able to help his peers.

Staff used this same approach with Jake. Staff reflected back to him his prior success at teaching his peers about the dangers of drugs and addictions in groups he co-led with staff. Staff noted that the peers learned a lot and that they seemed to pay attention better and were more motivated when he led the groups. Since he had done such a great job using his skills and has personal experience working hard to manage his anger, staff asked if he would be willing to share that experience and skill in groups. Jake then met with staff and set up a lesson plan that he shared with peers. The lesson plan consisted of some anger management skills that were relevant to Jake, and the meeting to help Jake teach these skills to another person was as good a "therapy" session as one would ever hope for. Jake was also encouraged to step up as a leader in groups when topics came close to his own experience and successes. Jake relished his role as leader and showed increased motivation and participation in all of his groups, not just the groups he led. Staff also noted that Jake was better able to accept support and feedback from staff when he was agitated and upset, noting that he was much less likely to become defensive or shut staff out as he had in the past. The peers also benefitted since Jake was speaking about problems they had in common. They were less defensive getting advice from him than from staff.

Ironically, many people who are unwilling to put themselves in the role of being students are thrilled to act in the role of teachers. In the teacher role, they are much more receptive to learning, to being students. In reality, you can't be a good teacher unless you are also a good student. The challenge for staff is to be willing to allow clients to teach and help us. Some staff who are psychologically invested in remaining in the helper role can have more difficulty with this than clients. They may need to see themselves as better (healthier, smarter, more capable) than clients. We tell them that it actually takes much more skill to work "one down," allowing a client to grow by having them help you, then it does to supervise or instruct them. Staff who understand this often advance dramatically in their clinical skills.

The Client Who "Won't Use His Skills"

A consulting psychologist receives a referral about a difficult client who "won't use his skills." How, the treatment team asks, can they help a person who refuses to make use of the skills they have been teaching him? The referral contains the following information:

> George has been in a residential program for many years. He has average intelligence with some capacity for abstract thinking. He signs fluently in ASL. He exhibits obsessive compulsive traits. His central theme is "I'm short, I'm ugly, everyone hates me." He becomes extremely upset by slights real and imagined, and then he tantrums and engages in self-injurious behavior. Due to his insecurities, when he has a friend or girlfriend, he tends to want all of their undivided time and attention. When the friend or girlfriend has something else to do, George becomes anxious, depressed, irritable, and sometimes explosive and self-injurious in his behaviors. When he has a girlfriend, he will give the person whatever she asks for, such as food and money, in order to keep her interested. One week he depleted his bank account and missed paying 1 month of rent, because he bought his girlfriend a series of expensive gifts.
>
> Staff and peers tried to engage George in other positive activities so he would obsess less about his girlfriend, but he frequently sabotaged these efforts. For example, a male peer invited George to his apartment to join a guys' get together. George accepted and was looking forward to the evening. When the time of the get together arrived, he refused to attend and stayed home alone.

Throughout the years, staff have worked with him on a host of skills, for example: journaling, considering alternate perspectives of the situation (such as when he misreads facial expressions in other people), relaxed breathing, walking away from stressful situations, seeking staff to talk to before he blows up, and so forth. By this time, when staff sat with him to help him calm down, he identified all the skills he should have used, and how to use them. When staff caught him as he was beginning to escalate, he could sometimes reverse the tide, but not always. There were some days, at home, when he approached several different staff within an hour stating he needed to talk about the same issues (i.e., how everyone hates me). Staff were willing to talk with him, but they knew he already just spoke with another staff person, and that this endless attention seeking, without *doing anything* to help himself, was counter-productive. Staff worried that if they turned away from him, he would perceive it as rejection and hurt himself. If they responded to every request to rehash the same complaints, they would be reinforcing these maladaptive behaviors. The fundamental goal that staff had for George was for him to use some of the coping skills he knew about. But, staff complained, George 'won't use his skills. He continues to hurt himself and other people. What should they do?"

Skill training, like all forms of mental health treatment, works best with clients who understand it well and are highly motivated to achieve results. As we have seen, mental health and rehabilitation programs have many clients who don't fit this profile. The simplified skill training approach presented here is designed to address the pretreatment problem of clients neither understanding nor wanting to collaborate in the treatment process. The simple model helps overcome the gap in world view between client and counselor/team and the strength-based approach helps elicit motivation. George appears to be an example of a client who "gets it" but doesn't seem to get better. He can "talk the talk but not walk the walk." On first glance, his problem does not appear to be skill deficits, but rather motivational deficits. Also, George is intelligent and signs well. He knows the purpose of psychotherapy. He has a schema for the process. All of this suggests the treatment focus should be on motivational enhancement strategies rather than skill building. However, the psychologist keeps open the possibility that more subtle skill deficits are still a problem. The psychologist asks the treatment team to consider several questions.

First, is he really "in treatment," or are there major pretreatment challenges still occurring?

As discussed above, there are many reasons clients are pretreatment. Most of the reasons have to do with attitudes, lack of motivation, and ambivalence about change. With language and learning challenged clients, the barrier may be the lack of a shared model of the treatment process.

This does not appear to be George's problem. Staff insist he knows about coping skills.

Most difficult treatment clients have to be coaxed along in the process. It can help staff to recognize this is long term work, that the pretreatment challenges of eliciting informed engagement may occur as long as the treatment work. Motivation may be an issue for most or all of the treatment. There is no magic. There is only "best practice."

Are there any reasons, the psychologist asks, why George might prefer to stay sick?

Clients like George, typically, have difficulty taking responsibility for their own development. They may have "secondary gain," which is that they get great satisfaction in staying in the patient role. If "getting better" to them means possibly losing a great deal of institutional and social support, they have good reasons to resist getting better. If they grew up in a family where they were viewed as the "poor, handicapped child," and if they have parents who continue to treat them, even though they are adults, as though they are incapable, incompetent, and in need of protection from the harsh, cruel world, they probably have an identity heavily rooted in this idea of themselves. They will not give up this identity, and the other perceived benefits of staying sick, easily in exchange for the unknown and frightening world of being an independent, healthy, grown-up. George constantly seeks out staff to talk about how he is short, ugly, and everyone hates him. He appears to like the social reinforcement that comes from talking about skills he might have used, but didn't. The alternative, actually using the skills to achieve stated goals, is much scarier to him than staying sick.

Following this search for secondary gain, the psychologist asks whether there are family or environmental barriers to George taking responsibility for his own development.

What systems, or what people, are invested in keeping him in a patient role? Very often there are family members who enable by never expecting the person to show responsible, competent behavior and by protecting the person from negative consequences. Was there a family member who gave George reinforcing attention whenever he acted pathetic and helpless? Was there a family member who invalidated or minimized mature, skillful behavior when George showed it? Were there any comparable people invested in keeping George in the sick role?

Sometimes the problem is not family but agency officials and legal authorities keeping clients in a dependent role. For instance, a client whose mother has always been his guardian has grown enough that it is becoming reasonable to consider dropping the guardianship. His mother vigorously opposes the idea and has an alliance with an equally infantilizing agency case manager. Sometimes, though not with George, clients engage in serious criminal behavior[8] but neither police nor judges hold them accountable. There are deaf persons who are savvy enough to "play the deaf card" to get excused from anti-social behaviors. Sometimes their lawyers advise them to do just this or do this for them. If we are working with a client whom the police will not arrest, no matter what he does, it is very likely that this police enabling will be more powerful than any therapeutic program staff can put together.

In George's case, there were no family or agency people invested in him staying sick. However, he was still acting out the sick, helpless, pathetic role he learned as a child even as the people who taught him this role were long gone.

George may understand recovery as learning skills but he appears to be, at best, ambivalent, about using these skills. Thus, pretreatment strategies were very much needed. Staff will usually do better if they understand that he is not fully on board, that progress will be limited until we can get him more on board, and that eliciting responsibility taking on his part is a major aspect of our pretreatment challenges. In other words, coaching him to use his skills will not work. A treatment plan that says, "George will identify feelings and use designated coping skills" will not work. Rather, staff need to use pretreatment strategies designed to elicit motivation. It appears that George either fears change or does not believe he can change. Staff need to find non-threatening ways to present him with evidence of his own capacity for change. They need to help him *discover* his own capacity for getting better.

The psychologist asks the team leaders what exactly they mean when they say he "won't use his skills." He is wondering whether the way staff think, and how they work with George, is counterproductive. He explores whether staff have become stuck conceptualizing treatment compliance and progress in rigid, "all or nothing" terms. For instance, when staff work with George, do they make black and white judgments like "he won't use his skills," overlooking instances when, in fact, he did use skills? Skill building work is not just about skills. On a deeper level, it is about stories; the stories we tell, and we get clients to tell, about their own development. Staff always have a great variety of "data" to attend to. There are instances of George doing well, appearing to make progress (e.g., times he does use skills, does go to social events, does cope without harming himself), and other instances of apparent backsliding. When staff construct the story about the meaning of their work with clients, what data do they attend to? Do they attend only to the data which shows lack of progress? If so, they aren't doing strength-based work. Do staff get so rooted in the story of what George can't, or won't do, that the larger narrative, shared with him, is only about his limitations. Is the story staff construct about George that he's stubborn, oppositional, non-compliant, and that if only he tried harder, he'd succeed? Such common narratives are dead giveaways that the staff do not know how to recognize and build upon skills and strengths.

It is helpful to invoke the story of the farmer trying to get his cow into the barn. First the farmer stood behind the cow. He pushed the cow and when that didn't work, he hit the cow with a stick. The cow just stayed in place. What was wrong with the cow? Did the cow have a "stubborn personality"? Did the cow have a psychiatric disorder, like "stubborn cow syndrome?" Finally, the farmer goes in front of the cow, holds out some grass, and coaxes the cow to come into the barn with kind words and the offer of grass. Now the cow walks into the barn. Has the personality of the cow changed? Do we now have a cow with a "cooperative personality?" Has the cow been cured of its mental disorder? Obviously, the "personality" of the cow appears to change in response to how the farmer treats it.

Thus, another question to ask in the treatment of George is how does the staff interact with him? Metaphorically speaking, do staff stand behind George with a stick or stand in front of him with a handful of grass? Do staff use a "one up" approach, telling him what he should do or do they use a "one down" approach, sharing the treatment dilemma, worrying out loud, and asking him what to do? George has repeatedly shown that he will resist staff directives to use his skills. Do staff continue to use this ineffective approach? Or do staff use therapeutic techniques, like skillful questioning, designed to elicit engagement?

It is very common for direct care staff to oversimplify and misrepresent this cognitive behavioral therapy approach as meaning little more than telling people to use their skills. For instance, were staff frustrated with George and impatient with him, and did they just blow him off by telling him to "use your coping skills?" This is not treatment. It is superficial and glib, and it is likely that clients who are pretreatment will respond with irritation and resistance. Clients usually pick up on the fact that they are being pushed away, and quite often, because they lack better coping skills, they will just "up the ante" with more dysfunctional behavior. Discussions with George's team revealed that this dynamic was part of the problem. Staff threw empty directives at him: "focus on yourself," "walk away," "use your coping skills," which he dutifully ignored. Indeed, George interpreted such brush offs as further evidence that he was "short, ugly, and everyone hated him." Not even staff, in his mind, wanted to talk to him. In order to get staff to attend to him, he had to be "sicker." He had to act crazy. In fact, George wasn't refusing to use his skills. He really didn't know how to do better.

Following this assessment, the psychologist could offer suggestions for how to engage George in treatment. In a nutshell, staff needed to stop telling him, one-up, what to do and instead, help him discover, one-down, his own capacity for change. How is this done?

First, it is done by staff searching tenaciously for evidence of skills and strengths George already had and helping him identify and label these skills. Anything George did which was even remotely adaptive and healthy could be used as evidence of his skills. For instance, he handled a difficult conversation well. Someone said "no" to him but he did not tantrum or hurt himself. Instead, he used the distraction skill of watching TV. He asked for assistance from staff and then coped successfully for 10 minutes while staff attended to something else. How did he manage to cope for that *long* 10 minutes? Another time, he helped someone else and took care of a stray cat. Where did he get such good helping/caretaking skills from?

In fact, because George had strong ASL skills and was intelligent, he had already identified in his therapy fairly advanced coping skills like identifying cognitive errors such as making assumptions, jumping to conclusions, using black and white thinking. He had learned how to make "I statements" and frequently did so. Each time he used one of these skills, staff learned to notice and *wonder* about it. "So, you are noticing your thinking patterns. You notice when you jump to conclusions. You stop yourself and reconsider. Then you come up with another idea. Help me understand this. I thought you were stupid. Is this something that stupid people can do?"

As Meichenbaum has explained, good questions are much more therapeutically useful than good statements (Meichenbaum, 1994). It's probably fair to conclude that George, like many "handicapped" people, has learned helplessness. He expects staff to fix him even as he won't let himself get better. Rather than attempt to answer his desperate cries for help, especially with empty directives like "use your coping skills," it is far more therapeutically useful for staff to play dumb, and share the therapeutic dilemma with him.

"Are you feeling lonely? Do you remember your counselor talking to you about the difference between being alone and feeling lonely? What was that difference again? Are you alone now or feeling lonely? How serious a problem do you think that is right now? Are you going to die? How did you handle this yesterday? Do you feel that was effective? How satisfied are you with your ability to handle emotions like this? Do you want to feel more satisfied or are you content with your progress? Do you want your life to stay as it is now? I understand that you feel that no one wants to be your friend? Is that something I can fix? Can we force people to be your friend? Who is the only person who can make, or not make, a friend for you? I understand you feel sad. What do you want to do about that?"

Fortunately, George had the sign language skills to understand this conversation. The challenge of this work is much more formidable when the client lacks the language or cognitive capacity for this conversation. Of course, staff must also have the sign language skills to have this conversation with George and, a much greater challenge, with clients who have much poorer language abilities. If George were in a non-signing environment, it would be exceptionally difficult for staff to do this strength-based work. Staff could not tell him what he did well. Indeed, they would not be able to perceive most instances when George did use skills.

In George's case, what ultimately helped break through his log jam was not staff exhorting him to use skills, but staff consistently, over a long period of time, pointing out to him instances in which he already did use the skills. When he did something skillful, staff would *wonder* what it meant about him. Staff learned to ask: "What skill did you just use?" "What does it say about you that you can do this skill?" Since many of his peers lacked this capacity for examining and changing thinking patterns, staff could also ask him to compare his ability to do this with that of his peers. What does this say, they would ask, about his skills compared to theirs? What does this say about his intelligence?

Staff also drew upon Motivational Interviewing, another pretreatment strategy. Staff conceptualized change in terms of shades or degrees and they helped George evaluate his own progress. Staff presented him with all the data (challenges he faced, times he used some skills, partial successes) and had him evaluate how he did. Staff could use a self-monitoring form in which George rates his own degree of progress. Taking the cue from Reality Therapy (Glasser, 2000), staff would follow this up by asking him to evaluate *his* degree of satisfaction with his progress. Staff might ask him to rate how much he shows a "willing attitude, 0 to 10." They then might ask him to identify "skills I used in this situation." A third question might be "other skills I could have used but didn't." Then, staff ask George to fill in a thermometer which measures "successful skill use, 0 to 10." Finally, they ask him to evaluate his own progress with a scale that says, "happy with results, 0 to 10."

George's staff eventually learned to avoid offering him any evaluative opinions. Only George's opinion really mattered. When he complained to staff some more about how short, ugly, and hated he was, staff learned to resist the bait. They stopped taking this on as their problem. They stopped offering facile reassurance or trying to provide the friendship that George said he wanted. They ask variations of the Reality Therapy questions: Are you satisfied with this result? If not, are you willing to do something to change it?

Thus, it really wasn't true that George wouldn't use his skills. The problem was more that he and his staff were stuck in a problem saturated narrative that prevented them from discovering together the skills and strengths he did have. Once staff started constructing with him a more strength-based narrative, suddenly they discovered that George had more skills than anyone had realized. The more they discovered together these skills, the more they found that George was actually willing to use them. George's story changed, and he began to find a different identity than being fat, short and hated.

Conclusions

What is the heart of culturally and clinically competent residential treatment for deaf persons?

There is a complex web of language, cultural, disability, and developmental issues to consider. For some deaf persons, the cultural model of

Deaf people provides the best lens through which to understand their experience. These are people who are comfortably fluent in ASL or bilingual. They may have graduate school education, professional jobs, or be highly skilled trades people, and they may be healthy "grass roots" members of the Deaf community. They have families and friends and rich lives. Some of these people staff our programs. With other deaf people, a disability perspective is helpful but the disability isn't deafness. The disability is language deprivation, which usually has a devastating impact upon psychological development. At the most extreme end are deaf clients who are virtually alingual. And still another pole are deaf people who *do* consider their hearing loss to be a devastating disability, who *are* looking for help to adjust to or overcome this disability. These persons usually don't relate to the cultural model of Deaf people. Staff in Deaf treatment programs need competencies, therefore, in an array of perspectives: insights from cultural, medical, disability, developmental and rehabilitation frameworks are all useful, sometimes.

The cultural perspective, however, needs to be the dominant one *because it provides the basis for genuine respect for deaf people, full communication access and empowerment, and the creation of a setting where deaf person's skills and strengths can be noticed and built upon.* Quality Deaf programs are signing programs which have made serious efforts to make themselves culturally affirmative. The next consideration is to ensure the staff and program are clinically competent.

This is easy to say and hard to do. The barriers deaf people face to getting the education and training they need means that in most places there are a shortage of qualified deaf applicants. Most Deaf programs are bicultural or multicultural with hearing and deaf people who are culturally diverse in many ways. Cross-cultural conflicts are normal and inevitable, yet it is the rare program which handles them well. And if these cultural and language challenges were not enough, there is still the issue of getting the treatment right for clients who are so vastly diverse.

Deaf and hearing people exist in the same cross-cultural context as between other linguistic majority and minority groups. The struggle that deaf people face for equal participation in all social domains, including medical and mental health care, is conducted mainly against hearing people, and often against those same hearing people who see themselves as helping deaf people. Issues of inclusion, respect, and empowerment inevitably play out in the treatment programs, and well they should. Treatment programs are supposed to be inclusive, respectful and empowering, and it's quite hard for programs in which hearing people dominate to develop such qualities, no matter the good intentions of the staff or the quality of the program otherwise. Other minority groups have made this point over and over. Programs that serve minority communities need to embody the values and perspectives of that community and need to work exceptionally hard to be staffed by qualified members of those communities.

And yet, cultural competence does not ensure clinical competence. Cultural affirmation is not the same thing as skilled mental health treatment. And in the real world, where there are many standards of care to satisfy, and some persons who can be exceptionally difficult to help, it's rare to find a team of people all of whom have all of the skills, knowledge base and personal sensitivities one needs. The team needs to be culturally and clinically competent and to work all this out in an effective, respectful dialogue with each other.

This is the complicated reality of what it takes to do this work well. The unfortunate reality for most deaf persons in need of mental health care, is that, if they get any treatment at all, the only accommodation provided is an interpreter. Sometimes the "interpreter" is a signer with neither the skills nor credentials to be in that role. In the worst instances, nothing at all is provided. The deaf person is just expected to speechread. In these cases, the gap between available services and ideal services can be staggering. The available services may actually be harmful.

When deaf people are placed in hearing programs, there is often a great search for a counselor who can sign. If such a counselor is found, he or she is expected to make up for all the treatment the deaf person is not getting everywhere else. This is often an unfair and unrealistic expectation. Most clients in residential treatment need residential treatment. If all they needed was a signing outpatient psychotherapist, it is very unlikely that anyone would be paying the vastly greater costs associated with residential care. Indeed, one purpose of residential treatment is to help very disabled people develop the skills they need to be able to live on their own and get by with a much more limited intervention, that of occasional outreach and weekly outpatient treatment. Long term outpatient treatment is also disappearing as a treatment model and available service.

Psychiatric rehabilitation is geared towards persons with severe mental illnesses. Some deaf persons have severe mental illnesses, but often the deaf persons in residential treatment programs have an array of problems related to mental illness, language deprivation, communication barriers, developmental deficits, neurological impairments, substance abuse and multiple kinds of trauma. Quite a number of clients have severe behavioral problems which adds another level of difficulty to the work (Austen & Jeffery, 2007; Vernon & Greenberg, 1999). Residential treatment programs typically serve clients who have complex challenges and for whom weekly 1-hour counseling sessions are an insufficient intervention. They need to develop culturally and clinically competent milieu settings, be they group homes, day treatment, partial hospital, or employment programs. In this chapter, we've discussed a number of the adaptations necessary to make residential treatment both culturally and clinically effective for deaf people. These include:

1. The creation of specialized Deaf treatment settings such as deaf group homes and day treatment/partial hospitalization groups and programs.
2. The staffing of these programs primarily by qualified deaf persons.
3. The provision for extensive staff development efforts to train staff in strength-based work and various "best practices" for helping clients develop psychosocial skills.
4. Attention to the various pretreatment challenges including the challenge of clients lacking a conceptual map or schema for the treatment process. Providing such a map with a developmentally attuned approach to psychosocial skills.
5. Formal skill training groups, borrowed from Dialectical Behavior Therapy, the Boston University Center for Psychiatric Rehabilitation, the UCLA Center for Research and Treatment on the Development of Psychosis, the Illness Management and Recovery (IMR) model, and from other cognitive behavioral treatment approaches, but adapted for the needs and abilities of deaf persons.
6. Attention to these adaptations that make treatment groups "deaf friendly." These include running the groups in ASL, attending well to the fund of information about treatment that clients have and filling in gaps, using action oriented formats like role play, minimizing English-based materials and drawing upon pictorial-based materials (for those clients who are low literacy), using narrative therapy techniques such as story telling and helping clients construct strength-based stories about themselves
7. Informal skill training, using methods like identifying skills clients already have, collaborative problem solving, and putting clients in the helper and teacher role.

There is good news and there is bad news. First the bad news. Deaf residential treatment and Deaf mental health care in general, is complicated. One has to learn all about mental health care and then one has to learn all about deaf people, including learning, if one doesn't know it already, a new language and learning how to assess and work with people who have vastly different language competencies. One also has to learn how to manage complicated social and political realities between deaf and hearing people.

Now the good news. Many people and programs acquire these skills and do this work exceptionally well. Deaf people, like hearing people, recover, get better, become more skillful and happy, when they are provided the right treatment settings. This is complicated, but it is not, as they say, "rocket science." The main barriers are attitudinal, especially the widespread ignorance that "all you need is an interpreter" and the assumption that the optimal treatment environment for most deaf people is with hearing peers. For deaf people with complicated emotional, behavioral, and language challenges, Deaf residential treatment needs to be as sophisticated as these clients are deserving.

Notes

1. The authors of this chapter would like to thank Michael Harvey, John Gournaris, and Alison Albrecht for their careful chapter reviews and suggestions.
2. Deaf people can sometimes have auditory hallucinations. See Chapter 2 in Glickman, 2009.
3. See Chapter 4 for a discussion of the "catchment area" problem.
4. See Chapter 2 for more on this.
5. What term should we use to describe the people we work with? "Patients" comes out of a medical context and may be appropriate for persons served in a hospital, but is not appropriate for community-based residential treatment. "Clients" is better, but some people object to this term also, saying it still emerges out of a medical model where professionals act upon subjects, called clients, who are not empowered agents in their own right. "Consumers" seems more applicable to people who purchase services on the open market. At Advocates, which is heavily influenced by the peer lead Recovery movement, the preferred term is "people we serve" or "persons with lived experience." In this chapter, we mostly use the word "client," but we mean by this someone who is choosing to enter into a "treatment" relationship. The pretreatment discussion is about fostering the collaborative, informed agents who choose to be engaged in activities designed to help them develop and grow in ways they find meaningful.

   Having said this, however, we want to add that these are concerns that native English speakers raise. In over 30 years of doing this work, I (first author) have never heard a deaf person complain about being called a "patient" or "client" and ask to be called instead a "person with lived experience." This is an example of how the language of the Recovery movement doesn't always translate into the Deaf experience.
6. Entirely capitalized words represent glosses for signs, indicating roughly how the concepts would be signed. Glossing like this is not intended to be a translation from English and does not capture many of the grammatical features of ASL. It does, for those familiar with ASL, suggest particular sign choices.
7. An example of the use of self-monitoring, an effective CBT technique that easily fits with a one down style. See Glickman (2009) and Chapter 4 (this volume) for more on this.
8. See Chapter 9.

References

Anthony, W. A. (2007). *Toward a vision of recovery for mental health and psychiatric rehabilitation services* (2nd ed.). Boston. MA: Center for Psychiatric Rehabilitation, Boston University.

Austen, S., & Jeffery, D. (Eds.). (2007). *Deafness and challenging behavior*. West Sussex, England: Wiley.

Bellack, A. S., Mueser, K. T., Gingerich, S., & Agresta, J. (1997). *Social skills training for schizophrenia: a step-by-step guide*. New York, NY: Guilford Press.

Cohen, M., & Mynks, D. (Eds.). (1993). *Assessing and developing readiness for rehabilitation services*. Boston, MA: Center for Psychiatric Rehabilitation at Boston University.

Glasser, W. (2000). *Counseling with choice theory: The new reality therapy*. New York, NY: Harper Collins.

Glickman, N. (2009). *Cognitive behavioral therapy for deaf and hearing persons with language and learning challenges.* New York, NY: Routledge.

Greene, R. W., & Ablon, J. S. (2006). *Treating explosive kids: the collaborative problem-solving approach.* London, England: Guilford Press.

Hanna, F. J. (2002). *Therapy with difficult clients: Using the precursors model to awaken change.* Washington, DC: American Psychological Association.

Klima, E., & Bellugi, U. (1979). *The signs of language.* Cambridge, MA: Harvard University Press.

Linehan, M. (1993a). *Cognitive behavioral treatment of borderline personality disorder.* New York, NY: Guilford Press.

Linehan, M. (1993b). *Skills training manual for treating borderline personality disorder.* New York, NY: Guilford Press.

Meichenbaum, D. (1994). *A clinical handbook/practical therapist manual for assessing and treating adults with post-traumatic stress disorder.* Waterloo, Canada: Institute Press.

Meichenbaum, D., & Biemiller, A. (1998). *Nurturing independent learners: Helping dtudents take charge of their learning.* Newton, MA: Brookline Books.

O'Hearn, A., Pollard, R., & Haynes, S. (2010). Dialectical behavior therapy for deaf clients: Cultural and linguistic modifications for outpatient mental health settings. In I. Leigh (Ed.), *Psychotherapy with deaf clients from diverse groups* (2nd ed., pp. 372–292). New York, NY: Oxford University Press.

Pollard, R. Q., Dean, R. K., O'Hearn, A., & Hayes, S. (2009). Adapting health education material for Deaf audiences. *Rehabilitation Psychology, 54*(2), 232–238.

Rollnick, S., Miller, W. R., & Butler, C. C. (2008). *Motivaltional interviewing in health care.* New York, NY: Guilford.

SAMHSA. (2009). Illness Management and Recovery, *Practioner Guides and Handouts.* Rockville, MD: U.S. Dept. of Health and Human Services, Substance Abuse and Mental Health Services Administration, Center for Mental Health Services.

Steinberg, A. G., Loew, R. C., & Sullivan, V. J. (1999). The diversity of consumer knowledge, attitudes, beliefs and experiences: Recent Findings. In I. W. Leigh (Ed.), *Psychotherapy with deaf clients from diverse groups* (pp. 23–43). Washington DC: Gallaudet University Press.

Sue, D. W., & Sue, D. (2008). *Counseling the culturally diverse: Theory and practice* (5th ed.). Hoboken, NJ: Wiley.

Sussman, A., & Brauer, B. (1999). On being a psychotherapist with deaf clients. In I. W. Leigh (Ed.), *Psychotherapy with deaf clients from diverse groups.* Washington, DC: Gallaudet University Press.

Trikakis, D., Curci, N., & Strom, H. (2003). Sensory strategies for self-regulation: Non-linguistic body-based treatment for deaf psychiatric patients. In N. Glickman & S. Gulati (Eds.), *Mental health care of deaf people: A culturally affirmative approach.* Mahwah, NJ: Erlbaum.

Vernon, M., & Greenberg, S. F. (1999). Violence in Deaf and hard of hearing people: A review of the literature. *Aggression and Violent Behavior, 4*(3), 259–272.

Volz, J. R., Snyder, T., & Sterba, M. (2009). *Teaching social skills to youth with mental health disorders.* Boys Town, NE: Boys Town Press.

6 Substance Abuse Treatment and Recovery

Adaptations to Best Practices when Working with Culturally Deaf Persons

Debra Guthmann and Cynthia Sternfeld[1]

What is unique or different about substance abuse treatment for deaf persons? The naïve person would say "nothing"; an addict is an addict. A somewhat more informed person would say that the treatment sometimes needs to occur in sign language or that at least an interpreter must be used. This person recognizes that there are language differences but may not appreciate the diversity of language skills among deaf people. Particular considerations include the high numbers of language dysfluent clients found in rehabilitation settings and the common fund of information gaps (Pollard, 1998) and Deaf cultural factors that require accommodations well beyond the provision of interpreters. To take some common examples, the 12-Step model of treatment, which is the oldest, most widespread, and familiar, is often very difficult for a subset of deaf persons, those with language and learning challenges (Glickman, 2009), to understand and use even when the steps are translated into American Sign Language (ASL). Common concepts used in cognitive behavioral therapy (CBT) such as triggers, warning signs, risk factors, and even the notion of "relapse prevention," may not be part of the established fund of information about the world that some deaf consumers begin with when in treatment. Glickman (2009) has described how these concepts sometimes present translation difficulties. Translation difficulties are not the only barriers. Deaf people at all functional levels participating in hearing substance abuse treatment programs often feel disconnected from their peers and, valid or not, use the lack of deaf-accessible treatment as a reason for not engaging in recovery efforts (Guthmann, & Graham, 2004).

The authors and contributors of this chapter are experienced substance-abuse counselors specializing in treatment with deaf persons, and many of them also have a strong background in the area of mental health. They are all well-versed in the evidence-based approaches to substance-abuse treatment now used: 12-Step programs, CBT, which includes relapse prevention work, motivational interviewing (and other "pretreatment" strategies), and harm reduction (HR) treatment. They have all struggled to find ways to adapt these recognized best practices for treatment with deaf consumers.

For more than three decades, researchers have attempted to document concerns about the unique challenges related to substance abuse treatment for persons who are deaf. A number of experts agree that the prevalence of alcohol abuse is at least equal to or greater than the hearing population (Boros, 1981; Guthmann & Graham, 2004; Guthmann & Sandberg, 1995, 1997, 1998; Isaacs, Buckley, & Martin, 1979; Johnson & Locke, 1978; Lane, 1989; Watson, Boros, & Zrimec, 1979). Estimating the epidemiology of substance-use disorder (SUD) among persons who are deaf is difficult because the population is considered low-incidence and language and cultural barriers exist. Some researchers contend that deaf individuals at greatest risk for SUD are those who are socially isolated, less connected with the Deaf or hearing communities, and less fluent in ASL (Guthmann & Blozis, 2001). For some of the reasons mentioned above, it is assumed that the actual percentage of deaf persons with SUD may be higher than first thought.

Over these past 30 years, some advances have been made related to service provision for deaf clients in need of substance-abuse treatment, but the growth one would expect to see in service delivery has not occurred. Indeed, just the opposite appears to be happening. Rather than an increase, the number of programs available nationally appears to be decreasing. In 2008–2009, an informal survey was undertaken among national-level professionals who work within the Deaf Community to identify programs providing specialized substance-abuse treatment (Titus & Guthmann, 2010). Of the nine specialized residential programs identified in 2008, only five remained 1 year later, and, as of 2011, only four of the programs were still open. Of the programs that closed or no longer provide substance abuse treatment for deaf individuals, three provided adolescent programming, thus leaving an even larger gap in service for this population. Reasons for closure for both adolescent and adult programs include loss of funding, lack of specialized staff, and, in one case, low census. A similar trend is noted for specialized outpatient programs. Of the seven outpatient programs cited in 2008, six remained in 2011; loss of funding was behind the closures.

The lack of specialized programs combined with decreased funding for existing services force providers to find creative approaches not only in individual treatment but in the creation and continuation of services to deaf people in need of treatment. Over the past decade, there has been a boom in the development of treatment interventions in the hearing community. Many of these methods were developed using government or private foundation dollars and are supported by an evidence base. Professional training opportunities in the hearing world abound. However, these resources are not yet accessible to deaf counselors or clients. Evidence-based treatments have yet to be adapted for deaf substance abusers.

Prior to the opening of some specialized treatment programs, the only option for deaf individuals was to attend treatment with limited (if any) interpreter access. Once specialized services grew, the staff and clients discovered effective means of working together to adapt available materials to be linguistically accessible and culturally affirmative. Creative approaches have been utilized to offer a continuum of services to deaf people in need of treatment. When services are available, clinicians have found the use of storytelling, visual metaphors, and active treatment activities such as role playing vital when working with this diverse deaf population. More recently, technology has been used to create language accessible adaptations of substance-abuse materials, which enables providers to better serve their deaf clients. Technology has also greatly improved the level of care that a client can access through the use of video phone, online webcam meetings, and other supports.

This chapter provides an overview of best practices in substance abuse treatment followed by a discussion of best practices in adapting such approaches for deaf consumers. These adaptations follow these themes: (a) The use of narrative therapy techniques, such as storytelling and visual metaphors; (b) creative uses of technology; (c) active treatment (focused around therapeutic activities, rather than discussion alone); and (d) translations and adaptations of English-based materials, including the development of pictorial tools. Consistent with the emphasis on storytelling techniques, this chapter will illustrate treatment principals and adaptations through a series of case stories. Finally, the importance of specialized Deaf substance abuse treatment programs will be discussed. All these creative adaptations were developed in such programs.

Irrespective of approach, relapse remains a common occurrence, particularly with newly recovering individuals. Skills that a client learns while in treatment can provide a foundation for relapse prevention as well as knowledge that will support the client in coming back for help even after relapse.

Best Practices in Substance Abuse Treatment

Cognitive Behavioral Treatment Model (CBT)

CBT involves individuals learning how their thoughts, feelings, and behaviors (especially drinking/using behaviors) are connected—and how to break those connections. The counselor helps the person analyze his or her environment and ways of responding to cues to use alcohol or drugs, and establish new patterns of response to those cues. Cognitive behavioral therapy is related to cognitive therapy, which is a system of psychotherapy that attempts to reduce excessive emotional reactions and self-defeating behavior by modifying the faulty or erroneous thinking and maladaptive beliefs that underlie these reactions (Beck, Wright, Newman, & Liese, 1993). CBT is particularly similar to cognitive therapy in its emphasis on the functional analysis of substance abuse and identifying cognitions associated with substance abuse.

In the initial sessions of CBT, the focus is on learning and practicing a variety of coping skills, only some of which are cognitive. Initial strategies stress behavioral aspects of coping (e.g., avoiding or leaving the situation, distraction, and so on) rather than thinking one's way out of a situation. This type of program requires participation in relapse prevention groups as well as training in cognitive, behavioral, and abstinence skills. The goals of treatment are for the client to develop ways of coping, an enhanced sense of self-efficacy, and modification of expectations of the substances effects. CBT attempts to help clients recognize the situations in which they are most likely to use alcohol and/or other drugs, avoid these situations when appropriate, and cope more effectively with a range of problems and problematic behaviors associated with substance abuse (Guthmann, Dickinson, & Sandberg, 2010).

When a client is in treatment, the clinician and client use the functional analysis process to help identify the client's thoughts, feelings, and circumstances before and after the drug and/or alcohol use. This analysis helps the clinician and client assess high-risk situations that may lead to substance use. It also provides insights into some of the reasons the individual may be using alcohol and/or other drugs (e.g., to cope with interpersonal difficulties, to experience risk or euphoria not otherwise available in the client's life). Later in treatment, functional analyses of episodes of chemical use may identify those situations or states in which the individual still has difficulty coping. CBT is usually seen as a short-term treatment and is intended to produce initial abstinence and stabilization. Skills training is most effective when clients have an opportunity to practice new skills and approaches within the context of their daily routine and learn what does and does not work for them as well as to discuss new strategies with the clinician.

CBT frequently utilizes exposure therapy as part of recovery (Monti, Kadden, Rohsenow, Cooney, & Abrams, 2002). One aspect of this is to provide clients with opportunities to experience stressors and practice responses to these stressors. One common stressor for deaf clients is frustration with communication and barriers to accessing treatment. It is not uncommon for a client to seek services and do "everything right" and then to show up to find that the services are not accessible. By the time clients arrive at treatment, they may have an attitude that hard work, patience and perseverance don't pay off. Intentional managing of communication related stressors can be incorporated into a Deaf treatment program because there is shared understanding of the communication dilemma, an appreciation of what this means for deaf people, the ability to empathize and strategize on how to handle these challenges, and the ability to practice. Hearing settings, by contrast, all too often just trigger maladaptive coping, like drinking, by exposing deaf clients in the treatment setting to the same triggers they experience in the rest of their lives.

Like some of the other approaches and techniques addressed in this chapter, CBT is compatible with a variety of treatments including self-help groups such as Alcoholics Anonymous (AA), family and couples therapy, vocational counseling, and parenting skills training. The characteristics that distinguish CBT from other treatment approaches include: functional analyses of substance abuse (that is, close analysis of the situations, stressors, emotions, and thoughts that trigger substance use); individualized skill training in recognizing craving, managing thoughts about substance use, problem-solving, planning for emergencies, recognizing seemingly irrelevant decisions, substance refusal skills; examination of the clients cognitive process related to substance use; the identification and debriefing of past and future high-risk situations; and the encouragement and review of extra-session implementation of skills and the practice of skills within sessions (Morgenstern, Blanchard, Morgan, Labouvie, & Hayaki, 2001; Waldron & Turner, 2008).

Motivational Interviewing

Motivational interviewing (MI) is a brief psychotherapeutic intervention to increase the likelihood of a client's considering, initiating, and maintaining specific change strategies to reduce harmful behavior. MI is founded on principles of motivational psychology, client-centered therapy, and stages of change in natural recovery from addiction. MI treatment includes components common to most brief interventions for addictive behavior that have been empirically tested (Bien, Miller, & Tonigan, 1993). MI is not a treatment model but a clinical tool used in many treatment programs and is a directive, client-centered counseling style for eliciting behavior change by helping clients to explore and resolve ambivalence (Miller & Rollnick, 1991). The examination and resolution of ambivalence is its central purpose, and the counselor is directive in pursuing this goal with the client. The goal is for the counselor to work with the client to resolve their ambivalence about recovery and then to commit themselves to the treatment process.

MI techniques work with deaf consumers as well as they do with hearing counterparts if the counselor and consumer are able to communicate fluently in ASL. The counselor is able to watch sign selection and mirror sign choice when using reflection techniques. This lets the consumer know two things—first, that the counselor understood what the consumer said, and second, that the counselor was really attending to the clients feelings. While empathic listening and effective communication are always vital in counseling, they have a deeper level of importance with deaf clients whose more common experience in treatment settings is that they are not understood on the surface level of language, much less the deeper level of feelings and meanings.

MI stresses that, in order to have change occur in a client's life, it needs to be the client resolving the ambivalences and doing the work not the counselor. Ambivalence takes the form of a conflict between two different courses of action (e.g., indulgence versus restraint), each of which may have a perceived positive and negative side associated with it. The counselor's task is to facilitate expression of both sides of the ambivalence struggle and guide the client toward an acceptable resolution that triggers change.

Motivational interviewing emphasizes that the counselor should not try to persuade the client to resolve the ambivalences by trying to point out the urgency of the problem as this can increase client resistance and diminish the probability of change (Miller et al., 1993; Miller & Rollnick, 1991). The style of counseling used with MI usually involves asking good questions, not lecturing clients about what they should do. More aggressive strategies (that have been used at times in traditional 12-Step programs) may push the clients to make changes when they may not be ready. Although not confrontational, the counselor should be directive when helping the client examine and resolve their ambivalences. The primary assumption with MI is that the lack of ambivalence is the main obstacle that needs to be overcome in order to initiate change. The specific strategies of motivational interviewing are designed to elicit, clarify, and resolve ambivalence in a client-centered and respectful counseling atmosphere (Miller & Rollnick, 1991). When using MI the counselor is very attentive and responsive to the client and resistance and denial are not seen as client characteristics but as feedback regarding the therapist behavior. Readiness to change is not a client trait, but a fluctuating product of interpersonal interaction. Client resistance is often a signal that the counselor is assuming greater readiness to change than is the case, and it is a cue that the clinician may need to modify their strategies. The therapeutic relationship is seen as a partnership and the clinician respects the client's autonomy and freedom of choice. To successfully implement the treatment approach, the counselor must also be proficient in using open-ended questioning, affirming the client's experiences, reflecting listening, and summarizing.

The 12-Step Model

The 12-Step model is based on the 12 Steps of recovery originally written by Bill Wilson, the co-founder of Alcoholics Anonymous. This model of treatment is one of the most widely used approaches and is characterized by a thorough and ongoing assessment of the client and of multimodal therapeutic approaches. It may include group and individual therapy, family education and support as well as other methods. A multidisciplinary team of professionals (e.g., counselors, psychologists, nurses) plan and assist in the treatment process for each client. The assumption is that abstinence is the prerequisite. Treatment provides tools and a context for the client to learn new ways of living without alcohol and other drugs. This type of treatment can be used on an inpatient or outpatient basis. Alcoholism is considered a multiphasic illness that affects a client physically, mentally, and spiritually. Therefore, treatment from alcoholism is more effective when it takes all of these aspects into account during the course of treatment.

The 12-Step model considers chemical dependency as the primary problem with an emphasis on the concepts of powerlessness over the use of chemicals. Another important concept in the 1 model is that the individual adopts the norms and values of a new social group, namely a 12-Step group, and shifts to a reliance on "a power greater than myself" rather than a reliance on will power. Finally, abstinence is the only acceptable goal of treatment and recovery. Twelve-Step treatment typically involves group therapy, educational lectures, recovering persons as counselors, multidisciplinary staff teams, therapeutic milieu, therapeutic work assignments, family counseling; use of 12-step programs, daily meditation literature, sober recreational activities, and structured daily routine (Guthmann & Sandberg, 2001).

The Minnesota Chemical Dependency Program for Deaf and Hard of Hearing Individuals (the Minnesota Program) is a specialized treatment program that provides innovative and creative inpatient and outpatient treatment on a national basis to deaf individuals from a variety of backgrounds. The Minnesota Program has used the 12-Step model successfully with their clients in treatment, but the key has always been breaking down the steps so they are more concrete and using a combination of drawing, role play and storytelling. The client shares examples from their life experiences by describing the components of their drawings in 1:1 situations with the counselor as well as to their peers and counselors when in group. The adaptation to the 12-Step model, developed at the Minnesota Program, has been written about in a number of publications (Guthmann & Graham, 2004; Guthman, Lybarger, & Sandberg, 1993; Guthmann, Sandberg, & Dickinson, 1999, 2010; Guthmann & Sandberg, 2003).

Harm Reduction

Harm reduction is any program or policy designed to reduce drug-related harm without requiring the cessation of drug use. Interventions may be targeted at the individual, the family, community, or society. Not all interventions intended to minimize the adverse consequences of substance use are harm reduction. The primary focus of harm reduction is on people who are already experiencing some harm due to their substance use (Guth-mann & Sandberg, 2001). Harm reduction and methadone maintenance treatment (MMT) can provide basic services to some difficult-to-engage clients and a reduction of some high-risk behaviors such as injecting and needle sharing (Phillips & Rosenberg, 2008). If a clinician is using a harm reduction model, the first priority is on reducing the various negative consequences of drug use rather than on eliminating drug use or ensuring abstinence. As a result of their use, clients may have multiple conditions which may complicate their recovery process. Illnesses that result from disregarding medical conditions, accidents resulting from drunk driving, arrests related to drug-related behavior, and diseases resulting from sustained, long-term substance use all can serve to complicate the treatment process. Providing opportunities and supports for clients to learn skills and get help to reduce negative consequences of their use, leaves the door open for the client to access higher levels of service when they are ready. For a deaf client who enters treatment with very specific language and learning needs there may be great value in attempting to lessen the severity of the impact of their drug use. In addition, deaf clients who may have a number of complicating health, social, or legal factors may use these problems as a reason to continue to use rather than to get sober. Rules that keep them out of treatment become one more barrier. Deaf clients who may have been using multiple substances and negative behaviors in place of coping skills will need time and opportunity to develop these skills before they become ready to eliminate these harmful behaviors. A client who is willing to stop drinking but not willing to give up marijuana has exhibited a desire to change behavior. Highlighting the desire for change rather than the resistance will keep the door open for more work to be done in the future as well as an opportunity for connection to a helping system where prior experience may have been one of disenfranchisement.

Abstinence is the ultimate goal for those using illegal drugs since this would reduce drug-related harm completely. It is hoped that all individuals who use illicit substances will eventually come to give them up entirely. Proponents of harm reduction recognize that there will always be illicit drug use and that many people are simply unwilling or unable to give up drugs entirely but nonetheless could benefit from intervention. Harm reduction accepts that some use of mind-altering substances is a common feature of human experience. It acknowledges that, while carrying risks, drug use also provides the user with benefits that must be taken into account if drug-using behavior is to be understood. Ambivalence is such a strong factor in drug abuse that, when the abstinence mandate is in effect, many people will just avoid addiction services.

Helping people avoid harm has also been an established part of the alcohol field for many years. Examples include promotion of responsible drinking, controlled drinking interventions, avoidance of drinking and driving, and low-alcohol content beverages. Other approaches may also include finding a safer route of drug administration, safer substances, reduction of harmful consequences of drug use, reduction of frequency of drug use, reduction of the intensity of drug use, and the reduction of the duration of drug use. Several European cities have developed facilities known as tolerance zones, injection rooms, health rooms, or contact centers where drug users can get together and obtain clean injection equipment, condoms, advice, and /or medical attention.

Harm reduction approaches to addictive behavior are based on three central beliefs: (a) Excessive behaviors occur along a continuum of risk ranging from minimal to extreme—addictive behaviors are not all or nothing phenomena. A drug or alcohol abstainer is at risk of less harm than a drug or alcohol user; a moderate drinker is causing less harm than a binge drinker; a crystal meth smoker or sniffer is causing less harm than a crystal injector. (b) Changing addictive behavior is a step-wise process, complete abstinence being the final step. Those who embrace the harm reduction model believe that any movement in the direction of reduced harm, no matter how small, is positive in and of itself. (c) Sobriety simply isn't for everybody. Although bold and radical, this statement requires the acceptance that many people live in horrible circumstances. Some are able to cope without the use of drugs, and others use drugs as a primary means of coping. Education is needed to help people in the Deaf community better understand the risks involved with their use. A harm reduction approach can provide support and education by keeping deaf people engaged with the hope that they will understand why abstinence rather than continued use may be a better solution for them.

As has been discussed, accessible treatment programs are few and far between. Individuals seeking treatment may likely have a history of family and friends enabling their sick behavior. Many deaf clients may have been told, "If you do this one more time...." Clients who have experienced empty threats may not understand that the zero tolerance and abstinence-only requirements in treatment programs are real. A deaf client, who tests the limits and gets kicked out of treatment, may not have other options. The harm reduction approach that focuses on client choice and education creates room for learning while empowering the client to make choices that advance their goals of living a manageable (sober) life.

We know that, when students go to college, regardless of if they are deaf or hearing, there may be an increase of exposure and experimentation with alcohol and drugs. Therefore, college is an important time to make harm reduction programs available. Individuals may find themselves in situations where they are drinking alcohol and violating campus rules, putting them in jeopardy of not being able to continue at college if a zero-tolerance approach is used. While expulsion sends a clear message, it leaves the student without any additional knowledge or resources to deal with possible addiction; further disenfranchising the student from potential help. Additionally, as is the case with counseling and treatment programs, accessible, Deaf friendly college programs are rare. When a hearing student is asked to leave a college or university setting because of drug/alcohol violations, there are other post-secondary options for the student to consider. This is not the case for many deaf students. A harm reduction approach can provide support and education by keeping deaf people engaged with the hope that they will understand why abstinence rather than continued use may be a better solution for them. Deaf students need strong academic programs as well as programs that support learning essential life skills. Post-secondary settings have a role in teaching these concepts. As an example, a recent change made at one university seemed to work well with their deaf students. Instead of offenders being removed from campus residential settings after a drug offense, they are required to live on campus so they can have greater access to education and support from staff and peers. This shift also serves to address the problem directly rather than just moving the parties to off-campus locations.

Best Practices: Adaptations That Make a Difference

The remainder of this chapter will explore various adaptations that counselors have created when working with deaf clients. Although the primary goal of this chapter is to provide the reader with ideas and information for specific counseling interventions, it is important to note that in almost every domain of treatment adaptations are required. This includes in the screening and assessment domain which is not discussed here except to note that almost all such assessments are heavily dependent upon the ability to read written English. Recently, we've seen some adaptations in the form of instruments developed using American Sign Language (Alexander, DiNitto, & Tidblom, 2005; Dennis, Chen, & Funk, 2006; Guthmann & Moore, 2007; Titus & Guthmann, 2010).

Adaptations to Best Counseling Practices for Diverse Deaf Consumers

When working in clinical settings with clients who take in information visually as opposed to auditorially, the use of visual examples and metaphors can become a primary counseling strategy. A metaphor is defined by the *American Heritage Dictionary, Fourth Edition* (2006) as "an implied comparison made between two unlike things that actually have something important in common." The word "metaphor" itself is a metaphor, coming from a Greek word meaning to "transfer" or "carry across." Metaphors "carry" meaning from one word, or idea, to another. A visual metaphor is the representation of a person, place, thing, or idea by way of a visual image that suggests a particular association or point of similarity. A metaphor is something used to explain or describe something else including perceptions, experiences, beliefs, or emotions. Visual metaphors are used to paint a picture of a concept and can then begin to help connect that concept for translation to other issues. Metaphors are basic mechanisms through which people make sense of the world, and visual metaphors seem to be particularly useful when working with a variety of clients. (Lakofff & Johnson, 1980). Storytelling is considered a metaphorical process because the stories contain an implied comparison with the life of the person being told the story. Storytelling and visual metaphors have proved effective at helping clients visualize future goals and understand their role in making them happen. Using visual metaphors and imagery provides a more participative and enjoyable experience and creates a climate in which people are more open to the messages and content of conversation.

Glickman (1996) suggests that many techniques from the narrative therapy school (White, 1995, 2007; White & Epston, 1990) are good linguistic and cultural matches with many deaf clients. Techniques such as *externalizing*, as it applies in narrative therapy, is a highly visual questioning intervention where clients are encouraged to create visual representations of *problems* so that the issue is seen as separate from the individual. Externalizing may work especially well with ASL users as the language lends itself to the creation of visual pictures that can then interact with the "narrator" of a story (Freedman & Combs, 1996). The use of storytelling as a clinical tool to use with deaf clients has been raised as a viable approach for a number of years (Isenberg, 1996).

Storytelling is a surprisingly sophisticated information processing tool. Storytelling is so much a part of our daily lives that we seldom think of it as something separate. If you ask a friend or acquaintance that you have not seen for some time how things have been, they will tell you at least one, if not several stories. If you go into a bookstore, you find shelves filled with stories. If you are a member of a self-help fellowship, such as AA, you go to meetings to share stories about what happened and what things are like now. If you are a parent, storytelling is one of the earliest activities you share with your children. The central religious texts of every major religion are essentially collections of stories. Storytelling is as close to a universal means of teaching as exists anywhere, and storytelling has also long been considered an important part of the "oral" tradition of Deaf Culture (Padden & Humphries, 1988). When telling a story, we express our understanding of the meaning and significance of the relationships between events. When we tell personal stories or hear other people's stories, we may get insight into our behavior and learn that our experience maybe shared by other people. Sharing common experiences can create a positive perspective. This is the process that the founders of self-help groups discovered as helpful in changing behaviors. Further, if we change the way we tell a story, by modifying how we respond to specific experiences, we may create new behavioral possibilities in responding to those same experiences in our life (Parker & Wampler, 2006).

In Deaf Culture, storytelling is a rich part of how the community shares information and events. Ask any person who has ever asked a culturally Deaf person a yes or no question, and you will get an overwhelming percentage noting that the deaf individual answers questions by telling a story from beginning to end. Assessors doing intake evaluations have to allow for time in the session for storytelling, and to realize this is not a defense mechanism to monopolize, but a cultural tendency that puts the information in a package that makes sense conceptually. Storytelling is a way to capture the whole picture. Deaf people may feel that providing specific information without the whole story doesn't make sense. In addition to treatment settings, this has proven challenging in court settings where attorneys want the deaf defendant or witness to answer a short brief question. The story of David illustrates this challenge.

David was deaf from birth and lived with his hearing family who did not sign. David was an alcoholic. He had four prior driving under the influence (DUI) convictions when he was involved in an accident that involved alcohol. David was interviewed by his attorney several times with an interpreter and each time he told the same story from beginning to end. He was not the driver, but the passenger, and the driver had fled the scene. He had to leave the car out of the driver's side because his side of the car was damaged and the door was jammed. He left his blood on the steering wheel. Each time he told this story he used gestures to show exactly how he left the car. The problem was he was not able to answer individual questions about the story posed to him by his attorney. He had to retell this story each time. The attorney and interpreter tried a variety of methods to get him to understand that he needed to say "yes" or "no" but he was not able. He eventually was found unable to stand trial because his attorney pled with the judge that he would not be able to control him on the stand, especially during cross examination.

Storytelling is, for example, a vital part of the Alcoholics Anonymous 12-Step model and participants are encouraged to tell and retell their stories. In treating substance abuse in deaf people, three excellent activities that encourage the client to tell his or her story are The Feelings Collage, the Life Lines project, and the People, Places, and Things activity.

Feelings Collage Project

Staff asks the clients to think of three difficult (hard) feelings and two positive (good) feelings they have experienced in the past and gives them large pieces of paper to glue magazine pictures onto. Clients are to think of something other than people to show the feelings. An example would be to use a fire with deep red colors, a volcano, or a twister full of black rage. These examples could be used to demonstrate the feeling of anger. Clients should take their time and really focus on the feelings they are putting on the paper. Additionally, clients can use the same idea to put down three negative feelings and three positive feelings.

Life Lines Project

Within Deaf Culture, it is fairly common for conversations to center more on events than emotions—the "what happened?" rather than the "how did it feel?" In order to create a step to move from the former to the latter question, Life Lines are helpful. It is fairly common when asking someone in treatment to tell about their history, they may cover all of the terrible things that happened—thinking that the focus of treatment is all of the "bad stuff" they did. A life line that focuses on the positive events can be the beginning of a strength-based platform to begin the work of recovery. The client can use any kind of format. As an example, ask the client to create a train track, a river, or a road (anything that a person can travel). Ask the client to draw their mode of travel on a large piece of paper. If the client creates a train track, they can make a train to put on the track that could move along the track. The client can use the same process if they choose the river. They can demonstrate a boat moving through the water. If the client selects the road, they can demonstrate with a car, truck, bus, or bike moving along the road. The client should pick just one mode of transportation. Ask the client to begin placing their happiest memories along the "river, road, or train track of life." The client should start at birth and travel to the present. The client should write down their happiest memories along the way. The idea of this activity is for the client to see the good things in their lives. This can also be connected to a concept of Higher Power when working within a 12-Step framework. This activity can also be modified to ask the client to review memorable or pivotal moments in their life. The Life Line activity lends itself well to be in a 1:1 or group setting. Creating a concrete visual representation from abstract concepts can help create a context for discussion and exploration with the client. The Life Line activity can also become the tool for a client to prepare to tell their own AA Story if they are asked.

People, Places, and Things (PPT) Activity

In the People, Places, and Things Activity, concrete objects like blocks are used to represent and aid reflection of different aspects of one's life.

Mike came to treatment through the court system. He had been arrested for drunk driving and possession of drugs on a night he had intended to commit suicide. Mike identified as an addict. He wanted help. He felt like a failure and had deep shame. He tried to share his emotions in group, but communication barriers caused him to feel more lonely and isolated. He felt his own father had never wanted to learn to sign or communicate with him. Mike believed his father was ashamed of him and felt deeply pained by this. Each time Mike struggled with communication, he became overwhelmed with feelings of shame and abandonment. In treatment, Mike's counselor Kevin started to talk with him about how people, places, and things could impact his sober life. One of the activities used with Mike involved blocks. Kevin started with red, blue, and yellow blocks and placed them in front of Mike. He asked Mike to imagine that each color of blocks represent aspects of his drug use. The red blocks represented the people, places, and things that made it easy to use drugs. The blue blocks represented the aspects of using drugs that he liked. Last, Kevin asked Mike to imagine that the yellow blocks represented the things Mike liked to do that had nothing to do with drugs at all—feel-good things that Mike could do while sober.

Kevin asked Mike to start with the red blocks and to pull out one block for each of the people, places, and things (PPTs) that reinforced his use. Mike separated them out from the group of blocks and pushed them toward Kevin. Second, Kevin asked to pull out a blue block for each positive feeling he got from his drug use. After pushing aside the blue blocks, Kevin asked Mike to use the yellow blocks to identify the things that he could enjoy doing sober and things that are good about being sober. Mike struggled to think of fun things he had done while sober and things that felt good about being sober.

Kevin discussed with Mike how the different colors of blocks have changed from many red, blue and yellow blocks down to a few yellow and just a couple of red and blue. Kevin pointed out to Mike that they have less blocks now. Mike acknowledged that a lot of those blocks were not helpful for him. Kevin points out that Mike may always have some of those unhealthy things in his life and that now it is his job is to find, develop, and increase those healthy behaviors represented by the yellow blocks. Kevin asked Mike what he needs to do to deal with the red and blue blocks, the PPT's, thoughts and emotions that will come up in recovery. They discussed that every recovering person has to deal with triggers and difficulties that arise. Kevin explained to Mike that in treatment he will learn problem solving, social and decision making skills as well as ways to have sober fun. Kevin summarized that sobriety is about managing the PPT's while creating a fulfilling sober life.

Visual Metaphors: Creating Connections and Understanding

One example of the use of visual metaphors can be found in the work of a client named Alice.

Alice is a new client to a hearing counselor who is fluent in ASL. Upon arriving at the office, Alice introduced her husband who drove her to the appointment. After brief introductions, Alice's husband asked if there was a coffee shop nearby and what time he should come back to pick up his wife. He left and the session began. Alice conveyed the following information in the first 10 minutes of her first session: She stated that she is a retired, 63-year-old deaf woman. She said that she enjoys gardening and that she grows vegetables and sells them at a farmer's market on the weekends to supplement her pension. Alice has been married to Bob for 33 years and they have two grown, hearing children and five hearing grandchildren. Alice comes from a big deaf family and confidentiality is very important to her. She asked if the counselor knew her maiden name and whether she could trust that none of her siblings or members of the Deaf Community would find out about her coming to counseling.

Alice had come to counseling at the urging of her children who believed she was addicted to Xanax. Alice explained that her doctor told her to use Xanax when her stress became unmanageable and that she should take no more than two Xanax pills per day. Alice admitted that she took 4 to 6 per day and that she has twice run out of her prescription before she was supposed to but believed that her use of the medication was reasonable given her situation. She indicated that before starting Xanax she had been anxious, had difficulty sleeping, had lost a lot of weight, and was diagnosed with hypertension. When asked what she hoped to gain from counseling, Alice stated that she wanted to find a way to calm down without using so much Xanax. She also indicated that she would like to figure it out in a few sessions because the drive to the signing counselor's office was very long. Although her husband didn't mind driving, she felt bad that it took up his whole morning to bring her. The counselor then used a visual metaphor to help convey that therapy takes time and that rushing through the process can be counter-productive.

The counselor noticed that Alice had beautiful fingernails and complimented her on how nice they looked. Alice enjoyed the compliment and said that she loved getting manicures. The counselor asked Alice how long it took from start to finish to get a manicure and Alice explains that it took at least an hour. The counselor asks if it is possible to get a good manicure in 10 minutes. Alice laughs and says that it's possible but it if you don't take the time the polish will probably get dented and dull and you'd have to get it done all over again. She would rather take the time and do it once and have it last longer. The counselor explained to Alice that counseling is a process that takes time too and you can do some work quickly and feel a little better but it may not be as useful and long lasting if you rush through it—much like a manicure. The metaphor enabled Alice to understand this concept in a way that resonated with her experience.

As the counselor learned more about Alice's family and her many responsibilities, the counselor asked Alice if she felt like she was running a marathon while pushing a full wheel barrel. Alice laughed and said that was true. The counselor asked Alice what was in her wheel barrel. She described all of the people she took care of; her grandchildren, her parents, and her husband. She thought about her situation and added that her house and her parent's home were also in the wheel barrel. Without prompting, Alice noted that the Xanax helped keep her calm but it made her feel slow and sometimes forgetful. She signed to the counselor that it kind of makes her run with the wheel barrel like she's drunk, weaving all over the place, and shared that frequently when she took Xanax she forgot things and had to repeat her steps. It was like pushing the wheelbarrow over the same path again. She considered the possibility that Xanax might actually be making her daily responsibilities more difficult.

Alice then added that she had a car accident a few weeks ago and ever since her husband has been driving her around. From a counseling perspective, it is an interesting development: Alice's need for a driver also gave her company in her lonely situation. If Alice were to stop needing a driver, would she stop getting her husband's help? What other metaphors could be used to explore this new dynamic between Alice and her husband? When metaphors are helpful in creating cognitive connections for clients, counselors can continue to refer back to them during future sessions. The wheelbarrow metaphor could be used as new burdens were uncovered. Alice could be asked, "Is the wheelbarrow full now? Can you keep it straight up or is it falling over? Can you keep pushing it forward or is it wobbling? Can your husband help you push the wheelbarrow or is he off to the side, ignoring you while you work? Does he even get in the way?" The metaphor is built as a powerful way of describing her life situation.

Another issue for Alice involved her concern about gossip within the Deaf Community. Creating a visual picture, the counselor asked Alice to think about a basin of water with a rubber duck and a sponge. Alice was asked to think of this as the "gossip and garbage" that can exist in the Deaf Community. She asked Alice to think about whether she wanted to be the duck or the sponge. She could absorb it and feel horrible and sink or let it roll off her back and focus on working her program. Alice loved this analogy and said she felt like a sponge all the time and that if she was already saturated from her stress at home, she didn't need the stress of the Deaf Community to add to that. Because Alice is a gardener, the counselor could also draw upon planting and growing metaphors. These should resonate easily with Alice.

Adaptations Made Possible by New Technology

The value and potential of technology to advance the field of counseling with deaf individuals cannot be understated. The level of access that technology has afforded the Deaf Community has been monumental. The impact of these advances for deaf people who are isolated struggling with substance use or other mental health disorders can be significant. During the past decade, the Internet has become an additional treatment platform for a range of mental health and substance abuse disorders (Day & Schneider, 2002; Griffiths, 2005; King et al., 2009; Pull, 2006). Existing research indicates therapy via the Internet or videoconferencing ("behavioral telehealth," "telemental health," "telepsychiatry," or "e-therapy") has equivalent outcomes to therapy delivered via traditional face-to-face interactions (Day & Schneider, 2002; King et al., 2009; O'Reilly et al., 2007).

The Deaf Community is very tuned into technology, and many individuals regularly use text messaging, email, video phones, and the Internet. It takes less than an hour to train a new deaf AA sponsor in how to use the video conferencing software that is now available. The primary means of communication in the Deaf Community, when not person-to-person, involves the Internet. The "Deaf Off Drugs and Alcohol" (DODA) program at Wright State University is part of a project focusing on e-therapy which is funded by the Center for Substance Abuse Treatment (CSAT) and has been using technology to fill some of the gaps. DODA is able to provide clinical support for clients within Ohio, and will refer those in need of a higher level of support to programs within Ohio (where they advocate for interpreters to be provided) or specialized inpatient programs for deaf individuals such as The Minnesota Program. One of the program components includes the provision of Web-based 12-Step meetings run by deaf facilitators who are in recovery; 12-Step meetings are held with up to 10 participants from across the United States. Group participants access the meeting by clicking on a web link invitation sent to interested parties. All participants can see each other in individual boxes on the computer screen, and images are large enough to communicate in ASL. DODA has an array of technology that is used with program clients. These technology-based applications include teleconferencing software, video phones, email, text messaging, voicemail, and Internet hosted pages on mainstream social networking sites.

The video conferencing software used at DODA allows multiple users on computers to see and sign to one another in ASL using computer cameras. The technology also extends to assessment capability. Videophone (VP) and video conferencing approaches have been especially helpful in providing services to persons who are deaf and has become an "industry standard" procedure. A VP permits one-on-one video conversations between two people who can see each other on the air, whereas video conferencing software permits multiple windows so that multiple people or images are possible on one screen. Videophone companies are funded by the government to provide free, at home service to deaf persons that have high speed Internet access. Videoconferencing is web-based and allows persons to communicate directly with an entire group, with a practical limit of approximately ten persons at a time. The actual number of persons at one time is dependent upon the specific software license purchased and the skill level of the person leading the group. A drawback of both of these technologies is that they require a high speed Internet connection, and this service is not always available or affordable. The success of e-therapy will assist in expanding to the newly identified population targeted for this project. Text messaging is very common in the Deaf Community and has been used in the DODA Program. If a client does not call in for their appointment or does not answer at the appointed time, it is possible to send a quick reminder via text messaging that the appointment time has arrived and encourage the individual to keep the appointment.

Earlier in the chapter we met Mike. DODA facilitated his treatment and provided aftercare as well. Mike returned home with energy and jumped into his out-patient treatment with DODA support and webcam AA meetings and groups. Mike came back to life. He began to do things he hadn't done in years, opening doors to his soul that he had forgotten were there. Old habits die hard, and being back in his home state, even with support Mike began to isolate again. But this time it was different. He caught himself isolating. He would reach out to DODA by VP and say, "Hey, I need to talk. I'm isolating and that will lead me back to using drugs." Mike understood the path to recovery is paved with hard work and keeping your tool box close by at all times. Mike continued to monitor himself, his thinking and his mood. He had medical issues that caused him to be exposed to medications that triggered his addiction and "stinkin thinkin" but the difference was that he reached out now and asked for help, just a call away on the VP. Help can be a counselor on a webcam, an online AA meeting, or connecting through VP with friends he met in a recovery group.

Currently, the DODA program recruits persons in recovery who are deaf to serve as sponsors for AA groups. These persons are trained in use of the software in one hour or less, and this includes a discussion of suggested "group rules" (such as only one person "talking" in ASL at a time). At least one AA or NA meeting is held daily via this technology and the offerings will be expanded in the new project period. Another distinct advantage of online support groups is that meetings can be anonymous. The video conferencing software allows deaf individuals to attend group treatment sessions remotely. Use of video phone and video web conferencing connections also allow for persons who are deaf and attending inpatient treatment at the Minnesota Program to maintain connections to their own communities in order to plan aftercare and sobriety programs.

It is difficult for deaf individuals to access linguistically appropriate recovery support materials. DODA, with permission from the Hazelden Foundation, began producing daily mediations in American Sign Language. Video content comes from the book *Twenty-Four Hours a Day* and is interpreted by a team of ASL Interpreters. Staff from DODA also work with Deaf-specialized treatment programs (notably the Minnesota Program) to coordinate for community transitions following the residential treatment episode. These services are primarily provided by video phone or teleconference technology that utilizes computers with cameras. Another advantage of this approach is that deaf people are much less likely to know each other than when deaf people attend AA meetings in their local area. This lessens the concern about confidentiality which can keep deaf people from attending some Deaf 12-Step meetings.

The following was written by Robert, a deaf client who utilizes online support:

Sometime, I have seen people on a webcam, they're all from AA and NA deaf meetings and I really like this one better than regular in person meetings because some of the deaf people who are chemically dependent and tell many stories about themselves, some of them are similar stories as mine. It making me feel so good that I'm not the only one who has this problem. They've so inspired me. I felt more comfortable to admit myself to them. We understood each other why we done this our shortcoming and took wrong paths, we found on right road to recovery and embraced from dark side!

Finally the number of deaf have joined this DODA and used the web conferencing on the Internet where all having the meeting online. I am involved too. I love it! I felt more safer than to be isolate myself. If this DODA doesn't exist, I wouldn't be alive or survive. The DODA is work for me. Yes I was afraid at first but with your services it made my stay helpful and I learned a lots and meet may new friends but I do not want to go again.

I'm talking to case manager of shelter. She told me that I will see lady will help me about something. I was said oh my god. Same old story I've been looking it for several years. I met lady. She work for DODA. I ask her what is that DODA means. She explains to me. I was yelled out by myself "Can't be have program for deaf!" I was looking for program in Texas, Florida, and Georgia – then I went back to my hometown in Ohio. So that day I was depression so Thank God Dayton has DODA. This could be save my life Now I'm real excited about program. Now I enroll this program—wow it is real helpful me better path because I was homeless for almost 10 years (on-off) Now I got nice place apt. so I can't believe it what happen to me. So I do believe DODA will be good program for who is deaf addict it. I said thank God I'm re-born I would like it be help other deaf people in Ohio. I know many deaf peoples live around here so they need help. I'm possible be there for them later.

DODA: Bridging the Gap for Other Treatment Providers: Charles

Charles was referred to a treatment program that serves hearing clients. The counselors at the program knew that Charles had a hearing loss but did not know the extent of the loss or what the implications were for treatment. The counselors reached out to DODA and one of their counselors, Elise, to collaborate in order to provide Charles with appropriate services. A few days later Elise drove an hour and a half away from her office to assist in the assessment of Charles. Elise walked into the room where Charles and a counselor were sitting and attempted to talk to Charles, looking him in the eye and introducing herself. Charles obviously was struggling to read Elise's lips so she signed to him. He immediately began signing back to Elise. Elise was able to efficiently gather

Charles's background information. She learned that his drug of addiction was alcohol, but because he had always maintained a home for himself and a freelance job where he was his own boss, he felt he did not have a problem. In assisting the assessor to help Charles look at the seriousness of his situation, Elise asked Charles about his drinking. He said he liked the taste of beer but that it was not a problem for him. Charles was very thin. Elise asked Charles about his eating habits. Elise then asked Charles if he was really hungry and if Elise had both a sandwich and a beer but just offered him just one of the two items, which one would he take. Charles said he wanted both. Elise told him he can't have both he has to choose just one. He smiled and Elise saw a look in his eye that is called the "ah ha" moment, and Charles said, "I'd take the beer." From that point on Elise was able to talk to Charles about the fact that his response indicated he might in fact have a problem with alcohol and, at this moment, Charles decided he did in fact want to do well and complete this program. Elise helped the program to identify his accessibility needs and provided support in securing these services.

In treatment, through the use of a functional analysis, Charles was able to identify some of the thoughts and feelings that surrounded his drinking. He was able to recognize situations, thoughts and feelings that could be triggers for drinking. Initially, Charles did not see his hearing loss and communication issues as a part of any of his problems although his story seemed to indicate that these were indeed factors relevant to his substance use and recovery. Charles was the only deaf person in the facility, and no one there signed. He refused an interpreter because he saw himself as a hard-of-hearing person who could read lips. Although the staff did not feel communication was great, they used some strategies such as typing to him if questions were not clear. In addition, DODA installed a web cam, and DODA staff met with Charles along with the agency staff to ensure he was getting the information he needed to learn about his drinking and addiction. Later in his treatment program, issues around being deaf and feelings of rejection came to the surface. When these issues came up, the treatment staff reached out to DODA to help them navigate these issues of identity and self-worth. DODA staff was able to consult with the staff regarding Deaf Culture and family dynamic issues as well as provide direct counseling support to Charles via the webcam.

Active Treatment Including Role Plays and Structured Activities

There is a risk in recommending action-oriented approaches for deaf consumers as some individuals may think this means that deaf people are less intelligent, less verbal, and less capable of abstract thinking than hearing people. It is problematic to generalize about deaf people since the differences are as great as those found among individual hearing people.

However, we have repeatedly observed that treatment approaches that utilize activities to promote insight resonate with many deaf consumers. Glickman (Chapter 5, this volume) believes that this has something to do with the structure of ASL and the tendency of the language to build abstractions out of specific examples. It may also have to do with a more visual orientation to life, but probably the language struggles that many deaf people have play a role as well. The point here is not that abstract insight-oriented approach are avoided. In fact, all four of the best practices described above require abstract thinking. The point is that action promotes discussion and insight and is culturally a good match with many deaf people. What follows are a number of case studies illustrating action oriented treatment that resonated with particular deaf consumers.

Active Treatment Strategies: Ann

Ann came to treatment to deal with her alcoholism in order to keep her job. During treatment, Ann participated in an activity called Standing Up For Assertive Behavior. Clients were given an interactive informational workshop on various aspects, behaviors, and symptoms associated with aggressive, passive, passive-aggressive, and assertive roles. Clients were given eight scenarios to use to develop strategies for how they would assertively approach each situation. Clients were told they will be practicing their assertiveness skills on the counselor. Using role-playing scenarios the counselor interacted with the clients to challenge their old behaviors of passivity, aggression, and passive-aggressiveness. The clients took turns observing the counselor and a participant client going through a chosen scenario. The counselor is always the "aggressor" in these scenarios, while the participant client is challenged to act assertively. Non-participatory clients are to observe and discuss various behaviors, feelings, and feedback that they noticed during the interaction. After each scenario, the clients who participated in the role play discussed any observations and feelings they had during the scenario. At the end of each scenario, the group discussed how to fine tune the approach to become more assertive and practiced it several more times until they felt comfortable with it.

This activity enables clients to demonstrate a wide range of responses while going through the role play scenarios. Clients frequently express feeling angry, overwhelmed, exasperated and frustrated. After several practice rounds where clients practice being assertive, there is typically a shift in their demeanor. Clients become eager to improve their assertiveness skills. This activity helps clients see what the new behaviors might look like while practicing their skills and discussing the merits and challenges of each response. The participatory/visual example is one that is self-reinforcing and provides opportunities for coaching and commentary.

For Ann, this was a pivotal exercise. Because of her addiction, Ann's world had become so small and isolated that she had only limited, work-related interaction with people. As she became more isolated, she would retreat further, feeling afraid and overwhelmed. The role play and the understanding that she could find and develop an assertive "voice" were a possibility she hadn't considered.

A few weeks into treatment, Ann came to the counseling session complaining about how she was annoyed that her mother and brother kept calling her and preaching to her about being sober and losing weight. This caused her to feel put down, angry, and disrespected, all of which were potential triggers. Ann was also stressed out because the women at work kept asking her why she wouldn't eat the cakes and cookies they brought in and were offended by this behavior. The counselor used a visual metaphor to initiate a discussion with Ann. The counselor picked up a basket of small toy cars and placed them on the desk. The counselor explained to Ann that the path to sobriety sometimes feels like driving on a road. Sometimes getting healthy and/or staying sober feels like a goal that you are driving toward. He explained to her that many days we can focus on moving forward and following the program but sometimes we get distracted and veer off the path. Staying focused is hard. It's like when you learned how to drive. At first it's hard to stay in the lines on the road and pay attention to all the things going on while you are driving. Sobriety is the same. It's easy to get distracted and veer off the path. There will always be distractions (or triggers) in life. The important thing is to stay on track. At this point the pair discussed ways in which these triggers might be a distraction from Ann's goal of getting healthy and sober. The counselor also reviewed with Ann that she has a choice to use again as well and together they can look at the possible outcomes of such a choice. Lastly, the counselor asked Ann about the strategies and the people, places, and things that will support her and what things help her to remember this in her moments of pain and doubt.

When working with deaf clients, it is critical that we acknowledge and respect that clients may feel that their options in terms of people, places and things are limited. They may not know any sober deaf friends or may believe that they have burned too many bridges in the Deaf Community to connect with people who once judged or rejected them. In a small community, it is not always easy to re-invent yourself, and this is true in the Deaf Community. Clients may feel as though they are second class citizens in their hearing families after years of family members, in the midst of a story, looking to the deaf member and saying, "I'll tell you later," or "It's not important." These clients and their families may need support and skills to establish a new, healthy relationship that allows the client to participate fully.

Active Treatment Strategies: Quinn

Sometimes we create an activity that is in itself a metaphor. Many clients struggle with anger and resentment. One client, Quinn entered an inpatient treatment program with a lot of resentment toward his family, friends, and people who had hurt him in the past. It was clear that he needed help letting go of these resentments, but he has a hard time trusting and talking with people about his issues. Quinn's counselor brought in a bunch of rocks and asked Quinn to paint on each rock a different feeling about a particular event or person that he has resentment or anger towards. Quinn painted on approximately 15 rocks. After the paint had a chance to dry, the counselor asked Quinn to tell him about each of the rocks he had painted. After Quinn described the emotion behind the rock, the counselor placed all of the rocks into a backpack and asked Quinn to wear the backpack until the next group meeting. When it came time for group, everyone asked Quinn about the backpack. The counselor asked Quinn to explain what was in the backpack and asked Quinn how it felt. Quinn remarked that the bag was really heavy, and he was tired of dragging and lugging the backpack all over the place! The group quickly caught on, as did Quinn, that holding on to anger and resentments does the same thing to our spirit; it weighs us down, it makes us tired, and we start to get sick of it, almost angry toward it. The group explored ways to let go of the anger and resentment and agreed that talking about it was a good place to begin. Quinn and his counselor decided to walk down to the river and toss the rocks. As he threw the rocks into the river, Quinn described in great detail events that had angered him. The counselor asked him to picture what life would be like without the anger around the various events. The counselor asked Quinn to direct all the anger he had towards that letting go when he threw the rock into the river. Quinn repeated this several times until the rocks were gone. Afterwards, Quinn remarked how much lighter his backpack felt, and how much better he felt throwing the anger rocks into the river. Quinn and the counselor discussed how being able to let go of our anger and resentments, helps our spirit feel lighter, just like his backpack felt lighter. Quinn still had a hard time talking about his past with others, but it was clear that some doors had been opened for him. He started to connect how much better he felt with talking about his past and by the end of treatment he was able to openly discuss his anger and resentment in group and with his counselors.

In the case of Quinn, language and cultural differences may have played a part in his resentment and anger. Some deaf clients may not be able to clearly express the resentments they may feel towards people who have hurt them. For hearing people, the ability to speak directly to a person and tell them how they feel can be very healing. Many deaf individuals are not able to do this without the assistance of a third party and/or technology. In the absence of the ability to give voice to resentments, this activity can be a beginning to the process of articulating exactly what the issues are and realizing how hurtful the resentments can be. The rocks become a reminder of how "unmentionable can become unmanageable" and that they can greatly limit the person who continues to carry them instead of letting them go.

Active Treatment Strategies: Tessa

Tessa is 20 years old and the only deaf person in her large family. When Tessa first arrived in the Intensive Outpatient Treatment Program (IOP), she was having difficulty with staff and other clients in the program. She would have outbursts and then end up feeling badly that she caused a scene. Her counselor Rick used an activity to help Tessa have greater awareness about how impulsivity impacts her life. Rick used a visual metaphor and embedded this in an activity. He came to his session with Tessa with two eggs. He explained that one was a raw egg and the other hard boiled. He asked Tessa to drop each of the eggs on the floor. She looked at him like he was crazy and he told her that it was alright—that they would clean it up together. So she dropped the eggs. The raw egg oozed out all over the place. The hardboiled egg got a little dent but was intact. Rick explained that the raw egg represents raw emotions before you have time to work through and process them. The hardboiled egg represents the way people deal with things when they approach them with time and consideration. If you drop the hardboiled egg, it bounces but is not the same mess as the raw egg. Rick also asked Tessa how it felt to always be cleaning up raw egg? She giggled and said that treatment was like the boiling water that would help her to become a solid egg. The work with Tessa continued, and one day she came to group and shared that she was exhausted from having to think so hard. She was realizing that she had always just done things that others wanted her to do. She never realized that each time she agreed to "go along with something" that she was making a choice. The understanding that not choosing is also making a choice, made her feel awake and alive and a little overwhelmed. She was enjoying that she was in charge of her life but dealing with the weight of the responsibility as well. Tessa learned that feeling overwhelmed was a big trigger for her. She tended to crave marijuana the most when she felt like she couldn't handle the stress of school, tutoring, and counseling. Tessa made posters for herself to remind her to slow down, to take a breath, and to find ways to make the tasks more manageable. Rick used some other activities to help Tessa see how the stress and other triggers were affecting her. Rick used The Thermometer activity (see below) to help Tessa look at her stress and her coping in a different way.

Rick used a full water bottle that had 10 marks drawn down its side at half-inch increments and the numbers 1 through 10 written on it. The number 10 indicated the top or the fullest point of the bottle. Rick asked

Tessa to imagine that in order to get through the day and stay clean, she needs to have a full or almost full bottle of water—at 9 or 10. The level of water represents her resolve to stay clean and her ability to handle stress. The lower the water, the more chance she will end up craving pot. He asked her what happens to her commitment to sobriety when she is overwhelmed—when the level of commitment goes down? She indicated that she feels disconnected from her goal of sobriety and thinks about getting high. Rick reflected back to Tessa that each time she feels over-whelmed, her strong commitment to sobriety diminishes. Tessa agreed. Rick explained that the water level represents her feelings around her ability to be clean. The less water, the less strong she might feel about sobriety. In this case the level of the water is much like the fuel that runs a car's motor, you can't get far without fuel. Keeping your tank full is the work of recovery.

Rick asked Tessa to give an example of the last time she thought about getting high. She laughed and said it was earlier that morning. She had delayed finishing an assignment because she wasn't sure if she understood it and emailed her teacher for an explanation about the assignment. She stayed up all night to complete the assignment and then went to email it to her teacher and her Internet connection was lost. She had to drive to the coffee shop to email her assignment and worried she would be late for her counseling appointment. Rick asked Tessa to pour off a little bit of water for each of the stressors she experienced in the past 12 hours. There were seven: (1) confusion about the assignment; (2) worrying if the professor would email her an explanation about how to do the assignment back in time; (3) staying up all night to get the assignment done; (4) double-checking the format for the paper; (5) problems with the Internet; (6) having to go to the coffee shop; (7) and making it to counseling on time. Tessa poured off a little water for each of these stressors and she realized that she had almost no water left. Rick asked Tessa what she thought this meant for her. She said that some of the things that caused her stress, she could control and some of them she couldn't. Tessa indicated that she needed to find ways to deal with things so that they would not become stressors, such as waiting until the last minute to finish her paper. Tessa clearly understood that she needed to do whatever she could to manage her stress and take care of herself. Rick asked Tessa what point on the thermometer would indicate when she starts to think about getting high. She indicated that probably when the level hits a 6. Rick asked how this knowledge could help her. Tessa was clear that, if she was having a stress-ful day, she needs to get support, take time to take care of herself and also to see what she can do to reduce her stress level.

Rick asked Tessa to create a list or a picture of what she wanted for her future. Tessa came into their session with a framed poster that she proudly showed Rick. Tessa decided to make the assignment like something she had seen on T.V. It was a "vision board" that had pictures and words that represented all of the things that Tessa wanted for herself. In the center of the vision board was a picture of Tessa with a big smile. Rick admired the wonderful picture of Tessa. She told him she put it there to remember what he had taught her, that the choices were hers and that the success or failure would be hers as well. That is why she put a picture of herself in the center. She acknowledged to Rick that one of her old behaviors is focusing on others instead of herself.

Prior to completing the program, Tessa made a Relapse Prevention Map (see Figure 6.1). The assignment was to draw a map of Tessa's triggers as well as solutions to address the triggers. The assignment was to identify 10 triggers and 10 solutions. When Tessa completed her map, she and Rick explored each of the potential solutions for anticipated triggers. While having the discussion, Tessa came to understand that, for her, the most important part is remembering that she has multiple options for any possible problem that arises.

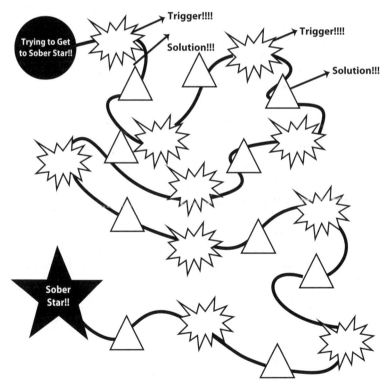

Figure 6.1 Relapse Prevention Map.

Active Treatment Strategies: Sam

Sam was referred to the Minnesota Program as a result of legal trouble. He was Native American and lived on a reservation in a very remote area. Upon arrival, Sam had never used amplification and had never received any specialized educational services. Sam communicated using gestures only. He knew no formal sign language and he could not read or write. Sam knew he was sent to Minnesota because of legal problems but was not fully aware of what would happen once he arrived in treatment.

Although clients like Sam are not representative of all culturally deaf clients, they do exist and need services. In order to serve clients like Sam, specialized treatment programs may need to utilize a Certified Deaf Interpreter (CDI) or another interpreter who is has the requisite communication skill set. Staff worked diligently with Sam, continuously asking for feedback about his experience and understanding. When working with a client with language challenges, it is important to watch for times when the client may isolate or shut down as a result of feeling overwhelmed or confused.

In helping Sam understand the difference between alcoholic and non-alcoholic beverages and his choices, staff asked him what items that he drank looked like. Staff used Sam's description and a calendar where he could indicate when the event he was describing had occurred. Staff drew a picture of Sam in the drunken state he described. He had wet his pants, he had thrown up, and he had a black eye but could not remember why. This picture helped Sam understand the concept. Next, using the calendar, staff asked Sam how he was feeling today. Sam explained that he was clean, his clothes were clean, his body was not hurting, and he felt okay. Staff then drew a picture of Sam in his present state. Next, using pictures of various alcoholic and non-alcoholic beverages, staff asked Sam to place the picture cards on the drawing of him that matched the result. Sam was able to clearly indicate which alcoholic drinks cause him to be in a drunken state and which non-alcoholic drinks kept him in a sober state. Each time he indicated where the picture card should be placed, staff would sign "drunk" or "sober." Later in the week, staff brought Sam to the store and asked him to identify the "drunk" (alcoholic) beverages and the "sober" (non-alcoholic) beverages. Sam seemed to understand quite clearly this difference.

Upon his arrival, staff used drawings to create a drug chart and determine his drug(s) of choice. Sam indicated that he used alcohol primarily and through Sam's *drawings*, they determined that he drank vodka, beer, and wine. He also drew a picture of a joint, indicating that he used marijuana. Throughout treatment, staff used gestures, drawings, and role play to help Sam understand expectations of his participation in the program, step work, and other recovery concepts.

It is important to remember that, when working with language-challenged clients such as Sam, information gaps are common and require the provision of extensive basic education. Going into the community to provide hands-on experience help clients learn and apply new concepts that can't be brought to life in the treatment setting. This type of approach would typically only be done in a Deaf program with staff who are aware of this information gap.

Although language challenges caused misunderstandings with Sam while in treatment, he knew that everyone there had in common with him a problem with alcohol and/or drugs and that their common goal was not to use them again. He also learned the routine of the group structure and how to participate. When it was his turn to talk about an assignment he would do so using pictures. In time, Sam became more and more skilled and was able to describe and explain the impact that alcohol and drug use had over his life. When Sam went to a 12-Step meeting, he recognized that everyone was there for a similar reason. Although he couldn't read the Steps on the wall, he understood that they represented the effort of people trying to stay sober and that if he went to a meeting like this on his reservation, people there would also be trying to stay sober. For Sam, attendance at 12-Step meetings would support in his effort to stay sober as well as to provide camaraderie.

One pivotal moment for Sam happened one day toward the end of his time in treatment. Sam was frustrated and annoyed with one of the cafeteria workers. Sam came back to the unit and sulked in his room. One of the other participants asked Sam what was wrong and Sam waved him away. After a short time, Sam went back to the other participant and started to try to explain what had happened. The conversation was not exactly clear but Sam taking the step and reaching out to get support was significant. Later in group, Sam told the group (through gesture and sign) that the guy that helped him was his friend and that, "friends help me sober." Sam had never had any one to talk to about his frustrations. It was an important understanding for Sam to realize that he could choose not to isolate. And this might help him to stay sober.

Sam successfully completed treatment and returned home to a very isolated environment where alcoholism was abundant. There were some addictions/recovery resources in his home community but these resources were not accessible. During family week, Sam and his family were given their contact information and there was a discussion about ways that Sam might be able to utilize the limited services that were available such as 12-Step meetings and other recovering people on the Reservation. After returning home, Sam was able to maintain his sobriety for about ten months at which time he relapsed. Sam was able to return to treatment in Minnesota and, much like other clients who may relapse and return to treatment, he felt bad about having started using again. This time in treatment, he was better able to express himself through pictures and signing. Sam had a very positive and successful treatment experience. He looked and felt better than he had in a very long time. He stayed in treatment for another 40 days and returned to the reservation.

Pairing Active Treatment and Other Supports

It is important to remember that after learning to use various activities, interventions, and supports, the counselor must decide how and when to utilize them. More often than not, the approach requires a variety of responses. In the case of Stan, it was important for the counselor to utilize active treatment strategies and at the same time reach out to DODA for other support.

Stan was a 30-year-old deaf man in a mainstreamed treatment program. One day, on the unit, Stan became very angry after a group session. After group, some of the men were laughing as they walked out of the room. Stan became resentful because he did not know what they were laughing at and he thought they might be laughing at him. Frequently in group he did not share because he was never sure if he understood the conversation. He never let anyone know this because he didn't want to appear dumb. On this particular day, Stan had shared some feelings. He quickly assumed that his sharing may have been off target and he was angry that these guys were laughing at him. Stan went to his counselor and told her that he wanted to quit the program. After discussing these feelings with the counselor, Stan came to realize that he frequently believes that others are laughing at him, and the resentment and anger and feelings of rejection become a trigger for his drinking. Stan admitted to the counselor that his intention was to leave the program and go drink at the first bar he could find. The counselor used an activity to help Stan better understand and recognize his triggers. Using a popcorn popper, she started to discuss the stressors in everyday life. She asked Stan to talk about stress. For each stressor, she asked him to put a handful of popcorn kernels in the popper. As Stan talked about situations that have occurred in his life that added to his stress such as addiction and using substances to deal with stress, she asked him to pour on a little oil and then a trigger or an incident occurs and plug in the popper. As the popper heated, the counselor educated the Stan about the physiological effects of anger and stress. The popcorn begins to pop and that can be equated to losing one's temper/blowing up/being out of control. The counselor asked Stan how they can stop the popcorn from popping. Stan said to "pull the cord" or "unplug." Together Stan and his counselor talked about ways to deal with anger and brainstormed ideas that had worked in the past such as how Stan could "unplug" by walking away, taking a time out to relax, or running cold water on his hands. The term "unplug" was also used during the counseling sessions as a way to explain the concept of emotionally disengaging or not losing the moment to emotion and anger.

By exploring his frustration and anger, Stan was able to look at how he analyzed the situation and to identify and practice new ways of thinking and new ways of responding to triggers. This intervention provided a foundation for much of the work Stan did while he was in treatment.

One outcome was that Stan decided that he needed greater communication access because he was deaf and that the need had nothing to do with his intellect (as he thought others would assume was the case). Stan had grown up with the flawed notion that being deaf was the same as being dumb. He thought that the less deaf he appeared the better. This was particularly difficult for Stan because he came to realize that through his entire life, he had struggled to prove he could survive without interpreters. Now, in treatment when he felt like he lost all of his dignity because of problems caused by his drinking, he was coming to realize that he wasn't fooling anyone about how deaf he was. At this time, the counselor reached out to DODA for additional support around communication access as well as how to address these very profound identity issues for Stan.

Aftercare

As we consider the continuum of services for substance abuse prevention, assessment, and treatment, we need to keep in mind that aftercare is perhaps one of the biggest challenges. For many counselors, trying to put together aftercare plans for clients is like putting together the pieces of a puzzle. There are few states that have a fully accessible aftercare support services i.e., counseling, 12-Step meetings, sponsor availability, etc. Some states have tried to focus their resources on setting up outpatient and aftercare counseling support, knowing that they can successfully refer a deaf client to an out of state specialized treatment program such as the Minnesota Program as long as there are support services available in the clients community when they complete treatment and return home.

In the 12-Step community, counselors often hear that these are "excuses" for not wanting to go to 12-Step meetings. When hearing people in recovery hear deaf people in recovery complaining about the lack of access as reasons for not going to meetings, they inevitably interpret these to be excuses or other examples of "stinkin thinkin" that addicts use. However, to deaf people, the lack of communication access and the emotional distance between deaf and hearing worlds, are valid concerns. Counselors may perceive these as excuses where clients see them as genuine barriers. The truth may lie somewhere in between.

Conclusions

In this chapter, we have described some of the ways that substance abuse counselors who specialize in work with deaf persons have adapted best practices in contemporary substance-abuse treatment for a diverse group of deaf clientele. While the nature of this work requires us to generalize, we always remember that each deaf person is a unique individual and that diversity among deaf people is as varied as among hearing people. That said, it is still striking how often counselors who do this work find that similar strategies for adapting treatment seem to resonate with large numbers of deaf clients. The adaptations for language are the most obvious, but what isn't obvious is the enormous diversity in language abilities that deaf clients possess. The naïve clinician imagines one just "signs" or uses an interpreter. The deaf treatment specialist pays great attention to assessing and matching communication abilities and will have to draw on additional communication specialists, such as deaf interpreters, for help with some clients. The specialist substance abuse counselor also works with deaf people who are fluent in English, ASL, or both, some of whom have college and graduate degrees and may have very little in common with the more severely language-dysfluent consumers. Simultaneous adapting for all these consumers, who can be present in the same treatment program, is a specialized skill in itself.

Wherever we find treatment specialists with deaf people, we also find that other kinds of adaptations are commonly made. In this chapter, we discussed adaptations to the four models of best practice in substance abuse work: cognitive behavioral therapy, the 12-Step model, motivational interviewing, and harm reduction. The additional adaptations that talented clinicians everywhere make involve more use of narrative therapy techniques like storytelling and creative metaphors (with visual metaphors being most appropriate), treatment activities as a promoter of insight and motivation, the creation of pictorial tools and signed translations/adaptations of treatment materials, and the creative use of technology.

These kinds of treatment adaptations don't happen as easily outside of specialized Deaf treatment programs. Naïve hearing clinicians don't know what they don't know, so they don't know why and how to adapt treatment for deaf consumers. Where specialized Deaf treatment resources do exist, clients usually must still struggle when returning to communities where no comparable resources are found. National programs available over the Internet, like the DODA program, have potential to address this for those deaf consumers sophisticated enough to use these computerized resources. Still, the knowledge needed to build on these adaptations emerges out of the experience of specialized Deaf treatment programs and can disappear as these programs lose funding and support. If this were to happen, we'd all be naïve as to what deaf consumers who have addiction problems need as part of their treatment and recovery process.

Note

1. This chapter contains contributions from Jason Valentine, Elly Carpenter, Shannon Englehart, Cindi Cassady, and Sandy Castle.

References

Alexander, T., DiNitto, D., & Tidblom, I. (2005). Screening for alcohol and other drug problems among the deaf. *Alcoholism Treatment Quarterly, 23*(1), 63–78.

The American Heritage Dictionary of the English Language, Fourth Edition. (2006). New York, NY: Houghton Mifflin.

Barnett, J. E., & Scheetz, K. (2003). Technological advances and Telehealth: Ethics, law, and the practice of psychotherapy. *Psychotherapy: Theory, Research, Practice, Training, 40*(1-2), 86–93.

Beck T. A., Wright, F. D., Newman, C. F., & Liese, B. S. (1993). *Cognitive therapy of substance abuse.* New York, NY: Guilford Press.

Bien, T. H., Miller, W. R., & Boroughs, J. M. (1993). Motivational interviewing with alcohol outpatients. *Behavioural and Cognitive Psychotherapy, 21,* 347–356.

Bien, T. H., Miller, W. R., & Tonigan, J. S. (1993), Brief interventions for alcohol problems: *A Review. Addiction, 88,* 315–336.

Boros, A. (1981). Activating solutions to alcoholism among the hearing impaired. In A. J. Schecter (Ed.), *Drug dependence and alcoholism: Social and behavioral issues* (pp. 1007–1014). New York, NY: Plenum.

Day, S. X., & Schneider, P. L. (2002). Psychotherapy using distance technology: A comparison of face-to-face, video, and audio treatment. *Journal of Counseling Psychology, 49,* 499–503.

Dennis, M. L., Chen, Y. F., & Funk, R. R. (2006). Development and validation of the GAIN Short Screener (GSS) for internalizing, externalizing and substance use disorders and crime/violence problems among adolescents and adults. *American Journal on Addictions, 15,* 80–91.

Freedman, J., & Combs, G. (1996). *Narrative therapy: The social construction of preferred realities.* New York, NY: W.W. Norton.

Glickman, N. (2009). *Cognitive behavioral therapy for deaf and hearing persons with language and learning challenges.* New York, NY: Routledge.

Glickman, N. (1996). What is culturally affirmative psychotherapy? In N. S. Glickman & M. A. Harvey, *Culturally affirmative psychotherapy with deaf persons* (pp. 1–56). Hillsdale: NJ: Erlbaum.

Griffiths, M. (2005). Online therapy for addictive behaviors. *Cyberpsychology and Behavior, 8,* 555–561.

Guthmann, D., & Blozis, S. (2001). Unique issues faced by deaf individuals entering substance abuse treatment and following discharge. *The American Annals of the Deaf, 146*(3), 294–303.

Guthmann, D., Dickinson, J., Sandberg, K. (2010). An application of the Minnesota model: An approach to substance abuse treatment of deaf and hard of hearing. In I. Leigh (Ed.), *Psychotherapy with deaf clients from diverse groups* (pp. 349–371). Washington, DC: Gallaudet University Press.

Guthmann, D., & Graham, V. (2004). Substance abuse: A hidden problem within the D/deaf and hard of hearing communities. *Journal of Teaching in the Addictions, 3*(1), 49–64.

Guthmann, D., Lybarger, R., & Sandberg, K. (1993). Providing chemical dependency treatment to the deaf or hard of hearing mentally ill client. *Journal of the American Deafness and Rehabilitation Association, 27,* 1–15.

Guthmann, D., & Moore, D. (2007). The Substance Abuse in Vocational Rehabilitation Screener in American Sign Language (SAVRS-S-ASL) for persons who are deaf. *Journal of the American Deafness and Rehabilitation Association, 41*(1), 8–16.

Guthmann, D., & Sandberg, K. (1995). Clinical approaches in substance abuse treatment for use with deaf and hard of hearing adolescents. *Journal of Child and Adolescent Substance Abuse, 4*(3), 69–79.

Guthmann, D., & Sandberg, K. (1997, January/February). Deaf Culture and Substance Abuse. *Counselor Magazine,* 29–32.

Guthmann, D., & Sandberg, K. (2001). Models of alcohol and other drug treatment for consideration when working with deaf and hard of hearing individuals. *Journal of the American Deafness and Rehabilitation Association, 34*(3), 28–42.

Guthmann, D., & Sandberg, K. A. (2003). Culturally affirmative substance abuse treatment for Deaf people: Approaches, materials and administrative considerations. In N. S. Glickman & S. Gulati (Eds.), *Mental health care of deaf people: A culturally affirmative approach* (pp. 261–303). Mahwah, NJ: Earlbaum.

Guthmann, D., Sandberg, K., & Dickinson, J. (1999). Chemical dependency: An application of a treatment model for Deaf people. In I. Leigh (Ed.), *Psychotherapy with Deaf clients from diverse groups* (Chapter 16). Washington, DC: Gallaudet University Press.

Isaacs, M., Buckley, G., & Martin, D. (1979). Patterns of drinking among the deaf. *American Journal of Drug and Alcohol Abuse, 6*(4), 463–476.

Isenberg, G. (1996). Storytelling and the use of culturally appropriate metaphors. In N. S. Glickman & M. A. Harvey (Eds.), *Psychotherapy with deaf people* (pp. 169–184). Hillsdale, NJ: Erlbaum .

Johnson, S., & Locke, R. (1978). *Student drug use in a school for the deaf.* Paper presented at the annual meeting of the National Conference on Drugs, Seattle, WA.

King, V. L., Stoller, K. B., Kidorf, M., Kindbom, K., Hursh, S., Brady, T., & Brooner, R. K. (2009). Assessing the effectiveness of an Internet-based videoconferencing platform for deliverly intensified substance abuse counseling. *Journal of Substance Abuse Treatment, 36,* 331–338.

Lakofff, G., & Johnson, M. (1980). *Metaphors we live by.* Chicago: University of Chicago Press.

Lane, K. E. (1989, April). Substance abuse among the deaf population: An overview of current strategies, programs and barriers to recovery. *Journal of American Deafness and Rehabilitation Association, 2*(4), 79–85.

Lipton, D. S., & Goldstein, M. F. (1997). Measuring substance abuse among the Deaf. *Journal of Drug Issues, 27*(4), 733.

McCrone, W. (1994). A two year report card on Title I of the Americans with Disabilities Act. Implications for rehabilitation counseling with deaf people. *Journal of American Deafness and Rehabilitation Association, 28*(2), 1–20.

Miller, W. R., Benefield, R. G., & Tonigan, J. S. (1993, June). Enhancing motivation for change in problem drinking: A controlled comparison of two therapist styles. *Journal of Consulting and Clinical Psychology. 6*(3) 455–461.

Miller, F. G., & Lazowski, L. E. (1999). *The Substance Abuse Subtle Screening Inventory-3 (SASSI-3) Manual.* Springville, IN: The SASSI Institute.

Miller, W. R., & Rollnick, S. (1991). *Motivational Interviewing: Preparing people to change addictive behaviour.* New York, NY: Guilford Press.

Monti, P. M., Kadden, R. M., Rohsenow, D. J., Cooney, N. L., & Abrams, D. B. (2002). *Treating alcohol dependence: A coping skills training guide* (2nd ed.). New York, NY: Guilford Press.

Morgenstern, J., Blanchard, K., Morgan, E., Thomas, J., Labouvie, E., & Hayaki, J. (2001). Testing the effectiveness of cognitive-behavioral treatment for substance abuse in a community setting: Within treatment and post-treatment findings. *Journal of Consulting and Clinical Psychology, 69*(6), 1007–1017.

O'Reilly, R., Bishop, J., Maddox, K., Hutchinson, L., Fisman, M., & Takhar, J. (2007). Is telepsychiatry equivalent to face-to-face psychiatry? Results from a randomized controlled equivalence trial. *Psychiatric Services, 58*, 836–843.

Padden, C., & Humphries, T. (1988). *Deaf in America: Voices from a culture*. Cambridge, MA: Harvard University Press.

Parker, T. S., & Wampler, K. S. (2006). Changing emotion: The use of therapeutic storytelling. *Journal of Marital and Family Therapy, 32*, 155–166.

Phillips, K. T., & Rosenberg, H. (2008). The development and evaluation of the harm reduction self-efficacy questionnaire. *Psychology of Addictive Behaviors, 22*, 36–46.

Pollard, R. (1998). Psychopathology. In M. Marschark & M. D. Clark (Eds.), *Psychological perspectives on deafness* (Vol. 2, pp. 171–197). Mahwah, NJ: Erlbaum.

Pollard, R. Q., Dean, A., O'Hearn, A., & Shapiro, L. (2009). An application of the Minnesota Model: An approach to substance abuse treatment of deaf and hard of hearing. In I. Leigh's *Individuals: Psychotherapy with deaf clients from diverse groups* (pp. 372–392). Washington, DC: Gallaudet University Press.

Pollard, R. Q., Dean, R. K., O'Hearn, A., & Shapiro, L. (2009). Adapting health education material for Deaf audiences. *Rehabilitation Psychology, 54*(2), 232–238.

Pull, C. B. (2006). Self-help internet interventions for mental disorders. *Current Opinions in Psychiatry, 19*, 50–53.

Rollnick S., & Miller, W. R. (1995). What is motivational interviewing? *Behavioural and Cognitive Psychotherapy, 23*, 325–334.

Titus, J. C., & Guthmann, D. (2010). Addressing the black hole in substance abuse treatment for Deaf and hard of hearing individuals: Technology to the rescue. *Journal of the American Deafness and Rehabilitation Association, 43*(2), 92–100.

Waldron, H. B., & Turner, C. W. (2008). Evidence-based psychosocial treatments for adolescent substance abuse. *Journal of Clinical Child & Adolescent Psychology, 37*, 238–261.

Watson, D., Steitler, K., Peterson, P., & Fulton, W. K. (1983). *Mental health, substance abuse, and deafness: Proceedings, First National Conference, Mental Health, Substance Abuse, and Deafness, Rochester, NY, 1981* (Readings in Deafness: Monograph No. 7). Silver Spring, MD: American Deafness and Rehabilitation Association.

Watson, E., Boros. A., & Zrimec, G. (1979 Winter). Mobilization of services for deaf alcoholics. *Alcohol Health and Research World*, 33–38.

White, M. (1995). *Reauthoring lives: Interviews and essays*. Adelaide, South Australia: Dulwich Centre Publications.

White, M. (2007). *Maps of narrative practice*. New York, NY: W.W. Norton.

White, M., & Epston, D. (1990). *Narrative means to therapeutic ends*. New York, NY: W.W. Norton.

Wilson, J. A. B., & Wells, M. G. (2009). Telehealth and the Deaf: A comparison study. *Journal of Deaf Studies and Deaf Education, 14*(3), 386–402.

7 Culturally Affirmative Adaptations to Trauma Treatment with Deaf Children in a Residential Setting

Karen Bishop

Introduction: Some Traumatized Deaf Children

Robert was admitted to the Walden School at age 10, after spending several weeks in an inpatient child psychiatric hospital[1] for aggressive behaviors at home and school. The Department of Children and Families had taken custody and determined that he could not return home but rather needed admission to this specialized residential treatment facility for deaf children with emotional and behavioral problems.

When Robert came to the program, he had only been in the country for 6 months (2 of which had been spent in an adolescent inpatient psychiatric hospital where he had 1 hour of American Sign Language [ASL] interpreting daily) after moving to the United States from Haiti. Robert's mother decided to come to the United States a year ahead of him to start a stable life in America, and then send for him to join her. While his mother was in the United States, Robert was left in the care of his grandfather who states that he "had the run of the island." We interpreted this to mean that he had no structure, formal education, or communication and that he was able to roam freely. In essence, he was a feral child.

Because Robert received no formal education in Haiti, he had not been exposed to a signed language. His mother and grandfather, the only two people in his family, speak Haitian Creole. Robert had no ability to speak Creole and would use only gestures to communicate with his mother and grandfather. His mother would use gestures to communicate with him, but in actuality, there was almost no communication between them.

Initially when he arrived in the United States, Robert was sent to a public school that had a small mainstream program for deaf students. He soon began having significant problems in school, getting into fights with peers, refusing to leave school grounds at dismissal, and one time bringing a small pocket knife to school, which, because of zero-tolerance laws, was viewed as a weapon. He had multiple suspensions within the six short months he was there. He also had significant problems at home, leaving the house at night and wandering the streets of Boston, shoplifting in local stores, and becoming physically assaultive towards his mother when she tried to set any limits with him. The police were called to the home when Robert attacked her, hitting her hard enough to cause a head injury. This incident, the last of many, resulted in the psychiatric hospitalization. After spending several weeks in a psychiatric hospital, he was placed at Walden School.

When Robert arrived, his behavior was out of control. He could not understand or follow directions or rules. He became aggressive in response to any expectations. He pushed teachers and peers, stormed out of the building many times, kicked holes in walls, threw objects, and damaged anything within his reach. For example, when he was expected to do his laundry and clean his room (with staff assistance) or compromise to select a TV program with his peers in the dorm, he flew into a rage. Physically big for his age, he intimidated those around him with threats or occurrences of assault. Both staff and students were fearful of him.

Robert's working diagnoses were Intermittent Explosive Disorder, Communication Disorder, Language Disorder, and Mild Mental Retardation. Later, after we knew him better, we would also diagnose him as having Post-Traumatic Stress Disorder and Reactive Attachment Disorder. Once he developed ASL skills, we were able to determine that he was not mentally retarded. Being so linguistically dysfluent just made him appear so.

David is a deaf child who arrived at the Walden School Program at age 8, never having used a signed language before. He has a caring and supportive intact family (with one older brother and a 2-year-old sister). He was adopted at approximately age three from a foster home where his deafness went undetected and where there was suspected sexual abuse. He has a cochlear implant which enabled him to hear some speech sounds. He could no longer live at home because of safety concerns. In addition to frequent physical outburst when he was told no, he would leave the house in the middle of the night and wander for hours, often being brought home by the police. Most concerning was the extreme self-injurious behavior that he displayed when things did not go his way. He would scratch his arms and legs with sharp objects and bang his head off the walls and floor until he bled. When he arrived at Walden School, he would regularly defecate in his pants and in the shower and handle his own feces. Without provocation, he would strip naked and run wild through the building and on the grounds, sometimes leaving campus and attempting to go to neighbors' homes. Walden School staff had never seen behavior like this before in our over 20 years of serving deaf children with trauma histories. His diagnoses on arrival at age eight were Reactive Attachment Disorder, Moderate Mental Retardation, Obsessive Compulsive Disorder, Mild Cerebral Palsy, and Pervasive Developmental Disorder.

Robert and David represent two of the many children and youth with complex life stories who are served at Walden School. Many of these children have been so linguistically deprived that they arrive nearly alingual.

Many are neurologically compromised and virtually all of them have been abused, neglected and traumatized in many ways. They almost always arrive frightened, and either aggressive or self-harming, having minimal understanding of where they are and why or what is expected of them, and most have "attachment disorders," which make initial bonding with them even more challenging. Some, like David, have never been in school before, and others, like Robert, have failed prior schooling attempts, usually in linguistically inappropriate mainstreamed environments. Most of these children are exceptionally difficult at first to engage in any collaborative treatment process.

This chapter is about mental health care with these traumatized deaf children. The focus is on the issue of how this trauma work with deaf children is different than such treatment with traumatized hearing children. How does a specialized Deaf treatment setting like Walden School work with these children? What will be different about the "trauma informed care" in such a setting? What special issues will arise and what adaptations will have to be made? Walden School provides a "culturally affirmative" treatment setting for Deaf children, but culturally affirmative means more than having deaf staff and hearing signing staff. It means changing the mental health treatment itself in ways that fit deaf children we work with. What does this look like? How is it done?

Starting with theoretical models influencing the work at Walden School, this chapter will discuss the approaches used at Walden School to provide treatment to language and learning challenged deaf youth, specifically approaches used to help these two youth above and others like them settle into the program and begin treatment. Providing trauma treatment to deaf youth poses unique challenges, but providing trauma treatment to deaf youth with language and learning problems poses an even greater challenge, and work with this latter group will be the focus of this chapter.

The Walden School

Walden School, The Learning Center for the Deaf's residential treatment program, is a nonprofit, nationally recognized educational program located in Framingham, Massachusetts. The program serves a diverse population of students who range in age from 8 to 22 years, and it accepts students from all over the United States. Most of the Walden School students reside at the school, although there are a small number of commuting students who are able to live safely at home. All students who come to the program, in addition to being deaf or hard of hearing, have serious emotional and behavioral challenges resulting from organic dysfunction, mental illness, or a history of childhood abuse and/or neglect. Many have complex trauma histories, some have cognitive limitations, and some have come from language-deprived environments. Often they have co-occurring diagnoses and multiple problems, one confounding the other. These children typically get referred to Walden School after other educational and residential settings have failed them.

Some students come to Walden School with age-appropriate, sophisticated ASL skills and intact cognitive functioning. For these students, traditional insight oriented therapy, along with milieu therapies and family therapy, is usually very effective. These services are adapted for signing deaf students. Students who arrive with strong sign language skills are often easier to serve because of the shared language with staff. All Walden School students have challenging behaviors and need a therapeutic treatment program, but when they arrive with language skills, staff can at least discuss with them the reasons for their placement and try to collaboratively set some goals.

The greatest challenge to providing trauma treatment for deaf children and adolescents is adapting that treatment to fit the language, learning, and clinical challenges of these students. Residential treatment programs that serve deaf children (and there are only a few in the United States) are unlike treatment programs that serve hearing children. To begin with, deaf people are a low incidence population, and deaf children with emotional challenges are an even lower incidence population. Because there are small numbers of these children nationally, the children served tend to have a wide range of diagnostic profiles, language skills and functional abilities. There are many residential programs for hearing children in the United States, and several in Massachusetts. These programs have the ability to specialize in particular clinical problems such as eating disorders or sexual offending behaviors. Deaf treatment programs must cast a broader net, serve every deaf child or adult in need, and then tailor the treatment approach to the individual needs of each student. This is easier said than done.

The main difference from hearing programs are the communication challenges, the huge range in communication abilities, the large numbers of severely language-deprived and -dysfluent children, and the need to adapt everything so that it is linguistically and conceptually suitable for students with such diverse communication needs.

Another difference is the role that "culturally affirmative treatment" plays. Treatment services are provided in American Sign Language, adapted for each student. Large numbers of deaf staff work at every level, and that physical and social environment is designed by and for deaf people. Deaf staff are role models for deaf children who see themselves and their future in the deaf adults around them. Deaf adults are also linguistic role models for children, particularly those with language and learning challenges, and will intentionally teach language to these children as a parent would teach a child.

At least 50% of all Walden School staff are deaf, and all staff must possess at least a second language fluency in American Sign Language. Currently, deaf staff represent over 75% of the direct care positions at Walden

School. Walden School staff have diverse backgrounds. Of the deaf staff, some are native signers and have deaf parents. Others are from hearing families where they were the only deaf members. Some have been raised at residential schools for the deaf while others graduated from mainstream programs in their hometowns. Regardless of their backgrounds, all deaf staff are native users or have second language fluency in ASL. They all consider themselves culturally Deaf, bicultural, or multicultural.

While it is imperative to have deaf staff and a linguistically accessible environment so children can communicate directly with their caregivers and therapists, much more is necessary to be considered a culturally affirmative treatment environment.

> Treatment programs for Deaf children must also address the variations in Deaf children's language fluency, the importance of Deaf culture in deaf children's development, and the power dynamics that exist between culturally Deaf and culturally hearing people. They must recognize the value of Deaf adult role models, as well as the boundary challenges faced by professionals who are members of the Deaf Community. They must work with families that do not share a native language with their Deaf children. (Vreeland & Tourangeau, 2003, p. 239)

The focus of this chapter is on treatment of those deaf students who come to Walden School without age-appropriate ASL skills. Some of these youth have cognitive delays, some have been deprived of early language, some are from other countries where there has been no formal education, and some have experienced such early significant trauma that their ability to learn language to this point has been compromised. Glickman (2009) refers to deaf people with this general profile as "language and learning challenged (LLC)," which is how they will be referred to in this chapter. Their lack of fluency in any language makes these children especially difficult to treat. It means that helping them develop language skills, especially in ASL, becomes an essential element of the treatment program.

Models of Treatment of Traumatized Children

The National Child Traumatic Stress Network (NCTSN; 2004, 2006) indicates that the prevalence of abuse among deaf children is significantly higher than that of their hearing peers. According to Sullivan, Vernon, and Scanlan (1987), deaf children are more vulnerable to neglect, emotional, physical, and sexual abuse than children in the general population. They reported that 50% of deaf girls have been sexually abused (as compared to 25% of hearing girls), and 54% of deaf boys have been sexually abused (as compared to 10% of hearing boys). According to Tate (2009), there are approximately five million deaf people needing mental health treatment.

She reports that deaf children and adults are three to five times more likely to have a serious emotional disturbance than their hearing peers.

There is very little written on the subject of treatment of traumatized deaf children and adolescents. The few resources that are available mostly focus on how a hearing therapist can secure an interpreter *as if that were all that mattered.* The NCTSN (2004) addresses therapy adaptations in four bulleted points suggesting visual modalities, refraining from using writing to construct narratives, using the interpreter to teach signs, and the need for teaching socialization and safety skills.

Because there are so few resources for treatment of this low incidence group, those doing this work must draw upon established best practices in treatment of traumatized children and adapt them. Each clinician usually begins the process of adapting anew, without guidelines or much established materials to draw upon. Some clinicians do this very creatively, yet their knowledge and methods are usually not passed on to other people. It should not be presumed that trauma treatment for deaf children is the same as trauma treatment for hearing children. *Just add interpreters!* The unique cultural and language differences make the matter of adaptation very central. In particular, the need to teach basic language skills as part of treatment to so many deaf children adds a whole new level of complexity and challenge.

Several theoretical models for trauma treatment have influenced the work at Walden School. The first and most prominent is the cognitive behavioral therapy (CBT) approach, especially that part of it fashioned by Donald Meichenbaum. As described in detail in Glickman's (2009) book, this approach to CBT is essentially about the teaching of psychosocial skills and the development of more life affirming self-stories. CBT is used at Walden School to teach students coping skills and to teach them the connection between their thoughts, feelings, and behavior.

In Glickman's 2009 work, another key point is that skill training must be developmentally appropriate. Students will vary enormously in the kinds of coping skills they can draw upon, but in the Walden School program, where the student population is mainly children with severe language and learning challenges, more developmentally simple coping skills are drawn upon most often. Many of these skills are sensory-movement-based and are illustrated with pictures using the Boardmaker[2] Program and digital photography of the students' images. Coping skills must be individually tailored to each youth and are developed keeping the individual student's needs and abilities in mind. Each student in the program has an individually tailored list of coping skills used when the need arises.

Walden School also draws heavily upon the collaborative and relational approach to treatment exemplified by the work of Ross Greene (R. Greene, 1998; R. W. Greene & Ablon, 2006) and Lorraine Fox (2004, 1994, 1987). Both Greene and Fox stress how healing can only occur in the context of collaborative, egalitarian relationships. Treatment is done *with* children, not to them, and this emphasis helped move Walden School away from such behavioral techniques as level systems and reinforcement programs.

Fox's main theme is that "children with "damaged egos" (sense of self), from past or current life circumstances, are unable (not unwilling) to see things as we see them, or as we would like them to see them" (Fox, 1987). Her pioneering work in the field of residential treatment helped reframe treatment work from focusing on helping children follow rules (compliance) to focusing on helping children understand and heal from past trauma and become negotiating partners in their own treatment. Greene makes the same points when discussing how children develop behavior problems from lack of skills, not lack of motivation. Both R. Greene and Fox's (1994) work cautions that compliance should not be the goal of treatment. They argue that compliance oriented environments actually perpetuate abuse of children. Fox has worked closely with Walden School staff, always emphasizing that it is a "coercion free" environment that helps children heal.

Greene's model of "collaborative problem solving" centers on what he first called "3 baskets" and later reframed as "3 plans" (R. Greene, 1998; R. W. Greene & Ablon, 2006). Almost every conflict that occurs can be conceptualized as Plan B, something that can be solved collaboratively. Non-negotiable Plan A issues are mostly safety concerns. Plan C refers to less important struggles which the staff choose not to fight at this time.

At Walden School these Plan C issues might include choosing not to insist that a teenager greet his teacher at the start of the day or avoid profanity when teaching skills to decrease assaultive behavior is the priority. Greene's plans are important because they emphasize the idea of identifying and solving problems with students, not for them, most of the time. Greene's theoretical framework, consistent with Meichenbaums' and most of contemporary CBT, helps staff remember that the key reasons for student misbehavior are skill deficits, not attitudes or motivation, and that staff's job is to help the students develop these skills. Greene's work also promotes an egalitarian, respectful treatment milieu, which minimizes the likelihood of students acting out in reaction to bossy behavior from staff. With Greene's reframe, as with Fox's, we've come to believe that "children do well if they can." This is crucial to the treatment work at Walden School because as Greene emphasizes, people intervene based on their assumptions about the reasons for a child's behavior.

Greene's (1998) description of common psychosocial skill deficits in "explosive" children is especially on target for understanding Walden School children. He describes language and executive function deficits that virtually all Walden School children have, and devotes considerable time to the development of language and "mental flexibility" skills. Greene was describing hearing children and may not have realized just how, with deaf children, his insights about language and cognitive flexibility skills are even more relevant. Language development—not just in terms of words for emotions, but also literally in terms of communication skills—is a core component of the Walden School work.

In addition, the work of Michael White has been influential at Walden School. (White, 1995, 2007; White & Epston, 1990). Students come to Walden School with a story. The stories are never the same, but the common element in most is that the youth blames him/herself for previous failure, for removal from the home, and in many instances for the abuse inflicted upon them. Sometimes the youth lacks detail and have re-created a story with themselves as the culprits instead of the person who has survived an ordeal. Making sense of their story is the treatment work. During the course of their treatment, youth learn to tell their story, sometimes for the first time, or re-tell their story, this time with more developed language and greater understanding of the events. This is a tremendously difficult journey and must come much later in the child's treatment because of the traumatic content, and also because the students need to develop basic language skills first.

An example of this is a young child who came to the Walden School program who had been physically and sexually abused and neglected prior to age 5. When he first arrived and told his "story," all he was able to tell us was that he was afraid of fish. At the time he had very little ability to talk about this, although he would become extremely hypervigilant, experience flashbacks, have increased anxiety and frequent outbursts of anger when he thought there was fish on the menu. Finally, after some time, the biological mother told us that while she temporarily lost custody, he was placed in a foster home (at age 4 through age 6), and, when he would not eat the fish (which was a regular menu item on Saturday nights), his foster mother would stick his head in the toilet, threatening to drown him, take it out, and then force him to eat the fish. He would eat it, only to vomit it up and then be beaten and forced to clean up his own vomit. After learning this, we were finally able to help him piece together that he was not actually "afraid of fish" but afraid of his foster mother and the severe abuse he suffered at her hands.

The work of establishing basic language is part of what Glickman (2009) refers to as "pretreatment." Glickman notes that mental health treatment must be a collaborative process involving informed and consenting persons, and when these conditions aren't met, the consumer and the process are both "pretreatment." Persons who are pretreatment don't understand or agree to the treatment process. Children or adults without the language skills to conceptualize the treatment process are by definition pretreatment, so a focus of this early stage of work is literally to give them the language for a "map" of the treatment process. Glickman argues that describing the process of work with clients as "learning skills" is a relatively simple map, one that can often be conceptualized with pictures or role playing. However, when deaf children have very little formal language, even this "simple" map may be too abstract. Developing basic language skills thus becomes an essential pretreatment task. The development of language skills in deaf children as part of the treatment process is one of the key differences between our work and that of work with hearing children.

While our clinical work starts in the pretreatment stages (basic vocabulary development along with developing of vocabulary for emotions), the work of developing a cohesive narrative comes later in the youth's treatment and only after they have developed basic language and self-management skills. For the young child mentioned above, much pretreatment work focused on his ability to cope when he was served food in the cafeteria he didn't like. It took staff almost a year to help him appreciate that all he had to do was say "No, thank you. I don't like that," and move on to the next menu item. This was very basic skill development, but it was pretreatment because he wasn't yet a collaborating partner in the treatment process.

The collaborative/relational model needs to be embedded in a larger framework of strength-based work. Influenced by the work of Brendtro, Brokenleg, and Van Bockern (2002), and described in detail by Vreeland (2007), Walden School has moved to a strength-based treatment model called the Circle of Courage. The Circle of Courage is a model of youth empowerment, based on the Native American belief that children must always be treated with respect and dignity. The model embraces four core values (referred to as "spirits"): belonging, mastery, independence and generosity—represented on a medicine wheel—one quadrant representing each core value. Walden School has used the Circle of Courage as the foundation of treatment and uses it to identify strengths and needs and establishes goals with children.

The authors further contend (much like Greene and Fox) that children are "troubled" because they live in hazardous environments. The goal of the model is to empower children and to provide them with opportunities to build relationships (belonging), develop skills and competencies (mastery), make meaningful choices that impact their lives (independence), and give to others (generosity). An important principle throughout the Circle of Courage is that it starts from identifying what skills the child already has. Noticing and labeling skills that students already have is also a key pretreatment strategy to bring children into the treatment process (Glickman, 2009).

At Walden School, this strength-based approach starts at the referral process by identifying (with the student and family) any strength(s) the youth currently possesses. Most students will not be willing to identify their problems before they see this attention paid to what skills and positive qualities they have. In these initial stages of pretreatment, it is common for youth to assert that they have no strengths, given that they have experienced multiple failures at previous placements or at home and school. Thus, during the referral process, it is the parents' role to point out existing strengths and later the staff person's role to look for these strengths and point them out when they notice them in the milieu.

For students with particularly challenging behavior, the strengths may seem insignificant in comparison to child's problems. It can be difficult to find something to praise about the child who is destructive and assaultive. But it is imperative for staff working with the child to find something genuine to praise frequently throughout the shift, even if it is something as simple as the youth being able to walk through the cafeteria to get food without hitting anyone. Sometimes strengths can be found not in the explosive behavior but in the recovery. For example, the student took less time to calm down, used some self-soothing skills to do so, and made some kind of repair to the person or environment. Sometimes they show skills in how they discuss calmly afterwards what happened and make a new plan for better behavior. The task for staff is to find the gem of skillful behavior sometimes among all the stones of problem behaviors that students show.

As youth progress through the program, their treatment work, their social skills work, and their skill development is categorized under the four spirits of the Circle of Courage. For example, Elizabeth, who was having social difficulties with peers mostly attributed to poor hygiene and her need to drive people away from her, had outstanding organizational skills and loved to plan and decorate for parties. Trying to capitalize on her strengths, we allowed her to plan and organize a tea party for several students in the program. The plans were elaborate, and it took her quite some time to get the party organized. She showered, and then her guests arrived. This was a therapeutic moment for several students. Some had never been invited anywhere before and were happy to be included. Elizabeth had never set up and ran a successful social event. Once the party was over, the therapist and staff working with Elizabeth were able to process how much better it feels to allow other students to develop relationships with her than it did to drive them away and feel lonely.

There is much written about working with traumatized children who are hearing. Particularly relevant to the treatment at Walden School are two outstanding books: *Collaborative Treatment of Traumatized Children and Teens* (2007) by Saxe, Ellis, and Kaplow, and *Treating Traumatic Stress in Children and Adolescents* (2010) by Blaustein and Kinniburgh. These authors, like most others in trauma treatment today, understand that traumatized persons go through various stages in the healing process. Blaustein and Kinnibuurgh describe the fundamental clinical challenges for traumatized children as: (a) forming attachments; (b) learning self-regulation (coping); (c) developing critical competencies (the belief of that they can control their own fate, problem solve, and develop a positive and coherent sense of self); and (d) Integrating or finding new meaning for the trauma one experienced. Their concept of the clinical stages are evident throughout both the pretreatment and treatment work at Walden School. Many of the students, particularly those with language and learning challenges, enter the school needing to start with the first two stages: forming attachments and learning self-regulation skills. Forming attachments are particularly challenging for some of the students not only because of their traumatic backgrounds and attachment disruptions, but because they often lack ASL skills that would allow them to converse and develop relationships. Staff are working simultaneously with these youth to develop an attachment while teaching them language.

Saxe and colleagues (2007) describe the emotional states that are often seen by youth who have traumatic backgrounds and processes by which their resulting disruptive behaviors may be addressed: (a) Regulating—the calm state that traumatized children experience; (b) revving—a triggered state where coping skills are employed to regulate emotions; (c) re-experiencing—the child is flooded by memories and re-experiencing of traumatic events; and (d) reconstituting—the child is returning to their regulated state and is able to use existing coping skills to re-engage with his surroundings.

Staff see children in all these states and learn to adapt their interventions to them. For instance, most of the work of teaching self-regulation skills occurs when the child is in the regulated states. It is here that we can provide children the opportunities to practice coping skills in relation to known triggers. Children who can demonstrate effective coping while in a regulated state often can't access the same coping skills when revving or re-experiencing and staff can be confused by this. They can think either that the treatment "isn't working" or that the child is refusing to use skills that they have demonstrated they know. Teaching staff about the emotional states and their relationship to recovery helps staff understand why the skills don't generalize from regulated to disregulated states easily and how we build competencies in coping over time, with the children practicing their skills in increasingly real life situations.

In summary, Walden School's treatment program emerges out of these best practices: cognitive behavioral therapy's focus on psychosocial skill building; narrative therapy's approach to story reconstruction; a strength-based focus; pretreatment strategies for educating, engaging, and motivating students; relational work and collaborative problem solving; and an understanding of the phases of trauma-informed care. All of these best practices must be adapted considerably for our deaf students, especially those with severe language and learning challenges.

Adaptations of Trauma Treatment for Deaf Children with Language and Learning Challenges

Trauma treatment for deaf children is adapted at Walden School in the following ways:

1. Adaptation for language

The first "adaptation," if you will, is that treatment must be provided in a linguistically accessible environment. This is primarily because language development is a core goal of the program for all its educational and therapeutic benefits. Sign language is the only language the child can acquire naturally and effortlessly, and only Deaf programs can provide this needed language exposure. As noted, some of the children referred to Walden School have developed their emotional and behavioral problems partly because they have been raised in linguistically inaccessible home and schools settings. This can only be rectified in a Deaf setting where every treatment venue (classroom, counseling sessions, group treatment, recreation, dorm life, etc.) provides opportunities for language development. At Walden School, most of the staff are native or near native ASL users. They have a well-developed sense of how to adapt their language to fit the communication needs of each student. Matching a student's language means not only making sure that there are agreed upon signs for specific words, but also making sure the student understands the concept being presented. Sometimes this means asking the student to repeat what has just been said in his/her own word. Sometimes it means the staff and student role-play the situation. Sometimes it means calling upon staff who are known for their exceptional language skills who supplement the competent but not exceptional skills of other staff. It also means constantly checking in to make sure that the concept being presented is being understood.

Often complex concepts need to be "unpacked" or broken down into simpler concepts. A concept like "coping skills" is a good example. There are signs for "coping," but students must have fairly well developed vocabulary, and many examples must be provided, before the abstract notion of "coping" is understood. For those with language and learning challenges, this concept needs to be broken down into very small "sub-concepts" such as explaining that sometimes (the student) gets upset. And when he is upset, there are things he can do to make himself feel better such as, going for a walk, riding a bike, putting lotion on his hands, playing with his handheld device. Doing these things is a way to "cope (using the sign here, knowing that the student will not understand yet). When he does these things, he will begin to feel better. He will begin to "cope" with the feelings he had before that felt negative. Over time, with much repetition, the student will begin to understand that choosing from a list of things to do when he is upset is called "coping skills."

Part of the work is also teaching affective vocabulary skills. Although this is part of any trauma treatment, it needs to be adapted further to meet the needs of deaf students with language and learning challenges. The youth who come to the program, even those with LLC will usually have such basic affective vocabulary as "sad," "mad," and "happy." The goal is to teach the children to expand their repertoire to include emotions such as frustrated, shy, afraid, disappointed, worried, etc. Teaching emotion words is a common therapy task, but the problems these students have go deeper as they are being taught basic vocabulary and sentence structure at the same time that they are learning to identify emotional states. This is often done with pictures of emotions and staff role playing situations that fit specific emotions.

Over time, staff see evidence that the child's language is improving as he is able to spontaneously produce language that was not there before. Each vocabulary word and concept needs to be elaborated upon and modeled for the youth. Staff use visual aids and role-play as key teaching strategies. Often staff will set up scenarios to teach these concepts. In one situation a student, Olivia, would always use the word MAD for a variety of emotions. She was either mad or she was happy; there was nothing else. When Olivia was in school, and her pencil would break, she would sign MAD and start banging on the desk. If the teacher tried to intervene and tell her to stop, she would strike whoever was around her. She was unable to simply tolerate the frustration of the broken pencil, sharpen it, and get back to work. The goal was to teach her "frustrated" and to help her find a solution to the broken pencil to minimize her frustration. So, the staff person with her set up a role-play where he was working on a paper in school and his pencil broke. He signed FRUSTRATED and then got up and sharpened his pencil. Then, he signed RELIEF or WHEW and went back to work with his sharpened pencil. In addition, using the Boardmaker Program, the teacher developed three pictures, one with a girl holding a broken pencil and punching the desk with a red X through it, the second was a girl with a broken pencil making the sign frustrated, and the third showed the girl standing by the pencil sharpener with a smile on her face. This set of pictures was set out on her desk as a visual support to remind her to sharpen her pencil when it broke and to teach her the word frustrated. All the staff in the unit knew she was working on the concept of being frustrated, so when they saw her in the milieu signing mad when she was actually frustrated, they fed her the sign for frustrated. Over time she added that to her repertoire of signs. This type of teaching of basic vocabulary and emotion vocabulary goes on constantly in the milieu.

David, the child described at the beginning of this chapter, arrived at Walden School at age 8 never having used a signed language before. Initially, it was extremely difficult to think about how to provide treatment to someone with almost no language skills. David would have a very difficult time following simple directions via sign language. While some of this could be attributed to resistance, mostly this difficulty was due to his lack of language skills. After arriving, he became much more aggressive and self-destructive. Staff understood this to be a reaction to his placement in an unfamiliar environment, away from home, with people who used "voice off" ASL, which he had never seen before. His aggression was severe enough that staff had to physically restrain him numerous times throughout a day. When he was restrained, he would urinate in his pants, an indication of how frightened he was, and also a sign that the restraints, while judged to be necessary, were possibly traumatizing him further[3]

David's pretreatment work included constant exposure to American Sign Language, just as parents would expose a child to their language. Every time he expressed an emotion, positive or negative, staff were there to give him the signs for his emotion. The same was true for exposure to sign language for words pertaining to his environment, schedule, and daily conversations. Language exposure was also provided when he displayed inappropriate behaviors. If, for example, in frustration he hit someone, staff would first ensure safety for David and those around him. Once David has regained control, staff would "debrief" with him by showing him a picture of him hitting someone with a big red X through it. Then the staff person, who was hit, would tell David he or she was hurt and sad. Staff would say: YOU HIT, WRONG, ME HURT, SAD.

Almost immediately we saw David begin to sign more, although at this point it was merely rote repetition. He would hit someone and then immediately say, HIT WRONG, YOU SAD. In addition, as the staff got to know David better and could identify sources of anger, they were able to intervene early, when the first sign of frustration and anger were apparent, and ask David if he was frustrated or mad. These pretreatment strategies continued for months, but there was gradual evidence that David was beginning to understand and label simple emotions.

At a later point, staff wanted to explain the concept of "trigger" to David. Trigger is a more abstract concept, the idea that something precedes and provokes a resulting behavior. As the concept of trigger is frequently used in CBT, a sign corresponding to the English word has started to be used more commonly. To teach this sign and concept, the staff person used the narrative therapy technique of telling a story. In ASL, he signed to David roughly as follows:

ME SCHOOL FINISH. WANT BICYCLE. SMALL HOUSE GO-IN. SEE BICYCLE—MY TIRE FLAT. MAD. BICYCLE (plural marker), KICK, KICK, KICK, KICK. ALL–BICYCLE-CLASSIFIER FALL-OVER. (After school was over, I wanted to go biking. I went into the shed and saw that bicycle had a flat. I got very angry, kicked all the bicycles, and they fell over.) The staff person then used the sign TRIGGER and signed TIRE FLAT. TIRE FLAT TRIGGER ME. MAD. BLOW-UP. (The flat tire triggered me, made me angry, and caused a blow up.) The staff person repeated the story and the use of the sign TRIGGER and then brought in another staff person, asking David to tell the story to him.

Given David's challenges, he was not able to repeat the story in a coherent way. He was able to say MAD BIKE. (David understood the emotion and that the story had a bike in it.) The staff person needed to retell the story to the other staff person, while David watched, taking in the story for a second time. Then the staff person tried to elicit the story from David by coaxing him to repeat as much of it as he could. This came in the form of questions, which also helped the staff determine what vocabulary and concepts David already had:

Staff: ME WANT WHAT?
David: BIKE
Staff: MY BIKE OKAY?
David: BIKE BROKE (here the staff person would say TIRE FLAT)
Staff: ME MAD WHY?
David: BIKE BROKE
Staff: TIRE FLAT
David: TIRE FLAT
Staff: TRIGGER WHAT?
David: BIKE BROKE
Staff: TIRE FLAT
David: TIRE FLAT

This type of exchange happens dozens of times throughout the average day within the milieu, and, in addition, the exercise will be repeated using different stories. Essential to this process are deaf adults who can be language role models and are able to adapt their use of language to the child. This simply cannot happen outside an ASL environment.

Staff want David to have the language skills to be able to understand why he is living at Walden School, what kind of place this is, and what skills we hope he will learn. Staff want to give him a "map" of the recovery process which at this point consists of identifying things that bother him (triggers), his emotional reaction, and his behavioral choices. Staff want to be able to discuss with him how to build upon this foundation to help him find a place in the world. When David can do this, he'll become an informed participant in the treatment process. Right now, the work is foundational, is pretreatment, and a key component of that is language development, both basic language vocabulary and structure and the emotional vocabulary he needs as part of his trauma recovery.

2. The adaptation of a pretreatment focus

As we saw, David was not ready to collaboratively set goals and design a treatment plan. He could not yet be an informed, consenting consumer of the mental health and educational services we were offering. Following Glickman (2009), we find it useful to conceptualize his stage of readiness as "pretreatment" and to consider our work with him at this time to be pretreatment oriented. This is true for most of the children when they first arrive at Walden School. This has led us to understand that a significant portion of our work is pretreatment and to arrange and conceptualize our services accordingly.

Pretreatment is a very complex part of treatment at the Walden School Program. Sometimes the youth understands why she is there, but most times she does not. The youth typically arrives with diagnostic labels and having experienced repeated failures in previous programs and/or at home. The first challenge is how to engage the student in the therapeutic process as a partner, not as a problem to be fixed. This is done at Walden School by giving long, focused attention to helping students understand what the school does and why they are here. Staff know that our students usually have much larger fund of information gaps than hearing children their age and that absolutely everything must be explained.

For example, Christopher, a student who has been in the program for approximately eighteen months, has been saving his allowance to buy a used PlayStation Portable (PSP) from a friend in his neighborhood. On a recent home visit he met his friend and bought the PSP. When he returned to the program, Christopher's mother called, reporting that her son had returned to the program with a stolen PSP in his possession. Apparently Christopher's friend had stolen his brother's PSP and sold it to Christopher. The therapist was trying to explain this to Christopher, who insisted that it wasn't stolen because he paid for it. It took Christopher, who had neither the language skills nor the world knowledge to understand the concept of receiving stolen property, three or four sessions of role playing before he understood that his friend had no right to sell the PSP to him since it did not belong to him.

This example brings up another adaptation that needs to be addressed during the pretreatment stage. It is not uncommon for even the deaf child who comes to Walden School with intact language to be missing crucial world knowledge—to have what Pollard (1998) refers to as "fund of information gaps." Treatment for these children has to include teaching them basic information that hearing children usually pick up through incidental learning. Christopher's fund of information gaps includes appreciating that the PSP was in fact stolen even if he bought it.

Gaps in fund of information are also shown by Roger, a young man in our program, who would spend some vacations and holidays in the Bronx with his family. Roger had several hearing friends that he would hang around with, and, although he considered himself street-wise, he was actually quite naïve. When he was out with these friends one night, they asked him if he would mind holding a bag for him while they were out. They were hanging on a street corner when the friend began a drug deal. The police came, the hearing friend ran when he heard the sirens, and Roger was left standing on the corner holding a bag of marijuana. When he was arrested, he emphatically told the police, "But it's not my bag, it's not my bag." It took much work for Roger to understand that it did not matter that he was holding the bag of marijuana for a friend. He was left holding the bag, which made him at least an accomplice to a crime. Roger also didn't understand that his friend had set him up as the "fall guy."

Roger's language and fund of information deficits contributed to considerable naiveté, which made him vulnerable to this kind of exploitation. Most of this was beyond his present language capacity to understand. Pretreatment work needs to have a strength-based focus because relationships will form, and students will join discussions, much more easily when centered on what they do well.

Pretreatment work with David, beyond teaching language, had to involve identifying his strengths, a difficult task given that he was so new to the program and behaving aggressively. Staff all agreed that he was eager to please and liked positive feedback (a thumbs up, a smile, a pat on the back) whenever he did something pro-social. Staff began praising every time he was in the unit and not aggressive. They found skills and strengths when he did not show the problem behavior and showed any positive behaviors.

Another child who came to Walden School with aggressive behaviors was both an all-star basketball player and extremely kind and gentle with younger children. When asked what his strengths were, he could only state that he was good at basketball. While this was true, being kind and gentle with younger children was a strength he possessed that we could also use for treatment. Despite his aggressive outbursts, he was able to serve as a youth "big brother" for a younger student. This helped him feel a sense of pride and success. Eventually, he was able to, at times, discuss controlling his outbursts because he wanted to be a good role model for his "little brother." When students at Walden School begin to have these kinds of experiences, they begin to shed the negative labels (and stories) they have of themselves.

As Glickman (2009) notes, there are no clear lines between pretreatment and treatment work. Much of what is done in pretreatment, such as identifying and building upon skills, is also done in treatment. The difference has more to do with the level of awareness and engagement a student has in the treatment process. Students in treatment are informed and willing participants. They are active agents in their own development and recovery.

Pretreatment at Walden School includes all the strategies used to ready a student for treatment, including relationship building, identifying strengths and skills the child already possesses, building affective vocabulary, and the initial identification and development of coping skills. Pretreatment is also helping the child understand the reason for placement and engaging them, to the extent possible, in initial goal setting. All of this is done in an environment designed to teach language at every opportunity.

3. Action-oriented and visually based treatment interventions

So far we have discussed two areas in which trauma-based residential treatment is adapted for our deaf students. The first is the infusion of language development into every aspect of the work. The second, which takes into account common language and fund of information gaps, is the prolonged pretreatment focus. Language development is a crucial part of this pretreatment work. So is working from a strength-based focus. Relationship development is also crucial, but it is not emphasized in this chapter because it is not a difference from work with hearing children. We understand that psychological development and recovery from trauma only occur in the context of relationships, and that establishing safe, warm, and nurturing relationships with our students is another foundation for all the positive growth we want to promote.

Beyond these, we've found that particular kinds of pretreatment or treatment interventions are more effective with our students. Most of them do best with a very action oriented intervention style which makes great use of pictures and other visual media and minimal use of written English tools. As their language skills, information about the treatment process, and motivation to participate develop, we can make more use of traditional language-based therapies. Until that point, our therapists do much of their work alongside direct care staff in the treatment milieu. Upon arrival, each student develops a Skill Building Plan as part of the Circle of Courage Program. The Skill Building Plan is used to identify strengths and triggers, what the child does well and what makes a child angry or upset, and what soothes and comforts him/her.

Developing a skill building plan with these students requires many adaptations for deaf students. The staff person needs to expand upon and "unpack" the concepts (like trigger, coping skills, social skills, etc.) included in the plan. In addition, there is much time devoted to what happens within a person's body when he is upset and what options he may have to stay calm. There are also discussions about what staff should and should not do when the child is upset. For some students, being physically touched—a pat on the back, rubbing his arm—helps calm a child. For others, being physically touched in any way escalates the situation. Typically, the advocate will need to role-play many of the concepts from the meeting in order for the child to begin to understand.

Because of language deficits in our population, we draw heavily upon sensory-movement-based interventions for coping skills (Trikakis, Curci, & Strom, 2003). For one such student who gets upset and acts out aggressively, one of his coping skills is to rock in a rocking chair with a weighted blanket on his chest. So, for him, when hitting, staff would teach him the word mad, and then he would choose from a list of three pictorial representations of coping skills: rocking, going outside for a walk, or laying between two heavy beanbag chairs. After staff assist the child in choosing a coping strategy, they walk him through the process of practicing the skill. This is done through role playing using the coping skill to respond well to the stressor. As this is done, staff model the vocabulary for describing what is occurring. Language development and skill development occur simultaneously. Staff will also take pictures of the student using his coping skills as a visual prompt the next time the child experiences a stressor.

One student, who had significant language and cognitive challenges, chose the coping skill of taking a beach towel, sitting foot to foot with staff and twisting the towel between the two of them. In order to promote his use of this skill when actually stressed, he was scheduled three times a day to practice this skill with staff. At each practice session, staff would remind him that when he was angry, they would get him the beach towel. After quite some time of practicing in this way, the student was able to accept the towel from staff and twist it when upset. It is important for staff to continue to help the child choose one of the listed coping skills when upset. Only after the child is able to choose a coping skill when it is actually needed will she/he begin to generalize that skill.

One technique that staff use to "join" the student in treatment and to act as role models is to openly talk with students about their own coping skills. Both staff and students hang pictures on their doors of their preferred coping skills. This also helps establish skill building as a common therapy metaphor in the program.

Meichenbaum's framework for teaching coping skills was what he termed "stress inoculation training," which was divided into three areas: conceptualization, skills acquisition, and application (Meichenbaum, 1977, 1985). Although the terms used at Walden School are different, the focus follows Meichenbaum's framework. At Walden School, the conceptualization area would be to "join" the child in understanding what treatment is about and to collaborate with the child in that treatment. Skill acquisition occurs when the student is beginning to identify, with much assistance from his therapist and staff, individual coping skills. After several years of doing this kind of work, there is now a menu of options at Walden School that some students prefer to choose from. And the application of skills is exactly the same as Meichenbaum delineates: using the skills in the milieu, at home, or in the community, when they are actually needed. Meichenbaum has also described the importance of having people teach skills they are learning to others (Glickman, 2009; Meichenbaum & Biemiller, 1998). At Walden School, we frequently ask students to teach skills they are learning to other students or sometimes to staff.

Visual supports are used in two more significant ways within the program. Many students, and certainly all of the language and learning challenged students, have visual schedules for both their school and residential schedules. This allows them the opportunity to follow their schedules somewhat independently and not rely on constant prompts from staff. This is done routinely throughout the program. Individually, visual supports are used to assist students with specific issues they are trying to master. For example, one young man struggles with hygiene issues. He will go into the shower and literally step under the water and step back out in less than three seconds. Visual supports were put in place to help him master the steps to showering. Using a pre-packaged curriculum that was visually oriented, we were able to break down the steps of taking a shower into 15 visuals for him to follow. To further reinforce the concepts, we had a childcare worker role-play taking a shower using each visual card as a prompt for the student to reinforce what he was seeing. Ultimately, the youth was able to take a shower independently, and we were able to move onto the next skill he needed to learn.

Visual aids were a key part of our work with David. Staff created a pictorial schedule (another common treatment adaptation) that guided him through every step of his school day and residential schedule. The schedule included pictures of the behavior, the sign, and the English word he was learning. There was a copy of this schedule in his classroom, bedroom, and unit, and he had a small copy that he carried with him throughout his day. Each time he was successful in following his schedule—and this was noted by checking off the block on the schedule for that activity—staff praised him enthusiastically.

Two more adaptations used frequently (and often together) are role playing and creating dialogues between two staff where they talk about the student's challenge and model how he or she should respond. Some students have the language skills to discuss conflicts and problems with peers and staff, but many do not. They need staff to unpack and walk them through each situation, role playing and labeling what had occurred and modeling skillful responses. Staff do this through staging dialogues where one might role-play the child and the other might role-play the other player. Role playing is so common at Walden School that it's really the bread and butter of treatment in a way that dialogue would be with more linguistically sophisticated persons. Role playing is an action-oriented, exposure-based technique, but even in role playing staff are teaching students language.

For example, role-plays are used to resolve conflicts. When a conflict arises in the milieu, staff will act out the situation that just happened with the children involved in the conflict watching. When finished, the two students are then asked to go through the situation again and see if they can come up with the same resolution that does not involve physical fighting.

As in stress inoculation, role-plays are also used to help a child prepare for a potential stressful event by anticipating the stressor, identifying and practicing relevant coping skills. For example, after being in the program for a short time, Katie, a young girl, was *sometimes* able to safely manage herself on trips home. Her parent had worked out that, when she had a safe week, meaning no physical outbursts that required restraint for the previous 72 hours, she would be able to go home for the weekend. If the week was not great, there was an option for Katie to go home for part of the weekend. Each week on Friday, her mother would come to the program for family therapy, part of which was to discuss her behavior for the week and determine if going home was an option and, if so, for how long. In the individual therapy session prior to the family therapy session, the therapist role played with Katie the three scenarios that could happen: going home for the full weekend, going home for part of the weekend, or not going home at all. The therapist played the role of the Katie, and Katie played the role of the parent. Of course, it took several sessions before Katie, playing the role of her mother, "decided" that "Katie" could not going home for the whole weekend. The therapist made up cards depicting all three scenarios, and had Katie choose one each session to practice with. When Katie (as mother) told the therapist (as Katie) that she wasn't going home, the therapist then modeled appropriate versions of being disappointed and mad.

Therapists often also model the internal self-talk we want a client to develop, an example of what Meichenbaum refers to as "self-instructional training." In this situation, the therapist signed "out loud" the following self-talk:

> ME REALLY WANT HOME FRIDAY, SATURDAY, SUNDAY. MOM SAID NO, ME AGGRESSIVE THURSDAY, BACK WALDEN SCHOOL SATURDAY. ME MAD! ME HIT MOM! ME HIT MOM, MOM CANCEL. ME ACCEPT—TWO DAYS. ("I really want to go home for the whole weekend. But my mother said I have to come back a day early because of my behavior. I'm mad! I feel like hitting her. But if I do, my whole weekend will be canceled, and I really want to go home. I better accept just two days.")

While the therapist modeled this self-talk for Katie, she watched but was not able to take it all in. The language and emotional challenges were still overwhelming her.

The therapist recognized this and unpacked it further.

Therapist: MOM COMING TODAY.
Katie: ME HOME. (A STATEMENT, NOT A QUESTION)
Therapist: YOU BEHAVE THIS WEEK, SAFE?
Katie: YES, SAFE, SAFE! EVERYDAY!
Therapist: TWO-OF-US, ASK MOM SOON. IF NO, DO-DO?
("If mom say no, what will you do?")
Katie: ME MAD! REALLY MAD!
Therapist: IF HIT MOM, CANCEL HOME.
Katie: ME CONTROL.

After this session, the therapist met with Katie's mother and planned the next session with all three of them. Walden School interpreters, who are familiar with student language skills, are used in this family session. The parent and therapist review the week's events in front of Katie—both any negative issues that came up as well as, even more importantly, the times she was able to use her coping skills effectively. The therapist (who is deaf) was able to modify her language when talking with Katie, and then again when talking with her mother. Working closely with the interpreters, the entire conversation was accessible to Katie.

The dialogue technique is similar to the use role of plays. The role-play technique is often used with students with language and learning challenges because they are not able to linguistically process a conflict or situation that has come up in the milieu. Showing a role-play of the situation; either with two staff or with a student and a staff person illustrates the points being taught. A typical adaptation, particularly when trying to teach conflict resolution skills, is the use of a dialogue between two staff to help illustrate a more appropriate way for children to handle a conflict. For example, two students each want to ride in the front seat on a field trip. The two staff people leading the trip stop and have a dialogue between themselves while the two students watch. The dialogue is kept simple and demonstrates how they negotiate taking turns in who sits in the front seat. They indicate agreement by shaking hands.

Once this has been modeled, each staff person helps one of the two students involved in the conflict negotiate his side. The staff lead the two students to a compromise and have them shake on it. This type of situation and staff intervention is repeated frequently in the milieu as each situation arises. Eventually, student copy the simple conflict-solving method that was modeled for them.

The Role of Clinical Staff at Walden School

The clinical staff at Walden School work mainly in the treatment milieu, not in the sanctity of their offices. Students who are in treatment, who actively and self-consciously make use of counseling, go to the therapist's office for formal sessions, but more often than not the therapist works in the milieu, taking advantage of teachable moments and training and assisting milieu staff.

The therapy process itself is adapted for our students. It is a rare student who has the language skills, cognitive sophistication, and motivation to make use of more traditional "talk" therapy in a therapist's office. Even in these instances, therapy tends to be very action oriented, using role playing, therapy games, and the visual arts. For example, one student was having difficulties with interpersonal boundaries. Often he was hugging female students, and even when they asked him or told him to stop, he would continue to do it. When asked about it, he said simply, "It's Deaf Culture." Showing very little understanding in his therapy sessions of this being a problematic behavior, he was given an assignment by his therapist. Before the next therapy session, this student was assigned to go to at least ten deaf male staff and ask what they would do if a female asked not to be touched. He was also instructed to ask if being told no and refusing to accept it, was part of Deaf Culture. This technique, combined with role-plays was successful in improving his interpersonal boundaries.

We can illustrate this by returning to David, our 8-year old described above. When he came to the program, one of his presenting problems was that he lacked social boundaries. He would lunge at anyone he saw; hugging them and not letting them go (this included both on campus to people known and unknown, visitors, and in the community). When staff intervened to tell him it was not appropriate to hug people in that way, he became aggressive. If the person receiving the hug attempted to set a boundary, he still became aggressive. It was unclear at first whether the aggression was due to having his wish to hug someone thwarted or due to his feeling overwhelmed by the complex linguistic information he was receiving.[4]

Staff designed a multi-layered intervention. In "therapy" the clinician lead the student to identify people in his immediate and extended family that were people he could hug. There was high motivation from David to participate because he wanted both to hug people and adored his family, so he would participate in the therapy sessions. The staff who worked most closely with David were included in the list of people who could be hugged because David lived at Walden School seven days a week. This list was made into a picture book, again using the Boardmaker Program and pictures that David kept with him. The therapist worked with David to understand that other staff and other people not on the list were not to be hugged, but to be given a "fist-bump" to say hello. The therapist then communicated this list with all the staff that needed to work with David in the milieu.

David carried his book around with him and when he attempted to hug someone, staff would prompt him to look and see if that person was on the list. If the person was on the "hug list," then it was allowed, if the person was not on the hug list, the staff then prompted David to give a fist bump. Once the initial intervention was designed and communicated, the "therapy" sessions began to focus on skills acquisition. Each time a session was scheduled, David was prompted to bring his "hug binder" with him and their session was literally walking around campus, doing little errands, in the same rote places twice a week so David could practice the targeted skills in a controlled environment. Equally important was "training" the adults he was passing/visiting while doing those errands to ask, "Where's your hug list?" if he attempted to hug them. Initially, David needed to be prompted often, but, ultimately, David was able to spontaneously follow his hug list within the controlled places he was brought on his errands.

The next step was to help David transfer those skills when working with another staff person. The place chosen was within his work readiness program where he was both with different staff and would travel to different areas of campus than the initial controlled environment. Staff taught David's work readiness teacher the same intervention. After some initial relapses, David was able to also travel around this less contained environment and hug only those who were on his hug list.

Embedded in this process, in addition to trying to get David to learn appropriate social boundaries, was the goal of teaching David language. Ultimately, when he got the hugging under control, the next goal was for David to ask someone how he/she was instead of just giving a hug. Eventually, this required language development, turn-taking skills, eye-contact skills and more.

The Walden School team was doing a form of stress inoculation or exposure treatment with David but adapted for his very rudimentary language skills and need for an active and visual learning approach. Walden School staff also integrated individual and milieu treatment so key skills are learned and used across all settings. All staff taught the skills and all staff taught David language though the clinicians took the primary lead in designing and implementing the treatment plan with David. When David was ready, he was able to teach others about the goals in his treatment plan.

Summary and Conclusions

As practiced at the Walden School, Deaf mental health care is similar to, and different from, mental health care of traumatized hearing children with emotional and behavioral challenges. The Walden School children have language and learning challenges, attachment problems, extreme emotional dysregulation and very challenging behaviors just as traumatized hearing children do. However, the language variation seen in deaf children is far more extreme, from many children who are alingual or semi-lingual to others who are skilled ASL users. Because it is their deafness that they have in common, other variables, like strengths, cognitive functioning, clinical problems, and functional abilities, vary much more widely than is typically seen in hearing treatment settings. For most of these children, language development is a core function of treatment, and all of the children need a signing environment, very attuned to their language abilities, in order to grow. It is the language differences that most characterize a culturally affirmative Deaf treatment program like Walden School.

The Walden School strives to build its treatment approach around standards of best practice as they are currently understood. As we've discussed, the principal treatment strategies we've drawn upon are:

1. The cognitive behavioral therapy focus on psychosocial skill building developed by Donald Meichenbaum as modified for deaf persons with language and learning challenges (Glickman, 2009).
2. A pretreatment focus which includes heavy emphasis upon language development.
3. Strength-based work which strives to build upon skills students already have rather than correct deficits.
4. Collaborative treatment in which students are taught skills for communication, coping, problem solving, and conflict resolution.
5. A narrative-therapy focus upon creation of life-affirming self-stories.
6. An understanding of the effects of multiple kinds of severe trauma on child development and a staged process of recovery from this trauma.
7. Integrated "seamless" treatment between milieu, classroom, and counseling sessions.

All these best practices have to be adapted for deaf children. They are adapted in particular for the language and cultural differences, a visual and active, hands-on learning style, and the fund of information gaps that most of our students come to us with. Adaptations we've described specifically are as follows:

1. The need to build language development into every aspect of treatment, sometimes starting from scratch.
2. The need to give students basic information about the world that they've never received previously to actively address their fund of information deficits.
3. Extensive attention to the pretreatment challenges of getting informed, motivated treatment engagement. This includes giving students a simple map for the treatment process, usually through the idea of skill building.
4. An action-oriented approach to treatment with role playing, active skill practice, modeling, and dialogue construction being central features. When students are ready for traditional therapy, this is provided, but this active treatment style is still used; use of pictorial and visual aids as substitutes for written English-based tools, or use of written English that matches a student's reading ability.
5. An emphasis upon milieu treatment, with therapists more often working with children and staff in the milieu and organizing treatment approaches than sitting with them in a formal office therapy session.

When placed in a culturally affirmative treatment setting even the most complicated and complex deaf children can make significant gains. Robert, described earlier, is an example. He was initially diagnosed with mental retardation. Once he developed language skills, that diagnosis was removed. When he began at Walden School, he was not safe enough to visit home. We are now working with his mother to step him down to a lower level of care that would have him home for extended vacations and every weekend. He is now able to engage in dialogues about his behavior and is planning to take classes on the main campus of the Learning Center for the Deaf.

David, although not ready to live at home yet, is able to go home on a regular basis and sleeps at home overnight on holidays. He no longer poses a risk to himself or others (including his younger sibling at home) and has almost no self-injurious behavior. He is now able to converse in simple American Sign Language and can discuss his behavior. He is no longer hugging everyone he walks by but says, "Hi, I'm David, how are you?"

Notes

1. It should be noted that there are currently no inpatient child psychiatric hospital units for deaf children in the United States. The only inpatient unit serving deaf and hard-of-hearing patients in New England is Worcester State Hospital, which has a small unit serving Deaf adolescents (ages 14 and up) and adults.
2. Walden School uses The Boardmaker Program and its supplemental discs PCS Sign Language I, II, & III, published by Mayer-Johnson. They are used throughout the program to make visual supports for students. The program produces signs, pictures, and English words together.
3. Although restraints are deemed necessary when a student's safety is at risk, through the guidance of Fox (2004) at Walden School they are also considered "treatment failure" and staff members are debriefed to determine where an intervention would have been beneficial so the situation did not escalate to needing to use restraint.
4. While the Walden School staff working directly with David knew to modify their language to "match" his when intervening, other people that David was trying to hug would not because there were so many people, it was difficult to make sure all knew to do this. This may have caused the frustration that led to aggression.

References

Blaustein, M., & Kinniburgh, K. (2010). *Treating traumatic stress in children and adolescents: How to foster resilience through attachment, self-regulation, and competency.* New York, NY: Guilford Press.

Brendtro, L., Brokenleg, M., & Van Bockern, S. (2002). *Reclaiming youth at risk: Our hope for the future.* Bloomington, IN: Solution Tree.

Fox, L. E. (1987). Teachers or taunters: The dilemma of true discipline. *Journal of Child and Youth Care Work, 3,* 39–54.

Fox, L. E. (2004, January). Understanding the impact of restraint on sexually abused children and youth. *Residential Group Care Quarterly Newsletter, 4*(3), 1–5.

Glickman, N. (2009). *Cognitive behavioral therapy for deaf and hearing persons with language and learning challenges.* New York, NY: Routledge.

Greene, R. (1998). *The explosive child.* New York, NY: Harper Collins.

Greene, R. W., & Ablon, J. S. (2006). *Treating explosive kids: The collaborative problem-solving approach.* London, England: Guilford Press.

Meichenbaum, D. (1977). *Cognitive-behavioral modification: An integrative approach.* New York, NY: Plenum Press.

Meichenbaum, D. (1985). *Stress inoculation training.* Elmsford, NY: Pergamon Press.

Meichenbaum, D., & Biemiller, A. (1998). *Nurturing independent learners: Helping students take charge of their learning.* Newton, MA: Brookline Books.

National Child Traumatic Stress Network. (2006). *White paper on addressing the trauma treatment needs of children who are deaf or hard of hearing and the hearing children of deaf parents.* Los Angeles, CA: Author

National Traumatic Stress Network. (2004). *Facts on trauma and deaf children.* Los Angeles, CA: Author.

Pollard, R. (1998). Psychopathology. In M. Marschark & M. D. Clark (Eds.), *Psychological perspectives on deafness* (pp. 171–197). Mahwah, NJ: Erlbaum.

Saxe, G., Ellis, B., & Kaplow, J. (2007). *Collaborative treatment of traumatized children and teens: The trauma systems therapy approach.* New York, NY: Guilford Press.

Sullivan, P., Vernon, M., & Scanlan, J. (1987). Sexual Abuse of Deaf Youth. *American Annals of the Deaf, 132,* 256–262.

Tate, C. (2009, July). Mental health and deaf individuals. Paper presented at the *Sixth National Summit of State Psychiatric Hospital Superintendents,* St. Louis, MO.

Trikakis, D., Curci, N., & Strom, H. (2003). Sensory strategies for self-regulation: Non-linguistic body-based treatment for deaf psychiatric patients. In N. Glickman & S. Gulati (Eds.), *Mental health care of deaf people: A culturally affirmative approach* (pp. 203–238). Mahwah, NJ: Erlbaum.

Vreeland, J. (2007). A comprehensive model for reducing/eliminating the use of physical restraint in residential treatment for deaf children and youth. In S. Austen & D. Jeffrey (Eds.), *Deafness and challenging behaviours: The 360 perspective* (pp. 231–246). Chichester, England: Wiley.

Vreeland, J., & Tourangeau, J. (2003). Culturally affirmative residential treatment services for deaf children with emotional and behvioral disorders. In N. Glickman & S. Gulati (Eds.), *Mental health care of deaf people: A culturally affirmative approach.* Mahwah, NJ: Erlbaum.

White, M. (1995). *Reauthoring lives: Interviews and essays.* Adelaide, South Australia: Dulwich Centre Publications.

White, M. (2007). *Maps of narrative practice.* New York, NY: W.W. Norton.

White, M., & Epston, D. (1990). *Narrative means to therapeutic ends.* New York, NY: W.W. Norton.

Appendix 7A   Student Skill Building Plan

Student Name: _____Date: _____

I. Strength-based Skill Building Plan
MY STRENGTHS: Circle your strengths and add more!

I like some things about myself	I like my room to look & feel nice
I care about how I look	I care about my schoolwork
I take care of my body	I can make things with my hands
I care about people's feelings	I have at least one hobby
I enjoy making people laugh	I play sports
It is important for me to help others	I am a good listener
I can handle some frustration	I can ask for help when I need it
I know how to share	I know how to be patient
I know how to make a good decision	There are adults who care about me
I can participate in activities with others my age	I have friends who care about me

_____

_____

_____

II: Strength-based Skill Building Plan
GOAL SETTING (relevant to the 4 core values)

1. What do you like best about yourself?

2. What are your favorite things to do?

3. What things could you teach others to do?

4. What are you proud of?

GENEROSITY　　　　**BELONGING**

INDEPENDENCE　　　　**MASTERY**

III: Strength-based Skill Building Plan
MY COPING STRATEGIES

1. What makes me very upset? What makes me lose control?
   (Circle your answers)

People don't listen to me　　　People tease me　　　People don't believe me

Failing in school, sports, etc.　　People yelling　　　I don't understand something

People touch me　　　I feel embarrassed　　　I feel lonely

_____

_____

2. I know I am getting upset/angry when.......
   (Circle your answers)

I start sweating   My heart beats faster   I am restless

I clench my teeth   I yell   I cry   I swear   I pace

I can't listen/pay attention   My head hurts   I clench my fists   I rock

I want to hurt myself   I want to hurt other people   I want to run from staff

I want to destroy things   _____

3. What helps me calm down and stay in control?
   (Circle your answers)

Time alone in   Listening to music   Hugging a stuffed animal   Watching TV
my room

Bouncing a ball   Talking w/ staff   Drawing/coloring   Talking w/ my therapist

Going for a walk   Twisting a towel   Lying down   Deep breathing   Yoga

Exercising   Ripping paper   Pacing   Putting water on my face

Sitting w/ staff   Reading a book   Writing in a journal   Play a game

8 Training of Mental Health Professionals

Yesterday, Today, and Tomorrow

Patrick J. Brice,[1] *Irene W. Leigh,*
Martha Sheridan, and Kendra Smith

Introduction

Training of mental health professionals to work with deaf clients, including those who are culturally Deaf, is a topic that has been addressed in the literature rarely, if at all. However, with increased focus on services for low-incidence populations with unique needs, the need to ensure the competency of professionals who provide these specialized services has become more critical in this era of accountability. Ensuring the competency of mental health professionals who work with the populations focused on in this book has been the unique focus for the authors of this chapter. All of us are part of the second and third waves of mental health clinicians with expertise in serving deaf clients with various linguistic and communication requirements. All of us have had significant exposure to what it means to grow up deaf in hearing environments, whether through personal exposure to deaf people, being deaf ourselves (Leigh and Sheridan), or through coursework and interaction with deaf people (Brice and Smith). This in part has sensitized us to the specific training needs of the students we have worked with in our training programs (clinical psychology, counseling, and social work) at Gallaudet University. To understand the importance of specialized in-depth training, we start by looking at the past and how it has evolved in terms of the need for mental health-specific training. We then turn to an exploration of issues related to the deaf population that require specialized training to ensure that mental health clinicians working with deaf people are competently prepared to provide the best possible mental health services. We also address how this training is best delivered and examine training issues that have emerged.

Historical Antecedents

The treatment of individuals with mental health issues has a long history, going as far back as approximately 3,100 BC, perhaps even farther (Merkel, 2003). Reviews of this history show how people were focused on diagnosing individuals with mental illness and creating treatment plans. We can only conjecture how training might have been accomplished, perhaps through mentorship, group lectures, and demonstrations, as was done for those being trained in medicine. Considering all the varied treatments that were attempted, including, for example, benevolent patience, sorcery, religious prayers focusing on a supreme being, chaining, purging, bath rituals, diet, neglect, cruelty, and a host of other approaches, it seems plausible that training evolved as time went on. We know of the physician and philosopher lectures in Greek and Roman times, continuing all the way to the establishment of asylums and hospitals for the insane in the 9th century, thereby setting the stage for ongoing grand rounds to discuss patient conditions and diagnoses.

The 1700s and 1800s witnessed the expansion of hospitals for the mentally ill and the beginning of reforms in mental institutions, led mostly by physicians who specialized in the emerging discipline of psychiatry. Quiet environments, strong relationships with doctors, and use of medication became more of the norm, taught through example, although significant abuses continued to exist until laws protecting this disadvantaged population of psychiatric patients were formulated (Gottstein, 2002). Medical doctors continued to focus on classifying categories of psychiatric conditions and developing treatment approaches including but not limited to talk therapy, hypnosis, and medication, following various theories about mental illness, such as psychoanalysis, ego psychology, and behaviorism.

If conditions were less than stable for psychiatric patients who could hear, what were they like for patients who were deaf? With limited use of spoken language, particularly when auditory technology was nonexistent, how could those who were born deaf and experiencing mental health problems be understood and treated? Historical records document that it was not until the 1500s or thereabouts that formal efforts to teach deaf people were attempted. These efforts laid the foundation for the establishment of schools for the deaf in the 1700s, starting in Europe, and then spreading to the United States in the 1800s (Branson & Miller, 2002; Eriksson, 1993; Moores, 2001).

It is now known that deaf persons with mental health problems were typically isolated in psychiatric wards, ignored by staff, and left to fend for themselves without access to communication or to sign language interpreters (Burch & Joyner, 2007; Rainer, Altshuler, Kallman, & Deming, 1965; Vernon, 1969). The first outpatient mental health clinic and the first inpatient psychiatric ward for deaf people began as part of the very first full-scale research project on the mental health of deaf people that was begun in 1955 under the auspices of the New York State Psychiatric Institute (Rainer, 1967; Rainer et al., 1965). During this project, mental health professionals learned "on the job" how to work with deaf people, albeit with the assistance of educators of the deaf. At that time, Edna Levine, a psychologist and pioneer in addressing the mental health issues of deaf people, made it abundantly clear that "clinical competency and flexibility are as essential as are familiarity with the development and developmental hazards of the deaf, and knowledge of their varied modes of communication and language usage" (Rainer et al., 1965, p. 176).

The New York State Psychiatric Institute spawned additional centers providing direct service for deaf mental health patients. At Michael Reese Hospital, Dr. McCay Vernon, a psychologist who had training in deaf-related issues, was part of a seminal federally supported research project led by the famed Roy Grinker, M.D., which resulted in a 1969 report on the psychiatric diagnosis, therapy and research on the psychotic deaf (Grinker et al., 1969). In Washington, DC, St. Elizabeth's Hospital Superintendent Luther Robinson, M.D., a psychiatrist by training, took an interest in the deaf patients isolated at that institution and instituted a ward for these patients together with ground-breaking training programs that included deaf as well as hearing interns in mental health fields (Robinson, 1978). And, in San Francisco, Dr. Hilde Schlesinger, a psychiatrist at the Langley-Porter Neuropsychiatric Institute, began an outpatient program that served both deaf adults and children. These individuals were in the forefront of a new wave of psychiatrists, psychologists, counselors, and social workers who recognized that deaf persons with psychiatric conditions could be returned to the mainstream if their mental health needs were appropriately diagnosed and understood and quality service delivery models were established.

However, the training efforts created by these programs were sporadic and consisted primarily of workshops or short courses rather than graduate programs per se. Based on a national survey, Levine (1977) demonstrated that, despite these new training endeavors, a large majority of those providing mental health services to deaf clientele had absolutely no preparation for working with or communicating with them. She organized the 1974 Spartanburg Conference in order to focus on the preparation of psychological service providers to work with deaf clientele (Levine, 1977). This conference generated a list of competencies that were essential if one was to provide at least adequate service, including an understanding of Deaf-related issues, communication, psychological implications, diagnostic approaches, and how to work comfortably with deaf clientele, that should be expected of psychologists, competencies that are still relevant today. The conference also endorsed the importance of professional qualifications based on accreditation guidelines in addition to knowledge about the deaf population.

Prior to this, Gallaudet University and the Rochester Institute of Technology established undergraduate social work programs in the early 1970s (Sheridan, White, & Mounty, 2010). Subsequent to the Spartanburg conference, in-service training programs for service providers were instituted throughout the country (Levine, 1980). As for specialized graduate professional training programs per se, the first MSW program providing training to deaf graduate social work students was established at the University of Maryland (1978–1983). A small number of other programs emerged, and, like the University of Maryland, were funded by short-term grants to fill a void in Deaf mental health services. The School Psychology Program at Gallaudet University was established in 1979 as a direct response to the Spartanburg Conference recommendation for the development of graduate education programs to prepare competent psychologists, in this case psychologists who could provide adequate psychological evaluation and treatment of deaf students. This was followed by the Gallaudet University Mental Health Counseling Master's degree (established in 1986). Gallaudet University's graduate social work program (MSW) was established in 1989, and the university's Clinical Psychology Ph.D. program was established in 1990.

Few other specialized programs exist (Pollard, 1992–93). Even to this day, professionals will get their specialized training and add the deafness component separately either through individual coursework or a certificate program. However, their numbers are still inadequate to meet the critical need for qualified mental health clinicians. We continue to find professionals serving deaf clients who lack expertise or training (e.g., Leigh, Powers, Vash, & Nettles, 2004), clearly a situation that is ethically questionable. Unfortunately, "quality mental health services for deaf clients have only recently become an aspiration rather than an oxymoron" (Leigh & Gutman, 2010, p. 3). This goal requires competent service providers. We need to know: What are the issues involved in creating a strong coterie of mental health clinicians who can competently serve deaf people? What knowledge base and special skills must they acquire and what kind of personal development, such as the multi-cultural sensitivities and self-awareness, must they experience? And how should training be provided?

The Need for Specialized Training

The naïve observer may wonder why graduate training programs specializing in mental health practice with deaf and hard-of-hearing people are needed, particularly in view of this shortage of specialist clinicians, and may ask, "Why not just provide American Sign Language (ASL) interpreters in mental health settings, and for deaf students in academic settings?" Or even, "Why not just take a few ASL classes?" The answers to these questions are complex and multifaceted.

Leigh and Gutman (2010) note the critical importance of specialized competencies such as those developed at the Spartanburg Conference (mentioned earlier), in particular, linguistic understanding of and ability to communicate with deaf people, cultural awareness, and ability to interpret ethical paradigms relative to small population dynamics. Language competency is one aspect that demands critical attention. While it is true that language is one factor that needs to be taken into consideration for effective services, broad language diversity exists among people who are deaf and hard of hearing. Deaf people are frequently referred to as a language minority and many seen in mental health settings may have experienced severe language deprivation in their formative environments, leading to language dysfluency (Evans & Elliott, 1987; Glickman, 2009; Pollard, 1998). This phenomenon alone presents critical challenges in diagnostic and treatment processes for the mental health clinician. The language dysfluency observed in deaf consumers of mental health services may appear to the untrained clinician to be a thought disorder (Glickman, 2009; Leigh & Pollard, 2011). Although deaf consumers may in fact experience thought disorders, the ability to distinguish these disorders from language dysfluency requires special training and considerable practical experience (Evans & Elliott, 1987; Glickman, 2009; Pollard, 1998). Qualified sign language interpreters trained in mental health interpreting are in short supply and cannot advise clinicians on diagnostics, culturally appropriate assessments, and interventions, as these are outside their areas of expertise (Glickman, 2009; Karlin, 2003). Even with the best of interpreters, the process is not perfect. Mistakes in interpretation do happen, considering that the presence of a third party undoubtedly complicates clinical dynamics (Harvey, 2003).

Deaf clients, likely due to the various causes of hearing loss, often present with intricate neurological, medical, or cognitive profiles. While the diversity, cultural, and linguistic factors discussed here are critical to effective service provision, it is also imperative for clinicians to be familiar with the many medical, neurological or cognitive factors which may be associated with being deaf and may complicate the diagnostic picture. Sign language interpreters can be useful, but the clinician must still have a knowledge base that goes beyond that required for working with hearing people.

Within educational training programs, sign language interpretation involves a cognitive process of analyzing and processing the meanings of what is communicated. This process creates a time lag (Harvey, 2003) that makes it impossible for the deaf person to participate equally in classroom discussions "in perfect temporal synchronicity" (p. 121). Content distortion may take place in the process of interpreting, and may be influenced by the interpreter's training and experience, understanding of the message, intrapersonal issues, and the infeasibility of interpreting all of "the subtle nuances, innuendoes, body position changes, facial cues, etc." (Harvey, 2003, p. 121). For example, Sheridan recalls missing the point of a professor's message in a class at a hearing university when a highly qualified interpreter incorrectly signed "purse money" rather than "parsimony." Students learn that this dynamic would be complicated even further in mental health settings where a deaf client experiences language dysfluency. In clinical situations such as this, a second intermediary interpreter such as a Certified Deaf Interpreter (CDI) is sometimes introduced to assist with language matching. Time lags and content distortion exist in this situation as well.

Classrooms with skilled signing faculty and classmates largely resolve the difficulties associated with classroom interpreting. However, while superior, this is still not a perfect situation. At Gallaudet University, students and faculty are required to pass an American Sign Language Proficiency Interview, and some departments may require additional measures such as observations of situations that require fluency in ASL. Still, not everyone shares the same level of fluency, particularly if they have entered their training program as new or early users of ASL. Despite this, the signed interaction provides opportunities for spontaneous clarification and in-depth probing that are very difficult to achieve with even the best interpreters.

To be effective in practice with this population, clinicians must have not only knowledge of language and communication aspects as well as solid training in relevant mental health disciplines, but also knowledge of the diverse biopsychosocial experiences, identities, sociocultural realities, and social constructions of deaf and hard-of-hearing people, as well as knowledge of their educational preferences and experiences, their developmental and family issues and experiences, civil rights, multisystemic and multicultural issues, strengths and resources available to them, and political and oppressive forces in their lives (Sheridan & White, 2008). Additionally, they must have knowledge of culturally and linguistically appropriate assessments and interventions, as well as theoretical applications (Evans & Elliott, 1987; Glickman, 2009; Leigh, 2010; Pollard, 1998; Sheridan & White, 2008). Furthermore, clinicians must constantly work to evaluate and adapt existing empirically supported interventions to practice with deaf and hard-of-hearing people. Further research is needed to establish evidence-based practices with this population. Another important component of practice is the awareness of power issues inherent in the clinical relationship and their effects on transference and counter transference (Glickman, 2009); for example, the role that speech, language, and stigma have played in consumers' lives which may continue to affect the dynamics of the clinical relationship.

Although it is not possible in the scope of this chapter to discuss every ingredient necessary for successful practice, it is important to note that trust, an important foundation in practice with any population, is much more likely to develop with culturally competent and aware practitioners. A culturally competent clinician who is able to communicate effectively with the deaf client is generally preferred (Cohen, 2003) and is able to facilitate effective engagement with clients who are deaf (Sheridan & White, 2008). All of these aspects emphasize the need for specialized training.

Benefits of Training with Specialization in a Deaf-Centric Academic Immersion Milieu

In addition to the professional education requirements set forth in the accreditation standards of each profession, training programs at Gallaudet University also offer courses that prepare students to practice specifically with deaf and hard-of-hearing people. Thus, the graduate programs in counseling, social work, and psychology at Gallaudet offer professional degrees in the respective disciplines that prepare students specifically for practice with deaf and hard-of-hearing people. This is in contrast to a degree obtained in one of these disciplines from a generic program with no specific focus on practice with this population. The unique nature and mission of Gallaudet University as a bilingual (American Sign Language and English), "diverse, multicultural institution" (Gallaudet University Mission Statement, 2007) affords an environment where trainees are deeply immersed in the language, culture, and community of deaf people on a daily basis. This section will highlight the unique advantages offered by training programs in counseling, social work and clinical psychology at Gallaudet University, which specialize in professional practice with deaf people.

The majority of students at Gallaudet University and approximately 50% of its faculty are deaf. Classes are conducted in ASL and English and life on campus is "Deaf-centric." Thus, students in social work, clinical psychology, and counseling are exposed to the language and culture of deaf people on a daily basis. Classroom and campus communication is accessible to deaf and hearing students alike. The Deaf-centric immersion nature of Gallaudet means that the dynamics of the classroom and campus encounters may often times serve as a microcosm of professional experiences to come. A salient feature is that Gallaudet University is a deeply valued institution in the international Deaf Community. Training at Gallaudet comes from a place that upholds the tradition of values dear to its community. Furthermore, Gallaudet University faculty have diverse sub-specializations in their work and research with deaf and hard-of-hearing people that is unparalleled in generic programs. With this, faculty are able to share numerous examples of practice applications to the deaf experience.

An important aspect of professional development in any discipline is the development of a professional identity. Students at Gallaudet live, learn, and interact with a distinct group of peers and faculty who facilitate the development of a specialist identity beyond that of their discipline, a specialist identity that encompasses the understanding of deaf-related issues. This provides students and graduates with a network of professional peers and gives them a grounding and a power base (Glickman, 2009) that is absent in generic programs. It also can provide them with a network of colleagues, all of whom understand the need to advocate and explain their role as specialists for deaf clients, especially when others may not understand that role.

Case discussions in the classroom are nurtured by the experiences and perspectives of peers and faculty mentors. Students discuss, for example, how mental illness is manifest in people who are deaf, and critically evaluate the utility of various theories, assessments, and interventions for practice with a diverse deaf and hard-of-hearing population. Faculty provide guidance to students across all curricular areas as they explore applications to professional practice with the deaf population. Students discuss the complexities of their work, share resources, and collaborate on research projects with others who share the same interests and challenges. Faculty with specialized knowledge and skills to practice with the deaf population are able to guide students through ethical challenges unique to work with this population (Brice, 2002; Peoples, 2002) and in developing an understanding of the social forces of oppression in the history of deaf people as well as in current contexts. This deepens the learning experience in a way that cannot be achieved in a generic program where students are isolated in their specialization. Professional development and identity are further enhanced through immersion in campus life and extra-curricular activities. As in any field of practice and with any population there are many questions still unanswered regarding effective practice. But this is where we have the opportunity to deeply explore, and critically evaluate, what we know, and what we need to learn more about. Furthermore, student research projects, theses, and dissertations contribute to our knowledge base of effective practice with this population.

The immersion milieu at Gallaudet allows students to experience the diversity and various constructions of deaf people. They observe and experience, sometimes firsthand, the sociopolitical dynamics of the Deaf Community. There are multiple opportunities for the development of professional self-awareness in relation to this diversity. This is facilitated through individual and group dialog and learning activities with faculty and peers. These self-awareness experiences happen for all students regardless of their background and experience with Deaf culture. These shared interactions allow students to develop new understandings of the many ways of being deaf in the world, and of what they bring to the professional relationship. Furthermore, interaction in the classroom and campus life provide students with rich access to diverse life stories, educational, social, community, employment, and deaf member family experiences well beyond the textbook. College and graduate students face unique developmental experiences (Whyte & Smith, 2010) and culturally competent faculty are able to respond to their personal and professional growth needs.

Additionally, the Gallaudet milieu serves as a model for organizational and professional behavior. It provides opportunities to learn normative behaviors related to such things as obtaining and using interpreters, use of space (e.g., appropriate arrangement of seating which allows all to see what is being signed), and attending behaviors (e.g., eye contact). The environment offers opportunities for ASL tutoring, and access to video phone equipment and other technologies. Students and graduates who have seen what genuine access for deaf people looks like through their experiences at Gallaudet, and have seen what deaf people can accomplish in such culturally affirmative environments, are better able to negotiate and advocate for appropriate accommodations at their internships and agencies. Another advantage of mental health specialization at Gallaudet University and the Deaf-centric academic milieu is the extensive collection of Deaf-related references and periodicals available in the University library. Furthermore, researchers at Gallaudet University are knowledgeable about the special practical and ethical considerations of research with deaf people (see, for example, Pollard, 1992, 1996).

Deaf-centric teaching approaches at Gallaudet University are consistent with Deaf cultural values and support deaf and hearing students alike. Deaf and hearing students typically participate equally in role plays, class discussions, and activities related to professional development. In contrast, deaf and hard-of-hearing students attending other universities have reported being discouraged from participating in such activities due to the discomfort of the professors or lack of appropriate communication access. Deaf and hearing faculty at Gallaudet specialize in professional practice with the deaf population and have the capacity to be judicial in appraisals of student performance and their appropriateness for the profession (Peoples, 2002; O'Hearn & Pollard, 2008).

The culture of accessible interactive communication in the Gallaudet milieu facilitates deep learning and does not stop when class is over. Much learning takes place outside of the classroom through informal social interaction, study groups, lunch discussions, dorm chats, weekend outings, and through observations of situations, behaviors, and communication. This brings a depth and breadth to the training that is unparalleled in a generic program. For deaf students in mainstream generic training programs who are dependent on interpreters or one-on-one communication, this very important aspect of interactive learning tends to diminish or stop when class is over and the interpreter leaves.

Challenges

The professions of clinical psychology, counseling, and social work all value continued professional development. The professional training programs at Gallaudet recognize that even though a Deaf-centric academic milieu greatly enhances student learning, no program can teach everything there is to learn. For students who come to Gallaudet University as new signers, acquiring a fluency in ASL in the span of their graduate career can be a challenge. The large majority of students do achieve this through ASL classes and immersion experiences, while a small percentage struggle but remain committed to ongoing professional development. Sometimes students will enter their program part-time or postpone graduation in order to sufficiently advance their sign language skills prior to entering professional practice.

For some programs, identifying quality internships is challenging. Programs work continuously to build relationships with organizations and to expand options for student placements. Programs continuously seek internship placements nationally and, for some, internationally, which provide students with sufficient exposure to deaf clientele as well as quality supervision. This also means that interpreter services may be necessary for deaf students in order to make supervision or other didactic activities accessible. Given the growing shortage of interpreter services and expanding need on Gallaudet's campus and in the Washington metro area, this is no small challenge.

Recruitment for graduate programs at Gallaudet is another area of continuing effort. The pool of potential applicants is small. Yet, this challenge is also a blessing because smaller programs allow for a more amenable faculty/student ratio.

Training Goals

Does the focus on practice with deaf and hard-of-hearing people distract from the depth of generic practice issues? How do programs balance accreditation requirements with the preparation for practice with deaf people? In short, the answer is to ask much more of our students compared to generic training programs. Each of the mental health programs offered at Gallaudet University has been fully accredited by its professional accreditation bodies, demonstrating that all professional competencies are covered and achieved in the curriculum. At Gallaudet, however, that is not enough. All programs find ways to integrate knowledge and skills related to working with deaf people into their courses.

It is, perhaps, first necessary to acknowledge that while the training goals of the three mental health disciplines described here are generally comparable with those in generic programs, they differ from each other because the disciplines differ from each other. The goals for training psychologists are not exactly the same as training social workers or counselors. Additionally, these differences can also be attributed to the fact that no pre-packaged, articulated pedagogy for such (specialized) training exists. All three disciplines offer nationally-accredited advanced degrees in the mental health professions, ensuring that curricula meet, and often exceed, the standards set by their respective disciplines. As these standards are widely available to the public through the affiliated professional organizations, they will be not covered here. Instead, what follows focuses on the training philosophy and goals that are unique to programs designed to prepare students for work with deaf and hard-of-hearing clients.

Training Philosophy

As noted earlier, the programs within the Departments of Counseling, Social Work, and Psychology were developed, in large part, as a result of the Spartanburg Conference and a growing recognition of the need for training programs that would integrate cultural competencies with accreditation standards. For social work, this has historically been a value base in the profession (Cross, 2008) with its focus on the person in the context of the environment. In recent years, the professional organizations of each of the major mental health disciplines have also embraced and articulated multicultural competencies necessary for the treatment of clients and the training of mental health professionals (e.g., ACA, 1996; APA, 2003; NASW, 2000). Thus, it is the philosophy and practice of each program that competency as clinicians requires, among other things, knowledge, skills, and dispositions/values specific to working with the linguistically and culturally diverse population of deaf and hard-of-hearing clients.

It is also a foundational belief that such training is most successful through experiential learning within the cultural context of the trainees' future clients. This includes having faculty, supervisors, and peers who are deaf or hard of hearing, as well as fieldwork experiences working with deaf and hard-of-hearing clients.

Knowledge Dimension

Core foundation courses provide students with knowledge appropriate to each discipline, preparing graduates from each program to obtain professional credentials and/or licensure in their respective fields. Additionally, the curriculum for each program contains content specific to serving the mental health needs of deaf and hard-of-hearing clients, largely provided by three methods: first, it is infused throughout these core foundation courses; second, it is taught in "specialty" courses and/or curricular activities; and, lastly, fieldwork placements or practica are done at agencies, schools, or programs serving deaf and hard-of-hearing populations.

Infusion of content related to deaf and hard-of-hearing clients happens in numerous ways. Deaf faculty and hearing faculty with clinical experience working with deaf and hard-of-hearing clients are able to contextualize the content material relevant to the target population. For example, instruction on the professional code of ethics might include discussions about the unique nature of working as a mental health professional with deaf and hard-of-hearing clients, such as issues of competency, confidentiality, and managing multiple or overlapping roles while working in a small, close-knit community (Leigh & Gutman, 2010). Case studies of deaf clients are another vehicle used to illustrate contextual cultural stressors, diagnostics, assessment, treatment, and preventive measures with this population.

While infusion is a cornerstone of professional preparation at Gallaudet University, specific courses and other curricular activities are also developed by each of the three departments to provide additional key knowledge and skills related to mental health services with deaf and hard-of-hearing clients. These offerings are consistent with the unique needs of the respective disciplines and, thus, take on different forms. Graduate Social Work programs typically have an advanced year concentration beyond the foundation in generalist practice. Gallaudet's MSW program is unique in its ability to offer an academic immersion experience in a concentration area (deaf/hard-of-hearing populations). In addition, all student interns work with deaf clients. In the clinical psychology and mental health counseling programs, the majority of courses integrate the current knowledge base in psychology/counseling and deaf people into the learning outcomes. There is an additional course focused solely on the experience of being deaf, and all students will conduct at least some (if not all) of their clinical training with deaf clients.

Finally, through fieldwork or externship placements with deaf and hard-of-hearing clients, students in the three programs have additional learning opportunities to enhance their knowledge through supervision and by working closely with other seasoned professionals.

No matter which method of delivery, the curricula also address the myths, assumptions, and errors often associated with the mental health needs of, and services for, deaf and hard-of-hearing populations. For example, the long-standing, yet erroneous, belief that deaf people lack language and higher order cognitive skills has led many psychotherapists untrained in working with this population to believe them to be unlikely candidates for in-depth, insight-, or psychoanalytically or cognitive-oriented interventions (Sussman & Brauer, 1999). Supervisors can also identify and help trainees "unpack" countertransference reactions that result from working with deaf clients, such as beliefs about deaf people's abilities, fears in the therapist related to miscommunications, or attitudes towards accommodations.

In addition to myths and assumptions, the following topics also are viewed as important for mental health practitioners working with deaf people to know and understand. These include: historical and emerging perspectives on deaf and hard-of-hearing people; deaf member families and family development; dimensions and intersections of diversity among deaf and hard-of-hearing people; the Deaf Community and Deaf Culture; language and communication (development, diversity in communication, issues and implications); educational systems, choices and implications; identity issues; cochlear implants; biopsychosocial aspects of being deaf throughout the lifespan; audiology; audism; assessment and diagnosis with deaf people; interpreting in mental health; adaptations to various psychotherapy and counseling practices needed to accommodate deaf people; and models of disability and ethnic diversity. All these issues must then be woven together since culturally competent practice with deaf and hard-of-hearing persons requires understanding multiple layers of diversity within the population related to the deaf "piece" interacting with all of the other aspects of human diversity that is true for deaf people as well as hearing.

Skills Dimension

Students develop skills through application in much the same way as students in any advanced mental health-related degree program. Opportunities for skill building are provided in the classroom (e.g., role plays and simulated sessions) and in supervised fieldwork placements. Students learn to make cultural adjustments to therapeutic interventions, as needed, based on continuing assessment of the specific ingredients of the therapeutic process and relevant cultural factors of the deaf or hard-of-hearing client(s).

Of particular importance in working with any client is the ability to communicate effectively. With deaf and hard-of-hearing persons this can mean using a signed language, such as ASL. The common assumption that training professionals through traditional accredited mental health programs and then having them take courses in ASL suffices, clearly does not hold; it typically takes 2 to 5 years to complete an advanced degree in a mental health related field and at least as long to achieve the appropriate proficiency in a second language (ILR, 2011). Achieving language proficiency in a second language is influenced by many factors, including social/cultural factors, age, educational background, and oral and literacy skills in the native language. Parsing language fluency even farther, Cummins (1991) identified two levels of proficiency: Basic Interpersonal Communication Skills (BICS) and Cognitive Academic Language Proficiency (CALP). It is estimated that achieving BICS in a second language requires 2 to 3 years of instruction. CALP, necessary for effective communication in a clinical setting, requires a minimum of 5 to 7 years of language instruction *at the immersion level* (Cummins, 1991), though some do acquire fluency faster if they have solid immersion experiences. The Interagency Language Roundtable (ILR) of the U.S. Foreign Service Institute cites comparable time and immersion requirements. For example, Level 4, "Advanced Professional Proficiency," of the ILR Language Level Rating is defined as "able to use the language fluently and accurately on all levels normally pertinent to professional needs" (ILR, 2011), and is estimated to develop in 5 to 8 years of *full-time* use of the language. ASL curricula are typically designed to teach BICS, not CALP, and students in classes rarely have full immersion experiences. Yet, this very inadequate level of language exposure is the main way most adults learn ASL, and the result is that there are many beginning signers who see themselves, and are seen by equally uninformed employers, as qualified to counsel deaf people. A much higher standard for sign language skill is promoted at Gallaudet where people learning ASL as adults have something much closer to a full immersion language learning experience.

Mental health training programs conducted in ASL have the benefit of instruction and faculty/peer interaction being conducted in the language of service provision. In addition, students learn the specialized vocabulary of the discipline in ASL—something not offered in a typical ASL course. They also receive support in developing communicative competence working with clients who represent a broad range of language skills—also not supported in an ASL course. Furthermore, students learn about how ASL and language diversity influence the assessment process, selection of assessment tools, and how ASL influences counseling and psychotherapy.

Values and Dispositions Dimension

In addition to knowledge and skills, best practices in multicultural curriculum development and training call for attention to the students' "attitude" or disposition in working with diverse populations. Core values of the professions of social work, psychology, and counseling form the basis of each discipline's code of ethics that guides professional behavior. Culturally competent helping relationships are possible only when the trainee develops self- and other-awareness, analyzes personal and systemic value biases, engages in the intentional exchange of cultural information, and makes empathic connections through mutual self-disclosure (Roysircar et al., 2003). Critical to providing opportunities for student engagement in these activities is interaction with deaf, hard-of-hearing, and hearing peers in the classroom. "Having a diverse group of students is critical to providing training that enhances multicultural competence and critical consciousness … it is the community of students in a given classroom, practicum setting, and program that provides the experiences, insights, questions, and critiques that drive and inspire learning" (McWhirter & McWhirter, 2007, pp. 398–399).

Working in small and/or special populations raises questions regarding the role of a professional's own identity, and how that influences his or her work. Smith (2007) studied identity development and drew parallels between deaf people preparing to work in the mental health field and those from other minority groups. Questions can arise with regards to which group a professional identifies. Is it the deaf client, for example, with whom a certain kinship may be felt, or is it with the larger group of mental health professionals? Trainees must address these questions and others like them as they develop their own professional identities and look toward their future careers.

Issues Unique to Training Deaf Professionals

Deaf mental health professionals offer something unique to deaf clients. Of all helping professionals, deaf mental health professionals have the ability to understand deeply the issues facing their clients and their clients' families. They are models of the possibility for success in a way that hearing professionals can never be. Deaf professionals also represent a sense of empowerment for the community; a leading role in setting the course for the future. In all of the graduate programs at Gallaudet, one part of the mission is to make professional preparation accessible to deaf and hard-of-hearing students, as well as hearing students wishing to work within the Deaf Community.

Beyond the content of training programs, the skills needed to work with deaf populations, and the challenges training programs face, some issues are unique to training professionals who themselves are deaf. At Gallaudet University, graduate training differs substantially from undergraduate education, with one of the major differences being the integration of deaf, hard-of-hearing, and hearing students in the same programs and courses. While there are a handful of undergraduate students who are hearing, they are the exception. At the graduate level, just about all programs are integrated.

Unique Needs of Deaf Learners

Perhaps one of the more obvious issues when teaching or training deaf students is the need for a friendly visual environment. And, in this sense, environment is defined broadly, encompassing things like lighting in the classroom, seating arrangements, visual distractions, and how material is presented. The classic image of the professor writing out statements on the black/whiteboard while describing an important point can never happen with deaf students present. More attention to visual presentations such as those in PowerPoint, captioned or signed videos, and graphics is necessary. While all audiences may benefit from improved visual presentations, the need is certainly greater with deaf students.

Bilingualism (ASL and English) and its variations exist not just between deaf and hearing students, but frequently are also manifested among signing and non-signing deaf students, or signing students who differ on how much they rely upon English word order in their communication. Deaf people who rely on spoken English may need computer-assisted real-time captioning (CART) or an oral interpreter, who mouths the words being spoken, to be able to access all of the lectures as well as class discussions and interactions that are typical of graduate classrooms. These discussions and interactions are an experience that can be immensely rewarding, but require appreciation of and responsiveness to the diverse language and communication skills of the students. Instructors may sometimes need to perform like air-traffic controllers, holding up some comments until everyone has finished comprehending a previous comment and has shifted attention accordingly. Rephrasing a comment or switching modalities (e.g., ASL to written English or vice versa) are also common techniques to ensure that everyone understands. When the entire group is comfortable and fluent in ASL, the communication is much easier, though the need to "direct traffic" rarely stops. A benefit of training in a specialized deaf environment (such as Gallaudet's) is that both sensitivity to and techniques for managing the communication exchange are developed through practice. This remains true whether a sign language interpreter is present or whether all present are fluent in the language being used.

While it may be politically awkward to discuss deaf people's ability to write in English, the fact remains that many culturally Deaf people, particularly those whose native language is ASL and who acquire English as a second language, struggle with the extremely complicated grammatical rules of academic English. Deciding how to approach that skill in graduate and professional education requires thoughtful reflection. Lowering grades because papers are not written with perfect grammar seems unfair at best and discriminatory at worst. On the other hand, most mental health professionals need to produce paperwork based on written English. It is certain that their work will be judged, rightly or wrongly, by the quality of their written work. It may not be the primary job of mental health training programs to teach writing in English, but neither can it be shirked. Finding the balance between making written English the "gold standard" and ignoring it completely requires great care. Attention to bilingual teaching methods can be helpful in this regard.

Faculty who have taught over the years realize that some extremely talented students also present with complicated learning profiles. Sometimes these involve formal accommodations in the classroom, such as extended time on examinations, extended time for turning in assignments, or having faculty notes available to the student. Other times, however, the faculty member has no documentation regarding the student's special needs, but nonetheless recognizes a need to modify the training or teaching approach to ensure success. There are a number of implications that follow from this. First is that additional faculty time will probably be devoted to students with complicated learning profiles. Second, these students may need more time themselves to complete the program. Third, academic support and resources must be sought out and employed appropriately.

Sometimes, frank conversations must take place between faculty and students about the student's unique learning needs. It is not unusual to give significant constructive feedback to students (deaf and hearing) on their work, only to have students say they had never heard that sort of criticism before. In fact, students will sometimes report the exact opposite, claiming they were applauded for their work. It may be that undergraduate professors had not required writing, or graded it so leniently that the students believed they were skilled, when in fact they had obvious weaknesses. For deaf students, education in a culturally affirmative university like Gallaudet may be a mixed blessing because, having shed most of society's prejudices about the presumed limitations of deaf people, faculty at Gallaudet typically hold deaf students to higher standards. Sometimes faculty have to tell deaf students that they need to do much better work. Naturally, these can be emotional discussions that are not always welcomed by either the student or the faculty member, but are common occurrences in professional preparation.

Along with the unique needs of deaf learners are the unique benefits and opportunities that accompany professional training. An obvious benefit is the beauty and fascination of a visual language and advantages of bilingual or even multilingual descriptions and presentations of ideas. A deeper and richer understanding of nuances of theories and cultures can be explored through the examination of the various ways different languages express concepts. Furthermore, when diverse cultures come together, the opportunity arises for understanding the layering and interaction of these cultures, as well as the points of common ground underlying all people.

Field Placements

Another issue when training deaf students relates to field placements or externships. While many deaf students do field placements in programs serving deaf clients, thereby fitting in nicely with the program, not all mental health training is available in that way. There are some skills, such as those related to specialty areas that cover, for example, working with particular disorders or learning about particular therapies or interventions, that must be learned first in general clinics or programs, and then adapted and applied to deaf clients. This raises a number of sensitive and potentially difficult issues.

The first issue relates to the receptiveness, willingness, and familiarity with deaf people on the part of the training sites. These characteristics, in our experience, vary widely from place to place. Some are quite familiar with deaf students and their needs and are exceedingly open and willing to integrate all students into their program. Others respond with skepticism regarding the student's ability to do the job, how they will communicate and fit in, how they can be supervised, and if interpreters will be present, how interpreters influence the work. For example, will clients be willing to meet with a deaf trainee who is communicating through an interpreter? There is also an additional burden, rightly or wrongly, placed on deaf trainees (and their program) to educate people from the training site on the lives and needs of deaf people. Students often gain wonderful skills from this experience, teaching others about Deaf Culture, ASL, adaptive strategies, etc. It is, however, something hearing students rarely face in this way.

Interpreters and their presence in mental health settings similarly raise very complicated issues. One of the first relates to funding. While deaf students are in school, the graduate programs are responsible for providing support, and therefore must obtain university-based funding for any needed interpreting services. Additional concerns include the following: how interpreters change the work, will clients work with a deaf professional through an interpreter, are interpreters allowed to have access to confidential patient/client information, and the like. However, when clinical psychology students go on internships, the issue of payment shifts. In clinical psychology, because the site pays interns, they become "employees," and as such, have rights under the Americans with Disabilities Act (1990). All the good intentions notwithstanding, many internship sites begin to waffle when they find they are responsible for at least partly (if not fully) funding the accommodations.

Deaf psychology students, even in today's more enlightened era, have had offers to interview with programs revoked when the sites learn they must fund an interpreter (Szymanski, 2010). Amazingly, these students are sometimes told outright that there is no way the site could afford the accommodations. Of course, legal action is an option, based on regulations for implementing the ADA. The reality, however, is that students who are desperate to obtain an internship to finish their training and move on with their careers may not be in a position to pursue legal action. They may also wonder how many places they can file complaints about, since these sorts of experiences are not isolated. This situation may not hold in all field placements, but it can be a very real issue for training directors and their deaf students who may have excellent qualifications and wish to pursue a training necessitating working in a primarily hearing environment, such as neuropsychology-based sites.

Deaf/Hearing Issues

There are no graduate training programs that serve *only* deaf students, and, to our knowledge, no clinical training programs (i.e., clinics or hospitals) where all of the staff and trainees are deaf. This means that deaf and hearing students and staff must train together, work together, and collaborate in many different ways. Once again, with two (or more) cultures coming together, the potential both for conflict and for dynamic learning is present (Glickman, 2009). For such interactions to be successful, however, many factors need to be addressed, either overtly or indirectly.

A major one is "hearing privilege." By virtue of the fact that a student is hearing certain benefits emerge. One obvious one is that hearing students can use telephones and have easier access to all information presented auditorally. The enormous rise in texting and email has evened out this playing field somewhat, but it is still easier for hearing students to receive calls from potential supervisors, placements, and hearing clients.

Wishing it away cannot simply change hearing privilege. However, deciding how to deal with this situation, both on the part of deaf and hearing trainees and professionals, can make a major difference in an experience. It is probably impossible to provide a recipe for how to approach and resolve an issue like an imbalance in power or access to information, but understanding that it is there and must be addressed is critical. Even such simple things as hearing people signing in public places in Deaf environments versus talking amongst themselves can have implications for relationship quality. While a standard recipe for coping with hearing privilege may not be possible, a common ingredient is that of humility, particularly on the part of hearing professionals. Professionals may come to believe they have answers or opinions regarding issues within their realm of expertise. Yet, it may be when the hearing person defers to deaf colleagues and clients—or can admit to being less than an expert and open to learning—that the working relationship flourishes.

When deaf and hearing students mix, issues of how to communicate, what language should be used, and what to do when not everyone is equally fluent quickly surface. At Gallaudet, some programs require a certain degree of ASL fluency to enter; others do not require fluency to enter, but require fluency to do field placements or externships and to graduate. Still other programs simply require a particular number of courses be taken in ASL as part of the curriculum. As in most cases, there is no easy answer. For example, requiring that everyone have fluency in ASL before entering a program can drastically limit the number of applicants a program receives. This could result in very small cohorts, or an "open door" admissions policy, which some accrediting agencies frown upon. The alternative, however, also leads to complications. Accepting students who are not fluent and expecting them to master a language in 2 or 3 years is a definite challenge for the novice. Additionally, as discussed earlier, trying to accommodate everyone's communication needs in a classroom of mixed signers and mixed hearing statuses can also be exceedingly challenging, particularly in an environment where ASL is expected to be the language of the classroom. Interpreters in the classroom can help, but are often not the most satisfying solution because of temporal delays in communication and the difficulties consistently finding interpreters who have the vocabulary and background necessary for the course. Given these complexities, it is useful for faculty to take the varied ASL and English competencies of the students into consideration and apply theories and methods of bilingual education. This is in keeping with Gallaudet's bilingual mission.

The limited number of field placements serving deaf clients also comes up when deaf and hearing students train together. All students who come to programs preparing mental health workers to work with deaf clients want experience working with deaf clients. Yet, if those sites or placements are limited, hearing students may feel conflicted about applying for sites that may be viewed as more appropriate for their deaf colleagues. Hearing privilege enters the picture here as well, since hearing students could rationalize that they have more options and therefore should not compete with their deaf classmates for these more limited placements, even if they want deaf-based experiences.

While these challenges certainly exist in deaf/hearing relationships, these relationships also present the opportunity for modeling professional collaboration. It is one thing to discuss how people grapple with these questions. It is quite another to actually do the grappling and show the larger world how rewarding and enriching it can be when two cultures come together with the goal of understanding each other. Modeling understanding, compromising (on all sides), educating, and advocating all come to the fore and allow students to work at activities that will become part of their professional careers. Deaf/hearing partnerships also present the opportunity for creative approaches to solving problems. Because deaf and hearing people bring different experiences, perspectives, and skills to the table, more possibilities exist for innovative approaches to training and providing treatment.

Employment

Ideally, training culminates in employment. However, unique issues arise for trained deaf and hard-of-hearing professionals. The problem of funding interpreters, as discussed previously for training purposes, particularly in field placements or internships, is also one that rears its head when deaf professionals enter the work force. It may be less of a problem if the professional works solely in a deaf oriented program, such as a deaf program in a clinic or hospital. However, deaf professionals who have larger goals and wish to establish new programs, train other professionals, conduct research on best treatments, and get advanced specialized training through, for example, paid postdocs, may need to pursue their careers in "mainstream" environments. Once again, graduates may be faced with the question of how funding for interpreters can be arranged. Given the very difficult economic times facing most countries right now and the limited budgets of most institutions, paying for an interpreter to accommodate a deaf professional may not be very easy to do. Similarly, programs for deaf clients that are faced with tighter budgets may be hiring less. This places some responsibility, therefore, on current professionals providing mental health services to deaf people to advocate for continued funding and to be in touch with policy makers in an active way to ensure that needed services are not curtailed. One must be creative in utilizing approaches. As Robert Pollard (1996) stated, "the daily presence of deaf professionals (and interpreters) has changed the culture of the Department of Psychiatry in wonderful and profound ways. The ripple effect from the Program for Deaf Trainees has been almost as gratifying as the program itself" (p. 393).

Future Issues

Technology is affecting all aspects of society, and there is no sign that the pace of change will slow down. There may be no greater impact of technology than that of cochlear implants (CIs). While it is clear that CIs do not make deaf individuals "hearing," this technology does enhance access to auditory information in an increasingly large number of people. Cochlear implantation, along with universal newborn hearing screening, is changing the characteristic of the deaf population. Graduate students at Gallaudet University who wish to study development in deaf children increasingly find that more and more of these children, including deaf children of deaf parents, are using CIs (Paludneviciene & Leigh, 2011). It is incumbent upon those of us doing training to look to the future and prepare for a Deaf Community in which many individuals have CIs. We must understand the unique meanings this presents for individuals and their families in order to facilitate development and adaptation.

Video technology, particularly in the form of "telehealth," is opening the door to accessibility in ways never before thought possible. While there is still much to learn about providing mental health services via a computer-aided video medium, the potential to bring services to populations in need is greater than ever, particularly for those with limited access to appropriately trained mental health clinicians. Serious questions do remain regarding telehealth. Can a professional viewed on a computer screen provide the same level of therapeutic relationship as in face-to-face therapy? How might emergency backup work in this situation? For whom is this approach effective? How might a deaf person who uses spoken language use this service? How do licensing and certification laws work with telehealth? Where must the professional be credentialed in order to provide services? What happens when the interpreter used is not familiar with local signs or when the deaf consumer is very language dysfluent?

The use of telehealth is not without problems. In Massachusetts, for example, psychiatric emergency rooms increasingly draw upon the MARTI video interpreting system to access interpreters after hours. The dependency upon MARTI developed after state budget cuts eliminated funding for after-hours interpreters. Emergency room clinicians may assume that provision of interpreter services through MARTI eliminates the need for on-site interpreters or, even better, specially trained clinicians. It can provide an illusion of successful accommodation when in reality there continue to be many barriers of understanding between the deaf consumer and the presumably hearing clinician. Thus, technological advances like this have advantages and disadvantages. The illusion of a "technological fix" can actually weigh against the employment of clinical specialists (N. Glickman, personal communication, July 2011).

There are also questions related to technology access. Does this approach lead to separate classes, those with economic resources sufficient to have computer and Internet access and those who do not? Clearly, economic issues continue to play an important role in service provision. Having economic resources may provide greater access to CIs and other forms of early intervention and support. This will ultimately affect who the clients are for mental health professionals working with the Deaf Community. The ethnic and racial backgrounds of the Deaf Community may change as a result of immigration trends. More limited economic resources also mean cuts in services, including much needed mental health services. Sadly, mental health services are often seen as secondary to other more basic (i.e., medical) needs. And services to low-incidence populations are easily cut with very little political impact or repercussions.

Yet, opportunities may never have been greater. Parents are receiving needed support earlier and earlier, and this helps them to resolve issues related to having deaf children (Adams, 2011). We know more than we ever have previously about the diverse and multifaceted developmental experiences of deaf and hard-of-hearing children and implications for educational opportunities. Advances in theories and methods of language development are an example of this. The strengths and resources of deaf and hard-of-hearing people throughout life, our communities, and organizations are recognized now more than ever before (for example, see Sheridan, 2001, 2008). Training programs in mental health continue to have bright and highly motivated young people entering the field with enthusiasm and creativity. ASL has gained acceptance as a language used in high schools and some colleges to satisfy foreign language requirements, and is no longer thought of as a "simpler" form of English. Research into issues important to the Deaf Community has never been more prolific. All these signs point to resources that are available to tackle the mental health needs of deaf and hard-of-hearing people and their families.

Note

1. All authors contributed equally.

References

Adams, E. B. (2011). *Hearing mothers' resolution of the identification of child hearing loss: An exploration of the reaction to diagnosis interview* (Unpublished doctoral dissertation). Gallaudet University, Washington, DC.

American Counseling Association (ACA). (1996). Multicultural counseling competencies and standards. Retrieved from http://www.counseling.org/Resources/Competencies/Multcultural_Competencies.pdf

American Psychological Association (APA). (2003). *Guidelines on multicultural education, training, research, practice, and organizational change for psychologists.* Retrieved from http://www.apa.org/pi/oema/resources/policy/multicultural-guideline.pdf

Americans with Disabilities Act of 1990, 42 U.S.C.A. §12101 et seq.

Branson, J., & Miller, D. (2002). *Damned for their difference: The cultural construction of deaf people as disabled.* Washington, DC: Gallaudet University Press.

Brice, P. (2002). Ethical issues in working with deaf children, adolescents and their families. In V. Gutman (Ed.), *Ethics in mental health and deafness* (pp. 52–67). Washington, DC: Gallaudet University Press.

Burch, S., & Joyner, H. (2007). *Unspeakable: The story of Junius Wilson.* Chapel Hill: University of North Carolina Press.

Cohen, C. B. (2003). *Psychotherapy with deaf and hard of hearing individuals: Perceptions of the consumer.* Binghamton, NY: Haworth Maltreatment and Trauma Press/ The Haworth Press.

Cross, T. L. (2008). Cultural competence. In T. Mizrahi, & L. Davis (Eds.), *The encyclopedia of social work* (20th ed., Vol. 1, pp. 487–491). Washington, DC: NASW Press and New York, NY: Oxford University Press.

Cummins, J. (1991). Language development and academic learning. In L. Malavé & G. Duquette (Eds.), *Language, culture and cognition* (pp. 161–175). Clevedon, England: Multilingual Matters.

Eriksson, P. (1993). *The history of deaf people.* Örebro, Sweden: SIH Läromedel.

Evans, J. W., & Elliott, H. (1987). The mental status examination. In H. Elliott, L. Glass, & J. W. Evans (Eds.), *Mental health assessment of deaf clients: A practical manual* (pp. 83–92). Boston, MA: College Hill Press.

Gallaudet University Mission Statement. (2007). Retrieved from Gallaudet University website: http://www.gallaudet.edu/x20518.xml

Glickman, N. (2009). *Cognitive-behavioral therapy for deaf and hearing persons with language and earning challenges.* New York, NY: Routledge.

Gottstein, J. (2002). *Psychiatry: Force of law.* Retrieved from PsychRights: Law Project for Psychiatric Rights website: http://psychrights.org/index.htm

Grinker, R., Vernon., M., Mindel, E., Rothstein, D., Easton, H., Koh, S., et al. (1969). *Psychiatric diagnosis, therapy and research on the psychotic deaf* (Grant number RD-2407-S). Washington, DC: U.S. Department of Health, Education and Welfare.

Harvey, M. A., (2003). *Psychotherapy with deaf and hard of hearing persons: A systemic model* (2nd ed.). Mahwah, NJ: Erlbaum.

Interagency Language Roundtable (ILR). (2011). Interagency Language Roundtable: Language skills descriptions—speaking. Retrieved from http://www.govtilr.org/skills/ILRscale2.htm

Karlin, T. (2003) "Umm, the interpreter didn't understand." Interpreting for individuals with thought disorder. *Views, 20*(4), 1, 10–11

Leigh, I. W. (2010). *Psychotherapy with deaf clients from diverse groups* (2nd ed.). Washington, DC: Gallaudet University Press.

Leigh, I. W., & Gutman, V. (2010). Psychotherapy with deaf people: The ethical dimension. In I. W. Leigh (Ed.), *Psychotherapy with deaf clients from diverse groups, 2nd ed.* (pp. 3–17). Washington, DC: Gallaudet University Press.

Leigh, I. W., & Pollard, R. Q. (2011). Mental health and deaf adults. In M. Marschark & P. Spencer (Eds.), *Oxford handbook of Deaf studies, language, and education* (2nd ed., Vol. 1, pp. 214–226). New York, NY: Oxford University Press.

Leigh, I. W., & Gutman, V. (2010). Psychotherapy with deaf people: The ethical dimension. In I. W. Leigh (Ed.), *Psychotherapy with deaf clients from diverse groups* (2nd ed., pp. 3–17). Washington, DC: Gallaudet University Press.

Leigh, I. W., Powers, L., Vash, C., & Nettles, R. (2004). Survey of psychological services to clients with disabilities: The need for awareness. *Rehabilitation Psychology, 49,* 48–54.

Levine, E. S. (1977). *The preparation of psychological service providers to the deaf. A report of the Spartanburg Conference on the functions, competencies and training of psychological service providers to the deaf. PRWAD Monograph No. 4.* Silver Spring, MD: Professional Rehabilitation Workers with the Adult Deaf.

Levine, E. S. (1980). *The ecology of early deafness.* New York, NY: Columbia University Press.

McWhirter, B. T., & McWhirter, E. H. (2007). Toward an emancipatory communitarian approach to the practice of psychology training. In E. Aldarondo (Ed.), *Advancing social justice through clinical practice* (pp. 91–118). New York, NY: Erlbaum.

Merkel, L. (2003). *The history of psychiatry.* Retrieved from University of Virginia website: http://www.healthsystem.virginia.edu/internet/psych-training/seminars/History-of-psychiatry-8-04.pdf

Moores, D. F. (2001). *Educating the deaf: Psychology, principles, and practices, 5th ed.* Boston, MA: Houghton Mifflin.

National Association of Social Workers. (2000). Cultural competence in the social work profession. In *Social work speaks: NASW policy statements 2000–2003* (5th ed.). Washington, DC: Author.

O'Hearn, A. M., & Pollard, R. Q. (2008). Modifying dialectical behavior therapy for deaf individuals. *Cognitive and Behavioral Practice, 15,* 400–414.

Paludneviciene, R., & Leigh, I. W. (2011). *Cochlear implants and the deaf community: Evolving perspectives.* Washington, DC: Gallaudet University Press.

Peoples, K. (2002). Ethical challenges in training professionals for mental health services with deaf people. In V. Gutman (Ed.), *Ethics in mental health and deafness* (pp. 99–122). Washington, DC: Gallaudet University Press.

Pollard, R. (1992). Cross-cultural ethics in the conduct of deafness research. *Rehabilitation Psychology, 37,* 87–101.

Pollard, R. (1992–93). 100 years in psychology and deafness: A centennial retrospective. *JADARA, 26*(3), 32–46.

Pollard, R. (1998). Psychopathology. In M. Marschark & M. D. Clark (Eds.), *Psychological perspectives on deafness* (Vol. II, pp. 171–197). Mahwah, NJ: Erlbaum.

Pollard, R. Q. (1996). Professional psychology and deaf people: The emergence of a discipline. *American Psychologist, 51*(4), 389–396.

Rainer, J. (1967). Background and history of New York State Mental Health Program For the Deaf. In J. Rainer & K. Altshuler (Eds.), *Psychiatry and the deaf* (pp. 1–4). New York: New York State Psychiatric Institute and New York University Center for Research and Training in Deafness Rehabilitation.

Rainer, J., Altshuler, K., Kallman, F., & Deming, W. E. (1965). *Family and mental health problems in a deaf population.* New York: Department of Medical Genetics, New York State Psychiatric Institute, Columbia University.

Robinson, L. (1978). *Sound minds in a soundless world.* Washington, DC: U.S. Department of Health, Education, and Welfare.

Roysircar, G., Webster, D. R., Germer, J., Palensky, J. J., Lynne, E., Campbell, G. R., … Blodgett-McDeavitt, J. (2003). Experiential training in multicultural counseling: Implementation and evaluation of counselor process. In G. Roysircar, D. S. Sandhu, & V. E. Bibbins, Sr. (Eds.), *Multicultural competencies: A guidebook of practices* (pp. 3–15). Alexandria, VA: Association for Multicultural Counseling and Development.

Sheridan, M. (2001). *Inner lives of deaf children: Interviews and analysis.* Washington, DC: Gallaudet University Press.

Sheridan, M. (2008). *Deaf adolescents: Inner lives and lifeworld development.* Washington, DC: Gallaudet University Press.

Sheridan, M., & White, B. (2008). Deaf and hard of hearing people. In T. Mizrahi & L. Davis (Eds.), *The encyclopedia of social work* (2nd ed., Vol. 2, pp. 1–10). New York, NY: Oxford University Press & Washington, DC: NASW Press.

Sheridan, M., White, B., & Mounty, J. (2010). Deaf and hard of hearing social workers accessing their profession. A call to action. *Journal of social work in disability and rehabilitation, 9*(1), 1–11.

Smith, K. L. (2007). *The experiences of Deaf counselors in developing their professional identity* (doctoral dissertation). Available from ProQuest Dissertations and Theses database. (UMI No. AAT 3255229)

Sussman, A. E., & Brauer, B. A. (1999). On being a psychotherapist with deaf clients. In I. W. Leigh (Ed.), *Psychotherapy with Deaf clients from diverse groups* (pp. 3–22). Washington, DC: Gallaudet University Press.

Szymanski, C. (2010). An open letter to training directors regarding accommodations for deaf interns. *APPIC E-Newsletter, III*(2), 16–17.

Vernon, M. (1969). The final report. In R. Grinker (Ed.), *Psychiatric diagnosis, therapy and research on the psychotic deaf* (pp. 13–37). Washington, DC: U.S. Department of Health, Education, and Welfare, Social and Rehabilitation Service.

Whyte, A., & Smith, K. (2010). Deaf college students. In I. W. Leigh (Ed.), *Psychotherapy with deaf clients from diverse groups* (2nd ed., pp. 261–280), Washington, DC: Gallaudet University Press.

9 Deaf People in the Criminal Justice System

Is a Culturally Affirmative Response Possible or Desirable?

Sue O'Rourke, Neil S. Glickman, and Sally Austen

Introduction

Many deaf people in the mental health system have challenging behaviors (Austen & Jeffery, 2007; Glickman, 2009; Vernon & Greenberg, 1999). Sometimes these challenging behaviors extend to anti-social and criminal actions which may bring them into the criminal justice system (CJS). Typically, the CJS is ill prepared to accommodate them, and deaf people, who often have experienced various forms of traumatization, victimization, and oppression, are further mistreated within the CJS. These deaf people are both victims and victimizers. Whatever the causes, some have become very dangerous people against whom society needs protection. On the other hand, many are badly in need of mental health and substance abuse treatment which can be even less accessible to them in the CJS than in the mental health system. Whereas the vast majority of deaf people, like the vast majority of hearing people, are healthy and productive members of society, the subgroup of deaf persons within the CJS, like the subgroup of deaf persons within the mental health system, contains a higher percentage of persons with what Glickman (2009) referred to as "language and learning challenges" (Miller, 2004; Vernon & Greenberg, 1999). They are highly vulnerable to abusive experiences within the CJS that are not intended to be elements of the constraints and even punishments that society imposes upon them.

This dialectic between deaf person as victim and victimizer, between a criminal justice system that sometimes fails to hold deaf people accountable for crimes on account of paternalistic assumptions, but other times subjects them to levels of mistreatment well beyond what their hearing counterparts experience, is explored through an imaginary conversation in this chapter. This conversation involves three people. A psychologist who specializes in work with deaf people provides necessary background about deaf people with behavioral challenges. A Deaf advocate comments, mostly from a culturally Deaf point of view, and advocates for the special needs of deaf people within the CJS. The Deaf advocate also challenges the psychologist and court official when they make questionable generalizations about deaf people and Deaf culture. A hearing court official argues back, from a no-nonsense, legal perspective, that all people should be held to the same standards of civil society, that deaf criminals are not deserving of special treatment, and that there is no place for paternalistic excuses for criminal behaviors in deaf people. This imaginary dialogue does not necessarily reflect how the arguments are played out in real life where, in fact, it may be the hearing court official who is more prone to the paternalistic biases that deaf people should be excused and "treated" rather than held accountable for bad behaviors. Sometimes it is the Deaf advocate, aware of how some deaf people may "play the deaf card" to get out of trouble, who may actually be harder on the deaf criminal.

Following this conversation, we present a discussion of best practice when working with deaf people in courts and prisons. In mental health treatment, we talk about "culturally affirmative" (Glickman, 1996; Glickman & Gulati, 2003) approaches with deaf persons as one form of best practice, but does this framework make sense in a forensic context which is not designed to heal? How does one accommodate the special needs of deaf persons in the CJS while still holding deaf criminals accountable for criminal behaviors? What "special treatment" should deaf defendants and criminals receive in a system designed primarily to contain and to punish, and only secondarily, if at all, to rehabilitate?

Psychologist:

Deaf people who offend are different from hearing people who offend. When you meet deaf people in the CJS, you'll notice that many do not seem like run of the mill criminals. Rather, some seem like people who are disabled cognitively, linguistically, socially and physically. Yes, we have deaf sociopaths (Vernon, Steinberg, & Montoya, 1999; Vernon & Vernon, 2010), but due to this pervasive language, cognitive, and psychosocial deficits, they are often not very skillful sociopaths.

In the United States, there have been three major studies of deaf prisoners. The first was a study of 97 deaf Texas state prisoners and focused on their language and educational abilities (Miller, 2004). The second was a study of 28 deaf individuals who were convicted, pled guilty, or were charged and awaiting trial for murder (Vernon et al., 1999). The third was a study of deaf sex offenders in a prison population (Miller & Vernon, 2003). All three studies found extremely high levels of both English and ASL incompetence such that, it was estimated, 20% to 50% of the prisoners were unable to receive due process, even if competent interpreters were provided.

We really don't have good data on deaf people in the CJS in Britain. The police and courts don't keep good records, and even when a criminal's deafness or language preference is noted, we rarely have other data about them. In Britain, using estimates of deaf people in the general population, we'd estimate that approximately 1 in 1,500 people are profoundly pre-lingually deaf. In 2005 a point prevalence study for the Department of Health indicated that there were 138 deaf prisoners out of a prison population at the time of roughly 80,000 (Gahir, O'Rourke, Monteiro, & Reed, 2011). This would suggest an over representation of deaf people in the prison population. Similarly, out of a population of around 500 patients in mental health hospitals in conditions of maximum security in the UK, we would predict 0.5 of a person in such facilities. In fact there have been a fairly stable number of around 10 such people at any one time. That's 20 times greater than one would expect given the percentage of deaf people in the population.

The data from the United States also indicates that deaf and hard-of-hearing people are substantially overrepresented in the CJS. A series of studies of prisons all over the United States showed that hearing loss severe enough to interfere with everyday functioning was two to five times more prevalent among prison inmates than among the regular population (LaVigne & Vernon, 2003; Vernon & Greenberg, 1999). A study by the American Speech and Hearing Association (ASHA) found that 10% to 15% of prison inmates in the United States have losses severe enough to warrant speech pathology, audiology special education and rehabilitation services (Jensema & Friedman, 1988). ASHA estimates that only 5% of the general population have hearing losses this severe (Vernon & Greenberg, 1999).

What do these figures suggest? That deaf people are more likely to commit crimes than hearing people? Both victimization and victimizing appear to be disproportionally high among deaf persons. A number of studies have found higher rates of maltreatment, physical and sexual abuse among deaf children than hearing children (Obinna, Krueger, Osterbaan, Sadusky, & DeVore, 2006; Sullivan, Brookhouser, & Scanlan, 2000; Sullivan, Vernon, & Scanlan, 1987; *White paper,* 2006). Other studies found higher rates of intimate partner violence among deaf adults (Anderso, Leigh, & Samar, 2011; Francavillo, 2009). This is one context for understanding what appears to be a high positive correlation between the experience of having a severe hearing loss in a hearing world and aggressive behaviors (Vernon & Greenberg, 1999). That deaf people are more often convicted? This is probably not true. That when convicted they stay in prison/hospital longer? It does appear to be true that once incarcerated it is much more difficult for a deaf patient or prisoner to be released back into the community (Baines, Patterson, & Austen, 2010).

Deaf Advocate:

It seems then that more deaf people get imprisoned, proportionally, than hearing people, and that when imprisoned, they stay there longer. This can't be because more deaf people are criminals than hearing people. It has to be because the criminal justice system is biased against deaf people.

Hearing Court Official:

What I've seen is just the opposite. Deaf people brought into courts and jails are treated much more leniently, because they are deaf, than hearing people. In fact, they are often let off. People feel sorry for them. If the CJS has a bias, it is actually in favor of excusing deaf people who commit crimes.

Deaf Advocate:

Then why are so many deaf people in the CJS?

Psychologist:

That's the question. Even with all the enabling that hearing people engage in, tolerating or excusing criminal behaviors in deaf people, there is still a high percentage of deaf people in prison. Why is this so? I think it's both because many deaf people develop what are called "challenging behaviors" which bring them to the attention of the CJS (Austen & Jeffery, 2007; Vernon & Greenberg, 1999) and also because the CJS, like society as a whole, does a pretty awful job of responding to deaf people. What I'd like to do is review why so many deaf people develop challenging behaviors, and how they find themselves involved in the CJS and the myriad ways that CJS officials respond to them.

Deaf Advocate:

Fine, but we've also got to talk about what it's like to be deaf and deal with police, courts and jails.

Psychologist:

Ok. Let's discuss the reasons for challenging behaviors first. One variable to consider early on is whether the deaf person has any cognitive impairment. When there is something neurologically wrong with the brain, one common result is poor impulse control and this leads to various kinds of problem behaviors. Most deaf people have average intelligence (Braden, 1994), and are not cognitively impaired, but the deaf population does have increased prevalence of disabilities some of which impact brain function in general or executive functioning (thinking and planning skills) in particular. Forty percent of deaf people have additional disabilities including subtle and not so subtle brain damage associated with their cause of deafness, for example meningitis, rubella, prematurity, or cytomegalovirus (Crocker & Edwards, 2004). There may therefore be neurological reasons for some types of offending which are akin to those seen in individuals with acquired brain injury or learning disabilities. Often, people who have these kind of brain problems also experience environmental stressors, like abuse, educational limitations, exposure to high crime areas and groups, which also influence them. It's hard to know how much of the behavior problem is due to cognitive impairment but it reasonable to think that brain pathology contributes to the problem.

Deaf Advocate:

I hope you are not suggesting that deaf people have bad brains. What about the most obvious problems that deaf people face, which are communication difficulties?

Hearing Court Official:

Whenever I start hearing people talking about "bad brains" or "bad environments," I'm getting ready to hear excuses made for bad behavior.

Psychologist:

I want to present to you, as best I can, a complex reality. Many people in the criminal justice system, deaf and hearing, have cognitive impairments. The main causes of deafness are also main causes for brain damage so that there is a disproportionate amount of brain damage in the deaf population, and some of this brain damage can contribute to violence (Vernon & Greenberg, 1999; Vernon et al., 1999; Young, Monteiro, & Ridgeway, 2000). It is perfectly reasonable to assume this is often a factor, even when we can't diagnose exactly what is wrong with the brain or know how much of problem behavior is caused by cognitive impairments. I know that talking about brain damage in *some* deaf people risks stigmatizing them further but cognitive impairments are very likely a factor in *some* offenders. Causation, though, is always complex. There are always many causes, and the choices people make are also causes.

Let's talk about these communication difficulties, especially those related to language deprivation. There is an enormous amount of research now into language deprivation in deaf children. Mayberry (2002) reported that many people who are born deaf experience severely delayed and impoverished language skills regardless of whether they sign, read, write, or speak. Gregory, Bishop, and Sheldon (1995) found that of their research sample of deaf students leaving school without graduating, 20% were not able to complete an interview in either speech or sign language despite being of normal IQ. Poor language impedes upon the ability to learn socially appropriate behavior (Kentish, 2007). When language skills are limited, there is a high likelihood the person will develop challenging behavior. This is easy to understand. When people don't have words or signs, they express themselves through behavior and they don't have the means to discuss and develop more appropriate ways of behaving. This is why we always teach children who are having a tantrum to "use your words." We know that having language is the key skill needed to control behavior.

Deaf Advocate:

You should not talk about language skill deficits in deaf people without explaining that most deaf people are raised without a rich exposure to the only languages they can acquire effortlessly and naturally, which are sign languages. There is nothing inevitable about deaf people having language problems. By far the main reason deaf people develop language problems is because they are not raised in a world of sign. When they do have a rich sign language environment, for instance when deaf children are raised by competently signing deaf parents, their language skills are much better.

Psychologist:

You are right about that. In deaf children of hearing parents (but rarely seen in deaf children of deaf parents), language deprivation is often linked to challenging behavior. In fact it is the case that deaf children of deaf parents do better than deaf children of hearing parents in many ways (Hindley, Hill, McGuigan, & Kitson, 1994). There are probably a number of reasons for this but access to an effective natural language is obviously a key factor. It is postulated that one reason why language deprivation leads to challenging behavior is that it impedes the development of a full "theory of mind" (the ability to think that others think differently from us or have different information from us) (Woolfe, 2001).

The origin of such behavioral difficulties, although organic in some cases such as deaf people on the autistic spectrum, often lies in early developmental experiences; being brought up in a linguistically impoverished environment where complex or subtle communication is not possible. For most deaf children, a linguistically impoverished environment is an environment without sign language. With no effective language, the child is exposed to visual gesture only, which may be sufficient for communicating about basic needs (e.g., "drink," bed,'" or "no"), but is woefully inadequate for discussing "why" or "because" or for reflecting on feelings and emotions. We therefore have a situation where many deaf adults, despite being of normal intellectual potential, do not develop psychosocial skills like coping with distress, problem solving, managing conflicts with other people, etc.

A leading scholar on the subject, Paijmans (2007) described the causal effect of poor language on executive functioning (the ability to observe one's own behavior and adapt it to different circumstances) and concluded that *"If either cognitive functioning or the ability to use language in thought and communication is disrupted, behaviour is likely to be maladaptive and inappropriate to the circumstances in which it occurs, and more likely to be perceived as 'challenging'"* (Paijmans, 2007 p. 105). In other words, the language deprivation that deaf children experience mostly because they are not raised with rich exposure to sign language often means they don't develop many crucial life skills. It also means they are vulnerable to developing severe behavioral problems.

Deaf Advocate:

Deaf children raised in deaf families are much more likely to develop good language skills and are therefore much less likely to develop behavior problems. What do we know about the language skills of deaf people in the CJS?

Psychologist:

There was one study of language skills of deaf people in a prison population. Miller (2004) studied the entire prison population in the state of Texas. She found that 50% of the deaf prison population read at or below the third grade level, using simple vocabulary and sentence structure. Twenty percent of deaf prisoners were judged to be linguistically incompetent, meaning they were not competent in either English or ASL. Another 47% of the deaf prisoners were ASL monolinguals. Most of the people in this latter group could understand the court proceedings as long as they were provided considerable education and very extensive accommodations were made in the communication process in the court (interpreters and deaf interpreters, and a much slower process of information exchange, allowing for consecutive interpreting) However, the educational and interpreting accommodations needed were rarely provided which meant that "20 to 50% of the deaf people arrested probably did not receive due process through their arrests, trials, and other legal proceedings, even with the provision of qualified sign language interpreters" (p. 118).

Language deprivation is one huge problem for deaf children. Others are isolation, confused identity, and low self-esteem. Isolation is an issue that follows many from cradle to grave (Austen, 2009). Due to social and educational policies and practices, many deaf children grow up socially isolated and then go on to struggle with isolation their entire lives. The 10% of deaf children who are born to deaf families, who tend to have social and linguistic role models, are more socially engaged and this is reflected in their higher self-esteem (Woolfe, 2001). Whilst in the past many deaf people attended specialist residential school and developed a peer group, mainstream education has become more common than specialist deaf education and many of the 90% of deaf people who have hearing parents grow up rarely meeting another deaf person. The tasks of childhood and adolescence are clustered around social communication: sharing interpersonal information, calculating norms and differences, finding one's place among one's peers. For deaf children who fail to establish a peer group, this isolation can lead to mental health problems and challenging behavior (Austen, 2009). Edwards and Crocker (2008) warn that the negative feedback a child with challenging behavior receives can negatively affect self-esteem which can result in further external displays of unhappiness such as more challenging behavior, or internalized displays such as anxiety, depressed mood and withdrawal.

Deaf Advocate:

You are completely neglecting the home many deaf people find in the Deaf Community. Many deaf people have rich social lives. Some find their social lives in the Deaf Community. Others are bicultural or multicultural. The idea of the lonely, isolated deaf person is a stereotype that fails to recognize how the Deaf Community and other deaf people, and their hearing allies I should add, become home for us.

Psychologist:

Yes, but many deaf people never find their way to the Deaf Community, and the widespread practice of educational mainstreaming has worsened this trend. There are exceptions to every generalization. There are plenty of happy, healthy, well-integrated deaf people, but you don't find them in the criminal justice system.

We're talking about reasons deaf people develop challenging behaviors. Social isolation is a reality for many deaf people. So also is lack of access to crucial information about the world (Pollard, 1998). Whilst many people fail to access information as a result of social isolation, poverty, oppression, mental health problems, poor education, abuse, illiteracy, sensory disability, or learning disability, deaf people are at increased risk of all of these variables (Austen & Coleman, 2004). An ability to learn the rules of behavior is impeded by a deaf child's lack of access to information, particularly information which hearing children pick up incidentally: overhearing a conversation, eavesdropping on their parents, listening to TV discussions. One leading Deaf mental health researcher commented that "the problem with deaf children is not that they can't hear, it's that they can't overhear" (Braden, 1994, p. 29). Lack of access to information can mean that the deaf person simply does not have the knowledge and skills to deal with life's difficulties in an appropriate manner or does not know the law or rules which govern how most people behave.

Deaf Advocate:

I think that you have to stress that all these problems are caused by society. They don't stem from anything inherent in being deaf. They stem from how hearing society responds to deaf people. There are also very few services available to help deaf people overcome such problems. Significant lack of services for deaf children and adults impacts on the ability of deaf people to receive the right care or education and to learn from their mistakes. From maternity services for a deaf mother, information for parents of a deaf baby, education services, mental health prevention services, mental health assessment and treatment facilities, habilitative housing, support through the criminal justice system, to the provision of services for deaf elders, the universal lack of services prevent deaf people from reaching their potential.

In terms of early intervention, whilst considerable efforts have been made towards early diagnosis of hearing loss (Hind, 2004), little is in place to offer equitable services to deaf people who begin to have difficulties. A hearing adult or child can access a myriad of services in the statutory, private and voluntary sectors. Low level interventions such as counseling can prevent problems becoming more serious. For the deaf person, it may be that the lack of linguistically appropriate services and funding problems may mean that minor problems have to become serious before the system rallies to offer some useful intervention.

I think you have to put the blame for these problems that deaf people have squarely on hearing people and hearing society. Look at the ways that hearing people respond to deaf people! Look at the low expectations they set for us!

Psychologist:

Yes, and then some deaf people live up to these low expectations. I know a deaf professional person who said this to me:

> *I don't bother buying a train ticket. If I get asked for my ticket on the train, I only have to sign that I am deaf and exaggerate my deaf speech and the ticket collectors run a mile. They will never prosecute me.*

Deaf Advocate:

A deaf professional said that? Shame on that person! You should know that many deaf people are appalled by that kind of attitude and behavior.

Psychologist:

True, but other deaf people seem to feel that because they have experienced so much prejudice and oppression, they are justified in taking advantage of hearing people, of "the system," whenever they can. They feel it is only fair.

Deaf Advocate:

You hear both arguments from deaf people. But most deaf leaders oppose that kind of abusive behavior. My mother, who was deaf, would always tell me to be proud of being deaf and that deaf people could do anything. She'd say, and most deaf professionals and leaders agree, that we don't advance our cause in society by playing the fool. We advance it by showing our best abilities.

Psychologist:

Remember that your deaf leaders and professionals, your most competent deaf representatives, are not the deaf people in the CJS.

In any case, the problem is that hearing people not only set low expectations, they don't set the same limits and rules as they do with other hearing people. A colleague of mine, who was leading an anger management session with some deaf patients, said to one of them:

So, if you get angry and damage something, like break a window or throw something at staff, what would be the consequences?

You know what the patient responded?

The staff would bring me a cup of tea and some biscuits.

Another colleague who is an administrator at a Deaf residential school in the United States tells the story of one of their deaf adolescents who was caught selling drugs on the school campus. The school authorities notified the police, hoping they would arrest the young man. Instead, the police took the young man out for ice cream, and then brought him back saying what a nice young man he was and how he promised never to do it again. The school authorities who actually tried to hold him accountable were furious, and the young man was certainly smart enough to figure out how he could use his hearing loss to his advantage.

Hearing Court Official:

Wow, that is truly outrageous.

Psychologist:

The difficulties that hearing people have setting limits with deaf people begins when the deaf child is born. The diagnosis of deafness is often a great shock to parents and the attitude of the parent about having a deaf child affects parenting style. Some parents regard their child's deafness as an impairment that needs to be corrected whilst others may regard it as an unexpected difference, which brings challenges that they expect to overcome. A child having a disability has been linked with both increased parental stress and with increased levels of behavior difficulties in the child, particularly where the parents find it difficult to adjust to their child's disability (Woolfson, 2004). The parents' confidence in their own ability to parent a deaf child has a big impact on their subsequent ability to discipline their child (Kentish, 2004).

Deaf Advocate:

This isn't true for most deaf parents of deaf children. They don't see being deaf as a tragedy. They are likely to see it as an opportunity to share a cultural identity and language. They may be quite happy their child is deaf, and feel very competent in raising a deaf child (Feher-Prout, 1996, cited in Kentish 2007).

You say that hearing parents don't know how to set limits with their deaf children. But sometimes it's just the opposite. Because they can't communicate with their deaf children, they do nothing but set limits. They can't explain, for instance, why the child shouldn't run across the street or go near the stove, so they just say "no" and punish and never let them do anything or take any risks. They don't provide reasons, and the child doesn't learn to use language to figure things out. Many deaf people I know have been traumatized by parents and school officials who did nothing but set limits, usually physically by spanking and other punishments.

Psychologist:

There is evidence for that too. Kentish (2007) reports that impaired communication between the parent and child can result in the parents being more likely to choose a physical response to child transgressions or to the child being withdrawn from the situation, rather than being verbally admonished. Knutson, Johnson, and Sullivan (2004) found that hearing mothers of deaf children, compared to hearing mothers of hearing children, used more physical discipline in response to depicted child transgressions and were more likely to escalate to physical discipline when the depicted child was described as persisting in the transgressions. In other words, deaf children are more likely to be raised by parents using physical discipline, not language-based discipline. The deaf child is not then required to think about the effect of their behavior on others or receive an explanation as to why their behavior was unacceptable. The consequence of these parenting strategies is that the child has less opportunity to learn from their mistakes. Kentish advises that, despite certain vulnerabilities, parents should not assume that poor social behavior is inevitable or that the parents' expectations of good behavior in the child should be diminished. Woolfson (2004) hypothesizes that where parents view their child's behavior through the lens of impairment, difficulties may be seen as an inevitable and unalterable part of being deaf, implying that they have no choice but to tolerate problematic behavior. Being deaf is sometimes regarded as a "tragedy" for which the parents feel they have to compensate the child so they are reluctant to upset or discipline the child. You get this collection of terrible parenting strategies. On the one hand, tolerating problematic behaviors. On the other hand, using corporal punishment (hitting) much more readily than they would with hearing children with whom they shared a language.

The result is that we hear story after story about deaf children who got away with bad behavior becoming adults who get away with bad behavior. We also hear about deaf people being physically and sexually abused, which means that authorities modeled bad behaviors for them. When parents can't communicate with their children, when they are overly physical and punitive, they are modeling poor problem solving and aggression. Whether getting away with bad behaviors, or having bad behavior modeled for them by parents who can't communicate with them, or both, deaf children are being taught to be aggressive. This doesn't always happen but it happens a lot. One deaf person whose parents tolerated his aggression told me,

My parents would tell my sister and brother off and smack them, but wouldn't discipline me at all. I think they thought I was behaving badly just because I was deaf. And they felt sympathy for me because I was deaf. Even if I was angry and started hitting out at people, they reacted with sympathy. I remember once that my father tried to send me to my room.... But my mother said, "Don't be hard on him. He can't help it—he's deaf."[1]

Another deaf person told me,

I really enjoyed being part of football violence. I would get excited about kicking people. Sometimes, we would hold someone's head down and then kick it. On one occasion I was taken to the police station but released without charge. On another occasion... a man was walking towards my gang so I picked up a bottle, smashed it and lost my head completely. I stabbed him in the face and it took off his nose. As a deterrent, the police said I was no longer allowed to watch home games.[2]

A deaf patient told a hearing counselor I know that

If the government reduce my benefits then I will have to get rid of my SKY TV, which will mean that I get bored, which will mean that I will start setting fires again.

The counselor replied,

But surely if you do that you will go to prison?

The patient then said,

No, last time when I set a fire in a block of apartments they just fined me £100.[3]

Hearing Court Official:

So, I can understand why hearing parents and school officials would excuse bad behaviors in deaf children, or at other times explode at them with physical anger, but I don't understand why court professionals would be more lenient on deaf people who commit crimes than on hearing people. By the time you are an adult, a crime is a crime, and the law operates under the assumption that people are responsible for their behaviors. Hearing people have traumatic childhoods also. We still send them to jail.

Psychologist:

Let's look at the reasons that professionals may treat deaf people who commit crime more leniently than hearing people who commit crime.

There is anecdotal evidence that deaf people who encounter the criminal justice system, particularly in the early stages of their criminal "career" are "let off." This evidence comes from two main sources:

1. from the experience of professionals asked to provide advice and reports to the courts in the matter of deaf people, in which the case is not pursued;
2. from deaf offenders themselves, their self-report and a knowledge of their history and the number of offences, which are not pursued until an escalation of offending means that they eventually are prosecuted and find themselves in prison or mental health services.

In examining the reasons why people make the decision to not prosecute deaf offenders we are again in the position of only having anecdotal evidence to draw upon directly. However a few studies looking at the difficulties faced by professionals working with deaf people in the CJS add weight indirectly to the speculation (Gahir et al., 2011; Smith, 2010).

We know that very few professionals in the CJS have any training in Deaf awareness and will have rarely encountered a deaf person. However, the failure to set boundaries is seen in clinicians, CJS professionals and families alike. If professionals who work with deaf people find it hard to assert boundaries, then how much harder will it be for others who have no prior experience with deaf people? There are a number of reasons why so many of these people have trouble setting limits and boundaries with deaf people.

First, there is the fear of being different

This situation arises when those around the deaf person have known him or her a long time and have generally tolerated negative behaviors. In such a situation, a new person may join the team, and feel that such behaviors should not be tolerated and considers being the first person to act differently by insisting on consequences being enforced. For the new staff member to take this action requires the courage to go against the collective opinion of the group, something that has been shown by Asch (1951) to be extremely difficult.

Second, there is the belief that somebody else will do it

Where a number of people are involved in the care of a deaf person with challenging behavior, each may expect one of the others to act, resulting in no one actually acting. This is known as "diffusion of responsibility." Imagine a case that over the years has involved a mental health team, social services, education services, and the client's family. Each may expect the other to take a lead in any criminal response and take the others' lack of action as evidence that nothing needs to be done. Equally, each may think that there are others who are more qualified or experienced to make that move. Bystander intervention studies from the 1960s onwards (Darley & Latane, 1968; International Ombudsman Association, 2009) have shown that the chances of a victim being helped by a bystander are more likely if the bystander is alone but becomes increasingly unlikely as the number of bystanders increases. Embarrassment at making an incorrect action is also known to inhibit bystander intervention. In the field of forensic work with deaf people, the victim is not so much someone who is being attacked at this moment but the potential future victims of the deaf perpetrators who are not been given a chance at protection by the inaction of staff in the present. This hypothetical danger in the future is even less tangible that a real danger one observes in the moment. If people believe that someone else will set limits around a danger that is real in the moment, they presumably would be even less likely to take steps around a hypothetical danger which somebody else may stop in the future. Thus, the easiest path for staff to take is to defer the hassle and risk of setting limits to someone else in the system of care.

Third, there is the fear of being ostracized from deaf people

It takes hearing people only a small step into Deaf Culture to discover that there are many ways to become labeled as having a bad attitude or being an oppressor. Being accepted into the Deaf Community is important to hearing professionals and is vindication of one's right and ability to work with deaf people. Hearing people may be so concerned to be politically correct and make such an effort to be non-discriminatory that they go to the other extreme of permitting unacceptable behaviors or choosing not to report crimes.

Sometimes, wayward behavior has been excused on the grounds of it being '"Deaf Culture." Membership of a minority culture is often used as a defense against criminal behavior, implying that the majority law does not apply. Although the Deaf Community as a whole does not defend violent behavior, individual deaf people may use Deaf Culture as an excuse for challenging behaviors. It is not just hearing people who tolerate challenging behaviors from deaf people. Deaf people can do this also. In fact, when deaf people argue that various forms of bad behavior are Deaf Culture, it becomes harder to conceptualize how a "culturally affirmative" response to challenging behaviors is appropriate. Must being culturally affirmative imply tolerating anti-social behaviors that are allegedly acceptable within a culture? It takes courage and good knowledge of a group to speak out against anti-social behaviors which members claim are socially sanctioned.

Deaf Advocate:

You've got this all wrong. While individual deaf people can say anything, just like individual hearing people can, the Deaf Community as a whole is not more tolerant of violence. I remember a story I read about a deaf patient on a culturally affirmative psychiatric inpatient program who was justifying his aggression as Deaf Culture. The hearing staff could not convince him this was a rationalization. It was only because they had a large group of deaf staff, and because these deaf staff were collectively willing to confront him that bad behavior was bad behavior, that he stopped using this excuse (Glickman, 2003a, p. 171). Deaf people often have a hard time being lectured to by culturally insensitive hearing people, but when you draw deaf people in as staff and allies, you have more tools to confront such challenging behaviors, not less.

Psychologist:

I guess you see deaf people taking both sides just as you see hearing people do. It can be very confusing deciding what Deaf Culture actually supports since people can attribute anything they want to it when that suits their purposes. I agree about the importance of deaf staff in a culturally affirmative setting (Cromwell, 2004). They have the credibility that hearing staff don't and can often be far more effective in challenging inappropriate behavior.

Fourth, there is the possibility of "hearing guilt"

This is the belief that because hearing people have oppressed deaf people, causing problems of low self-esteem, they therefore must tolerate bad behavior.

Hearing professionals presumably work in settings with deaf people in order to provide help. As a professional group aware of the difficulties faced by deaf people, they can acquire hearing guilt; feeling bad about what hearing people have done to deaf people and wanting to offer a different experience to their clients. In attempting to show understanding, a sympathetic and overly tolerant response to the inappropriate behavior may result. A psychology assistant told me this about a college experience:

> *I was one of five people at college who volunteered to spend break times with a deaf student who had cerebral palsy. Each day four of us would exchange gossip on how many times or how badly the deaf man had hit us with his walking stick. We accepted and expected this behavior. The fifth helper resigned the voluntary post as soon as she was hit for the first time saying, "His behavior is unacceptable and I do not have to put up with being hit." I was shocked. It had never occurred to me that we didn't have to put up with being hit. I thought it was part of the job; part of him.*[4]

Deaf Advocate:

I don't know what was going on there, but I suspect this deaf patient was in a hearing program. In the Deaf treatment programs I know of, a deaf man would not be permitted to hit people with a walking stick. I believe deaf staff would have been far less tolerant of such behavior than hearing staff. They would not have excused such behavior on account of Deaf Culture.

Psychologist:

There is the pathologizing of deaf people, the idea that deaf people are disabled or deficient and not responsible for their behavior. Professionals are not generally trained to work with deaf people and are as ignorant and prone to assumptions as the rest of the population. Those who are not used to working with deaf people frequently experience anxiety when having to do so for the first time, and, relying on oral and written communication skills, suddenly find themselves in a position where they are not understood and can feel extremely deskilled (Schlesinger & Meadow, 1972). Anxiety about doing the "wrong thing" and being inadvertently discriminatory can lead to paralysis and reluctance to operate in the usual way.

These professionals may experience confusion regarding the presentation of a deaf person. They may fall back unconsciously on prejudices they are unaware of, such as a presumption that deaf people are not competent or that deafness inevitably causes behavior problems. This leads to the notion that any aberrant behavior on the part of a deaf person is due to the hearing loss itself which, as an impairment or disability, requires sympathy and treatment rather than being dealt with via the CJS. This promotes a belief system in which it can become almost impossible for a deaf person to commit a crime. This unwittingly patronizing attitude on the part of professionals, whereby deaf people deserve sympathy and not punishment, may prevent deaf people taking responsibility for their actions at an early stage and may develop into entitlement beliefs.

Deaf Advocate:

Again, these are attitudes and behaviors that hearing people are far more vulnerable to than are deaf people. The idea that being deaf is a disability, that deaf people are not competent, that we deserve pity, comes from hearing people. Deaf people can spot a deaf con artist, or someone who uses his hearing loss to manipulate people, a mile away. Deaf people joke about how naïve hearing people can be, and how easy it can be to take advantage of them. If we had a more Deaf-centric way of raising deaf children, there would be much less tolerance for these kinds of paternalistic attitudes.

Hearing Court Official:

Let me tell you what often happens in court rooms. A deaf defendant is brought in, and immediately the court has to consider the time and expense involved in accommodating this person. In recent years, the courts have had to consider not only hiring interpreters but then hiring additional Deaf interpreters or Relays and then being told they have to modify the pace and flow of court proceedings in order to accommodate the interpretation process. If the crime is relatively minor, the court must consider whether it is "in the public interest" to devote the time and expense to adjudicating in this way. Court officials also believe that after putting out all this expense, the deaf defendant is likely to be released later due to sympathy from the jury. Court officials may conclude it's just easier to let the person go. If there is a local mental health resource they can refer the defendant to, they will be all the more inclined to do so.

Deaf Advocate:

It does take time and money to provide due process to deaf people in the CJS especially those deaf people who are not competent language users (LaVigne & Vernon, 2003). This should not provide a rationale for excusing criminal behaviors. However, if the charge is relatively minor, then a referral to a treatment program, if you can find one that works well with deaf people, may be the most fair and just response.

Psychologist:

But there are very few treatment programs well prepared to treat, or even manage, deaf people with challenging behaviors. It may be that some people are reluctant to report deaf people who engage in criminal behaviors because they know that treatment services are rarely available and that prison won't do anything but incarcerate the person. People may think, what's the point of calling the police?

The structure of services could almost be seen as encouraging poor boundary setting. For example, in the UK there are no deaf probation officers, despite their being plenty of deaf social workers. The systemic response to deaf people is overwhelmingly skewed towards referral for help, not limit setting through the CJS. Perhaps this reflects the expectation that deaf people will not require probation services (either because deaf people don't commit crimes or because it would not be worthwhile to send a deaf person through the CJS).

We respond in a similar way to deaf people who have sexual offending behaviors. We have strong evidence for a relatively high percentage of referrals of deaf persons to mental health facilities who have sexual offending problems (Young, Howarth, Ridgeway, & Monteiro, 2001). We also have evidence that a higher percentage of deaf persons in prison settings have sexual offending behaviors than hearing persons in prison settings (Miller & Vernon, 2003). However, there are far fewer treatment options for deaf persons with sexual offending behaviors than for hearing persons. With "low functioning" deaf people with sexual offending behaviors, we have virtually no treatment options. There has been some preliminary thinking on adapting sex offender treatment for deaf persons (Lemere, 2003) and some initial attempts to do so,[5] but this territory remains largely uncharted, even with the need.

With deaf sexual offenders, especially from the language and learning challenged group, one always has to wonder whether the problem sexual behaviors are mainly a result of deprivation of learning or what could be considered undersocialization. Perhaps, with the right communication and treatment environment, these behaviors would improve. For the vast majority of deaf persons with this problem, there are no counselors, much less treatment programs, with both the Deaf mental health care and sexual offending expertise needed.

Most hearing officials in a court will begin with the assumption that a deaf person with problem sexual behaviors who is arrested needs treatment, and that any use of the CJS and jails reflects cruel and unusual punishment. Defense attorney's certainly take advantage of the pity and paternalism that hearing people hold towards deaf people.

Deaf Advocate:

I want to point out some of the difficulties that deaf people have reporting crimes by other deaf people that they have witnessed or been the victim of. Sometimes deaf people don't know how to report a crime. Sometimes they are not sure what a crime is. Very often they are afraid of being misunderstood by the police.

While anyone who reports a crime can fear retaliation, deaf people have even more reasons to be afraid. The Deaf Community is very small and it can be the deaf person's only social outlet. To come forward to report a fellow deaf person can lead to being the subject of gossip and being ostracized. In addition, fierce loyalties and the belief that it is unacceptable to report a deaf person can lead to guilt at the thought of doing so and prevent such action.

A hearing person who speaks out against abuse or reports crime in their workplace or community has many opportunities to build up a social life elsewhere. A deaf person doing the same may have no such options, and the consequence of such action can be social isolation. This is particularly relevant to deaf professionals who may find huge conflicts of interest working within their own small community.

In addition, once a deaf person is known for committing a terrible crime, the Deaf Community may reject the person. I know of an instance where a linguistically impaired deaf man stabbed his girlfriend. She lived and received a lot of support from her local Deaf Community. The deaf man was eventually placed in a forensic hospital. He needed treatment and assistance from the Deaf Community but all the programs and most of the professionals who worked with deaf people wouldn't work with him. Deaf people know the high cost of facing rejection from the Deaf Community, and they have to weigh this also when they consider reporting a deaf person.

Psychologist:

The last reason that professionals who work with deaf people may be reluctant to report a deaf person who commits a crime is that it involves acknowledging that they were not successful in their work.

Within mental health services, care is taken to assess risk. Much time and effort is expended in developing treatment plans and strategies, all of which may be wasted if the person goes on to commit crimes and enters the CJS. When professionals report serious behavior problems, after tolerating or failing to address well less serious behavior problems, they can appear incompetent. Feelings of failure on the part of the individual professional or on behalf of the organizational leaders, often coupled with a lack of faith in the CJS to deal with deaf people appropriately, can lead to a reluctance to report crime. In addition to this, Deaf mental health services are often expected to be able to work with offenders even if this is unrealistic or beyond their expertise. Again, the presumption of the hearing people who refer these persons is that deaf people in trouble always need mental health care, not police or court intervention. When professionals in such settings assert that "treating" some deaf offenders is not appropriate, they run the risk of being seen as incompetent or uncaring by those with a more paternalistic view.

There are very few specialists and dedicated mental health programs for deaf people, and those which do exist face great pressure to be successful with every deaf client. Hearing programs and personnel generally realize that no program or person is successful with 100% of clientele, but specialists stake their reputations on their claim that they can do work that nonspecialists cannot. Specialized programs are very expensive and are constantly having to justify their existence. When they do not succeed in treating a high profile deaf person, such as a person whose challenging behaviors are especially severe and treatment resistant, or someone who is sociopathic and not mentally ill, it can provide fodder for those who question the need for such expensive, specialized services. They see lack of success with some high profile deaf criminal as evidence of the lack of lack of effectiveness of the program with the vast majority of its clientele who are more treatable. Hearing programs can fail with some clients and survive much more readily than Deaf programs.

Deaf Advocate:

You know, listening to you, you'd get the impression that deaf people have an incredibly easy time in the CJS. We get away with murder. When we do bad things, people offer us cookies. You are completely neglecting a very harsh reality of what deaf people actually experience when we come in contact with courts or when we are incarcerated. Remember that your own numbers suggest that the percentage of deaf people in the CJS is actually higher than it should be given our percentage in the population. So, clearly, deaf people are not all being excused for criminal behaviors. In fact, I'm wondering whether communication problems and other misunderstandings result in some deaf people being incarcerated unfairly. I'd like to focus on that.

Psychologist:

OK. Let's start with the experience of a deaf person being arrested. It is problematic to arrest a deaf person. The average police officer, not having met a deaf sign language user before, is likely to struggle with communication procedures. Most of the time, police officers do not have an interpreter on hand just in case they arrest a deaf person. They have to make the best of it. The deaf person may well not know why they are being arrested and may not understand the Police Caution in Britain or the Miranda warning in the United States,[6] whether spoken, written down, or delivered in sign language

Hearing Court Official:

Might it be easier, rather than deal with the awkward and embarrassing difficulties this presents, just to let off the deaf person with a warning (which they, of course, may not understand either)? You know this frequently happens. And some deaf people may even exaggerate their communication difficulties, not speak if they can, deliberately make strange noises or gesture in a way they know the police officer will find strange, just to get the officer to let them go.

Deaf Advocate:

Your concern is with deaf people being let off. Have you considered the issue of how traumatic being arrested can be for deaf people when it occurs? Being arrested is upsetting enough. Imagine not being able to communicate and possibly not knowing what you are being arrested for. You assume deaf people are trying to get away with something. Isn't it more reasonable to assume they are just trying to communicate? Sometimes they are making desperate attempts to make themselves understood by speaking as best they can, signing or gesturing, and the police officer misunderstands, jumps to conclusions about their being dangerous. The deaf person finds him or herself handcuffed behind their back, a truly aversive experience for a deaf person, equivalent to covering a hearing person's mouth. And then there is the worst case scenario, when police officers shout out to deaf people who don't respond. The police officer may draw the wrong conclusion and taser or shoot the deaf person. You need merely Google "deaf person mistakenly shot by police" to find plenty of examples.

Hearing Court Official:

Ok, that happens, but so does this. Even if the police decide to make an arrest, victims of deaf people are forever feeling sorry for the deaf person and dropping charges. For example, a deaf sex offender was eventually charged with sexually assaulting a woman in a shop. His exasperated family's comment was that he was always looking through windows at women in the neighborhood and had sexually assaulted a number of women in the local area and at his place of work, but no one would press charges as they felt sorry for him because he was deaf. They were very clear that, as a result, he felt he could pursue his tendencies to accost women and ask them for sex without fear of reprisals.

The clinician involved with a sex offender client 10 years before his incarceration in a medium secure facility said the following:

We all sort of thought he was pathetic rather than dangerous. Although his treatment of women was wrong, we often commented that the women had to take some responsibility for clearly telling him "No" as it was obvious from his looks and his voice that he has additional needs. When I heard that he had been caught having followed a woman home, broken into her house, and held a knife to her throat, I wondered how he had had gone from pathetic and harmless to threatening and dangerous. I guess the answer was in the myriad of clinicians who, like me, took no measures to make him aware of the inappropriateness of his actions.[7]

Deaf Advocate:

Hearing people and hearing society treat deaf people like children. What kind of communication skills did this deaf man have? Did people surround him converse in sign language so he'd have the ability to learn to communicate like anyone else? Did he receive education in a language he could understand? Did his parents or school personnel teach him social skills? What opportunities has he had to meet women, to date, to have sexual experiences? You take a man and make him completely powerless and then you are surprised when he acts in a desperate way. Where does the fault really lie?

Hearing Court Official:

Every criminal in jail, deaf or hearing, has a story about who has done him wrong. It's always everyone's fault except the person who does the crime. What's easier for a criminal than to blame society?

Psychologist:

We have laws that lay out the rights of criminal defendants and the responsibilities of police and courts to accommodate defendants with special needs. In Britain, appropriate accommodation to consider the deaf person's needs when under arrest is laid out in the Police and Criminal Evidence Act (PACE). The PACE guidelines indicate that an interpreter should be present when interviewing a deaf person. In the United States, the Americans with Disabilities Act requires that police officers ensure "effective communication" with people who are deaf or hard of hearing, and goes on to lay out what effective communication looks like. However, we all know that legal standards are not always observed in practice, and that the general ignorance people have about the language skills and deficits of deaf people and the interpreting process also occurs within the CJS. The possibility of misunderstanding and misjudgment is always there, and increases dramatically when the deaf person has poor language skills, limited life experiences and a poor fund of information about the world. In such situations, these communication barriers are not overcome by the presence of sign language interpreters (LaVigne & Vernon, 2003).

Deaf Advocate:

Well, we also know that interpreters are usually not provided during arrest procedures. When people claiming to be interpreters are provided, like the police officer or secretary who took a sign language class, they are often unqualified. And even when qualified interpreters are provided, this is no guarantee of effective communication, especially, as you say, with those deaf people who have poorer language skills. You talk about deaf people abusing the system. What deaf people see is the system abusing them. We are arrested. We are denied communication, including the ability to use our hands, during the arrest process. We are not informed of our rights, or even of why we are being arrested and what will happen to us, in a way we can understand. And everything we say and do, including misperceptions on the part of the police about such things as "he was angry and threatening" is used against us. How many times, when they say we were angry and threatening, were they misunderstanding based on their ignorance of sign language and Deaf Culture?

It doesn't get any better for us when we get into court. The same problems of communication access and ensuring that deaf defendants can participate meaningfully in their own defense occur. All the misunderstandings that hearing people have of deaf people play out in court. Hearing court officials make assumptions about deaf persons' level of competence and responsibility based on prejudicial stereotypes about deaf people, and they don't get the guidance they need to assure they are providing equal access.

With the linguistically incompetent group, the roughly 20% of deaf prisoners who cannot understand court proceedings even with an interpreter present (Miller, 2004), you have almost a guarantee of a miscarriage of justice. Again, the one researcher who has studied the language skills of deaf people in prison estimates that as many as 50% are denied due process because of language deficits or because suitable accommodations were not made for their special learning needs (Miller, 2004). Linguistic incompetence is virtually unknown in people of normal intelligence apart from people born deaf who were deprived of adequate sign language exposure growing up. It is not the usual reason people are found incompetent to stand trial (U.S.) or unfit to plead (Great Britain.) The usual reason is mental illness or mental incompetence. Linguistic incompetence is usually not recognized. Deaf people found incompetent to stand trial are presumed to be incompetent due to mental illness or mental defect, and are likely to face long periods of psychiatric hospitalization, which never address the problem of language incompetence and which wouldn't correct that problem even if it did. Thus deaf people can be arrested for relatively minor offenses, found incompetent, and sent for involuntary hospitalization for much longer periods than they would have to face if they were found guilty. The most famous case of this kind in Great Britain was of a deaf man named Glen Pearson. He was accused of stealing two light bulbs and £5.00 (about $8.00). He was found "unfit to plead" and forced to spend nearly 4 months in a psychiatric hospital. If he had just been found guilty, he probably would have been released with a warning or minor fine (Young, et al., 2000).

Then there is the horror of being deaf and in prison (Vernon, 2010). Prisoners may fear being raped, beaten, killed, or subject to other forms of violence. Anyone who is perceived as weak is especially vulnerable to such violence from both other prisoners and from prison officials. As you can imagine, deaf people are sometimes easy targets.

Very few prisons offer any accommodations for deaf prisoners. Although technological developments have assisted deaf people enormously in the community, they are of little help in a prison. Mobile phones are not permitted, nor emails, nor texting, and it is likely to be a battle to get funding for a text phone. Video phones are virtually nonexistent. General ignorance about interpreting is even worse in a prison. The majority of prison staff simply do not see the issue and think, for example, that a fellow prisoner using a voice phone and "interpreting" will suffice.

A deaf person in prison is unlikely to have any deaf peers or staff with the ability to communicate in sign language. Even when there is more than one deaf person in prison, they may be kept apart for fear that they might sign to each other and "plot" something. Teasing and bullying looms large in prison, and many deaf prisoners find themselves treated like the "village idiot" by becoming the butt of jokes with others mimicking sign language, poking fun at their voices, or simply being pushed around. If people in the wider society assume deaf people are incompetent, imagine the prejudice they are subjected to in a prison setting where they have no safe place, like the Deaf Community, and very good reasons to be afraid.

Within the prison service, part of the rehabilitation of offenders involves education and/or work. There are many examples of deaf prisoners being refused access to these activities simply because they are deaf; either because officials assume that they are incompetent or due to difficulties in obtaining funding for interpreters for classes. One ex-prisoner told me that he was furious about this as he wanted to receive this education partly because he wanted to improve his English and partly because prisoners got paid for attending education classes. He pestered and pestered to go to classes until, finally, the authorities agreed. He had no interpreters and a teacher with no deaf awareness who kept turning away from the class. He didn't feel he learned much but, by the end, *he had taught her* some basic skills in working with deaf students!

Prisoners show they are ready for parole by participating in these rehabilitation offerings. The consequences of lack of access to these programs depends on whether or not the deaf prisoner is serving a life sentence. For those on the time limited sentence, it means the deaf person is released having had no rehabilitation and is, therefore, more likely to reoffend. For the lifer who has reached his or her minimum sentence (tariff) before parole is considered, the issue is that parole is unlikely to be considered unless there is a demonstrable reduction in risk of re-offending. How is that demonstrated if not by attending treatment groups, showing an understanding of the offending process, and learning how to avoid reoffending? For the deaf person, unable to access such groups, the prospect is to remain in prison well beyond the tariff. Alternatively, prison authorities may waive this condition, potentially recommending someone for parole who has committed a dangerous offense and still holds the same beliefs and attitudes which led to the commission of the crime in the first place.

Getting an interpreter, however, is no guarantee of equal access. We've already seen that at least 20% of deaf prisoners are so significantly language impaired that they wouldn't benefit from the existing rehabilitation programs even if an interpreter was available. There are others who could benefit, but the rehabilitation offerings would need to be more tailored for them. If this is true in a mental health or educational setting, it is certainly true in a prison setting. These deaf prisoners get no rehabilitation while they are likely to be subject to multiple and unending kinds of abuse. You can see there is good reason for people to think twice before sending a deaf person to a setting where there is no chance of rehabilitation and considerable likelihood that mental health problems will be made far worse from the experience.

With no one to communicate with, no ability to contact the outside world, little activity, and no escape from teasing and bullying, it is hardly surprising that deaf people in prison are at risk for mental health problems.

Psychologist:

Many prisons will ask for an expert opinion regarding the mental health needs of deaf offenders. In the absence of the ability to communicate, there is every chance that a deterioration in mental health will go unnoticed. Those prisoners who act out their distress by, for example, smashing up their cells, may be more likely to be referred, whilst those who are quietly depressed and "at risk" are missed. In the event that deaf prisoners are assessed by a specialist psychologist or psychiatrist, untreated mental illness, personality disorder, or learning disability may lead to a recommendation to transfer to a specialist secure mental health facility. In this case there is an opportunity for appropriate intervention aimed at reducing reoffending. Those deaf prisoners without a mental health need will remain in prison without the opportunity for learning and development which will reduce their risk. Thus at the end of their journey from maladaptive childhood behavior, through minor criminal activity, to more serious crime leading to incarceration, they are still not in a position to learn to behave differently.

Hearing Court Official:

Well, you can't be suggesting that we just let deaf people who commit crimes go free? How should the legal system deal with deaf people who are accused or guilty of committing crimes?

Conclusions

Although, as noted above, research into deaf persons in the CJS is very limited, the overall picture we're describing is this: There does appear to be a positive correlation between the experience of having a severe hearing loss in a hearing society and being both the victim and perpetrator of challenging behaviors. Some reasons deaf people have high rates of such challenging behaviors were described above. It also appears that deaf people are significantly overrepresented in the CJS in the United States and Great Britain. At the same time, the dominant response of authorities from parents to teachers and counselors to police and courts, seems to be to excuse deaf people when they show less serious challenging and anti-social behaviors. It is likely that many deaf persons accused of crimes are not arrested, brought to trial, and convicted until their crimes are relatively serious. A paternalistic attitude of not holding deaf people accountable for challenging and anti-social behaviors appears to coincide with widespread violation of their rights. Indeed, it appears that one reason that deaf people are excused from arrest and trial is because CJS officials find it cumbersome to insure their rights are met. Thus, deaf people, who suffer more violence but also have higher rates of challenging behaviors encounter a criminal justice system that vacillates between treating them, on the one hand, as nothing but victims, and excusing challenging behaviors and, on the other hand, systematically violating their rights and traumatizing them further.

When deaf people are brought to trial, there is good reason to believe they are denied due process 20% to 50% of the time either because they are not linguistically competent to stand trial or because the court does not put in place the accommodations necessary to ensure they can participate competently in their own defense. Once incarcerated, deaf people are subject to all the horrors of the prison system with minimal attention paid to their communication needs, and one result of this is that they do not have access to education and rehabilitation programs that could provide them path a better path once released. Another result is that prison life is likely to traumatize them further, resulting in worsening mental health and greater likelihood of a repetition of criminal behaviors upon release.

These conclusions are offered as likely hypotheses based on the research and clinical/forensic experience available. More research is needed to verify these conclusions, and such research would be part of a culturally affirmative response to deaf offenders. But what would such a culturally affirmative response to deaf offenders in the criminal justice system look like?

It's much easier to discuss culturally affirmative mental health care of deaf people than a culturally affirmative response from the CJS because the mental health system is designed to heal and the CJS isn't. People who are viewed as disabled or disadvantaged elicit much more sympathy than those viewed as criminal. Still, there are many insights from the culturally affirmative model that are applicable to the CJS in designing interventions with deaf criminals that are more fair and balanced, that neither excuse anti-social behaviors nor victimize deaf persons further, that hold deaf criminals accountable while taking into account their special communication needs.

To begin with, within the culturally affirmative model, it is explained that people who work with deaf people need to be specially trained, that they need to have undergone some personal and cultural development, and they need to have acquired a particular body of relevant knowledge and specialized skills.[8] These three dimensions of self-awareness, knowledge, and skills, should inform their thinking and actions in responding to challenging and anti-social behaviors from deaf children and adults, both within and outside the CJS.

With regard to self-awareness, we've seen how paternalistic attitudes towards deaf persons contribute to the development of challenging behaviors. Low expectations for deaf people, the idea that they are not capable of behaving well, and shouldn't be held accountable for challenging behaviors, contributes to the phenomena of excusing these behaviors until they become more serious. Deaf people learn to "play the deaf card" from hearing and other deaf people who convey, in one way or another, the notion that "he or she is deaf and can't help it." Excusing anti-social behaviors from deaf people is not respectful or empowering. A culturally affirmative response surely must start from the attitude that deaf people are capable and should be held to the same expectations of civil society as hearing people. For example, when a deaf adolescent is arrested for selling drugs, or assault, or theft, it does them no help to divert them from the CJS on the grounds that they are deaf and therefore need help not incarceration. Such enabling behaviors from authorities teach deaf adolescents how to become career criminals.

At the same time, when deaf children are raised in disabling environments that deprive them of access to the only languages they can acquire effortlessly and completely, sign languages, which results in extreme kinds of language dysfluency and concomitant delays in the development of essential psychosocial skills, it seems essential that appropriate rehabilitation programs be available as dispositions for courts.

Deaf children, adolescents, and adults are in need of school, rehabilitation, and mental health programs to address effectively, in a linguistically and culturally appropriate manner, these challenging behaviors. As Deaf mental health care, as described in this book, becomes more of a practical reality, the hope is that parents, teachers, counselors, police, and courts will have more resources to draw upon, more disposition options other than jail. Ultimately, one hopes that personnel from the criminal justice systems and mental health systems could collaborate to fashion court ordered and probation monitored treatment that is linguistically and culturally appropriate, and to hold deaf defendants accountable if they fail to complete the treatment or go on to offend again. This "carrot and stick" approach is probably fair and balanced as long as the treatment resources are available.

The self-awareness dimension of this work refers to the working through of unexamined prejudices and biases about deaf people that prevent them from having all the rights and responsibilities of other members of society. This certainly must include greater respect for sign languages and Deaf Culture, and a breaking down of the barriers to achieve full inclusion of deaf persons in schools, employment, and all other dimensions of society.

The knowledge dimension refers to specialized knowledge about deaf people that anyone assessing or responding to them in the CJS should acquire. Knowledge of the diverse ways that deaf people communicate, the relationship between competency/fitness to plead and the kinds of resources and process adaptations courts are able to make, is especially essential. The skills dimension refers to specialized skills needed to do forensic work with deaf defendants. These dimensions are addressed in part in the previous dialogue and in the recommendations that follow.[9] Beyond that, a culturally affirmative response to deaf defendants must surely involve developing deaf forensic units and, if they are shown to have a mental health problem, deaf forensic hospital settings such as exist at various locations in the UK.

Mental health facilities for deaf people have developed over the last 40 years, but little attention has been paid to the plight of deaf people in the CJS. In considering whether the CJS can become culturally affirmative, this is not a merely a question of improving the lot of deaf people but also about enabling the legal process to be more effective. Taking findings from the mental health literature, we are able to make the following recommendations:

1. Improving process: Several authors make recommendations about access to interpreters, deaf relays, and monitoring of communication in court (LaVigne & Vernon, 2003; Vernon & Andrews 2011). The use of video for police interviews and in court would be a major step forward in assuring the safety of proceedings. The PACE guidelines in the UK recommend video recording police interviews with deaf people, but it is not obligatory and has funding implications which make it unlikely. In the UK, the use of appropriately qualified interpreters in court is mandatory. The practice of three interpreters working together is now commonplace in Great Britain; one interpreting, a second monitoring/assisting and a third resting.

   A recent development which goes some way to meet the need to monitor process is the introduction of intermediaries to work with vulnerable individuals in the CJS such as victims, witnesses and defendants. There are a number of deaf intermediaries who can work with the deaf defendant (or victim or witness) in court to explain the process, take time to explain concepts which are difficult to understand and alert the court to any difficulties. The intermediary often engages in some ad hoc Deaf Awareness training during the proceedings and informally monitors the communication process.

   The difficulties of providing appropriate accommodation for deaf people through the CJS can be overcome with expert support and advice without the necessity for an overly lenient approach. Such advice should be obtained early in the legal process. If the arrest and police interview is criticized after the event, for example, for not having a suitably qualified interpreter, this can compromise the case, leading to it being dropped, the person being "let off," with no attention being paid to the deaf person's needs for rehabilitation, and, of course, creating the risk of future victims. Although dealing with deaf people who commit minor offenses may seem overly complicated and expensive, the consequences of not doing so may be that the behavior escalates and we see greater numbers of deaf people in prison and secure mental health facilities having committed more serious crimes.

2. Dealing with linguistic incompetence: the courts do not cope well with the notion of being incompetent or unfit to plead due to linguistic incompetence (LaVigne & Vernon, 2003; Vernon & Miller, 2001). In the United States, linguistically incompetent deaf individuals may be incarcerated in secure mental health facilities for long periods of time, incarcerations that are not necessarily commensurate with the seriousness of the crime they committed, and where attempts to rehabilitate them or "make them competent" are doomed to failure (Vernon & Miller, 2001, 2005; Vernon & Raifman, 1997). The situation used to be much the same in the UK prior to the Glen Pearson case mentioned earlier, where being unfit to plead automatically led to a period in a high secure mental health hospital. As a result of his

appeal, when he was deemed unfit to plead, there is now the possibility of a "Trial of the Facts" involving a lower burden of proof and with the possibility of a range of dispositions if it is found that the person, in all probability, committed the crime. This means an incompetent defendant may receive treatment in in a less secure facility if that is appropriate to the crime and level of risk. UK courts still struggle with the notion of being unfit to plead due to linguistic incompetence or deprivation of knowledge and experience, as this does not fall readily within the classifications of mental disorder within the Mental Health Act (1983 amended 2007). Nevertheless, this has been successfully put forward as a reason for being unfit to plead both in Great Britain and the United States (Vernon & Miller, 2001). However, it is done on an individual basis rather than being more generally recognized.

3. Improving knowledge: Improved knowledge of deaf people and Deaf Culture on the part of professionals who work in the CJS, from police officers and prison staff to judges, would dramatically improve the situation for deaf people as well as the efficacy of the legal process. It is unrealistic to expect every professional within the CJS to have expert knowledge on deaf people. Yet, a basic awareness does not seem unrealistic. Most professions have a list of mandatory training which includes some aspect of disability and diversity awareness. Part of this needs to be the clear message that deaf people in the CJS are best served by the professionals seeking expert advice in order to deal with the case appropriately; making fair accommodation for the deaf person's needs without assuming incompetence or making excuses based on the person being deaf.

4. Research: Vernon and Greenberg (1999) point out that our knowledge about deaf people in the CJS is limited and needs to be improved via systematic collection of accurate data. Police, courts, prisons, and mental health facilities would benefit from keeping records of the number of deaf people in the CJS and the difficulties they encounter. In addition, it would make available vital information that would lead to research into the paths deaf people take into and through the CJS and, ultimately, to improved services.

5. Organizational change: There is growing acceptance in the field of mental health that deaf people are unable to access appropriate assessment and treatment unless this is delivered in sign language by skilled professionals in a culturally affirmative milieu. In the UK there are a number of specialist mental health hospitals at different levels of security which provide this, despite the difficulties of grouping deaf people with a range of difficulties together. The prison service would undoubtedly benefit from the same approach so that expertise can be developed, staff trained, and rehabilitation programs developed. There is resistance to this for a number of reasons, none of which seem

to be valid in our opinion. It is argued that prisons are of various levels of security, and that therefore a Deaf unit will not meet different security needs. With the numbers of deaf people in prison, small specialist units at varying levels of security would seem feasible. Prisoners are generally kept close to their home area, and sending prioners to specialist units goes against this policy. These same arguments have been used to oppose the development of specialized Deaf mental health programs.

People in the Deaf Community and professionals who work with them have long argued that the benefits of creating such specialized treatment programs far outweighs the costs of having to travel or being farther from home (Glickman, 2003b).[10] Prisoners are frequently moved from facility to facility, which, in the case of deaf prisoners, would need to change. However, when staff in a prison have developed some ability to sign, or other accommodations have begun to be made for them, there is less reason to move deaf prisoners to settings where there is even less awareness of their special needs.

It seems that the arguments against having small Deaf units in prisons are not robust and merely reflect an ongoing lack of understanding of the needs of deaf prisoners. However, until this issue is addressed, possibly as a result of a legal challenge under the Equality Act (UK, 2010) or Americans with Disabilities Act (1990), deaf people in prison will continue to be seriously disadvantaged compared to their hearing peers.

Returning to our imaginary dialogue, the last words in this chapter come from our Deaf advocate.

Deaf Advocate:

Since the mental health systems in wealthy countries like the United States and Great Britain still struggles mightily to serve deaf people well, then how much more serious remains the plight of deaf people in poorer countries where there is so little understanding of us or school, rehabilitation, or mental health services that meet our needs. I don't want to excuse criminal behaviors in some deaf people, but neither must we lose sight of the continuing plight of deaf people for such basic human rights and needs as having a language and being included fully within all the social institutions of a society. A culturally affirmative response to deaf people who commit crimes would have to include, at a minimum, addressing our communication needs appropriately in court, creating culturally and clinically competent treatment resources for issues like substance abuse and sexual offending, and bringing those deaf people who must be incarcerated, and who choose this, into prison settings with other deaf prisoners. At least there, we'd have the opportunity to communicate with other people, much less likelihood of being bullied, abused, or even murdered by hearing offenders or staff, and much greater likelihood that we could get technological access, like video phones, that we need to communicate with family, and rehabilitation offerings that would enable us to learn the skills to become safe members of society.

Indeed, it is only when you allow us to be incarcerated together that you can do the research that even begins to articulate how to provide deaf offenders with appropriate culturally affirmative rehabilitation. I appreciate the discussion above about not excusing challenging behaviors in deaf people, but I think we have a very long way to go before we have a criminal justice response to deaf people that approaches fairness and justice. It's quite easy to preach that deaf people should be held to the same standards of civil society as everyone else. Who can argue against that? It's much more difficult to create the social change, the fully inclusive educational, mental health, and rehabilitative institutions; the end of discrimination and oppression, the result of which would be more happy, healthy, and successful deaf people who don't have the challenging behaviors that bring them into the criminal justice system in the first place.

Notes

1. Adult who went through the whole CJS including a high secure psychiatric facility (Austen & Two Service Users, 2007).
2. Personal communication to Sally Austen.
3. Adult who had had no current criminal record and no contact with forensic services, personal communication to Sally Austen.
4. Personal communication to Sally Austen, 1983.
5. Nick Horne and Will Hough, personal communication to Sue O'Rourke, 2011.
6. The Miranda warnings originated in a U.S. Supreme Court ruling, *Miranda v. Arizona*, 384 U.S. 436, which set forth the following warning and accompanying rights, which police must communicate to persons when arresting them:
   • You have the right to remain silent;
   • Anything you say can be used against you in a court of law;
   • You have the right to consult with a lawyer and have that lawyer present during the interrogation;
   • If you cannot afford a lawyer, one will be appointed to represent you;
   • You can invoke your right to be silent before or during an interrogation, and if you do so, the interrogation must stop.
   • You can invoke your right to have an attorney present, and until your attorney is present, the interrogation must stop.
   The UK police caution refers to the requirement that, after informing the person he/she is under arrest, the officer will state:
   "You do not have to say anything. But it may harm your defense if you do not mention when questioned something which you later rely on in court. Anything you do say may be given in evidence."
7. Personal communication to Sally Austen, 2002.
8. See introduction and Glickman, 1996.
9. More is found in this text in Chapter 8 on the training of Deaf mental health specialists.
10. See Chapter 4, this volume.

References

American with Disabilities Act. (1990). Retrieved August 19, 2012 from http://ww.ada.gov/ last

Anderso, M. L., Leigh, I. W., & Samar, V. J. (2011). Intimate partner violence against Deaf women: A review. *Aggression and Violent Behavior, 16,* 200–206.

Asch, S. E. (1951). Effects of group pressure upon the modification and distortion of judgment. In H. Guetzkow (Ed.), *Groups, leadership and men.* Pittsburgh, PA: Carnegie Press.

Austen, S. (2009). Mental health and prelingual deafness. In J. Graham & B. D. Baguley (Eds.), *Ballantynes' Deafness 7th Edition* (pp. 202–212). Oxford, England: Wiley-Blackwells.

Austen, S & Coleman, E. (2004). Controversy in deafness: *Animal Farm* meets *Brave New World.* In S. Austen & S. Crocker (Eds.), *Deafness in mind. Working psychologically across the lifespan* (pp. 3–20). London, England: Whurr.

Austen, S., & Jeffery, D. (Eds.). (2007). *Deafness and challenging behavior: The 360° perspective.* Chichester, England: Wiley.

Austen, S., & Two Service Users. (2007). The deaf service user's perspective of challenging behaviour and restraint. In S. Austen & D. Jeffery D (Eds.), Deafness and challenging behaviour. The 360º perspective (pp. 3–16). Chichester, England: Wiley.

Baines, D., Patterson, N., & Austen, S. (2010). An investigation into the length of hospital stay for deaf mental health service users. *Journal of Deaf Studies and Deaf Education, 15*(2) 179–184.

Braden, J. P. (1994). *Deafness, deprivation and IQ. Perspectives on individual differences.* New York, NY: Plenum Press.

Crocker, S., & Edwards, L (2004). Deafness and additional difficulties in deafness. In S. Austen & S. Crocker (Eds.), *Deafness in mind: Working psychologically across the lifespan* (pp. 252–269). London, England: Whurr.

Cromwell, J. (2004). Training deaf professionals. In S. Austen & S. Crocker (Eds.), *Deafness in mind: Working psychologically across the lifespan* (pp. 317–328). London, England: Whurr.

Darley, J. M., & Latane, B. (1968). Bystander intervention in emergencies: Diffusion of responsibility. *Journal of Personality and Social Psychology, 8,* 377–383.

Edwards, L., & Crocker, S. (2008), Psychological processes in deaf children with complex needs. An evidence-based practical guide. London, England: Jessica Kingsley.

Equality Act. (2010). Retrieved August 19, 2012 from http://www.homeoffice.gov.uk/equalities/equality-act/

Francavillo, G. S. R. (2009). *Sexuality education, sexual communication, rape myth, acceptance, and sexual assault expeernce among deaf and hard of hearing college students* (Unpublished doctoral dissertation). University of Maryland, College Park.

Gahir, M., O'Rourke, S., Monteiro, B., & Reed, R. (2011) The unmet needs of deaf prisoners: A survey of prisons. *International Journal on Mental Health and Deafness, 1*(1) 58–63.

Glickman, N. (1996). What is culturally affirmative psychotherapy? In N. Glickman & M. Harvey (Eds.), *Culturally affirmative psychotherapy with deaf persons* (pp. 1–55). Mahwah, NJ: Erlbaum.

Glickman, N. (2003a). Culturally affirmative inpatient treatment with psychologically unsophisticated Deaf people. In N. Glickman & S. Gulati (Eds.), *Mental health care of deaf people: A culturally affirmative approach* (pp. 145–201). Mahwah, NJ: Erlbaum.

Glickman, N. (2003b). Culturally affirmative mental health treatment for Deaf people: What it looks like and why it is essential. In N. Glickman & S. Gulati (Eds.), *Mental health care of Deaf people: A culturally affirmative approach* (pp. 1–32). Mahwah, NJ: Erlbaum.

Glickman, N. (2009). *Cognitive behavioral therapy for deaf and hearing persons with language and learning challenges.* New York, NY: Routledge.

Glickman, N., & Gulati, S. (2003). *Mental health care of Deaf people: A culturally affirmative approach.* Mahwah, NJ: Erlbaum.

Gregory, S., Bishop, J., & Sheldon, L. (1995). *Deaf people and their families: Developing understanding.*, Cambridge, England: Cambridge University Press.

Hind, S. (2004). Newborn hearing screening: the screening debate in In S. Austen & S. Crocker (Eds.), *Deafness in mind. Working psychologically across the lifespan* (pp. 20–36). London, England: Whurr.

Jensema, C. K., & Friedman, R. W. (1988). Criminal justice and the deaf. Part II. *The Voice, 4*(7), 19–22.

Hindley, P. A., Hill, P. D., McGuigan, S., & Kitson, N. (1994). Psychiatric disorder in deaf and hearing-impaired children and young people: a prevalence study. *Journal of Child Psychiatry, 35,* 917–934.

Kentish R (2007), Challenging behaviour in the young deaf child. In S. Austen & D. Jeffery D (Eds.), *Deafness and challenging behaviour. The 360° perspective* (pp. 75–88). Chichester, England: Wiley.

International Ombudsman Association. (2009). Retrieved from http://www.ombudsassociation.org/

Knutson, J. F., Johnson, C. R., & Sullivan, P. M. (2004). Disciplinary choices of mothers of deaf children and mothers of normally hearing children. *Child Abuse and Neglect, 28,* 925–937.

LaVigne, M., & Vernon, M. (2003). An interpreter isn't enough: Deafness, language, and due process. Wisconsin *Law Review, 5,* 844–936.

Lemere, S. (2003). Towards culturally affirmative assessment and treatment of deaf people with sexual offending behaviors. In N. Glickman & S. Gulati (Eds.), *Mental health care of Deaf people* (pp. 305–326). Mahwah, NJ: Erlbaum.

Maybery, R. (2002). Cognitive development in deaf children: The interface of langauge and perception in neuropsychology. In S. Segalowitz & I. Rapin (Eds.), *Handbook of neuropsychology* (2nd ed., Vol. 8, pt. II, pp. 71–107). Dordrecht, The Netherlands: Elsevier Science.

Mental Health Act (1983 amended 2007). Retrieved August 19, 2012 from http: www. legislation.gov.uk/ukpga/2007/12/contents

Miller, K., & Vernon, M. (2003). Deaf sex offenders in a prison population. *Journal of Deaf Studies and Deaf Education, 8*(3), 357–362.

Miller, K. R. (2004). Linguistic diversity in a Deaf prison population: Implications for due process. *Journal of Deaf Studies and Deaf Education, 9*(1), 112–119.

Obinna, J., Krueger, S., Osterbaan, C., Sadusky, J. M., & DeVore, W. (2006). *Understanding the needs of the victims of sexual assault in the Deaf Community.* Minneapolis, MN: Council on Crime and Justice.

Paijmans, R. (2007). Neuropsychological, behavioural and linguistic factors in challenging behavior in deaf people. In S. Austen & D. Jeffery D (Eds.), *Deafness and challenging behaviour. The 360° perspective* (pp. 89–108). Chichester, England: Wiley.

Pollard, R. (1998). Psychopathology. In M. Marschark & M. D. Clark (Eds.), *Psychological perspectives on deafness* (Vol. 2, 171–197). Mahwah, NJ: Erlbaum.

Schlesinger, H. S., & Meadow, K. P. (1972). *Sound and sign: Childhood deafness and mental health.* Berkeley: California University Press.

Smith, C. M. (2010). An analysis of the assessment and treatment of problematic and offending behaviours in the deaf population (Unpublished doctoral dissertation). University of Birmingham, Birmingham, England.

Sullivan, P., Brookhouser, P., & Scanlan, J. (2000). Maltreatment of deaf and hard of hearing children. In P. Hindley & N. Kitson (Eds.), *Mental health and deafness* (pp. 149–184). London, England: Whurr.

Sullivan, P. M., Vernon, M., & Scanlan, J. M. (1987). Sexual abuse of deaf youth. *American Annals of the Deaf, 132*(4), 256–262.

Vernon, M. (2010). The horror of being deaf and in prison. *American Annals of the Deaf, 155*(3), 311–321.

Vernon, M., & Greenberg, S. F. (1999). Violence in Deaf and hard of hearing people: A review of the literature. *Aggression and Violent Behavior, 4*(3), 259–272.

Vernon, M., & Miller, K. (2001). Linguistic incompetence to stand trial: A unique condition in some deaf defendants. *Journal of Interpretation*, 99–120.

Vernon, M., & Miller, K. (2005). Obstacles faced by deaf people in the criminal justice system. *American Annals of the Deaf, 150*(3), 283–291.

Vernon, M., & Raifman, L. J. (1997). Recognizing and handling problems of incompetent deaf defendants charged with serious offenses. *International Journal of Law and Psychiatry, 20*(3), 373–387.

Vernon, M., Steinberg, A., & Montoya, L. (1999). Deaf Murderers: Clinical and Forensic Issues. *Behavioral Science and the Law, 17*, 495–516.

Vernon, M., & Vernon, M. (2010). *Deadly charm: The story of a Deaf serial killer.* Washington, DC: Gallaudet University Press.

White paper on addressing the trauma treatment needs of children who are deaf or hard of hearing and the hearing children of deaf parents. (2006). Los Angeles, CA: National Child Traumatic Stress Network.

Woolfe, T. (2001). The self-esteem and cohesion to family members of deaf children in relation to the hearing status of their parents and siblings. *Deafness and Education International, 3*, 80–95.

Woolfson L. (2004). Family well-being and disabled children: a psychosocial model of disability-related child behaviour problems. *British Journal of Health Pscyhology, 9*(1), 1–13.

Young, A., Howarth, P., Ridgeway, S., & Monteiro, B. (2001). Forensic referrals to the three specialist psychiatric units for deaf people in the UK. *Journal of Forensic Psychiatry, 12*(1) 19–35.

Young, A., Monteiro, B., & Ridgeway, S. (2000). Deaf people with mental health needs in the criminal justice system: A review of the UK literature. *Journal of Forensic Psychiatry, 11*(3), 556–570.

10 Deaf Mental Health Research

Where We've Been and Where We Hope to Go

Neil S. Glickman and Robert Q Pollard, Jr.

Introduction

In 2010, Johannes Fellinger, a psychiatrist, researcher, and founder of the Institute of Neurology of Senses and Language in Linz, Austria, invited second author Robert Pollard to collaborate on a review article examining the current status of Deaf mental health (DMH) research. The article had been solicited by the editors of *The Lancet,* a highly influential British medical journal read by physicians worldwide. Review articles solicited by *The Lancet* typically require the authors to collect and examine only very high quality research studies published in the past handful of years, thereby focusing the authors' opinions on only the best and most recent findings in a given field of study. I (Pollard) was told that *The Lancet* editors requested that the review article focus only on high quality *empirical* studies in the DMH field that were conducted in the past 5 years or so and, further, to limit the review to about 100 of these presumed recent, high quality empirical studies. This implausible directive conveyed *The Lancet's* presumption that a given medical topic, particularly one as broad as "mental health of deaf people" (as the article was ultimately titled) would indeed have a rich body of high quality, recent empirical research activity that the authors could draw from in crafting their review.

I was quite concerned regarding how Fellinger, his colleague, neurolinguist Daniel Holzinger, and I could produce a review that was consistent with *The Lancet's* expectations. My chief reservation was that the DMH field did not have anything approaching a sizable body of recent, sophisticated empirical studies to draw upon. For many reasons, among them the scarcity of qualified researchers, the available empirical literature in this field is quite limited in both quantity and quality. We nevertheless wanted to accept this unique and important invitation, knowing what a special opportunity it presented for putting DMH topics "in the spotlight" of one of the worlds' most widely read medical journals. To do so, of course, we had to reach farther back in time than the editors had presumed necessary and draw upon both rhetorical and empirical literature in the field. For example, few empirical studies we reviewed were well-controlled for matters such as: method or proficiency of preferred communication modality among the deaf research subjects, age at onset of deafness, degree of hearing loss, aided versus unaided hearing acuity, and a host of other variables that are very significant in understanding the nuances of the deaf population (Barnett, McKee, Smith, & Pearson, 2011). Despite these limitations, the article (Fellinger, Holzinger, & Pollard, 2012) has generated considerable interest in the topic of Deaf mental health care, in part due to the high visibility of *The Lancet*, our review's focus on clinical service equity issues as well as research-based issues, the simultaneous publication of a thought-provoking commentary and an editorial regarding our review, and the editors' wonderful decision to fund the production of a British Sign Language summary of the publication and post it on *The Lancet's* website, alongside the review, the commentary, and the editorial.[1]

Despite the aforementioned concerns regarding the dearth of high quality research in the DMH field, empirical studies regarding normal and abnormal psychological functions among deaf persons actually has quite a long history (Pollard, 1992a). Rudolph Pintner, publishing in the 1920s to 1940s, was one of the earliest and most prolific researchers in this field. He was interested in the measurement of intelligence in the deaf population, among other things. As discussed in this book's introduction, Pintner and associates published over 80 papers comparing deaf and hearing samples on intelligence and personality. Unfortunately, but not surprisingly for the time, they used biased measures such as written English tests in their studies. Accordingly, their findings, too, were biased and usually portrayed deaf people in a falsely negative light, concluding that deaf persons had lower intelligence and more psychopathology than hearing people (Vernon, 1995). Pintner's conclusions regarding the intellectual inferiority of deaf people were later reinforced by Helmer Myklebust who used English-based personality tests like the MMPI to conclude that deaf people demonstrated greater psychopathology than the general population (Pollard, 1992a). Thus, through the first half of the 20th century in the United States, there was active research in this field but, by current standards, it was badly done and quite negatively biased against deaf people. Yet, it was highly influential among other researchers and especially among mental health practitioners who sometimes encountered deaf persons in their work and looked to this biased research for guidance.

We view most DMH research published prior to the mid-1970s as highly suspect due to the lack of awareness, before that time, of American Sign Language as a valid and complex language, and the consequences that this lack of information had on how psychologists and psychiatrists viewed and wrote about deaf people. Virtually all researchers in the DMH field prior to and during the 1970s were hearing people who did not know sign language well and had little personal knowledge of the sociocultural characteristics of the (normal) deaf population. A review of research on the psychological characteristics of deaf people prior to the mid-1970s would lead one to conclude that deafness itself inevitably leads to limited intellectual functioning and a host of emotional and behavioral problems. Such conclusions still find their way into modern publications, when authors reach too far back in the literature to learn what is "known" about the psychological characteristics of deaf people.

One of the most serious consequences of this sad research history is how it has set-back the pace of pursuing much-needed knowledge in the DMH field. Since the mid-1970s, most DMH research has been aimed at "un-doing" this false and pathologizing research history. That is, most DMH research over the past 40 years has been aimed at challenging the older, biased research and demonstrating why the conclusions put forth in those publications are wrong. This crucial step had to be taken, of course, but it prevented the few qualified researchers in the DMH field from pursuing questions about deaf mental health that our colleagues in the hearing mental health research field were free to investigate. *In other words, DMH research is behind hearing mental research by at least 40 years.*

We are frequently asked by other researchers, research funding agencies, public mental health officials, clinicians, and many others, questions that would be easily answered if they involved the mental health of *hearing* people, such as basic questions about the epidemiology of various psychiatric disorders in the deaf population, or questions regarding what psychological tests are best used to investigate this or that psychiatric problem or personality characteristic regarding a deaf individual. It is downright embarrassing (and puzzling to the people asking us such questions) to have to constantly reply with "we don't know" or "that hasn't been determined yet."

Naturally, we want the Deaf mental health field to catch up, but catching up is easier said than done. First and foremost, there are extremely few researchers qualified to conduct DMH research (i.e., fluent in sign language, familiar with both normal and mentally ill deaf populations, trusted by the Deaf community (i.e., possessing "cross–cultural legitimacy" (Pollard, 1996)), skilled in research methodology, and with sufficient access to sizable numbers of deaf individuals willing and able to participate in a given research study). The number of qualified DMH *clinicians* has grown steadily in the United States in the past three decades, in no small part as a consequence of the Americans with Disabilities Act opening the doors of higher education more widely to qualified deaf persons interested in pursuing mental health careers. Yet, the vast majority of these persons pursue service-oriented careers. Understandably so, since the need for DMH service providers is so high, it's a compelling "calling" for a qualified, well-trained clinician. Yet, as a consequence, the number of qualified DMH *researchers* has remained pitifully low.

Obtaining research funding in the DMH field is a challenge as well. Within the National Institutes of Health (NIH), which funds the majority of health-related research in America, including research on mental health topics (especially via the NIH's National Institute on Mental Health (NIMH)), there is a common misconception that because there also is a National Institute on Deafness and other Communication Disorders (NIDCD) within NIH, that that institute would be the logical one to fund DMH research or other studies regarding the *health* of deaf people. But in reality, NIDCD's research priorities regarding deafness are preventing and treating hearing loss, not research on psychosocial or other non-audiological health matters regarding deaf people. In fact, it is the U.S. Department of Education, via its National Institute on Disability and Rehabilitation Research (NIDRR), which has funded the majority of American DMH research. The Department of Education, however, has a different mission than the NIH, so funding from that source for deaf mental health studies has not been consistently available.

There is reason for cautious optimism regarding the DMH funding picture, however, on several fronts. Advocacy efforts as well as good quality empirical publications by researchers in the field have drawn increased attention and recent funding from NIDRR, NIMH, and certain other NIH institutes that are coming to recognize that the deaf population is an understudied and underserved minority group worthy of research attention (Barnett et al., 2011). Even NIDCD has begun to fund some work on the "lives of deaf people" rather than just an exclusive focus on their hearing loss.

A Short History of Deaf Mental Health Research

In the introduction to this book, I (Glickman) discussed the handful of DMH programs developed in the 1950s and 1960s and the pivotal role of psychologist Edna Levine in advancing more culturally attuned and respectful study of deaf people. Other key names of this era were Schlesinger, Meadow, Vernon, Grinker, Mindel, and Denmark. Vernon essentially put to rest the prevailing idea that deaf people had below average intelligence (Vernon, 1995, 2005). He proved it was bias in the prevailing testing methods themselves that lead to such false conclusions. Schlesinger and Meadow were interested in the psychosocial development of deaf children and conducted research that demonstrated that no particular course of mental health or illness was set in stone just because a child was born deaf. Along with Vernon, they made strong arguments for the cognitive and emotional developmental value of sign language use. Grinker and some others began to explore psychotic symptoms in deaf inpatients. This era of research clarified the need for specialized DMH services (Altshuler, 1971; Altshuler & Rainer, 1968; Grinker et al., 1969).

During the 1970s and 1980s, NIDRR funded Schlesinger's Research and Training Center on Deafness and Mental Health at the University of California San Francisco (UCCD) for about 15 years. Most of the DMH research published in this period was authored by UCCD faculty and staff

(Hilde Schlesinger, Laurel Glass, Holly Elliott, J. William Evans, Bruce Heller, Kathryn Meadow, Asa DeMatteo, S. Margaret Lee, Mimi Lou, Daniel Langholtz, Michael Strong, Steven Fritch-Rudser, Daniel Veltri, Robert Pollard, and others) including a ground-breaking manual on mental health assessment of deaf clients (Elliott, Glass, & Evans, 1988). UCCD's work during this period covered a variety of topics including child development, psychosis, neuropsychological assessment and functioning, deaf-blindness, mixed deaf-hearing families, and sign language interpreters in mental health settings. The UCCD clinician/researchers examined normalcy as well as deviations from normalcy, and elucidated ways to evaluate, understand, and serve the mental health needs of deaf people more appropriately. Like other DMH specialists writing during this time, they were largely interested in "un-doing" previous bad research and service provision habits.

When UCCD's NIDRR funding ended in the 1990s, the volume and pace of American DMH research diminished markedly. Nancy and Greg Long and their colleagues at Northern Illinois University subsequently received NIDRR funding to study so-called "traditionally underserved" deaf people, that is, deaf people with low sign language fluency, little or no English literacy, and a range of psychosocial and developmental problems (Long, 1993; Long, Long, & Ouellette, 1993). Their research and that of the Arkansas Rehabilitation Research and Training Center on Deafness and Hearing Impairment at the University of Arkansas, under the leadership of Glenn Anderson and Douglas Watson, put even more focus upon this subgroup of multiply-challenged deaf people, especially their vocational training and placement needs (Anderson & Watson, 1985). My (Glickman) work on deaf people with "language and learning challenges" draws upon their research (Glickman, 2009). When the Northern Illinois University NIDRR funding ended, NIDRR funded a group in San Diego to focus on hard-of-hearing and late-deafened people. The San Diego group included Raymund Trybus, Thomas Goulder, and Karen Stika.

Deaf mental health work has been promoted through a few professional organizations. For more than four decades, the American Deafness and Rehabilitation Association (ADARA) has been the principal professional home in the United States for rehabilitation and mental health counselors working with deaf adults. In 1983, ADARA held a conference on "mental health and deafness" and published their proceedings (Heller & Watson, 1983). ADARA conferences have been held in the United States every 2 years. They usually alternate with biannual "Breakout" conferences, which have had different sponsors, and which have focused more on psychiatric rehabilitation practices with deaf persons, and less on vocational rehabilitation. In 1990, Greg Long and I (Pollard) established a "Special Interest Section on Deafness" within Division 22 (Rehabilitation Psychology) of the American Psychological Association. In Europe, there is an active European Society on Mental Health and Deafness which as of May,

2012 has been instrumental in hosting five World Conferences on DMH, the content of which is primarily research focused.

In the introduction, I (Glickman) review the DMH literature that emerged from the 1980s. Most of what was published from this period were descriptions of services or case studies, not empirical literature. I was a graduate student at Gallaudet College from 1981 to 1983, and I remember searching hungrily for anything published on the subject of DMH, and how little was available at the time. I can remember the excitement I felt at discovering the 1983 ADARA monograph as well as a 1981 book, *Deafness and Mental Health* (Stein, Mindel, & Jabaley, 1981) which I discussed in the introduction. At that time, anything written on the subject that didn't pathologize deaf people was groundbreaking.

I (Pollard) worked for UCCD from 1986 to 1990, and subsequently founded the Deaf Wellness Center (DWC) in the Department of Psychiatry at the University of Rochester Medical Center. In 1992, I received a grant from NIMH that established the DWC's "Program for Deaf Trainees," which has served as an internship and practicum site for dozens of deaf individuals pursuing careers in the mental health field. While a few have gone on to conduct research, the majority are in clinical service or service administration positions. In 2003, the DWC was awarded a 5-year grant from NIDRR to conduct research that, refreshingly, was not focused on simply "undoing" biased, old DMH research but was more forward-focused, illustrating a new style of DMH research based on what we know about *hearing* persons with mental illness and trying to bring that knowledge to bear on behalf of deaf people with mental illness. In fact, the title of that 5-year project was "Toward Equity." It consisted of a set of studies embedded within three topic areas: psychological testing, dialectical behavior therapy (DBT; a popular, evidence-based treatment approach used with hearing people), and sign language interpreter preparation for mental health work.

Each of these three topic areas has remained a focus of DWC research and scholarship, not only during the 5-year period of the "Toward Equity" grant but subsequently, through additional funding secured from NIDRR, the Fund for the Improvement of Post-Secondary Education (also housed within the U.S. Department of Education), NIH's National Institute on Drug Abuse, the State of New York, the Alaska Mental Health Trust Authority, the American Psychiatric Foundation, the Registry of Interpreters for the Deaf, the National Consortium of Interpreter Education Centers, the National Association of State Mental Health Program Directors, and various branches of the Centers for Disease Control and Prevention. Through this funding support, and the innovative, dedicated work of my DWC colleagues, we have produced more than 80 publications, 19 films (15 of them in American Sign Language for Deaf audiences) and other products that are benefitting deaf consumers, clinicians, and researchers alike. DWC staff are highly visible on the national and international stage and are often found presenting at conferences and workshops dealing with a host of issues relevant to DMH, sign language interpreting and, increasingly, public health issues affecting the deaf population. Our latest research forays in this latter regard are focused on intimate partner violence and suicide risk affecting the Deaf Community.

Deaf Mental Health Research Today

This brings us to the present state and short term future outlook regarding Deaf mental health research. The aforementioned Fellinger et al. (2012) article in *The Lancet* provides viewpoints based, to the greatest degree possible, on recent empirical research studies. The authors conclude that the mental health "disease burden" in the deaf population is greater than that noted in the general population. This higher incidence of mental health problems is exacerbated by a severe restriction in the availability of accessible, appropriate mental health services for deaf people. Johannes Fellinger, lead author of the article, is also an artist. His illustration (Figure 10.1) of this dual problem of increased disease burden and restricted access to care was published along with *The Lancet* review. The article stresses the need for specialists and specialized services in the DMH field, especially for those deaf people with intellectual disabilities and severe language deprivation. Research is cited which shows the importance of early access to effective communication for the subsequent emotional health of deaf children. Another recent review of the field (Leigh & Pollard, 2011) allowed for a somewhat broader, historical perspective than did *The Lancet* article and also is recommended.

Figure 10.1 The combined effects of increased disease burden and care limitations (by Johannes Fellinger, MD, 2011; reproduced with permission from *The Lancet* and Dr. Fellinger).

In the remainder of this chapter, we discuss a potential research agenda for the DMH field. We should note that the DMH research agenda does not just pertain to care and treatment but includes topics like epidemiology, mental illness disparities, diagnosis and assessment. It is a broader agenda than that addressed in this book on DMH care. The next section below draws out research implications emerging out of the work presented in the preceding chapters of this text, allowing for an important digression into the critical issues of trauma and violence involving deaf people. Then we will review the results of a groundbreaking conference on research priorities in the DMH field that took place in January, 2012.

Research Ideas Emerging from Earlier Chapters in this Book

In the introduction, I (Glickman) borrowed the "self-awareness, knowledge, skills" framework to structure ideas relevant to Deaf mental health care. We will now use this framework to discuss certain research topics or hypothesis that emerge from the chapters of this book, and then proceed to discuss the recent conference where a different framework was used to establish a Deaf mental health research agenda.

The Self-Awareness Dimension

The self-awareness dimension may be the most difficult to operationalize in research projects. It involves the study of attitudes, beliefs and behaviors pertaining to Deaf/hearing cross-cultural encounters. Yet, all these dimensions are potentially measurable. Components of Deaf identity have already been identified and initial scales developed (Glickman, 1996, 2009; Glickman & Carey, 1993; Leigh, 2009; Maxwell-McCaw, 2001). In Chapter 2 of this book, Gournaris and Aubrecht, drawing upon Hoffmeister and Harvey (1996), argue that deaf and hearing people, based on generally unconscious "relational postures," relate to one another in a set of predictable ways. They argue that greater cultural and personal self-awareness, as well as cross-cultural conflict resolution skills, could foster more productive collaborations between deaf and hearing people, and they recommend, in particular, more study of these proposed relational postures.

Deaf/hearing cross-cultural conflicts are illustrated through stories and imaginary dialogues in Chapters 1, 2, 5, and 9. As mentioned in the introduction, it is sometimes difficult to provide details about actual conflicts because this is sensitive for people who have experienced such conflicts. The difficulty of approaching this task aside, it is certainly my (Glickman's) perception that the greatest barriers deaf people face in receiving quality mental health care are attitudinal ones. These barriers are parallel, in my mind, to the attitudinal barriers faced by other minority persons. Thus, the study of how the identities, attitudes, beliefs, and behaviors of deaf and hearing people, in contact with each other, develop and interact, all comprise potential areas for useful research. The questions that emerge from such studies would parallel those emerging from other majority/minority cross-cultural contexts: how do deaf and hearing people develop in their understandings of themselves and each other, and what experiences for each group promote collaboration, mutual understanding, respect, and effective partnerships?

The Knowledge Dimension

In this book, certain aspects of the knowledge dimension have been emphasized. First, attention was drawn in Chapter 1 and 3 to the significance of sign language dysfluency for interpreters and clinicians working in mental health settings. While so much corrective work was done in the last part of the 20th century to establish that sign languages are true, legitimate languages and that the Deaf communities throughout the world use such minority-status languages, the fact remains that, chiefly because many deaf children have inadequate exposure to sign language, the actual language skills of deaf persons, especially those seen in clinical and forensic settings, varies enormously, and many are poor language users in any language. The widespread use of cochlear implants has not solved this problem and may well have aggravated it (Humphries et al., 2012). Outside of the United States and other developed nations, the poor language skills of many deaf people is primarily the result of a lack of deaf education services. Research focusing on accurate, detailed assessment of signed as well as spoken language skills of deaf persons, and drawing out the implications, especially for interpreters and clinicians, of working with deaf persons whose language skills are dysfluent in their "best" language would be incredibly useful.

In Chapter 3, Charlene Crump and I (Glickman) addressed strategies interpreters may use when working with deaf persons who manifest impaired language skills. We drew upon work done at the Deaf Wellness Center on this subject (Pollard, 1998). This subject needs much more attention, and more incorporation into interpreter training programs. It is already a focus of attention in the annual mental health interpreter training program offered by the Office of Deaf Services in the Department of Mental Health in the state of Alabama.

Language dysfluency has many clinical implications, as discussed in Chapters 1, 3, and 9. An especially important research need is to further the development of measures of sign language abilities so that such measures can provide a detailed, valid analysis of the vocabulary, grammatical, syntactic, and other linguistic abilities of signers, especially those at the lower ability levels. The most well-known existing sign language skills assessment tool is the Sign Language Proficiency Interview but this is used primarily to measure and describe more advanced ASL abilities of personnel who seek to work with deaf persons (Caccamise, Newell, & Mitchell-Caccamise, 1983; Newell, Caccamise, Boardman, & Holcomb, 1983). A newer instrument, the Profile of Multiple Language Proficiencies (Goldstein & Bebko, 2003) can be used to categorize abilities in spoken and signed English and in ASL. Presently, assessments of sign language abilities in deaf people *served* in mental health treatment settings tend to be descriptive and highly dependent upon the language skills of evaluators who may not always be qualified to make such judgments.

Developing new instruments, or refining existing instruments so that they can used to specify the presence or absence of specific grammatical and syntactic sign language features, would have many benefits. Such advancements would help clinicians differentiate between language versus thought disorder, which would significantly enhance the likelihood of accurate diagnosis of language dysfluency that has its origins in language impoverishment versus mental illness versus traumatic brain injury, stroke, and/or other causes. Furthermore, improved, more broadly focused sign language assessment instruments would help establish objectively the kind of skills hearing and deaf sign language interpreters working with a language-impoverished consumer might need. In addition, they would be useful in forensic settings when evaluators strive to determine whether deaf persons have sufficient communication abilities to collaborate with their attorneys, a necessary ability to be considered competent to stand trial. They would help establish for courts unfamiliar with the issue of linguistic incompetence that a person may be incompetent to stand trial while not having a major mental illness or mental retardation. Such instruments would be invaluable in elucidating the consequences of inadequate sign language exposure for deaf children, including those deaf children who do not benefit adequately from cochlear implants (Humphries et al., 2012). They would help establish why programs that serve deaf people need to have communication specialists who can assist in communicating well with deaf persons with poor language skills and thereby also help establish standards for communication competencies and resources in such programs.

In Chapter 1, I (Glickman) report that one of the lessons learned from the Westborough State Hospital Deaf Unit's 23 years of serving deaf inpatients was that a significant percentage of the deaf people served there fit a profile for a hypothesized disorder I call "language deprivation with deficiencies in behavioral, social and emotional adjustment" (Glickman, 2009). For deaf people who cannot access spoken language, being raised without early and consistent access to sign language often means they never develop substantive language abilities of any kind. Because of this, their "fund of information" (Pollard, 1998) about the world and their abilities to learn new information (which is dependent on stores of existing information and on adequate language and learning strategies) are compromised. Many fundamental cognitive skills are substantially impoverished by such language deprivation, making learning in childhood and through-out adulthood extremely difficult, including learning about social norms, legal versus illegal behavior and other matters. Accordingly, a substantial number of these individuals also develop a pattern of behavioral, social, and emotional disturbances including aggression, self-harm, a gross defi-ciency in interpersonal skills and perceptions, poor school and vocational attainment and, frequently, significant deficits in fundamental indepen-dent living skills such as money management, healthful living practices, and more. These persons comprise a significant percentage of the deaf clientele seen in clinical service settings and, as discussed in Chapter 9, are often incarcerated in prison and forensic hospitals as a result of running afoul of laws and behavioral norms they do not comprehend. These deaf persons are especially vulnerable to misdiagnosis because their low level of psychosocial functioning, dysfluent language, and behavioral problems can resemble the characteristics of some persons with major mental ill-nesses. They may have psychiatric disorders such as mental retardation, depression, or bipolar disorder, but their language and learning challenges often mean that the best practices in mental health diagnosis and care are not effective with them, even in the hands of skilled DMH practitioners.

This combination of highly challenging behaviors and limited treatment resources often means that the only tools available to help such individuals are residential or institutional confinement and medications. Often these persons are not able to make informed decisions regarding their medica-tions and other aspects of their care (although they remain legally empow-ered to do so because such authority has not been transferred to someone more capable via adjudicated means such as legal guardianship). Com-monly, they are prescribed heavy doses of medications which present their own dangers (Moncrieff, 2009; Whitaker, 2010). Because this cohort of deaf persons has been discussed, using different labels, in virtually every study of deaf inpatients (see Chapter 1 and Glickman, 2009), it would be helpful for research to establish the prevalence of deaf persons who have this hypothesized disorder as a co-occurring condition. This could lead to more realistic appraisals of the evaluation and treatment challenges involving this significant subset of deaf persons.

Mental health programs (or private practitioners) geared toward serv-ing the deaf population usually must serve not only deaf persons who are fluent in a signed, spoken and/or written language but also deaf persons with very impaired language abilities. These two ends of the deaf con-sumer spectrum present quite distinct challenges. It is far easier to adapt best practices in mental health care for deaf persons who are fluent sign-ers than for those who have significant language and learning challenges. Some of the latter group lack the cognitive building blocks necessary to identify and label their emotions or analyze and solve daily life problems. Some of these people cannot use the structural properties of language to organize and sequence events in time or clarify the distinction between actors and agents in a narrative. Sometimes they lack rudimentary under-standing of cause and effect or conditional ("if this, then that") relation-ships. Virtually always, such individuals lack abstract reasoning abilities necessary to draw inferences and develop insight. The vast majority of mental health and rehabilitation strategies used with hearing persons assume basic knowledge and skills in these areas, not to mention some ability to read and write. Most mental health practitioners outside the DMH field assume their clients, deaf or hearing, have these abilities. The ability to "unpack" and simplify abstract concepts, and teach key ideas and skills in a developmentally appropriate manner to deaf individuals with impoverished language and cognitive abilities, is an important part of the skill set that DMH clinicians must bring to this work. This is virtu-ally never within the skill set of non-DMH clinicians and, furthermore, non-specialist clinicians frequently do not comprehend the "realities of interpreting work" (Dean & Pollard, 2005) sufficiently to work effectively with this population, even in partnership with qualified sign language interpreters.

Documenting the prevalence, characteristics, and treatment needs of deaf persons with "language deprivation with deficiencies in behav-ioral, social and emotional adjustment" should be a research priority, not because we want to draw some false correlation (once again) between hearing loss per se and psychiatric disorders, but because we want to avoid costly diagnostic errors and, just as importantly, develop appropriate treat-ment approaches for this unique but sizable subset of the deaf population. Research that helps clinicians document the language and cognitive abili-ties of the heterogeneous deaf population, and then adapt best practices in treatment in light of an individual's unique pattern of abilities, would advance tremendously this field of clinical specialization.

The Problem of Trauma and Violence Involving Deaf People

Chapter 7 of this volume describes the trauma treatment program at the Walden School in Framingham, Massachusetts. It is the main place in this book where the widespread problem of deaf victimization (physical and sexual abuse, neglect, and communication isolation) is addressed. Chapter 9 addresses deaf people in the criminal justice system and the issue of deaf people who commit violent and other criminal acts. These topics deserve far more attention than they are given here, and both need to be a focus of the DMH research agenda.

There are very few trauma treatment programs like that at the Walden School, for deaf children or adults, yet there is mounting evidence that deaf people experience various forms of trauma disproportionately more frequently than the general population. There are a number of good dis-cussions of the issue of trauma in deaf people but only a few are based on empirical research (Anderson & Kobek, 2011; Anderson & Leigh, 2011;

Anderson, Leigh, & Samar, 2011; Barber, Wills, & Smith, 2011; Barnett et al., 2011; Schwenke, 2011; Sullivan, Brookhouser, & Scanlan, 2000). Some, like the content in Chapter 7, are discussions of trauma treatment approaches and programs (Merkin & Smith, 1995).

Sullivan, Vernon, and Scanlan (1987) present frequently cited data on the sexual abuse of deaf youth. They concluded that 54% of deaf boys are sexually abused as compared to 10% of hearing boys, and that 50% of deaf girls are sexually abused compared to 25% of hearing girls. However, Sebald (2008) questioned their methodology and conclusions and called for better quality research. She called for studies replicating those findings, identifying the long-term effects of childhood sexual abuse on children who are deaf or hard of hearing, describing the characteristics of the types of perpetrators who sexually abuse children who are deaf or hard of hearing, and identifying treatment interventions that take into account their unique communication needs.

A widely circulated paper on the trauma treatment needs of deaf and hard-of-hearing children (National Child Traumatic Stress Network, 2006) reports that the incidence of sexual abuse for deaf children is higher than for their hearing peers. According to this report, deaf boys are more likely to report abuse than deaf girls, whereas with hearing children girls are more likely to report abuse. The abuse often occurred in vans or buses when children are being transported to and from school. Approximately 20% to 25% of deaf children were abused both at school and home.

This paper (National Child Traumatic Stress Network, 2006) also cites work by Harvey (1996) which states that communication isolation itself can be traumatizing for deaf people. Communication isolation as a form of trauma is an experience largely unique to deaf people and worthy of research investigation. Sexual or physical abuse or other trauma experienced by deaf children who also have minimal language skills raises the question of whether trauma symptoms may manifest differently among different types of deaf people. Schild and Dalenberg (2011) hypothesize that deaf survivors of trauma experience more dissociation and less traditional post-traumatic stress disorder symptomatology than hearing survivors.

An empirical study reported by Kvam (2004) based on a self-administered questionnaire sent to 1150 members of the Norwegian Deaf Register, found that deaf females age 18 to 65 who lost their hearing before age 9 reported childhood sexual abuse more than twice as often as hearing females, and deaf males reported it more than three times as often as hearing males. The reported abuse was also more severe than that experienced by hearing children. Many deaf people look to Deaf residential schools as cherished places where they were first exposed to sign language and Deaf culture, often making life-long friends, yet Kvam's study showed that many also were victimized there, often by other deaf people. This difficult, counterposing situation is not an uncommon one in the United

States. Research that sheds light on the benefits *and* risks associated with residential education is extremely limited. Given the tremendous stakes involved, both positive and negative, high-quality empirical investigation of this complex, sensitive, and emotionally-charged topic is long overdue.

More recent research is finding that deaf female adults experience high levels of intimate partner violence (Anderson & Kobek, 2011; Anderson & Leigh, 2011; Anderson et al., 2011; Barnett et al. 2011). In one study, 72.7% of deaf women served in an outpatient mental health program reported psychologically abusive behaviors, and 56.5% reported a history of physically abuse from a partner (Johnston-McCabe, Levi-Minzi, Hasselt, & Vanderbeck, 2011). In another study of deaf Gallaudet college students, the overwhelming majority of the sample experienced partner-perpetrated psychological aggression within the past year, with one half of the sample experiencing severe psychological aggression. Surprisingly, over 75% of the survivors of psychological aggression did not label their experiences as abuse, raising several possible research questions regarding why that would be. Forty percent of the sample reported experiencing at least one incident of physical assault in the past year, with approximately 20% experiencing severe physical assault. Just as striking, nearly 80% of survivors of sexual coercion chose not to label their experience as sexual coercion (Anderson & Kobek, 2011). These findings suggest not only a high prevalence of intimate partner violence among deaf college students but a low level of knowledge (i.e., fund of information) about what constitutes intimate partner violence.

Thus, available empirical evidence and clinical reports indicate that deaf children and adults experience high rates of trauma, are at risk for unique forms of trauma such as language deprivation, and may manifest trauma symptoms differently than hearing persons—all of this in the context of scarce trauma research, as well as few trauma-focused prevention and treatment programs. Every aspect of this problem needs further study. Priority should be given to development of valid trauma assessment measures and research that would help establish suitable, effective prevention and treatment programs.

There are also some data and discussions, as reviewed in Chapter 9, about a higher incidence of *victimizing* (perpetrating) behaviors among deaf people, although the empirical literature here is even more sparse. Vernon and Greenberg (1999) present an overview of the issue of violence perpetration among deaf and hard-of-hearing people. They argue that the prevalence of brain damage, learning disability, communication disorders, educational retardation, unemployment and underemployment among many deaf persons creates poorer coping skills and greater frustration which tends to manifest in disproportionate levels of hostility and aggressive behavior. In Chapter 9, the authors discuss the disproportionally high prevalence of deaf people in the criminal justice system, and relate this to the widespread practice of our schools, law enforcement, and legal systems excusing "challenging behavior" in deaf people until these become too serious to dismiss. On the Westborough Deaf Unit discussed in Chapter 1, the primary reason we received referrals for inpatient care was that the deaf individuals in question had committed some kind of violent act which was presumed to be related to mental illness, but which was more likely related to the challenges associated with the hypothesized disorder of "language deprivation with deficiencies in behavioral, social and emotional adjustment." The prevalence of violent behaviors in the deaf clinical population also is reflected in a recent volume from Great Britain devoted solely to this topic (Austen & Jeffery, 2007).

The problem of high rates of intimate partner violence, coupled with ignorance about the nature of the violence, was cited above. A recent study from Canada, relying on anecdotal information, suggests that family violence is emerging as a serious problem in the Deaf Community there and recommends a comprehensive study (MacDougall, 2000). There is certainly reason to seek more solid empirical study on the incidence, nature, precursors to, and treatment of violent behavior among deaf people as well as the protective factors that may reduce the incidence and severity of such behaviors.

The Skill Dimension

Three of the chapters in this book address the crucial issue of adapting best practices in mental health and substance abuse treatment for deaf persons, a process that requires highly specialized knowledge and skills. In Chapter 7, as mentioned, Karen Bishop discusses adaptations of cognitive behavioral therapy, collaborative problem solving (Greene & Ablon, 2006), collaborative and relational trauma treatment approaches (Fox, 1994, 2004; Saxe, Ellis, & Kaplow, 2007), and narrative therapy approaches (White, 2007; White & Epston, 1990) for deaf children who have experienced various forms of abuse and trauma. In Chapter 5, Wendy Heines and I (Glickman) discuss adaptations of psychiatric rehabilitation approaches including cognitive behavioral therapy, illness management and recovery (SAMHSA, 2009), and collaborative problem solving. In Chapter 6, Guthmann and Sternfield discuss adaptations of best practices in substance abuse work such as 12-Step programs, motivational interviewing, cognitive behavioral therapy and harm reduction. All such treatment adaptation work is consistent with the work done at the Deaf Wellness Center on adapting dialectical behavioral therapy and public health information to make such information more accessible, affective, and culturally relevant for deaf adults (O'Hearn & Pollard, 2008; O'Hearn, Pollard, & Haynes, 2010; Pollard & Dimeff, 2006, 2007; Pollard, Dean, O'Hearn, & Hayes, 2009).

Everywhere one looks in the Deaf mental health field, qualified DMH clinicians are engaged in creatively adapting assessment and treatment materials and methods of all sorts, yet often without knowledge of what has been done elsewhere and in ways that are not well-coordinated nor sufficiently validated through empirical study of the outcomes of using such adapted materials and methods. Necessity being "the mother of invention" understandably drives these valiant efforts but to move the DMH field forward, rigorous research methodologies should guide and evaluate these adaptation efforts.

We've seen that such adaptation work often has common themes. One theme is the inadequacy of accessing standard treatment programs, for many deaf people, just by engaging the services of a sign language interpreter. O'Hearn and Pollard (2008) detail why such presumptions regarding "equal access" are seldom realized. Dean and Pollard (2005) provide more general insights into the "realities of interpreting work" that many consumers, both hearing and deaf, do not tend to appreciate, to the detriment of everyone involved in interpreted encounters. While some deaf people do prefer to receive mental health treatment in mainstreamed settings via the services of a qualified interpreter, many, especially the language and learning challenged group, do not appear to benefit from this approach.

A number of strategies are commonly used to adapt treatment for deaf people with language and learning challenges. These include: paying close attention to the (often differing) language abilities of the deaf people involved and accommodating them as best as possible; minimizing the use of English written materials and maximizing the use of pictorial and other visual aids; addressing fund of information gaps; utilizing engaging, action-oriented treatment approaches such as role playing and therapy games; allowing for, even promoting, the culturally preferred modality of storytelling; and having deaf people model and coach skills for other deaf people. Judging from the existing scholarship and clinical practices regarding Deaf mental health care, it appears that just about any treatment (or learning) approach designed for hearing persons requires *adaptation* to be effective with deaf consumers, not mere *translation* into sign language. Pollard et al. (2009) offer a particularly detailed analysis of this matter. Creating and validating effective, adapted treatment approaches for deaf people presents a virtually endless supply of desperately needed collaborative opportunities for researchers and clinicians.

A central premise of this book is that Deaf mental health care is a highly specialized field. Seventeen years ago, Pollard (1996) framed this argument in an article subtitled "The Emergence of a Discipline." For most deaf persons, treatment in mainstreamed settings via non-specialist clinicians working through sign language interpreters simply does not yield the same level of effective care as specialized clinicians accomplish. (Worse, we know that many unfortunate deaf persons are served in mental health settings by non-specialist clinicians who do not even employ the services of qualified sign language interpreters.) Effective Deaf mental health care simply must be provided by specialist clinicians in the vast majority of circumstances if we are to expect outcomes similar in quality as the standard of care that hearing consumers experience. In Chapter 4, Gournaris, Hamerdinger, and Williams present some preliminary data in this regard, but the question of whether, or under what specific circumstances, specialized deaf treatment programs are superior to mainstreamed programs that provide access via interpreters has not been empirically demonstrated nor have important related questions such as the cost-effectiveness of specialized treatment programs, consumer preference, and other matters.

The question of whether or not deaf persons can be served well through mainstreamed programs that utilize sign language interpreters is often debated. On the one hand, all the contributors of this book argue passionately for the importance of specially trained, sign-fluent providers, and related specialized service approaches and treatment centers. On the other hand, there will never be enough qualified Deaf mental health specialists to serve all the deaf people in need, and interpreters will always be an essential component of the service delivery system. Indeed, specialized Deaf treatment programs such as the Walden School and the Deaf Services Center, and Deaf treatment programs within larger hearing organizations, such as Deaf services at Advocates, Inc.,[2] even though they are staffed by a majority of deaf persons, still require a dedicated interpreting team. At Advocates, the interpreting team enables the many deaf individuals who work and receive services there to be included in the full range of events Advocates offers and to interact with family and community members who do not sign.

Deaf mental health specialists also strenuously argue for more and better interpreting resources, such as interpreters who have been specifically trained in mental health work, including both hearing sign language interpreters and Certified Deaf Interpreters. The Deaf Wellness Center has obtained research grants by arguing that the important research question is not whether deaf people should be served via interpreters as opposed to sign-fluent specialists but rather, given the necessity of interpreter-mediated treatment services in most U.S. public mental health programs, how to train interpreters so that they can be optimally effective in mental health settings. Several DWC publications address this issue (Dean & Pollard, 2001, 2005; Pollard, 1998). Mental health interpreter training programs, such as the yearly training institute offered by the Alabama Office of Deaf Services, are dedicated to improving the mental health practice competencies of interpreters, whether they work in specialized Deaf treatment programs or not. The "either/or" thinking (interpreters or specialists) is a moot issue, because we need all of the above. We need specialized providers, approaches and settings *and* we need highly trained interpreters who can work well in specialized or mainstreamed mental health service settings.

Another wide-open area of DMH research is program evaluation. Outcome-based program evaluation data is needed for virtually all public mental health services that deaf people receive, whether in specialized programs or mainstreamed settings. If we accept the assumption that serving deaf people often requires specialists (clinicians and interpreters), different or adapted approaches, and sometimes specialized service programs and settings, then we must acknowledge that we have next to no empirical knowledge regarding *evidenced-based practices* with deaf persons. This is another way in which the DMH field is about 40 years behind that of mental health work with hearing persons.

Deaf people face communication barriers so often that they, and many non-specialist clinicians, presume that circumventing some of these barriers, usually via interpreter services, is sufficient to create an effective treatment environment. That is to say, people often assume that if you have made certain (often minimal) communication arrangements, you will be able to provide effective mental health treatment. Consistent with O'Hearn and Pollard (2008), in Chapter 5 Wendy Heines and I (Glickman) argue against this notion. Beyond the significant challenges of offering effective access to mental health care for higher-functioning deaf persons, some treatment challenges, like addressing the needs of deaf persons with problematic, aggressive sexual behaviors, are so complex that effective treatment arguably is not offered anywhere in the U.S., especially when such problems involve the deaf language and learning challenged group. Everyone doing this type of work, and work in other highly-specialized DMH areas, is a pioneer.

Wherever Deaf treatment programs or independent specialists are working, their rarity and linguistic accessibility inevitably translates into considerable pressure to be "an expert in everything" that might afflict a deaf individual, that is, they bear a burden to respond to a wider range of clinical problems and client characteristics than anyone could be properly prepared for. This is an especially acute problem for new, highly trained (e.g., doctoral level) DMH professionals, such as those who graduate from the Deaf Wellness Center's Program for Deaf Trainees, who soon find themselves in positions of clinical leadership or independent practice due to the rarity and high demand for their skills. DWC supervisors frequently and directly address this problem that is "lying in wait" for these newly-minted DMH practitioners and program leaders.

At the programmatic (versus individual practitioner) level, this was certainly also the case at the Westborough State Hospital Deaf Unit where, over its 23 years, staff were asked to serve deaf people who really needed outpatient substance abuse treatment, residential mental health services, day treatment, specialized types of counseling such as that for sexual offenders, or who had committed crimes but were judged incompetent to stand trial, or who were just "high risk individuals" who needed to be placed somewhere safe. Furthermore, the patients referred to us presented not only the previously noted wide array of linguistic and cognitive abilities but other complications such as deaf-blindness, or any number of physical disabilities that sometimes were a consequence of syndromic or other hearing loss etiologies (e.g., CMV infection, rubella, etc.). The staff at Westborough were not trained to deal with the cacophony of medical, linguistic, cognitive, psychiatric, legal, family, and other challenges that came along. A great deal of learning had to be done "on the job," and staff always struggled with the more fundamental communication and cross-cultural challenges which sapped energy that otherwise might have been devoted to development of specialized clinical programming. As staff inevitably turned over, the accumulated expertise that had been learned on the job often failed to transfer to newer staff members.

In Chapter 4, Gournaris, Hamerdinger, and Williams describe their efforts as state administrators of public mental health services for deaf people, to create a high quality continuum of care for their deaf consumers. Yet, they struggle to create such systems of care in the absence of reliable data about the population they seek to serve (e.g., epidemiological data), not to mention data regarding the best evaluation, diagnostic, and treatment practices. To some degree, this is a "chicken and egg" problem. We need data to justify the establishment of specialized services, but we also need specialized services to allow us to conduct the research studies that would generate such data. For example, if there never were any specialized Deaf psychiatric inpatient units, it's unlikely that the hypothesized clinical disorder, "language deprivation with deficiencies in behavioral, social and emotional adjustment," would ever be given much attention. Similarly, because one state (Texas) created specialized prison units for deaf persons, it has been possible to study the language skills of deaf prisoners there, and identify the enormous problem of language dysfluency in that deaf prison population (Miller, 2004).

We also need more qualified DMH clinicians and researchers. In Chapter 8, Brice, Leigh, Sheridan, and Smith describe the training process for mental health specialists at Gallaudet University, one of the very few universities to offer such specialized training. Across the various mental health-related training programs at Gallaudet, however, the focus is primarily upon the development of clinical practitioners as opposed to researchers.

In spite of these challenges, Deaf mental health care, like all mental health care and all health care generally, ultimately must demonstrate its effectiveness via empirical research. We have to be able to demonstrate what clinical practices are most needed and most helpful for which deaf people under which circumstances. These are ultimately researchable questions. Many such questions have readily been answered as they pertain to hearing people. If the DMH research field was not so far behind, for the reasons noted above, we might have more of these answers today.

Perhaps we will in the decades to come but only if the research workforce and the funding support is in place to carry out this long-overdue work.

The NASMHPD Deaf Mental Health Research Priority Consensus-Planning Conference

In 2008, a number of individuals[3] collaborated to create the National Coalition on Mental Health and Deaf Individuals (NCMHDI). The mission of NCMHDI is "to create and modify public systems of care to adequately provide culturally and linguistically appropriate mental health and substance abuse services to humans with hearing loss" (NCMHDI, n.d.). This group is affiliated with the National Association of State Mental Health Program Directors (NASMHPD). NASMHPD is an important and influential organization, consisting of every U.S. state's director of public mental health services. The opportunity to bring Deaf mental health issues to the attention of such an influential body was very important. NASMHPD had already proven receptive to DMHC issues, hosting two conferences and producing two monographs relevant to DMH concerns (Critchfield, 2002; National Association of State Mental Health Program Directors Medical Directors Council, 2002). At a 2009 NCMHDI meeting, attended by Robert Glover, the Executive Director of NASMHPD, I (Pollard) gave a presentation on the history and status of research in the Deaf mental health field and advocated for convening a consensus-planning conference to set research priorities regarding DMH issues. Consensus-planning conferences are common in other areas of medicine, including psychiatry, and it seemed a worthwhile endeavor in light of how far behind Deaf mental health research was in comparison to the general state of knowledge regarding mental illness in the general population. Dr. Glover was very supportive of the idea. For three years, Glover, his dedicated associate Meighan Haupt, and I worked out the programmatic and financial details of the conference. The conference took place in January, 2012.

The vision for the conference was that it would bring together leading researchers, clinicians, administrators, consumers, and other stakeholders in the DMH field along with representatives from key government agencies involved in research funding and/or public mental health administration (NASHMPD, NIMH, NIDRR, SAMHSA). Also invited were a few mental health researchers who were not DMH experts but could offer the group cutting-edge information about the state of mental health research generally, so that the group could consider how this knowledge might be applied or adapted to deaf mental health research. Over the 5-day span of the conference, a series of five lengthy, semi-structured breakout sessions allowed the conference delegates to brainstorm, debate, and prioritize relevant research and research infrastructure priorities. The goal was to achieve consensus among this diverse group of participants regarding the research priorities that would be of most value to the DMH field, in particular, research that would inform and improve the delivery of public mental health services for the deaf population.

The conference deliberations were organized around three themes. The first, "disease burden," explored research topics related to how deaf people experience and manifest mental illness (e.g., epidemiology, assessment, and diagnostic issues). The second topic, "treatment," explored research topics related to the provision of mental health care to deaf people. The third topic, "research infrastructure," explored mechanisms that would expand the workforce, funding support, and other resources relevant to conducting DMH research.

An entire day of conference deliberations was devoted to the topic of disease burden and another full day devoted to the topic of treatment. During the first set of breakout sessions, conference delegates brainstormed and discussed potential research ideas relevant to that day's theme. Delegates were divided into three breakout groups. The membership of each group was carefully designed to include a balance of the different "types" of delegates present (e.g., researchers, administrators, consumers) as well as a balance of deaf and hearing delegates. In a plenary session, each group presented and explained the reasoning behind that group's "top 10" research ideas for that day's theme. Delegates then returned to their breakout groups to further debate the ~30 "top 10" ideas that had been generated by the three groups. (The research infrastructure theme was allotted a half-day and followed a slightly more streamlined procedure.) Following a methodology I had employed in a previous consensus-planning conference regarding regional Deaf mental health care services (Pollard, 1995), the breakout groups were instructed to debate and (hopefully) reach agreement on a two-dimensional rating (1–4) for each research topic. The first dimension was *impact*: to what degree would accomplishing that particular research idea or activity benefit public mental health services for deaf people? The second dimension was *feasibility*: how easy or difficult would it be (in terms of cost, time, workforce, or any other relevant criterion) to actually carry out that research idea or activity? These two criteria forced participants to consider not only the potential value of various research activities but also the real-world challenges that would affect the field's ability to accomplish those research activities.

Happily, the three breakout groups *were* able to reach consensus on both impact and feasibility rankings, across 37 ideas that were debated. Thus, each research idea received an *impact* ranking (1–4) and a *feasibility* ranking (1–4). This allowed us to "plot" each idea on an *impact-feasibility matrix* which could then serve as a blueprint for future action. Obviously, ideas ranked high in impact *and* high in feasibility are "low hanging fruit" that should be pursued with urgency. In contrast, ideas ranked low in impact as well as low in feasibility are likely not worth pursuing, at least not as a high priority. Other combinations of impact-likelihood ranking hold different implications. For example, ideas ranked high in impact but moderate or even low in feasibility might be well worth pursuing (because they were judged to be high in impact) but perhaps such ideas would involve high costs, or longer periods of time to accomplish, thus lowering their feasibility score. I (Pollard) emphasized this matter in a visit with each breakout group, comparing high-impact, low-feasibility ideas to President Kennedy's 1961 call for "landing a man on the moon and returning him safely to the earth ... before this decade is out." Many of the most important research accomplishments require considerable time, funding, and other resources to achieve. This does not mean they are not worth pursuing; in fact, the opposite is often true.

With the permission of NASMHPD, which first posted the conference results on their website (http://www.nasmhpd.org/), the impact-feasibility matrix is presented in Appendix 10.A. The full listing of the 37 consensus prioity research ideas is presented in Appendix 10.B.

Conclusions

The contributors to this book have all sought to outline the key themes, issues, and dimensions of the clinical specialty of Deaf mental health care. Three quarters of a century after the pioneering but misguided research of Rudolph Pintner into the intellectual functioning of deaf people, we have the foundations of a truly Deaf-affirmative approach to mental health, substance abuse and rehabilitative treatment for deaf people with mental illness. Unfortunately, in terms of basing this approach on science, we have far more questions than we do answers, far more presumptions and beliefs than we do facts, far more passion than empirically based reasoning.

At present, you are safe to pose nearly any question you can think of regarding DMH and presume our field does not yet know the answer to it, at least not with anywhere near the usual certainty with which we know things through empirical research in the hearing mental health field. We look forward to Deaf mental health research being conducted not only by individuals possessing the requisite knowledge and training in the conduct of high quality empirical research but also the skills and characteristics needed to conduct such research in an effective, culturally-affirmative manner. Among these crucial, additional characteristics are sign language fluency, cross-cultural legitimacy (Pollard, 1996), appreciation for community-based participatory research methods relevant to the Deaf community (Barnett et al., 2011), and knowledge and respect for the unique ethical challenges and mandates relevant to conducting research with this population (Pollard, 1992b, 2002) For all the future researchers who, we hope, will someday answer these questions, the DMH field presents fertile ground, just begging to be plowed, planted, and reaped.

Notes

1. See (http://download.thelancet.com/flatcontentassets/video/pop-up-pages/popup_video_S0140673611611434.html)
2. See Chapters 5 and 7.
3. Key players from the DMH field included Steve Hamerdinger, Brad Trotter, Barry Critchfield, Roger Williams, Robert Pollard, and especially Candice Tate.

References

Altshuler, K. (1971). Studies of the deaf: Relevance to psychiatric theory. *American Journal of Psychiatry, 127*, 1521–1526.

Altshuler, K. Z., & Rainer, J. D. (Eds.). (1968). *Mental health and the deaf: approaches and prospects*. Washington, DC: U.S. Department of Health, Education and Welfare.

Anderson, G. B., & Watson, D. (Eds.). (1985). *Counseling deaf people: Research and practice*. Fayettevilles: Arkansas Rehabilitation Research and Training Center on Deafness and Hearing Impairment.

Anderson, M. L., & Kobek, C. M. (2011). Is it abuse? Deaf female undergraduates' labeling of partner violence. *Journal of Deaf Studies and Deaf Education, 17*(2), 273–286..

Anderson, M. L., & Leigh, I. W. (2011). Intimate partner violence against deaf female college students. *Violence Against Women, 17*(7), 822–834.

Anderson, M. L., Leigh, I. W., & Samar, V. J. (2011). Intimate partner violence against Deaf women: A review. *Aggression and Violent Behavior, 16*, 200–206.

Austen, S., & Jeffery, D. (Eds.). (2007). *Deafness and challenging behavior*. West Sussex, England: Wiley.

Barber, S., Wills, D., & Smith, M. J. (2011). Deaf survivors of sexual assault. In I. Leigh (Ed.), *Psychotherapy with Deaf clients from diverse groups* (2nd ed., pp. 320–340). Washington, DC: Gallaudet University Press.

Barnett, S., McKee, M., Smith, S. R., & Pearson, T. A. (2011). Deaf sign lanauge users, health inequities, and public health: Opportunity for social justice. *Preventing Chronic Disease: Public HealthResearch, Practice and Policy, 8*(2), 1–5.

Caccamise, F., Newell, W., & Mitchell-Caccamise, M. (1983). Use of the Sign Language Proficiency Interview for assessing the sign communicative competence of Louisiana School for the Deaf dormitory counselor applicants. *Journal of the Academy of Rehabilitative Audiology, 16*, 283–304.

Critchfield, A. B. (2002). *Meeting the mental health needs of persons who are deaf*. Alexandria, VA: National Association of State Mental Health Program Directors.

Dean, R., & Pollard, R. Q, Jr. (2001). The application of demand-control theory to sign language interpreting: Implications for stress and interpreter training. *Journal of Deaf Studies and Deaf Education, 6*(1), 1–14.

Dean, R., & Pollard, R. Q, Jr. (2005). Consumers and service effectiveness in interpreting work: A practice profession perspective. In M. Marschark, R. Peterson & E. Winston (Eds.), *Interpreting and interpreter education: Directions for research and practice* (pp. 259–282). New York, NY: Oxford University Press.

Elliott, H., Glass, L., & Evans, J. W. (Eds.). (1988). *Mental health assessment of deaf clients: A practical manual*. Boston, MA: Little Brown.

Fellinger, J., Holzinger, D., & Pollard., R. (2012). Mental health of deaf people. *The Lancet, 379*(9820), 17–23.

Fox, L. E. (1994). The Catastrophe of Compliance. *Journal of Child and Youth Care, 9*(1), 13–22.

Fox, L. E. (2004). Understanding the impact of restraint on sexually abused children and youth. *Residential Group Care Quarterly Newsletter, 4*(3), 137–154.

Glickman, N. (1996). The development of culturally Deaf identities. In N. Glickman & M. Harvey (Eds.), *Culturally affirmative psychotherapy with deaf persons* (pp. 115–153). Mahwah, NJ: Erlbaum.

Glickman, N. (2009). *Cognitive behavioral therapy for deaf and hearing persons with language and learning challenges*. New York, NY: Routledge.

Glickman, N., & Carey, J. (1993). Measuring Deaf Identities: A Preliminary Investigation. *Rehabilitation Psychology, 38*(4), 277–283.

Goldstein, G., & Bebko, J. M. (2003). The profile of multiple language proficiencies: A measure for evaluating language samples of deaf children. *Journal of Deaf Studies and Deaf Education, 8*(4), 452–463.

Greene, R. W., & Ablon, J. S. (2006). *Treating explosive kids: the collaborative problem-solving approach*. London, England: Guilford Press.

Grinker, R., Vernon., M., Mindel, E., Rothstein, D., Easton, H., Koh, S., & Collums, L. (1969). *Psychiatric Diagnosis, Therapy and Research on the Psychotic Deaf* (No. Research Grant number RD-2407-S). Washington, DC: U.S. Department of Health, Education and Welfare.

Harvey, M. (1996). Utilization of traumatic transference by a hearing therapist. In N. Glickman & M. Harvey (Eds.), *Culturally affirmative psychotherapy with Deaf persons*. (pp. 138–147). Mahwah, NJ: Erlbaum.

Heller, B., & Watson, D. (Eds.). (1983). *Mental health and deafness: Strategic Perspectives*. Kansas City, Missouri: ADARA.

Hoffmeister, R., & Harvey, M. (1996). Is there a Psychology of the Hearing? In N. Glickman & M. Harvey (Eds.), *Culturally affirmative psychotherapy with Deaf persons* (pp. 115–153). Mahwah, NJ: Erlbaum.

Humphries, T., Kushalnagar, P., Mathur, G., Napoli, D. J., Padden, C., Rathmann, C., et al. (2012). Language acquisition for deaf children: Reducing the harms of zero tolerance to the use of alternative approaches. *Harm Reduction Journal, 9*(16), 1–9. Retrieved from http://www.harmreductionjournal.com/content/9/1/16

Johnston-McCabe, P., Levi-Minzi, M., Hasselt, V. B. V., & Vanderbeck, A. (2011). Domestic violence and social support in a clinical samplele deaf and hard of hearing women. *Journal of Family Violence, 26*, 63–69.

Kvam, M. H. (2004). Sexual abuse of deaf children: A retrospective analysis of the prevalence and characteristics of childhood sexual abuse among deaf adults in Norway. *Child Abuse and Neglect, 28*, 241–251.

Leigh, I. (2009). *A Lens on Deaf Identities*. New York, NY: Oxford University Press.

Leigh, I. W., & Pollard, R. Q (2011). Mental health and deaf adults. In M. Marschark & P. E. Spencer (Eds.), *Oxford handbook of deaf studies, language and education* (2nd ed., pp. 214–226). New York, NY: Oxford University Press.

Long, G., Long, N., & Ouellette, S. E. (1993). Service provision issues with traditionally underserved persons who are deaf. In O. M. Welch (Ed.), *Research and practice in deafness: Issues and questions in education, psychology and vocational service provision* (pp. 107–126). Springfield, IL: Charles C. Thomas.

Long, N. (1993, Winter). Historical overview of services to traditionally underserved persons who are deaf. *American Rehabilitation, 19*(4).

MacDougall, J. C. (2000). Family violence and the deaf. Retrieved from http://www. justice.gc.ca/eng/pi/fv-vf/rep-rap/deaf-sourd.html

Maxwell-McCaw, D. (2001) *Acculturation and psychological well-being in deaf and hard of hearing people.*Washington, DC: George Washington University. Doctoral dissertation

Merkin, L., & Smith, M. J. (1995). A Community based model providing services for deaf and deaf-blind victims of sexual assault and domestic violence. *Sexuality and Disability, 13*(2), 97–106.

Miller, K. R. (2004). Linguistic diversity in a Deaf prison population: Implications for due process. *Journal of Deaf Studies and Deaf Education, 9*(1), 112–119.

Moncrieff, J. (2009). *The Myth of the chemical cure: A critique of psychiatric drug treatment.* New York, NY: Palgrave Macmillan/St. Martin's Press.

National Association of State Mental Health Program Directors Medical Directors Council. (2002). *Reducing the use of seclusion and restraint. Part III, Lessons from the deaf and hard of hearing communities.* Alexandria, VA: National Technical Assistance Center or State Mental Health Planning (NTAC).

National Child Traumatic Stress Network. (2006). *White paper on addressing the trauma treatment needs of children who are deaf or hard of hearing and the hearing children of deaf parents.* Los Angeles, CA: National Child Traumatic Stress Network.

National Coalition on Mental Health and Deaf Individuals (NCMHDI). (n.d.). Retrieved from http://www.nasmhpd.org/NCMHDI.cfm

Newell, W., Caccamise, F., Boardman, K., & Holcomb, B. R. (1983). Adaptation of the Language Proficiency Interview (LPI) for assessing sign communicative competence. *Sign Language Studies, 41*, 311–352.

O'Hearn, A., & Pollard, R. Q, Jr. (2008). Modifying dialectical behavior therapy for deaf individuals. *Cognitive and behavioral practice, 15*, 400–414.

O'Hearn, A., Pollard, R., & Haynes, S. (2010). Dialectical behavior therapy for deaf clients: Cultural and linguistic modifications for outpatient mental health settings. In I. Leigh (Ed.), *Psychotherapy with Deaf clients from diverse groups* (2nd ed., 372–392). New York, NY: Oxford University Press.

Pollard, R. Q. (1995). Mental health services and the deaf population: A regional consensus planning approach. *Journal of the American Deafness & Rehabilitation Association, 28*(3), 1–47.

Pollard, R. (1998). Mental health interpreting: A mentored curriculum [Videotape and users' guide]. Rochester, NY: University of Rochester School of Medicine.

Pollard, R. Q (1992a). 100 years in psychology and deafness: A centennial retrospective. *Journal of the American Deafness & Rehabilitation Association, 26*(3), 32–46.

Pollard, R. Q (1992b). Cross-cultural ethics in the conduct of deafness research. *Rehabilitation Psychology, 37*(2), 87–101.

Pollard, R. Q (1996). Professional psychology and deaf people: The emergence of a discipline. *American Psychologist, 51*(4), 389–396.

Pollard, R. Q (2002). Ethical conduct in research involving deaf people. In V. Gutman (Ed.), *Ethics in mental health and deafness.* Washington, DC: Gallaudet University Press.

Pollard, R. Q, Dean, R. K., O'Hearn, A., & Hayes, S. (2009). Adapting health education material for Deaf audiences. *Rehabilitation Psychology, 54*(2), 232–238.

Pollard, R. Q, & Dimeff, L. (2006). Opposite action: An adaptation from the Deaf perspective [Motion picture]. Seattle, WA: Behavioral Tech.

Pollard, R. Q, & Dimeff, L. (2007). Practicing radical acceptance: An adaptation from the Deaf perspective (Motion Picture). Seattle, WA: Behavioral Tech.

SAMHSA. (2009). Illness Management and Recovery, *Practioner Guides and Handouts.* Rockville, MD: U.S. Dept. of Health and Human Services, Substance Abuse and Mental Health Services Administration, Center for Mental Health Services.

Saxe, G., Ellis, B., & Kaplow, J. (2007). *Collaborative Treatment of Traumatized Children and Teens: The Trauma Systems Theray Approach.* New York, NY: Guilford Press.

Schild, S., & Dalenberg, C. (2011). Trauma exposure and traumatic symptoms in deaf adults. *Psychological Trauma: Theory, Research, Practice and Policy* Advance online publication.doi:10.1037/a0021578

Schwenke, T. (2011). Childhood trauma: Considering diagnostiic and culturally sensitive treatment approaches for deaf clients. *Journal of the American Deafness and Rehabilitation Association, 45*(1), 158–173.

Sebald, A. (2008). Child abuse and deafness: An overview. *American Annals of the Deaf, 153*(4), 376–383.

Stein, L., Mindel, E., & Jabaley, T. (Eds.). (1981). *Deafness and mental health.* New York, NY: Grune & Stratton.

Sullivan, P., Brookhouser, P., & Scanlan, J. (2000). Maltreatment of deaf and hard of hearing children. In P. Hindley & N. Kitson (Eds.), *Mental health and deafness* (pp. 149–184). London, England: Whurr.

Sullivan, P. M., Vernon, M., & Scanlan, J. M. (1987). Sexual abuse of deaf youth. American Annals of the Deaf, *132*(4), 256–262.

Vernon, M. (1995). An historical perspective on psychology and deafness. *JADARA, 29*(2), 8–13.

Vernon, M. (2005). Fifty years of research on the intelligence of deaf and hard of hearing people. *Journal of Deaf Studies and Deaf Education, 10*(3), 225–231.

Vernon, M., & Greenberg, S. F. (1999). Violence in Deaf and hard of hearing people: A review of the literature. *Aggression and Violent Behavior, 4*(3), 259–272.

Whitaker, R. (2010). *Anatomy of an epidemic.* New York, NY: Crown.

White, M. (2007). *Maps of narrative practice.* New York, NY: W.W. Norton.

White, M., & Epston, D. (1990). *Narrative means to therapeutic ends.* New York, NY: W.W. Norton.

Appendix 10A   The Impact-Feasibility Matrix

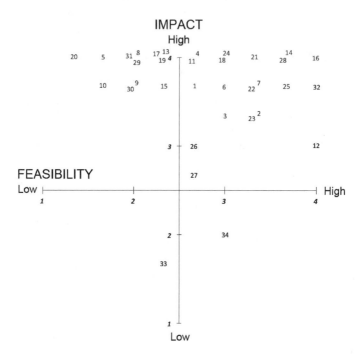

Appendix 10B   NASMHPD Deaf Mental Health Research Priority Consensus-Planning Conference

Final List of 34 Research Priorities

Disease Burden Theme

1. Investigate whether the prevalence of major mental illnesses or disorders in the deaf population, as measured by the *Kessler 6* and other priority measures, and adapted for communication suitability, is the same or different from the prevalence of these in hearing people.
2. Investigate the prevalence, methods, risk factors, and protective factors (e.g., resilience and social networks) associated with suicidality in deaf versus hearing populations.
3. Investigate whether there are disparities in how physicians (psychiatrists and primary care physicians) prescribe neurolepic medications for deaf versus hearing patients.
4. Investigate what variables, particularly language competencies, correlate with and predict overt acts of violent behavior in deaf people served in the mental health system.

5. Conduct a demographic study to define and measure the prevalence of deafness so that we can accurately measure utilization of services.
6. Determine whether the hypothesized disorder of "language deprivation with deficiencies in behavioral, emotional and social adjustment" is a valid and useful construct (see Glickman, 2009) *Cognitive Behavioral Therapy for Deaf and Hearing Persons with Language and Learning Challenges*, p. 333).
7. Investigate the prevalence of aggression, violence, and self-harm in deaf adults and children served in public mental health settings.
8. Taking into consideration how sign language and communication assessments are done in the deaf mental health field with deaf adults and children who have limited communication abilities (i.e., language-deprived or language-dysfluent), develop and standardize a communication assessment tool capable of documenting these individuals' communication strengths and weaknesses, and which is useful for planning and delivering appropriate services.
9. Develop, implement, and evaluate an instrument assessing trauma symptoms in deaf children and adults (inclusive of language impoverishment and adverse sociocultural experiences as possible sources of trauma) that is useful with individuals with varied linguistic competencies, including those with no formal language competencies (e.g., pictorial/visual modalities).
10. Conduct a longitudinal study of deaf children and youth, from birth through high school, comparing those identified as developmentally disabled with those not identified as such, to determine risk and protective factors associated with mental health, developmental, and substance abuse problems.

Treatment Theme

11. Adapt and validate existing best practices for addiction treatment and prevention, for use with deaf persons with diverse communication abilities and methods, who are served in the public mental health system.
12. Examine existing outcomes measures commonly required by the Substance Abuse and Mental Health Services Administration, and state and local mental health authorities, to determine the linguistic and sociocultural appropriateness of these measures for deaf individuals.
13. Employ longitudinal research methodology to design and evaluate the effectiveness of existing or new early intervention programs in fostering the mental wellness of deaf children and their families
14. Develop and examine the effectiveness of telehealth and web-based applications for psychoeducation and mental health and substance abuse service delivery to deaf individuals in multi-site locations.

15. Investigate the treatment effectiveness of various psychiatric medications with deaf persons with varying clinical presentations.
16. Create and evaluate a peer support program for deaf persons in recovery from mental illness.
17. Develop and investigate the effectiveness of treatment approaches to improve outcomes for deaf children, youth, and adults post-trauma, including sexual and physical abuse and the potentially traumatic experience of language deprivation.
18. Compare the cost, effectiveness, and consumer satisfaction of mental health services provided directly by communication-fluent service providers versus services provided through sign language interpreters working in partnership with non-signing providers.
19. Examine the effectiveness of methodologies used to adapt evidence-based practices for deaf people in achieving mental health and addiction recovery-related outcome measures.

Research Infrastructure Theme

20. Establish the policy and practice of listing American Sign Language on surveys that ask about language preference.
21. Create and make available a library of high quality research instruments and outcome measures translated into American Sign Language.
22. Establish and fund a national program (e.g., via "center grant" mechanisms) to conduct high-quality ASL translation of mental health-related measures.
23. Create a forum for mental health and addiction database sharing regarding deaf populations, which allows for secondary data analysis and intra-field research collaboration.
24. Create pre- and post-doctoral research fellowship opportunities and an associated placement network to increase preparation for deaf mental health research careers.
25. To improve recruiting, research agendas, and research methods, involve persons from the Deaf community early and intensively, throughout the research enterprise.
26. Work towards advancing awareness within the National Institutes of Health, especially the National Institute of Mental Health, and the National Institute for Disability and Rehabilitation Research, regarding the need for mental health and addiction-related research with deaf populations.
27. Increase the activity of persons in the deaf mental health field within national professional research organizations.
28. Facilitate research career information sharing and mentoring for deaf doctoral-level researchers in order to enhance their research skills, opportunities to secure fiscal support, and involvement with productive research enterprises.

29. Develop pipeline programs to foster interest and skills in deaf mental health research among students from elementary school onward, including employed persons. (This supports recommendations made in the report, "Building Pathways to Health Care Careers for the Deaf and Hard-of-Hearing Community—Final Report," March 2012. See http://www.rit.edu/ntiol/hccd/system/files/FINAL REPORT Building Pathways March 2012.pdf)

30. Establish and fund a program (e.g., via "center grant" mechanisms) to develop (rather than merely adapt) deaf mental health-related measures, and conduct multi-site validation activities.

31. Establish and fund a program (e.g., via "center grant" mechanisms) to develop and/or adapt products designed to educate and/or facilitate the recovery deaf persons in the public mental health system, useful across the entire range of deaf consumers' communication abilities.

32. Working with the National Association of State Mental Health Program Directors, foster collaboration and liaison with the NASMHPD Research Institute, Inc. to promote deaf mental health research.

33. Work with the National Institute of Health and similar agencies to expand their venues and opportunities for continuing education regarding deaf mental health research.

34. Pursue Small Business Innovation Research grants and other collaborative grants to develop and disseminate deaf mental health products.

Index